RELIGIOUS EDUCATION
between MODERNIZATION
and GLOBALIZATION

STUDIES IN PRACTICAL THEOLOGY

Series Editors

Don S. Browning

James W. Fowler

Friedrich Schweitzer

Johannes A. van der Ven

RELIGIOUS EDUCATION
between MODERNIZATION
and GLOBALIZATION

*New Perspectives on
the United States and Germany*

Richard R. Osmer
&
Friedrich Schweitzer

WILLIAM B. EERDMANS PUBLISHING COMPANY
GRAND RAPIDS, MICHIGAN / CAMBRIDGE, U.K.

© 2003 Wm. B. Eerdmans Publishing Co.
All rights reserved

Wm. B. Eerdmans Publishing Co.
255 Jefferson Ave. S.E., Grand Rapids, Michigan 49503 /
P.O. Box 163, Cambridge CB3 9PU U.K.

Printed in the United States of America

08 07 06 05 04 03   7 6 5 4 3 2 1

ISBN 0-8028-1284-8

www.eerdmans.com

To our families,

Who remind us always of the importance of religious education

And became good friends through this project:

Sally Taylor Osmer

Marianne Miller Martin

Richard Andrew Osmer

Mirjam Anne Schweitzer-Martin

Sarah Richardson Osmer

Paul William Schweitzer-Martin

Emily Virginia Schweitzer-Martin

Contents

Preface

This book first began to take shape almost half a decade ago through our participation in the International Academy of Practical Theology. The friendship and colleagueship growing out of our participation in this organization led us to realize that our research on religious education in our own national contexts — the United States (Osmer) and Germany (Schweitzer) — seemed to reveal trends that were parallel. We were intrigued and collaborated in a presentation to the Academy and an article published in the *International Journal of Practical Theology*. At that point, our focus was on the early twentieth century and the emergence of reform movements in religious education in both countries at approximately the same time. Through further conversations, we began to discern similar trends in both national contexts at other points across the century. As we approached the end of the twentieth century and turned toward a new century and millennium, it seemed worthwhile to take stock of the recent past and point toward the future of our field. The result is this book.

As will become apparent over the course of the volume, we have come to believe that the comparative perspective developed here is likely to become especially important in the future. The world is currently caught up in a period of rapid change through the emergence of interconnected systems of communication and transportation that are reshaping the polities, cultures, and economies of virtually all parts of our planet. It is extremely important during this present time of change to gain perspective on religious education. How did this field view the challenges before it over the course of the twentieth century? Do these challenges remain in force or have they changed to such an extent that new thinking is needed by this field? These are the kinds of questions that a comparative perspective allows us to explore, and they are precisely the focus of this book.

Sandra Kunz, a doctoral student in practical theology at Princeton Theological Seminary, served as our editorial assistant for this book. Her fine judgment and editorial skill were of tremendous help in the completion of the project, and for this we offer her our deepest thanks. Jana Strukova, also a doctoral student in practical theology at Princeton Theological Seminary, helped prepare the bibliographies on the American religious educators. Special thanks to her as well. We also wish to express our gratitude to President Thomas Gillespie and Dean James Armstrong of Princeton Theological Seminary, whose generous support during Osmer's sabbaticals made it possible for him to travel to Tübingen on two occasions to work directly with Schweitzer. This allowed us to conceptualize different parts of the book through the give and take of extended conversation and to give direct feedback on draft chapters. Part I was, in effect, written jointly. While individual chapters of Parts II and III were written by one or the other of the authors, they have been subject to critical feedback by the other. The comparative sections of Part II are the outgrowth of our common reflection on what we learned by comparing religious education in both national contexts.

Parts of this book also were written while both scholars were on study leave at The Center for Theological Inquiry, Princeton, New Jersey. Special thanks is offered to Wallace Alston, Director of the CTI, and Don Browning and Robert Jensen, who, successively, were the senior scholar for research during the times when each of us was at the Center.

Introduction

Many of the challenges currently experienced as "crises" by churches around the world are related to education. This should come as no surprise. The importance of education to the long-term vitality of a community has throughout the ages been recognized by theologians and philosophers alike. Augustine, Luther, Calvin, Schleiermacher, and Barth all found it necessary to address questions of Christianity and education. Plato, Aristotle, Kant, Rousseau, and Dewey, likewise, gave attention to education in their writings. It is therefore surprising that much contemporary systematic theology and theological ethics remains silent on this topic. It is largely left to those in the fields of practical theology and religious education to remind their fellow members of the academic community that the very future of the church is at stake in its education and that the "crises" of the contemporary church are deeply intertwined with its educational failures.

Much of this book is devoted to unraveling the challenges that modernization and globalization have presented to Protestant religious education over the course of the twentieth century. While its focus is largely on locating Protestant religious education theory in relation to the unfolding social contexts of the United States and Germany during this period, it is important to keep before us the larger issues at stake for the contemporary church. While religious education is in view, it serves as a window on the church and religion generally. The educational questions and issues with which religious education struggled during the past century remain with the church and lie at the heart of the challenges to which it must respond today. Let us begin, then, by reminding ourselves of several of the more important of these challenges.

1. The Inability of the Church to Incorporate Its Youth

A relatively obvious necessity facing every community that seeks to exist through time is an ability to incorporate new members. Communities that include families have typically viewed this sort of incorporation, in part, as a task of educating the young. This involves handing on a determinant cultural inheritance from one generation to the next. Equally important, however, it also includes the ongoing reconstruction of this inheritance in ways that allow each new generation to address the particular possibilities and challenges of its own time and place. In the long run, this sort of ongoing transmission and reconstruction is what keeps traditions alive. It is the means by which a community persuades its children and youth that the traditions it offers them have something of significance to contribute to their lives.

There are many indications that contemporary Protestant churches in the Western world are having tremendous difficulty carrying out this task.[1] In effect, they seem unable to persuade their youth that continuing affiliation with the church, except at the most superficial level, is worthwhile. Since the 1960s, social science has documented extensively the widespread departure of youth from participation in church life. In the United States, a four-step pattern has emerged: relatively high participation in the church during childhood; diminishing participation during adolescence; departure from the church during late adolescence and young adulthood; and the return of a small percentage to the church during their late twenties and early thirties.[2] As recently as 1988, the Gallup organization found that 82 percent of all adults in the American population received some sort of religious instruction as children, whether their parents were involved in the church or not.[3] While this percentage has declined over the past decade, it is still the case that far more children are involved in religious education during childhood than re-

---

1. For the recent international discussion see Mordechai Bar-Lev and William Shaffir, eds., *Leaving Religion and Religious Life*, Religion and the Social Order, vol. 7 (Greenwich: Jai, 1997); Leslie Francis and Yaacov J. Katz, eds., *Joining and Leaving Religion: Research Perspectives* (Leominster: Gracewing, 2000).

2. An overview of this pattern is found in Wade Clark Roof and William McKinney, *American Mainline Religion: Its Changing Shape and Future* (New Brunswick: Rutgers University Press, 1987). More focused studies include Dean R. Hoge, Benton Johnson, and Donald A. Luidens, *Vanishing Boundaries: The Religion of Mainline Protestant Baby Boomers* (Louisville: Westminster/John Knox, 1994); Dean Hoge, *Converts, Dropouts, Returnees: A Study of Religious Change Among Catholics* (New York: Pilgrim, 1981); and Roy Oswald and Speed Leas, *The Inviting Church: A Study of New Member Assimilation* (New York: Alban Institute, 1987).

3. *The Unchurched American . . . 10 Years Later* (Princeton, N.J.: Princeton Religion Research Center, 1988), pp. 25-29.

main involved. The critical time of departure is adolescence, during which participation in church life declines precipitously. In some traditions confirmation or similar ceremonies seem to be the marker event, as young people see this as a kind of graduation from the church school.[4] Initially, it was thought that this departure was only temporary and that young adults would return to the church when they had their own children.[5] While this has proven to be the case for some, however, many have chosen not to affiliate with any religious community, and they have not encouraged their children to participate in a religious community either.[6]

In Germany, the situation seems even bleaker, particularly when one looks at congregational education. Many congregations offer very little in the way of religious education for children under five, when Sunday school begins, and not a great deal more is offered to older children and adolescents. In Germany, only a minority of the children participate in Sunday school and less than 15 percent of Christian youth ever come in contact with Christian youth-work.[7] This places undue pressure on the efficacy of confirmation classes, which often last no more than ninety minutes per week over a period of no more than nine months. Once confirmation classes are completed, moreover, it is common for young people to rapidly curtail their participation in the church and then stop participating altogether, similar to their American counterparts.[8] Even if religious education is taught in German public schools and even if most children and adolescents participate in this subject, this clearly is not enough to secure their introduction to church and congregation.

4. One of the most telling findings of the Search Institute in this regard is the high rate of involvement of young people in the Evangelical Lutheran Church in America *through confirmation* and the very rapid decline of participation following confirmation. See Peter Benson and Carolyn Eklin, eds., *Effective Christian Education: A National Study of Protestant Congregations: A Report for the Evangelical Lutheran Church in America* (Minneapolis: Search Institute, 1990).

5. For an early discussion of this premise that is largely critical of the idea that parental responsibilities would bring large numbers back to the church, see R. T. Gribbon, *When People Seek the Church* (Mount Saint Alban, Washington, D.C.: Alban Institute, 1982).

6. The study of Hoge, Johnson, and Luidens cited above, *Vanishing Boundaries,* is particularly telling in this regard for it examines five hundred persons confirmed in the Presbyterian church who have now reached middle adulthood and, thus, have achieved a stable life structure, including parenthood. Slightly over 50 percent were in the unaffiliated sector of the population and, clearly, had not returned to the church.

7. The fact that there are no clear statistics on the quantitative scope of Sunday school participation is, perhaps, itself indicative of the predicament.

8. For a current overview and additional references see Friedrich Schweitzer, *Die Suche nach eigenem Glauben: Einführung in die Religionspädagogik des Jugendalters* (Gütersloh: Gütersloher Verlagshaus, 1996). It should also be mentioned that church attendance in Germany is much lower than in the United States.

Young people in both Germany and the United States commonly associate the church with older adults, if not the elderly. This is an accurate perception if the demographics of many Protestant churches are taken into account; in both countries, the "graying" of mainline Protestant congregations is a well-documented reality.[9] Worrisome as this perception is, it becomes even more alarming when placed alongside an additional body of research on adolescent religiosity. Social scientists in the 1990s discovered a new interest in religious questions among German adolescents, for example,[10] but neither was this interest directed automatically toward the church nor did the church seem to have any success in speaking to this new religious sensitivity. Tom Beaudoin found a similar expression of religious themes and questions in a recent analysis of youth culture in the United States.[11] Here, too, the church seems unable to tap into this adolescent religiosity.

The growing gap between the religious quest of the younger generation, on the one hand, and a traditional church of older adults, on the other, is a major challenge facing the Protestant church and Western Christianity generally. Obviously, many factors have contributed to this gap between adolescent religiosity and church participation, some internal to the life of the church and some best interpreted as external, contextual dimensions closely associated with modernization. The challenge before religious education and the church generally is to better understand why it has failed to incorporate its children and youth into the church and how it might respond.

2. The Increased Separation of the Church from Public Education

One of the most important dynamics of the relationship between education and Christianity has been the increased separation of public, state-supported education from the church. While there are important historical differences in the way this has unfolded in the United States and Germany, there also are certain similarities. These are most apparent if the separation of the church and public education is not viewed exclusively in legal terms but as a contin-

9. See Roof and McKinney, *American Mainline Religion;* Joachim Matthes, ed., *Kirchenmitgliedschaft im Wandel: Untersuchungen zur Realität der Volkskirche. Beiträge zur zweiten EKD-Umfrage "Was wird aus der Kirche?"* (Gütersloh: Gütersloher, 1990).

10. Jürgen Eiben, "Kirche und Religion — Säkularisierung als sozialistisches Erbe?" in *Jugend '92: Lebenslagen, Orientierungen und Entwicklungsperspektiven im vereinigten Deutschland,* vol. 2, ed. Jugendwerk der Deutschen Shell (Opladen: Leske und Budrich, 1992), pp. 91-104.

11. Tom Beaudoin, *Virtual Faith: The Irreverent Spiritual Quest of Generation X* (San Francisco: Jossey-Bass, 1998).

uum of social processes with various degrees of separation. While religious education was not an official part of the curriculum of public education in the United States over the course of the twentieth century, for example, many informal trappings of Protestant Christianity remained a part of its ethos — from prayers at the beginning of the day and at sporting events to unofficial Bible studies carried out by individual teachers. Likewise, while religious education remained an option in public education in Germany for much of the twentieth century, it often was treated as a marginal subject in the curriculum. In addition to this, religion was neglected in philosophies of education shaping the attitudes of the teaching profession. The separation of the church and public education, thus, can be viewed as taking place at various levels along the lines of a continuum. When this perspective is taken, similar patterns across both national contexts and, indeed, across Western Christianity are apparent.

In general, public education has gradually come to view religion as a purely private affair, a matter of personal preference and a choice best left to the individual. Legally, of course, this has been the official position across the twentieth century in the United States, but it increasingly has come to inform the attitudes and practices of teachers and the way religion is portrayed in curriculums as well. In Germany, certain political developments since the 1960s and the 1990s have represented a decisive step in this direction, attenuating the ties between school education and Christianity. Since that period, religion has been treated increasingly as privatized and as individualized, to speak sociologically. Many philosophers of education have developed theoretical perspectives based on the secularization thesis, portraying religion as being in a process of progressive decline. These philosophers influence teachers, and these teachers educate children — all according to the principles of religious privatism and individualism.

The impact of these changes in education can hardly be overestimated. The second half of the twentieth century has witnessed the expansion of educational institutions on a scale unseen in the past. Even the important impacts of the Reformation and Enlightenment were not of the same quantitative scale. Historically, it is fair to say that the second half of the twentieth century is the first period ever in which Western Christianity has been subject to the effects of highly secularized and secularizing mass education. Never before in history have so many people attended school for so much of their time every day or remained in educational institutions for such an extended period of time over the course of the life cycle.

The impact of this extended involvement in education and of religion's decreasing role in that education has been great and has been documented by a wide variety of empirical studies. In the United States, for example, Robert Wuthnow identified education as one of the most influential factors in the "restructuring of American religion" since 1945.[12] The more education persons receive, the less likely they are to participate in the traditional activities of the church — what Wuthnow refers to as an "education gap." Repeatedly, major studies since the 1950s in the United States have documented the secularizing effects of higher education in terms of religious participation and personal religiosity.[13] Sociological surveys of church membership in Germany since the 1970s have found similar data pointing to the so-called "educational dilemma" of the church: The more people participate in education, the less likely they are to be involved in the church. Yet the church seems to be more dependent on education than ever for the maintenance of its membership in light of the ever higher degree of religious diversity and the general weakening of ascriptive ties to the church.[14] In other words, the church needs an educated membership, yet education distances people from the church.

The separation between church and public education is thus a hugely important issue for the future of Protestantism and Western Christianity. Here again, the church's long-term future is intertwined with education in ways that often are ignored. The silence of theologians and ethicists on this issue in both Germany and the United States is deafening. Robert Lynn's astute observation in the early 1960s remains accurate four decades later: Protestant social ethics has failed to develop a "sustained critique of the public school and its policies" even though they "have developed a critical perspective upon almost all the sectors of American life. The most conspicuous exception is public education."[15] Here again, the challenges of the past century remain with us, even if the church's response must move in new directions.

12. Robert Wuthnow, *The Restructuring of American Religion: Society and Faith Since World War II* (Princeton, N.J.: Princeton University Press, 1988), p. 161.

13. See James Davison Hunter's summary of this research in *Evangelical Christianity: The Coming Generation* (Chicago: University of Chicago Press, 1987), pp. 165-78; see also Wuthnow, *Restructuring*, pp. 168-72.

14. The dilemma was first described by Ernst Lange in the 1970s; for a more recent interpretation see Rüdiger Schloz, "Das Bildungsdilemma der Kirche," in *Kirchenmitgliedschaft*, by Matthes, pp. 215-30.

15. Robert Lynn, *Protestant Strategies in Education* (New York: Association Press, 1964), p. 58.

3. The Growing Distance between the Family and the Church

As we shall point out repeatedly over the course of this book, the family historically has been one of the most important sites of religious education in Protestant Christianity. We will not take the time at this point to document this claim, nor will we unpack the complex interrelationship between changes in the modern family and the decline of its role in religious education. This too will be taken up at a later point. Our point at present is relatively simple: families in both Germany and the United States increasingly stand at a distance from the church and mediate attitudes toward it (and religion generally) that frequently have more in common with the religion-as-personal-preference perspective than with the religion-as-convictional-participation perspective commonly associated with church membership.

There are differences between Germany and the United States in patterns of familial involvement in the church. A fairly high percentage of American families still look to religious communities for help in inculcating moral attitudes in children and youth and in preventing their involvement in at-risk behavior.[16] In Germany, beyond baptism and confirmation, the vast majority of families do not expect much from the church in terms of education. These differences should not mask the underlying similarities, however. In both countries, parental goals for religious education do not focus primarily on nurturing children and youth into the church for the sake of the truth the church has to offer. It is one thing to look to the church for help in allowing youth to "survive" adolescence, something that continues to be the case in many American families. It is quite another to hope that they will come to recognize the truth of Christianity and allow their lives to be reshaped by this truth. Standing at a distance from the church, many families in effect view the church as a kind of helpmate in socialization and a relatively weak one at that. In Germany, many families are following a pattern of personal or private religion that is loosely related to the teachings of the church. Religious individualization seems to create an ever deeper gap between the church and the family.

4. The Lack of an Identity-Shaping Moral Ethos

When we stand back from the three issues that we have raised above — the failure of a graying church to incorporate its youth, the separation of the church from public education in the context of an increasingly educated pop-

---

16. Hoge, Johnson, and Luiden, *Vanishing Boundaries.*

ulation, and the growing distance of the family from congregational life — a matter of great importance in moral and religious education becomes apparent. Where will children and youth encounter an ethos through which they will acquire the intellectual and moral virtues of a Christian way of life? By *ethos*, here, we mean an ethic that is embodied in the practices of a community. Discussion of ethos in recent moral philosophy and Christian ethics has largely emerged out of the recognition that abstract ethical principles have little impact on the actual thinking and actions of persons unless they have been instantiated in the relationships, models, and practices of a community with which individuals identify.

In light of the foregoing analysis, we must ask: Where will such an ethos exist for Protestant Christianity today? We might hope that the family would provide such an ethos, but this has become highly unlikely in light of the privatized and individualized understanding of religion characterizing this setting. In public education, professional educators and teachers tend toward universalistic types of ethics — the discourse ethic of Habermas, the Declaration of Human Rights, or generalized affirmations of tolerance and fairness. Such ethics are chosen, in part, in hopes of finding a neutral basis for moral education in a multicultural and multireligious society. The gap between these abstract affirmations and their instantiation in the school ethos is readily apparent. And what about congregations? Certainly, the perception of youth that these communities are primarily for older adults makes it increasingly unlikely that congregations will fill this role. Even in those cases where children participate in the church school on a regular basis, we must wonder whether this alone can serve as a viable ethos by which religious and moral identity can be shaped. Attempts at extending the Sunday school in the United States through weekday programs have largely failed, and the possible impact of even the very best Sunday morning school hour is highly limited in comparison to the fifteen thousand or more hours of public education most young people receive by the end of high school.[17]

The questions with which this book deals, thus, are not merely abstract issues of little real consequence to the life of the church or to Christianity in general. Already, it is apparent that the most perplexing issues before church and Christianity are deeply intertwined with education, both within the church and in the family and public schools. Moreover, it is apparent that many of these issues can be understood only if the church is viewed in relation to changes taking place in its social context. This is the perspective that

---

17. Michael Rutter et al., *Fifteen Thousand Hours: Secondary Schools and Their Effects on Children* (Cambridge: Harvard University Press, 1979).

will guide our work in this book, and we will explore our thesis — that religious education (and the church) stands in an interdependent relation to its changing social context — in three parts. Part I of the volume will explore the importance of international, comparative research in religious education today and provide an overview of the comprehensive frameworks that we will use to describe the contexts of Germany and the United States: modernization, globalization, and postmodernism. Part II will examine paradigmatic figures and texts in twentieth-century religious education in Germany and the United States. These figures and texts will, first, be interpreted in relation to the unfolding social contexts of their respective nation, and, then, be compared with their counterparts across the Atlantic during the same period. Part III will point to the challenges before religious education as it enters the twenty-first century. Here, we will attempt to raise issues in the emerging global context that call for fresh thinking with regard to religious education.

I The Promise and Problems of Contemporary Religious Education

1 *Protestant Religious Education in Context: The Need for Historical and Comparative Perspectives*

Our Guiding Thesis

It is not difficult to point to changes of great significance taking place around the world today, from the emergence of a global economy and new systems of electronic communication to problems of social integration in rapidly changing societies and the hostility to the stranger this lack of cohesion has created. It will not be possible for practical theology and religious education to address these kinds of trends if they limit themselves exclusively to the development of practical methods and strategies. What is needed is a deeper analysis of the challenges faced by Christianity today, not merely for the sake of understanding but, more importantly, for the sake of perspectives that can guide Christian action in church and society. In this chapter, we will offer an initial overview of how we will respond in our book to this need.

Our guiding thesis is the following: *Protestant religious education stands in an interdependent relationship to the social contexts in which it is located and these contexts are best understood today on the basis of international, comparative analysis.* The core of this thesis is the interdependence of religious education theory and praxis with the social contexts in which they are located. It is impossible to understand the former without also understanding the latter. We will argue, moreover, that our understanding of social context needs to be extended beyond national communities because the comprehensive frameworks of modernization, globalization, and postmodernism bring into focus processes that are mediated through, but certainly stretch beyond, particular societies. Hence, our pursuit of a comparison of religious education in Germany and the United States.

Where can religious educators turn for help in understanding the social contexts in which they work? In addition to theology, the disciplines of social philosophy, sociology, social psychology, and social history, among others, offer pertinent interpretations of current social contexts. In general, such analyses tend to focus on topics like modernity, postmodernity, modernization, reflexive modernity, and globalization. Influential statements have come from Jürgen Habermas, Niklas Luhmann, Peter Berger, Ulrich Beck, Anthony Giddens, and Roland Robertson, among others.[1] In dialogue with the work of these persons, we will explore the relationship between social context, religious education, and Protestant religious education theory.

The thesis that religious education theory/praxis and social context are interdependent places us at odds, for the most part, with standard accounts of religious education in the United States and Germany, which tend to focus primarily on the *ideas* of prominent representatives of religious education theory in a particular country in isolation from the *cultural contexts* in which they took shape. We will examine these approaches in greater depth at a later point in this chapter. It is important to take special note of the term "interdependent" in the thesis statement offered above. We do not see religious education theory/praxis as merely one of the myriad by-products of complex social forces. It both shapes and is shaped by these forces. A significant subtheme running throughout this book, especially Part II, is our analysis of religious education theory as a form of rhetoric that attempts to address and, thereby, persuade a range of audiences or publics. While it is responsive to social trends and forces, it is not completely determined by them.

To put this somewhat differently, our dialogue and use of the comprehensive perspectives of modernization, globalization, and postmodernism is both *critical* and *constructive*. It is critical in a twofold sense, using such theories to form a critical perspective on twentieth-century Protestant religious education theory/praxis and, simultaneously, attempting to maintain a critical stance toward the comprehensive frameworks used in this analysis.

---

1. Jürgen Habermas, *The Theory of Communication Action*, vol. 1, *Reason and the Rationalization of Society*, trans T. McCarthy (Boston: Beacon, 1984), and vol. 2, *Lifeworld and System: A Critique of Functionalist Reason*, trans. T. McCarthy (Boston: Beacon, 1987); Niklas Luhmann, *The Differentiation of Society*, trans. S. Holmes (New York: Columbia University Press, 1982); Peter Berger, *The Heretical Imperative: Contemporary Possibilities of Religious Affirmation* (Garden City, N.Y.: Anchor, 1979); Ulrich Beck, *Risk Society: Towards a New Modernity* (London: Sage, 1992); Anthony Giddens, *Modernity and Self-Identity: Self and Society in the Late Modern Age* (Stanford: Stanford University Press, 1991); Roland Robertson, *Globalization: Social Theory and Global Culture* (London: Sage, 1992).

A brief word clarifying the latter is in order here. All of the social theorists mentioned above have both explicit and implicit normative claims built into their theories. Habermas is a case in point. Not only does he offer a normative theory of modernity as an "unfinished project," but also, within this depiction of modernity, he portrays religion, largely, as an evolutionary by-product of the past that is of little value in grounding contemporary post-conventional moral identities.[2] We will examine his theory of modernity in greater detail in the following chapter. In our view, this portrayal of the potential role of religion in the context of modernity is deeply problematic and is based more on Habermas's normative commitments than on empirical research into the role religion has in fact played in new social movements and civil society across the modern period. In engaging a perspective of this sort, the danger is allowing it to set the terms of analysis and debate. Accordingly, we view our dialogue with such theories along the lines of a critical dialogue in which the normative perspectives of theology are allowed to maintain their own point of view on the nature of religion and human community.

We also seek to develop a constructive perspective in this book. In Part III, in particular, the critical perspective of the preceding sections will open out to constructive proposals about the future of Protestant religious education. Our hope is that Roman Catholics, as well as members of Jewish, Islamic, and other religious communities, will find these proposals to be of interest. If our guiding thesis is true — that religious education stands in an interdependent relationship to its social contexts — then they too are confronted by challenges similar to those faced by Protestant communities. Our constructive proposals, thus, represent an invitation for dialogue among various different Christian communities and across different religious traditions. Many of us committed to a religious tradition share a common goal of promoting the well-being of our societies and the human community as a whole. This will be achieved only if religious communities develop new forms of education that nurture a commitment to the common good.

---

2. Jürgen Habermas, "Modernity: An Unfinished Project," in *Habermas and the Unfinished Project of Modernity: Critical Essays on the Philosophical Discourse of Modernity*, ed. Maurizio Passerin D'Entrèves and Seyla Benhabib (Cambridge: Polity, 1996), pp. 38-55. For Habermas's general view of religion cf. his *Theory of Communicative Action*. For a critical appraisal cf. Don S. Browning and Francis Schüssler Fiorenza, eds., *Habermas, Modernity, and Public Theology* (New York: Crossroad, 1992).

A Brief Comment on Terminology

Readers should be aware, from the beginning, that we are pursuing an international, comparative approach in this book. Our approach is international not only because we, as authors, were raised and now live on two different continents, but more importantly because we are addressing international processes of modernization and globalization — processes that cut across political, cultural, and economic boundaries. We will look at the development of religious education theory and praxis not only in the abstract but in relation to two concrete contexts of the Western world: Germany and the United States. This procedure will afford us with two case studies of the interdependence of religious education theory and social context, as well as affording us a perspective on trends taking place across national communities.

When two scholars from different cultures are writing together, difficulties about terminology are bound to arise. An important case in point for us is the term "Protestant religious education." There is no single term that conveys the same meaning across national and denominational boundaries or across different periods of history. While "religious education" and its equivalents in other languages — e.g., *religiöse Erziehung/Bildung/Religionspädagogik, éducation religieuse, religieus onderwijs* — may be considered the general category under which the educational praxis of different religious communities can be subsumed (a terminological use partially consistent with the present authors' use), there still remain a number of complex semantic and philosophical/theological problems. In some countries, "religious education," as opposed to "religious nurture," is understood to refer exclusively to settings that offer comprehensive education for children, such as public or private elementary or secondary schools. In other countries, the term is used to indicate that a theorist's methodological focus is not theology, but educational theory or the social sciences.[3] Similar complexities are present in the terminology of "Christian education." Over the course of the past century, some religious educators in the United States viewed this term as the only one that could be employed in a theologically responsible manner. At approximately the same period of time in Germany, followers of the theologian Dietrich Bonhoeffer eschewed this term altogether because of its association with the "German Christians" during National Socialism.[4]

---

3. For a discussion of religious education in the United States and the United Kingdom see Gabriel Moran, *Religious Education as a Second Language* (Birmingham, Ala.: Religious Education Press, 1989).

4. See the chapter on postwar Germany in Part II of this volume, especially the section on Oskar Hammelsbeck.

Still further layers of complexity can be added to this terminological difficulty. Before the twentieth century "catechetics" or "catechesis" was the most common term used to describe the field. These terms were criticized during the eighteenth century and the emergence of modern educational thinking for their "narrow" understanding of education. Some Catholic educators still consider "catechesis" the most appropriate term for educational activities in a church context, and a small number of Protestants have also adopted this terminology.[5] Recent interest in the adult catechumenate of the first centuries of the church's life and catechetical instruction of the Reformation period have led some to adopt the language of catechesis once again, often under the influence of the religious communitarianism of Stanley Hauerwas, William Willimon, and L. Gregory Jones.[6] As we shall see in Part II, John Westerhoff anticipated this use of catechesis in his mature work. Nevertheless, the term is currently used by only a relatively small number of Protestant educators.

In what follows we will, in general, use the term "religious education theory" as our most comprehensive expression, referring to school settings as well as to the congregation, to formal instruction as well as to nurture, and to the classroom as well as to the sanctuary. We will qualify this term with "Protestant" when we are referring to the religious education of Protestant communities. In Part II, we will try to be as specific and contextually sensitive as possible in pointing out the terminological arguments that unfolded in the specific context under scrutiny. As will become evident over the course of this study, we agree that it is both possible and desirable to bring theology and educational theory into dialogue, without forcing either to be defined too narrowly. This dialogue is not understood in the sense of a comprehensive *theologia* or *philosophia naturalis,* in which religious education in the Christian sense is defined exhaustively by the characteristics of religious education in general — an understanding which is prone to play down the historical

5. For a contemporary Catholic view see Wolfgang Bartholomäus, *Einführung in die Religionspädagogik* (Darmstadt: Wiss. Buchgesellschaft, 1983). For a Protestant plea for catechetics cf. Christoph Bizer, "Katechetische Memorabilien. Vorüberlegungen vor einer Rezeption der evangelischen Katechetik," in *Jahrbuch der Religionspädagogik,* ed. Peter Biehl et al., vol. 4 (Neukirchen: Neukirchener, 1998), pp. 77-97.

6. Stanley Hauerwas, *Character and the Christian Life: A Study in Theological Ethics* (San Antonio: Trinity University Press, 1975); L. Gregory Jones, *Transformed Judgment: Toward a Trinitarian Account of the Moral Life* (Notre Dame: University of Notre Dame Press, 1990); L. Gregory Jones, *Embodying Forgiveness: A Theological Analysis* (Grand Rapids: Eerdmans, 1995); William H. Willimon, *Making Disciples: A New Approach to Confirmation* (Inver Grove Heights, Minn.: Logos Productions, 1990); William H. Willimon, *Remember Who You Are: Baptism as a Model of the Christian Life* (Nashville: Upper Room, 1980).

and contextual specificity of the Christian tradition. Rather, the relationship between theology and education is viewed as both dialectical and dialogical, that is, as both mutually critical and mutually informative.

Problematics of Contemporary Religious Education: An Initial Examination

At the outset of this study, it may prove helpful to point to some of the problems that we consider basic challenges faced by the theory and praxis of contemporary religious education. From our perspective, there are a number of challenges that make it difficult for religious education to find its way successfully into the twenty-first century. These challenges arise at the interface of four audiences or publics to which religious education is related: the individual person, the family, the church, and the general public (including the state). These audiences have been the focus of historical Protestant religious education and in recent decades have been conceptualized in helpful ways by Robert Lynn, Lawrence Cremin, and others who have articulated an "ecological" approach to education.[7] Broadly speaking, by "ecological" these persons are referring to the way a range of institutions — including public schools, universities, the media, religious communities, business organizations, and families — educate the public. Sometimes these institutions work together in complementary ways; sometimes they seem to work against one another.

The approach adopted in this book is "ecological" in this sense, focusing on the "ecology" of Protestant religious education, including the church, the family, the individual person, and public education. While the last of these may puzzle American readers, they should keep in mind that in Germany religious education remains a part of the curriculums of state-supported schools. In addition to this, the contribution of Protestant religious educa-

---

7. See Robert Lynn: *Protestant Strategies in Education* (New York: Association Press, 1964); "The Public Schools and the Study of Religion," in *An Introduction to Christian Education,* ed. Marvin Taylor (Nashville: Abingdon, 1966); (with Elliott Wright) *The Big Little School,* rev. ed. (Birmingham, Ala.: Religious Education Press, 1980); "A Historical Perspective on the Future of American Religious Education," in *Foundations for Christian Education in an Era of Change,* ed. Marvin Taylor (Nashville: Abingdon, 1976). See also Lawrence Cremin: *American Education: The Colonial Experience 1607-1783* (New York: Harper and Row, 1970); *Public Education* (New York: Harper and Row, 1976). Similar approaches to a comprehensive understanding of the tasks of Christian religious education may be found in Germany, most notably with Karl Ernst Nipkow, *Bildung als Lebensbegleitung und Erneuerung. Kirchliche Bildungsverantwortung in Gemeinde, Schule und Gesellschaft* (Gütersloh: Gütersloher Verlagshaus, 1990).

tion to education in general is a frequent topic of discussion in the United States as well as in Germany, even if the interest in this topic is not shared by all educators. As will become evident below, the institutional processes of modernization have fractured the ecology of Protestant religious education, leading contemporary Protestant religious education to neglect one or another of these publics in various ways. To our way of thinking, there is no normative hierarchy by which these four publics or audiences are ordered. Though we will focus attention first on questions pertaining to religious education's role in the education of the public, this should not be construed as signaling that we consider this audience to be the most important one for religious education.

Religious Education and the Education of the Public

The public role of religious education is especially problematic today. Most institutions educating the public in Western society are highly secularized. Should religious education simply resign itself to being sidelined from the mainstream of public education? Or should it try to fight its way back into the public domain? Given the high degree of secularization typical of most institutions of public education, there is much uncertainty about which of these options religious education should choose. Examples of debates over this issue are readily apparent in both the United States and Germany. In the United States it is evident in the context of ongoing discussions about prayer in schools and school vouchers, while in Germany and other European countries it is apparent in discussions about religious education in school curriculums.

More is at stake than the question of religion's place in state-supported schools. From our perspective, the most important dimensions of this issue have to do with what is sometimes called the *paideia* of a community: the general process by which a society transfers its cultural achievements to the next generation.[8] How should we define the relationship between general education and religious education within this all-encompassing *paideia*? Should general and religious education be viewed as two complementary halves that, together, produce a meaningful whole, a view common among prominent representatives of American Protestant religious education across the twentieth century? Or, if both do not fit together, should religious education be seen as standing in tension with general education, often mounting a critique on behalf of religiously based values? Or have religious and general

---

8. Detailed references from this discussion may be found in Part III of this volume.

education just gone their separate, incongruent, and incompatible ways because they are completely different forms of learning that take place in completely different settings that have nothing to do with one another?

These questions are bound up with the issue of the state's relationship to religion in education.[9] For democratic countries the separation of church and state is understood as essential, as a prerequisite of freedom. But is this separation — as needed as it is and will continue to be — really an adequate way of framing every question having to do with the treatment of religion in public schools? Can we now think afresh about both the losses and gains of this separation, especially when it is applied monolithically to all matters pertaining to the teaching of religion in public education? A host of new issues and situations have emerged over the past century, unforeseen by those who introduced the separation of church and state in order to safeguard civil liberty. These can be posed in the form of questions:

- What is the task of education in the face of the current global increase in multicultural and mutireligious interaction?
- Is it reasonable to assume that public education should never address these tensions and conflicts?
- Can it address these adequately without attending to religion?
- Is intercultural learning possible if religion is not treated as part of the connection between culture and learning?

Beneath all these questions, the fundamental issue of the relationship between religion and the state remains, with its overriding question ever present: How is the state to take up religious issues within education without compromising its fairness and protection of religious liberty?

Within the philosophy of education, reflection on the relationship between religion and education issues in a kind of paradox: The more extensive the secularization of education and educational institutions has been, the more religion needs to be included in the curriculum. The process of secularizing education has not unfolded as simply and straightforwardly as some philosophers of education had hoped. There are at least two unintended side effects that cannot be overlooked.

First, the secularization of education in the public sphere has weakened

9. Regarding the United States, see Warren A. Nord, *Religion and American Education: Rethinking a National Dilemma* (Chapel Hill: University of North Carolina Press, 1995). Regarding Germany and the recent discussion there cf. Christoph Th. Scheilke and Friedrich Schweitzer, eds., *Religion, Ethik, Schule. Bildungspolitische Perspektiven in dyer pluralen Gesellschaft* (Münster: Waxmann, 1999).

religious education in the private sphere and in civil society. The advocates of the secularization of public education may not have imagined that this would hinder or diminish religious education in the family or in religious communities; nevertheless, the secularization of the school has been accompanied by a gradual weakening of most traditional forms of religious education, especially in mainline churches. This effect may partly be attributed to the secularizing effects public schools and secular universities have upon children and youth. Second, religious life as a whole has become more privatized. Traditional forms of mainstream religious education were based on the assumption that religion involved not only the private sphere but also the public sphere. In recent decades, highly individualized forms of religion have come to the fore, not only in the privatized forms of the historic religions but, even more extensively, in their fundamentalist derivatives, in the commercialized, marketplace religions of modern consumerism, and in the eclectic religious collaging of "Sheilaism"[10] and New Age syncretist religion. In this situation, the assumption guiding the philosophy of education's view of religion and education is no longer convincing. We can no longer assume that religious education does not need to be included in public education because it will "take care of itself" through other agencies in society.

The Church

The problematics of contemporary religious education go beyond the "external" relationship of the church and religious education in public educational institutions. Even in the churches themselves, there are internal ambiguities about religious education. Is religious education to be viewed primarily as a ministry in the church or as discipline in the academy? On the one hand, Protestants, since the Reformation, have viewed education as an integral aspect of church life, as may be seen in Luther's and Calvin's emphasis on catechetical instruction.[11] On the other hand, education and religious education became self-consciously academic disciplines in their own right with the rise of modernity, especially during the twentieth century. Since their emergence as disciplines based on the canons of modern scientific research and rationality, they have operated with a considerable degree of autonomy in their

10. Robert N. Bellah et al., *Habits of the Heart* (Berkeley: University of California Press, 1985), p. 221.

11. For an overview in English of Luther's and Calvin's emphasis on catechetical instruction, see Richard R. Osmer, *Confirmation: Presbyterian Practices in Ecumenical Perspective* (Louisville: Geneva, 1996), chaps. 4-5.

relationship to the church. They have insisted on their own educational agenda, which may be quite different than the church's expectations. Consequently, the church has become uncertain about religious education's role in the process of "traditioning" its members, at times even raising questions about whether its educational proposals actually hinder this task.

It is in response to this development that Charles F. Melchert raised the question, "Does the Church Really Want Religious Education?"[12] Some religious education theorists like John Hull in England have argued that "religious education," in contrast to the "religious nurture" of a particular religious community, necessarily entails an encounter with religious plurality.[13] Moreover, he believes that it also entails being exposed to various "outside" perspectives — the perspectives of philosophy and the social sciences on religion, as well as the perspectives of other religious communities. Is this intentional exposure to plurality an experience the churches should desire for their members? What does it mean to be a church member or, in the case of children and youth, to become a church member in the context of religious pluralism? And what does religious pluralism really mean for religious education? Should religious education be based on the detached, "objective," and critical approach of religious studies in order to maximize its educational efficacy? Or should it be confessional? If the latter, how should this come to expression in education — in terms of the faith community's general aims for its young or solely in terms of the individual teacher's theological position and religious identity? This question has particular force in German public school settings in which "confessional" forms of religious education are still a real possibility. But it has equal force in congregations as well.

Questions like these immediately lead to foundational issues concerning religious education as a discipline. How should this discipline be related to theology, religious studies, the philosophy of education, and the social sciences? As far as the process of education itself is concerned, is it true that, educationally speaking, "teaching about" religion is preferable to the "teaching of" religion? And if this were true, what does it imply for the relationship between Christianity and education? We will develop and defend a clear position on these issues: a stance for a pluralistic approach that does not claim to be neutral, detached, or objective but allows for an education that is theologically grounded but that still does justice to educational criteria as well. If we are to move beyond mere opinion on this matter, however, we must first de-

12. Charles F. Melchert, "Does the Church Really Want Religious Education?" *Religious Education* 69 (1974): 12-22.

13. John Hull, *Studies in Religion and Education* (London: Falmer, 1984).

velop principles and guidelines that make such a considered position possible. We also must scrutinize more closely the various problems religious education has encountered across the modern period.

The Family

Additional challenges to the field of religious education emerge out of its commitment to the family as a context of religious education. One of the many changes in family life over the course of modernization during the past two hundred years is that the "traditional family" has evolved into the nuclear family consisting of only two generations and a small number of children. In contrast to earlier forms, this modern family is separate from the workplace. It is located in the private sphere, which, at the same time, is strongly influenced by the media and by public education, since the children spend a considerable amount of their time in school.

Since religious education within the family has not been well researched, it is difficult to arrive at conclusive observations about this sphere of life. Survey data in both the United States and Germany continue to find that parents want their children exposed to religious education. Infant baptism and confirmation, for example, are affirmed by many Christian parents.[14] Yet we know little about how parents actually carry out religious education at home. Clearly, shifting patterns of child-rearing — "from obedience to negotiation," as one observer aptly put it — have affected religious education at home.[15] In addition, various forms of religious privatization seem to be operative in many families, often creating a situation in which religion is a heartfelt matter but never becomes a topic of conversation at the family table.[16]

14. A summary of much of the relevant survey data on the continuing interest of American parents in religious education for their children is found in Dean R. Hoge, Benton Johnson, and Donald A. Luidens, *Vanishing Boundaries: The Religion of Mainline Protestant Baby Boomers* (Louisville: Westminster/John Knox, 1994), pp. 109-15. For Germany, see Klaus Engelhardt et al., *Fremde Heimat Kirche. Die dritte EKD-Erhebung über Kirchenmitgliedschaft* (Gütersloh: Gütersloher Verlagshaus, 1997).

15. Peter Büchner, "Vom Befehlen und Gehorchen zum Verhandeln. Entwicklungstendenzen von Verhaltensstandards und Umgangsnormen seit 1945," in *Kriegskinder, Konsumkinder, Krisenkinder. Zur Sozialisationsgeschichte seit dem Zweiten Weltkrieg,* by Ulf Preuss-Lausitz et al. (Weinheim: Beltz, 1983), pp. 196-212.

16. For an overview of some of the difficulties facing religious education in the home, see Merton Strommen and Richard Hardel, *Passing on the Faith: A Radical New Model for Youth and Family Ministry* (Winona, Minn.: Saint Mary's, 2000). For a good survey on the German situation see Michael N. Ebertz, "Heilige Familie? Die Herausbildung einer anderen Familien-

In Part III of this book, we will describe more fully some of the research on the family that has taken place over the past two decades. The prevalence of divorce, the breakdown of social supports for families in civil society, the entry of women into the workplace, and changing roles of men and women in the home will be explored. Clearly, the "modern" family is evolving toward something new, what some commentators call the "postmodern" family form. These changes present both problems and opportunities for contemporary religious education. Some argue that one of the most important tasks before religious education is to provide families with moral and religious frameworks to guide the choices they must make in forming new family patterns in a time of rapid social change. Important differences between families should not be overlooked, nor should the significant variations in family patterns found across denominations and countries. But, as we will show in Part II, the family has largely disappeared as an audience in Protestant religious education.

By the loss of the family as an audience we mean that religious education theorists seldom address families, especially parents, directly. This sort of address was an important part of the reform movement of the sixteenth century. Luther, Calvin, and many others wrote tracts and short treatises addressed to Christian parents. They viewed the family as an important site of religious education, indeed, as the first setting in which the catechism should be taught. As the family and religion became increasingly privatized across the modern period, however, the role of the family as an audience for religious education theory has gradually diminished. While some of the representative figures examined in Part II have addressed church leaders responsible for the families in their own religious communities, they have not done so with the depth and breadth given to other settings. Very few have addressed parents directly. How to respond to the changing situations in families remains a key challenge for contemporary religious educators, a challenge that we will address over the course of this volume.

The Individual Person

One audience or reference point of religious education still needs to be mentioned: the individual person. What does religious education have to offer to the individual? What does it contribute to the formation of the self as it has

---

religiosität," in *Wie geht's der Familie? Ein Handbuch zur Situation der Familien heute,* ed. Deutsches Jugendinstitut (München: Kösel, 1988), pp. 403-13.

been described by various theorists of modernization? Is it true that ego identity, as Habermas claims, can no longer rest on a religious basis since all attempts at finding a religious basis for identity formation have become obsolete? Is it true that the social process of individualization has turned religion into one more ephemeral resource that the individual may use temporarily, only to discard at a later time? Not everyone has thought of religion in this way. Some, in the tradition of the early Schleiermacher and Romanticism's critique of the Enlightenment, have described religion's role vis-à-vis the individual quite differently. They consider religion a much-needed advocate for human experiences that are often ignored within the busy schemes of science and technology or utilitarian morality and economics. These are experiences relating to human finitude: mortality, meaning, and the deeper self.

Adolescence is a critical time in the development of individual identity. It is readily apparent in both Germany and the United States that adolescence has become a stage of the life cycle during which many young people leave the church, never to return. Precisely when they are attempting to construct a sense of themselves as individuals and to form an initial sense of the direction of their life, they find that the church and its education have little to offer. Moreover, adolescence is no longer viewed as the one crucial period in which a more or less permanent personal identity is achieved (à la Erikson).[17] Many contemporary psychologists and social theorists have begun to rethink the nature of the life cycle and to see personal identity as something that must be reworked repeatedly over the course of life. What sort of contribution does religious education have to offer to the life journeys of individuals? How might it overcome the common perception that confirmation marks the "end" of religious involvement, a view that confines religion to the time of childhood and early adolescence? Have the life journeys of individuals become so diverse that the church must develop context-sensitive programs that are responsive to the particular needs of those involved in specific congregations? How might it reach out to adults who have left religion far behind during adolescence but are haunted by a loss of meaning during the middle part of their lives?

These questions represent important challenges to contemporary Protestant religious education, but they should not be viewed as totally foreign to Protestantism's historic commitments. The individual was granted an important role in the churches of the Protestant Reformation: as a participant in the priesthood of all believers, as an arbiter of moral conscience, and as a servant of God in his or her vocation in the world. The church has theological re-

---

17. Erik H. Erikson, *Identity and Crisis* (New York: Norton, 1968).

sources at its disposal by which to support and address individuals. The changes pointed to above, however, invite fresh thinking on this topic, something to which we will turn in the final part of this book.

Deciphering the Problematics: The Analysis of Social Contexts

It has become apparent to us over the course of our work on this project that no one social theory is fully adequate to describe and interpret the socio-historical developments of the twentieth century. In part, this is due to the inherent limitations of any perspective that seeks to be comprehensive, a postmodern insight into the necessity of methodological pluralism. But just as important, it also is due to important changes in the social context that began to take place during the latter part of the twentieth century.

Until fairly recently, modernization theory has dominated the research and theory-construction of sociology. With the rapid emergence of global systems of communication, transportation, and economic exchange, it has become apparent to many social commentators that it is no longer adequate to make a particular society or nation-state the primary unit of social analysis, which modernization theory has consistently done. Over the past two decades, a variety of theories of globalization have begun to emerge, theories that describe and interpret the interconnected systems and cultural flows that characterize our world today. Some interpreters of culture have begun to describe this change in theoretical approach as the movement from modernity to postmodernity. Anyone even remotely familiar with the literature on postmodernity is aware that this term is used in a wide variety of ways today, from a critique of the autonomous, monolithic "subject" presupposed by modern theorists to an interpretation of the "culture-collaging" characteristic of globalization. At the same time, there are some who view this term as misleading, arguing that the changes being pointed to represent not an entirely new situation, but merely an intensification and acceleration of modernization.[18] They prefer terms like "second," "late," or "reflexive" modernity.

Our position is to affirm the importance of methodological pluralism, the necessity of using a variety of perspectives to describe and interpret adequately the social contexts of religious education in Germany and the United States

---

18. See, for example, Ulrich Beck, Anthony Giddens, and Scott Lash, *Reflexive Modernization: Politics, Tradition and Aesthetics in the Modern Social Order* (Stanford: Stanford University Press, 1994). Recently, Giddens has adopted the language of globalization, making it clear that these categories are not mutually exclusive; see *Runaway World: How Globalization Is Reshaping Our Lives* (New York: Routledge, 2000).

during the past century. Modernization theory remains important to us. We are convinced that concepts like institutional differentiation, cultural pluralism, and individualization, which took shape initially in this framework, are still useful and accurate as descriptive lenses. At the same, however, they do not fully capture the remarkable changes that have taken place in Europe and North America during the latter part of the twentieth century, changes sparked by such things as the expansion of higher education following World War II, the new social movements and cultural transformations emerging in the 1960s, the rapid spread of systems of electronic communication in the 1980s and '90s, the massive expansion of international trade and financial markets, and the widespread emergence of a sense that local communities, nations, and even the world as a whole have been put at risk by the very scientific and technological forces that were supposed to bring various threats to human life under control. Taken together, these cultural transformations have created a new social context in which the older categories of modernization theory, so closely tied to changes internal to national communities, must be supplemented by the new perspectives of globalization and postmodernism. In the following chapter, we will describe more fully how we are using these terms.

Because we have found some value in all of these theories, we operate with a degree of methodological pluralism in this book, drawing on a variety of frameworks to interpret the social context under discussion at any given point. This should not, we hope, appear as a kind of mindless eclecticism in which various perspectives are used indiscriminately and with little regard for their disciplinary integrity. Rather, we are striving for self-conscious and principled methodological pluralism in which multiple perspectives are viewed as necessary to the comprehension of complex phenomena. Here, we are breaking with those religious education theorists who have adopted the perspective of a single dialogue partner in social philosophy or the social sciences and have allowed this perspective to control their analysis of social context. It would be difficult, if not impossible, to adopt such an approach today. Not only do the multiple frameworks of modernity, globalization, and postmodernism each bring to light somewhat different insights, but each is also needed to understand the various social transitions taking place over the course of the twentieth century.

The Need for a New Approach

The major goal of this study, therefore, is a new understanding of religious education gained through a reconstruction of religious education theory against the backdrop of its social context. This is developed along three lines: (1) *historically*, through an examination of paradigmatic figures of Protestant religious education in their respective German and American social contexts during the twentieth century; (2) *systematically*, through an interpretation of the social context to which these figures were responding in terms of the comprehensive frameworks of modernity, globalization, and postmodernism; and (3) *comparatively*, through an examination of similarities and differences of representative figures in Germany and the United States across the twentieth century. The existing literature on the development of religious education theory in the twentieth century and earlier is lacking precisely this sort of threefold perspective we hope to provide.

A Review of the Literature

We will first survey two types of literatures of religious education theory, both of which we consider to be in some ways inadequate. These are (1) historical approaches that in some ways neglect the cultural context, and (2) works that take the social context into account, but view it through the lens of only one particular social theory.

In America, quite a few books that fit into the first category have been published with the title of *History of Religious Education* or *History of Christian Education*.[19] Such books usually offer a condensed summary of the writings of individual authors, who are frequently grouped together according to their theological interests, denominational background, or their role in professional associations, most commonly the Religious Education Association.[20] In addition to these sorts of historical accounts, there also have been various attempts to "map" the field by describing basic "approaches" or "types."[21] Although the sequencing of these typological approaches often reflects historical developments, such authors and editors tend to treat their

19. The most recent example is James E. Reed and Ronnie Prevost, *A History of Christian Education* (Nashville: Broadman and Holman, 1993).

20. See Stephen A. Schmidt, *A History of the Religious Education Association* (Birmingham, Ala.: Religious Education Press, 1983).

21. Kendig Brubaker Cully, *The Search for a Christian Education — Since 1940* (Philadelphia: Westminster, 1965); Harold Burgess, *An Invitation to Religious Education* (Mishawaka, Ind.: Religious Education Press, 1975); Jack L. Seymour and Donald E. Miller, *Contemporary Approaches to Christian Education* (Nashville: Abingdon, 1982); Jack L. Seymour and Donald E. Miller, *Theological Approaches to Christian Education* (Nashville: Abingdon, 1990); Mary C. Boys, *Educating in Faith: Maps and Visions* (San Francisco: Harper and Row, 1989).

typologies as ideal types. They do not attempt to reconstruct the religious education theory espoused in various works in relation to a systematic, theoretical interpretation of the social context in which they were written. This sort of reconstruction of religious education theory/praxis and its social context is the primary focus of our book.

The German literature in this vein is quite similar.[22] The general tendency is to group authors and publications together along the lines of particular "approaches," which frequently are placed in a historical sequence. Not only is this historical periodization of various approaches questionable (implying that certain perspectives disappear altogether once a temporal marker is passed), but few attempts are made to systematically interpret the relationship of religious education theory/praxis to developments in the sociohistorical context. Only recently have efforts been made in this direction.[23]

The second approach — i.e., using a systematic and comprehensive analysis of social context to account for the development of religious education — has been used primarily in Germany. These works are written by scholars who adopt one particular theory of modernity as a framework for interpreting the recent developments in religious education. For example, Helmut Peukert and Norbert Mette use an adaptation of Habermas's theory to project a theory of modernity and then interpret religious education theory/praxis within this framework.[24] Heinz Schmidt does something similar using Luhmann's theory.[25] Such attempts typically do not include a detailed historical analysis of religious education. Rather, they adopt a particular social scientific theory or certain concepts within such theories as their starting point and then apply them to the field. More recently, Karl Ernst Nipkow and Rudolf Englert have drawn on the threefold distinction between pre-modern, modern, and postmodern aspects of religious education in order to develop

22. To mention a few examples: Wilhelm Sturm, "Religionspädagogische Konzeptionen des 20. Jahrhunderts," in *Religionspädagogisches Kompendium. Ein Leitfaden für Lehramts-studenten*, ed. Gottfried Adam and Rainer Lachmann (Göttingen: Vandenhoeck und Ruprecht, 1984), pp. 30-65; Gerd Bockwoldt, *Religionspädagogik. Eine Problemgeschichte* (Stuttgart: Kohlhammer, 1977); with more emphasis on context: Godwin Lämmermann, *Religions-pädagogik im 20. Jahrhundert* (Gütersloh: Gütersloher Verlagshaus, 1994), and Christian Grethlein, *Religionspädagogik* (Berlin: de Gruyter, 1998).

23. See Karl Ernst Nipkow and Friedrich Schweitzer, eds., *Religionspädagogik. Texte zur evangelischen Erziehungs- und Bildungsverantwortung seit der Reformation*, 3 vols. (München/Gütersloh: Kaiser/Gütersloher Verlagshaus, 1991/1994); introduction, "Religionspädagogik seit 1945. Bilanz und Perspektiven," in *Jahrbuch der Religionspädagogik*, ed. Biehl et al., vol. 12 (1996).

24. Norbert Mette, *Religionspädagogik* (Düsseldorf: Patmos, 1994), with many references to Peukert's philosophy of education.

25. Heinz Schmidt, *Leitfaden Religionspädagogik* (Stuttgart: Kohlhammer, 1991).

new theoretical frameworks for the discipline — a point of view which is obviously related to our own.[26]

Of greatest importance to our work are the studies of religious education theory that combine historical and systematic reconstruction. For example, in the United States, the idea of *paideia,* as described by educational theorist Lawrence Cremin, has been developed by religious educators Jack Seymour, Charles Foster, Robert O'Gorman, and James Fowler (in conjunction with Martin Marty's understanding of the "public church") to describe the role of religious education vis-à-vis public life.[27] Their work has many affinities to our own. These authors have asked two important questions: (1) Has religious education theory maintained the public as one of its audiences? (2) Are congregations interested not only in raising future church members but also in transforming society? In many ways, they echo themes initially raised in the United States by the religious education movement in the first decades of the twentieth century, themes which attempted to argue for religious education's role in public life in the face of the secularization of the American school system. At approximately the same time, prominent religious education theorists in Germany began to articulate an almost identical set of issues — even though religious (confessional/denominational) education continued to have a place in state schools.

More recently, Achim Leschinsky of the Max Planck Institute and Humboldt University's faculty of education has reconstructed the development of religious education within the state school from the sociological perspectives of individualization and secularization.[28] His work deserves a longer comment, for it illustrates a point of view that is common in the United States as well as in Germany. Leschinsky argues that religious education in state schools is a remnant of an earlier era, a time when all schools were Christian institutions. Schools were often founded by the church, influenced and shaped by the surrounding Christian culture and tradition, and supervised by church officials as representatives of the state (at least prior to 1918-1919). For Germany, the separation of church and state came with the Weimar Republic, Germany's first democracy. This put an end to the close ties between church and school,

---

26. Karl Ernst Nipkow, *Bildung als Lebensbegleitung und Erneuerung. Kirchliche Bildungsverantwortung in Gemeinde, Schule und Gesellschaft* (Gütersloh: Gütersloher Verlagshaus, 1990); Rudolf Englert, *Religiöse Erwachsenenbildung. Situation — Probleme — Handlungsorientierung* (Stuttgart: Kohlhammer, 1992).

27. For detailed references to this literature see Part III of this volume.

28. Achim Leschinsky, "Glaubensunterricht in der Säkularität. Religionspädagogische Entwicklungen in Deutschland seit 1945. Entwicklungen in Westdeutschland," in *Christenlehre und Religionsunterricht. Interpretationen zu ihrer Entwicklung 1945-1990,* ed. Comenius-Institut (Weinheim: Deutscher Studien-Verlag, 1998), pp. 7-45.

leaving religious education intact as a school subject taught one to three hours per week. According to Leschinsky, this compromise between state and church, which was renewed in the German Constitution of 1949 (at that point applicable only to West Germany, but also in force in East Germany after 1990), never fulfilled its original promise. It could not guarantee the Christian character of school education.

From this point of view three postwar developments have eliminated any rationale for continuing to include denominational/confessional religious education in the state schools: (1) the secularization of German educational institutions and the general population; (2) the presence of a much higher degree of individualization among the population, with the result that individuals view themselves as the arbiter of their life's meaning and purpose, quite independent of established religious institutions; and (3) the increased reality of multiculturalism and religious pluralism in German society. Often the ensuing argument is for a model similar to the "multi-faith" religious education approaches found in England and to the religious studies approach (teaching "about" religion) found in some American public schools.[29]

While this position is challenging, we do not view it as adequate. We are not concerned merely with Leschinsky's particular argument, but the way it represents a perspective that is quite widespread among contemporary philosophers and social analysts of education. It is a position that is highly dependent on an understanding of secularization rooted in certain questionable assumptions of many modernization theories. While it is certainly true that the German and American state school systems have become increasingly secularized over the second half of the twentieth century, this perspective ignores the covert presence of secular "religious alternatives" within these schools, including the presence of civil religion, for example, and the affirmation of metaphysical materialism, which frequently accompanies theories of evolution. Likewise, while it is an empirical fact that mainline churches in Germany and the United States have decreased in membership and public support during this same period, this does not necessarily mean that religiosity has disappeared altogether. Indeed, many new individualized expressions of a search for ultimate meaning and spiritual community are quite evident, from the proliferation of self-help groups to the rise of New Age spirituality. Robert Wuthnow has documented this extensively in the United States.[30]

---

29. Paul J. Will, Nicholas Piediscalzi, and Barbara Ann Demartino Swyhart, eds., *Public Education Religion Studies: An Overview* (Chico, Calif.: Scholars Press, 1981).

30. Robert Wuthnow, *Sharing the Faith: Support Groups and America's New Quest for Community* (New York: Free Press, 1994).

José Casanova offers a critique of secularization theories that is based on the theoretical distinction between secularization and institutional/cultural differentiation.[31] According to Casanova, much secularization theory mistakenly portrays modernization as virtually identical with the disappearance or privatization of religion. If one views modernization as a process of institutional and cultural differentiation, he argues, a very different picture begins to emerge. Within modern, differentiated societies, religion is one of a number of institutions (including the economy, government, family, and systems of education) that operate relatively independently of one another. Empirically, religion has played a wide variety of roles in institutionally differentiated societies, sometimes in surprisingly public ways. It is by no means obvious, therefore, that state-supported schools, charged with the education of the public, should not find a place for religion in the *paideia* they seek to promote. In addition to this, we are not convinced that religious needs are best met by a type of detached, social scientific study "about" religion.

Christian Kahrs's study of religious education, which is limited to the time from approximately 1850 to World War I, avoids many of these shortcomings.[32] Kahrs is interested in the emergence of what he perceives as modern Protestant educational thinking during this period of time. The development of this kind of thinking, he argues, is a reaction to the cultural insecurities brought about by modernity. Since modernity is premised on the idea of an open future, the meaning of tradition must be redefined vis-à-vis this idea and must be no longer thought of as concerned merely with handing on the past. Moreover, Kahrs also views modern Protestant educational thinking as responding to the relativization of the Christian tradition under the influence of modern historical approaches. This is a topic that we will come back to in Part II.

Our own study follows the approach described earlier. Simply put, it is an attempt to combine (1) a detailed historical analysis of trends and paradigmatic figures within the twentieth-century development of Protestant religious education in Germany and the United States and (2) a systematic interpretation and comparison of religious education in these two social contexts as seen through the lenses of several comprehensive frameworks, most notably modernization, globalization, and postmodernism. This leads us to consideration of the methodological problems faced by this approach.

31. José Casanova, *Public Religions in the Modern World* (Chicago: University of Chicago Press, 1994).

32. Christian Kahrs, *Evangelische Erziehung in der Moderne. Eine historische Untersuchung ihrer erziehungstheoretischen Systematik* (Weinheim: Deutscher Studien-Verlag, 1995).

Initial Methodological Considerations

Theories of religious education, obviously, are not theories of modernization, globalization, or postmodernism. Likewise, comprehensive social theories of this sort normally give little, if any, attention to religious education. How to bring an interpretation of religious education theory into dialogue with an interpretation of the social contexts of twentieth-century Germany and the United States is therefore not something that is immediately obvious. The all-important issue is to bring both sides of our research together in a methodologically responsible manner.

There are many extremely complex questions involved in methodological considerations of this sort. For example, how can historically and culturally sensitive readings of specific social contexts be combined appropriately with theoretical perspectives like those of modernization theories?[33] How can the relationship between social context and theoretical reflection be portrayed in a nonreductive fashion?[34] These kinds of considerations, which are basic to the cross-disciplinary work of practical theology and religious education, will be addressed in depth in Part III, which sets forth our constructive proposals. In this chapter we will offer only an overview of the four primary interpretive levels taken up in the present study. These are the following:

The first interpretive level involves analyzing the development of religious education theory over the course of the twentieth century in the context of modernization, globalization, and postmodernism. Here, a historical understanding of religious education theory is placed against the backdrop of major social trends unfolding over the course of the twentieth century.

Second, we will give a fresh reading to major religious education texts, viewed as paradigmatic of trends occurring within both religious education and the social contexts of Germany and the United States. These texts are placed against the background of modernization, globalization, and postmodernity by posing two questions: (1) How do the authors themselves perceive their work with respect to what they view as the most important cultural and social changes of their day? (author's perspective); and (2) How do we, as interpreters looking "be-

33. See Robert Wuthnow, *Meaning and Moral Order: Explorations in Cultural Analysis* (Berkeley: University of California Press, 1987).

34. See Dominic LaCapra, *History and Criticism* (Ithaca, N.Y.: Cornell University Press, 1985).

hind" the authors' backs, discover and reconstruct interconnections between comprehensive social processes and the theoretical concepts and practical proposals these representative figures offered? (interpreter's perspective).

Third, we will construct a comparative perspective by examining in tandem figures from both Germany and the United States during similar periods. Since interpretive frameworks like modernization are extremely abstract and refer to trends that are widely pervasive in a given society, it is difficult to grasp the actual effects of these trends on the basis of the analysis of a single context. To claim that someone like George Albert Coe, for example, was responding to certain facets of modernization in American society is a relatively empty claim unless some point of comparison either within or beyond the American context can be posited.

Our fourth and final interpretive level involves an attempt to develop our own constructive proposals for religious education as it enters the twenty-first century. Against the background of the first three levels of interpretation (which together make up Part II of this book), we will attempt to describe significant contemporary challenges facing each of the audiences or publics of religious education (individuals, church, public *paideia*, and families) in the context of paradigmatic figures of the past century. Our hope here is to point the way ahead, that is, to indicate the kinds of challenges involved in the renewal of the ecology of religious education in general and Protestant religious education in particular.

Obviously, one of the most important dimensions of our work is its international and comparative focus. It is still relatively unusual for academic religious educators to reflect on their work comparatively, examining similar developments in different parts of the world. It will be one of our tasks in this volume to it make clear why we think this kind of comparative work not only is possible but is increasingly important for both religious education and practical theology.

We initially became convinced of the value of such cross-cultural comparative work when we discovered that our research as scholars in the United States and Germany had led us to pose, independently of one another, similar questions about the past and present of religious education in our respective countries. In book-length studies, both of us had pursued the idea that the major challenges facing religious education today would not receive an adequate or effective response as long as there was no in-depth historical analysis.[35] We both had come to the conclusion that the most important difficulties faced by religious education in the present were deeply intertwined with long-term cultural and social developments related to processes like modernization and globalization.

In conversations fostered by our mutual involvement in the International Academy of Practical Theology, it became clear to us that in pursuing historical work on our own countries, we were uncovering trends that appeared strikingly similar.[36] In both countries, for example, a religious education movement began at approximately the same period of time, the first decades of the twentieth century. In both cases, the movement was characterized by the term "reform." In both countries, representatives of these movements considered their work to be the origin of modern religious education, making use of a "scientific" approach in sharp contrast to catechetics and other forms of teaching in the "prehistory" of religious education. As we will see in Part II, these are not the only parallels. Developments in religious education theory on both sides of the Atlantic after 1945 and during the period beginning with the 1960s reveal a number of remarkable parallels, as well.

Such parallels are largely unknown — or perhaps better forgotten, since prior to National Socialism in Germany there was a real, if limited, exploration of the international dimensions of religious education.[37] Since 1945, a few studies focusing on religious education in Germany have been published in English,[38] and a few accounts of religious education in the United States have become available in German.[39] But no comparative work on both contexts has been done, as far as we know.

35. Richard R. Osmer, *A Teachable Spirit: Recovering the Teaching Office in the Church* (Louisville: Westminster/John Knox, 1990) and Friedrich Schweitzer, *Die Religion des Kindes. Zur Problemgeschichte einer religionspädagogischen Grundfrage* (Gütersloh: Gütersloher Verlagshaus, 1992).

36. Cf. Richard R. Osmer and Friedrich Schweitzer, "Religious Education Reform Movements in the United States and in Germany as a Paradigmatic Response to Modernization," in *International Journal of Practical Theology* 1 (1997): 227-54.

37. To mention the most important example: Otto Eberhard, *Welterziehungsbewegung. Kräfte und Gegenkräfte in der Völkerpädagogik* (Berlin: Furche, 1930). With references to the European discussion cf. George Albert Coe, "Religious Education," in *A Cyclopedia of Education*, vol. 5, ed. Paul Monroe (Detroit: Macmillan, 1911 [repr. 1968]), pp. 145-50.

38. Most notably Ernst C. Helmreich, *Religious Education in German Schools: A Historical Approach* (Cambridge: Harvard University Press, 1959).

39. For example, Manfred Kwiran, *Religionsunterricht in USA — ein Vergleich. Edukative und methodische Perspektiven amerikanischer Religionspädagogik — ein pragmatischer Ansatz* (Frankfurt am Main: P. Lang, 1987); concerning the Sunday school see Thomas Hörnig, *Mission und Einheit — Geschichte und Theologie der amerikanischen Sonntagsschulbewegung im 19. Jahrhundert unter besonderer Berücksichtigung ihrer ökumenischen Relevanz und ihres Verhältnisses zur Erweckungsbewegung* (Maulbronn: Verlag am Klostertor, 1991).

Some twenty years ago, Wolf-Eckart Failing recognized the importance of such research and made a plea that future scholars engage in international comparative research in religious education — a plea that has not been answered with respect to Germany and the United States.[40] Even if our sights are broadened and we take other countries and non-Christian religions into account, no more than a handful of international comparative studies can be found. To mention the major examples: Gabriel Moran on religious education in England and the United States; Fernand Ouellet on religious education in the United States, England, and Canada; Witold Tulasiewicz and Cho-Yee To on the educational practices of world religions.[41] In addition to these studies, some of the research in comparative education is of interest here — especially on countries such as Israel, Turkey, and Egypt in which religion constitutes an integral part of general education and its development.[42]

Although none of these studies has afforded us with a model for our own comparative work, they have played an important role in shaping the general background of our thinking. But a larger question remains: Why has so little comparative work been done on religious education? Why have there been so few attempts to compare religious education in different countries? Certainly, we believe that much can be gained from such international comparative work. What is the value of this sort of research? Four preliminary answers to this question can be offered, answers that hark back to what has been said in earlier sections of this chapter.

1. *Increasingly, the decisive developments shaping contemporary societies and our world as a whole are international in character.* In the past, this trend was described as the "internationalization" of life. Since the 1980s, these developments have been described in terms of the globalization of various aspects of life, including education and religious education. Due to the global scope of economic and political processes, individual societies and cultures are increasingly subject to similar, if not identical, forces and give evidence of similar developments. Well-known examples of such social trends are plural-

---

40. Wolf-Eckart Failing, "Ansätze einer vergleichenden Religionspädagogik. Eine Problemanzeige," *Der Evangelische Erzieher* 27 (1975): 386-98.

41. Gabriel Moran, *Religious Education as a Second Language;* Fernand Ouellet, *L'étude des religions dans les écoles: L'expérience américaine, anglaise et canadienne* (Waterloo, Ontario: Wilfrid Laurier University Press, 1985); Witold Tulasiewicz and Cho-Yee To, eds., *World Religions and Educational Practice* (London: Cassell, 1993).

42. For example, Bill Williamson, *Education and Social Change in Egypt and Turkey: A Study in Historical Sociology* (Basingstoke: Macmillan, 1987); Bernd Schröder, *Jüdische Erziehung im modernen Israel. Eine Studie zur Grundlegung vergleichender Religionspädagogik* (Leipzig: Evangelische Verlagsanstalt, 2000).

ization, individualization, and privatization. In light of these sorts of transnational developments, religious education theory must begin to work more self-consciously out of an awareness of the global nature of the forces to which it is responding.

2. *It is increasingly apparent that certain questions can be answered only on the basis of international, comparative research.* For example, in the United States it is often assumed that the "decline" of religious education in the family is widespread and is largely due to certain trends closely related to modernization, such as the entry of women into the workforce, the increase of single-parent families, and the absence of supports that in the past were provided in civil society. But without a comparative perspective, how is it possible to answer the following questions: (1) Are these kinds of trends an inevitable by-product of modernity or are they due to context-dependent factors such as government policies? (2) Is the decline of religious education in the home closely linked to modernization in all countries? (3) Have different religious communities in different settings developed effective "alternatives" to these kinds of trends? International comparative research allows us to discern different paths of religious education in the context of comprehensive, transnational processes in order to better understand their respective meanings.

3. *Practical theology and religious education stand in an independent, but mutually influential, relationship.* This reason is somewhat more complex. In light of our first two points, it should be apparent that we are working out of the assumption that religious education theory should be understood in the wider context of social, cultural, and religious developments. In our understanding, such analysis also is the task of practical theology. We are presupposing here an understanding of practical theology that does not view it along the lines of applied theology or as the "helpmate" of systematic theology, applying its findings to the various fields of ecclesial praxis. At a later point, we will describe more fully our own understanding of practical theology. While we will not take up the complex issue of the relationship between religious education and practical theology in this chapter, we can point out some possible gains for religious education of international comparative research in practical theology. Given the common need for sociohistorical analysis of religious praxis, practical theology and religious education must find new ways of cooperating based not on competition but on mutual understanding and reinforcement of each field's work. For us, viewing religious education and practical theology as interconnected does not weaken the equally important ties of religious education to educational theory, philosophy, and the social sciences. While maintaining its ties to these fields, religious education may benefit from taking part in international research under the rubric of practical theology.

4. *The ecumenical implications of international comparative research should also be noted.* Serious ecumenical efforts must include knowledge of other churches, Christian traditions, and, in the case of interreligious dialogue, other religious communities. Most commonly, these attempts at mutual understanding have been limited to doctrinal formulations and matters of polity (e.g., the role of bishops, mutual recognition of ordination, etc.). Frequently, little attention is paid to gaining any real understanding of grassroots religious practices (such as religious education) as they are actually conducted in different communities. Understanding these kinds of practices, however, may well be more important in fostering genuine ecumenical understanding at a congregational level than the dialogues of theologians and church officials.

In short, there are a variety of reasons for carrying out the sort of international, comparative research we are attempting in this book. Some of these point to the intrinsic value of academic research in fostering deeper and richer understanding. Others are motivated by matters of praxis. One question remains to be addressed in this methodological introduction: How have we decided which theories of religious education should be examined in this study? In light of the main interest of the study, it seems sensible to us to make our selections on the basis of the reception and influence of particular texts on developments in the field. Our goal in the present volume is not to discover authors or insights that have been overlooked in the history of religious education or forgotten in later times. Rather, we are interested in examining what might be called the "mainstream" of religious education theory. Our working assumption is that the very perceptions earning certain authors and texts a place in the "mainstream" of education reflect their attempt to address important social and ecclesial demands found in our analysis of social and historical contexts. We do not mean that the persons and texts selected are those we judge to be the most adequate for the period under consideration. Such judgments would necessarily vary widely. Rather, our concern is to focus on texts and persons who were widely recognized during the periods under consideration as having made an important contribution to Protestant religious education.

The dynamics of reception and evaluation are obviously complex, and the process by which "mainstream" publications are attributed their status is influenced by a range of factors. These include personal friendships, collegial relationships, nepotism, gender, institutional affiliation, and denominational background. In light of the aims of the present study, however, we consider this "mainstream focus" a workable approach.

2   Modernization, Globalization, and Postmodernism: Toward an Analytical and Cross-Disciplinary Framework

In the previous chapter, we began our exploration of the thesis that Protestant religious education stands in an interdependent relationship with the social contexts in which it is located and that these contexts are best understood today through international, comparative analysis. In this chapter, we will describe the frameworks used to understand the social contexts explored in Parts II and III. We will be using modernization and globalization as our two primary frameworks, and postmodernism as a third framework that is a subspecies of globalization. It may be helpful at the outset to indicate why we believe these sorts of frameworks are necessary in international, comparative research of the sort we are conducting in this project.

Direct comparisons of educational theory and praxis formed in one country to those of another country are notoriously difficult and often misleading. In large measure, this is due to the importance of contextual factors in both interpreting and evaluating the viability of educational theory and praxis. If the particularities of history and culture are bracketed out, many of the factors that make a particular program of education compelling in a specific time and place are removed from the picture. No doubt, this is one of the reasons that most attempts to import educational programs formed in one nation to another have failed so miserably. For example, many of the contextual factors that made the progressive education movement so compelling to teachers in the United States during the early decades of the past century — the presence of democratic institutions and the pragmatic orientation of American culture — simply were not present in Germany and many other countries in Europe during this period,[1] and attempts to import the ideas and practices of the progressive education movement met with limited success.

Such cultural differences that make importing educational practices difficult also make direct, point-by-point comparisons between two cultures' educational theories and praxes difficult. To make any such comparisons, some common bases of comparison must be adopted. We have adopted the social and institutional processes of modernization and globalization, which have influenced both American and German culture, as such common reference points — as frameworks for understanding these two societies and as lenses through which to view religious education theories in both countries. Some of the similarities in religious education theory that we have identified across these two national contexts can be explained, we think, by the common challenges posed by modernization and globalization in both countries. As we note these similarities we will, at the same time, attempt to keep before the reader the important contextual differences distinguishing Germany and the United States, placing limits on our use of modernization and globalization for comparative purposes. While these frameworks offer a vantage point from which similar processes and trends can be noted, they must be brought into dialogue with the historical and cultural particularities of each national context. Balancing a concern for both cross-cultural similarities and national particularities is what makes international, comparative research so difficult but also so important.

An approach based on modernization, globalization, and postmodernism as a common reference point for international comparisons has its limitations with respect to the fullness of history. If it is said that the United States and Germany have gone through parallel processes of modernization over the past century, such a view tends to exclude unique experiences, which have been important for the history of both countries. The United States did not go through a Third Reich, for example, and Germany was not involved in Korea or Vietnam. The relationship between black and white was an issue only for the United States in the 1960s, and Turkish workers and immigrants play an important role in Germany but not in the United States. Such historical differences between Germany and the United States cannot be overlooked, and the methodological value of using abstract concepts is not unlimited. Nevertheless, as we will see, it still makes sense to view the development of re-

---

1. Progressive education was closely related to the work of John Dewey. See Dewey's *Democracy and Education: An Introduction to the Philosophy of Education* (New York: Macmillan, 1928) for a statement of this perspective.

ligious education in both countries as a response to common challenges in both contexts.

Modernization, Globalization, and Postmodernism: Initial Definitions

Those familiar with contemporary social theory are quite aware that the terms "modernization," "globalization," and "postmodernism" are used in a wide variety of ways. Moreover, it is not uncommon for them to be portrayed as mutually exclusive. Given these different understandings, it is obvious that some sort of clarification of the way we are using the terms is necessary.

In ways that will be elucidated more fully below, we are using the terms "modernization" and "globalization" as historical-interpretative frameworks to point to key developments taking place during distinct eras. In the West, early modernization began to occur in the aftermath of the Reformation and Renaissance with the rise of the modern nation-state and the first impulses toward the creation of *national* cultural identities, political and judicial systems, and, to a lesser extent, economies. These early impulses were given their peculiarly modern form with the rise of modern science and the industrialization of the economy over the course of the eighteenth, nineteenth, and twentieth centuries. Science not only served as the basis for the ongoing technological innovation driving the industrialization of the economy but also as a cultural ideal of modern life, the very epitome of a humanity "come of age" and learning to rely on its own powers and reason. By "modernization," thus, we have in mind a range of processes closely associated with the emergence of the modern nation-state, the rise of modern science, and the industrialization of the economy between the eighteenth and twentieth centuries.

Globalization is, perhaps, best portrayed initially by way of contrast. It points to the diminishment of the nation-state as the center of cultural, political, and economic activity and a movement away from heavy industry as the primary focus of the economy. Three closely related "revolutions," beginning during the final two decades of the twentieth century, have driven globalization: (1) the technological revolution of the electronic media, emerging, largely, out of the invention of microprocessors for computers but also related to advances in other forms of electronic and satellite communication; (2) the emergence of a global economy, based on this technological revolution in the media; and (3) the collapse of both the Soviet Union and the bipolar structuring of interstate relations characterizing the Cold War, leading to the emergence of new multipolar forms of political organization. Obviously, modernization did not stop one day and globalization begin the next. Nation-states are still important centers of cultural, political, and economic activity, and scientific research and technological innovation continue to be important dimensions of contemporary life. But a significant shift has begun to take place, like the reconfiguration of colored pieces of glass when the end of a kaleidoscope is turned. The same colors are there but they are arranged in a different pattern. We are in the very early stages of globalization. While it is apparent that the institutional and cultural patterns of modernity are changing, it is unclear at this point exactly what new configurations will emerge.

"Postmodernism" is used in a more limited way in this book. It is a kind of "subspecies" of globalization. We are not so much interested in a particular philosophical definition of the postmodern, the sort of definition that might emerge, for example, by identifying this concept closely with the thinking of Foucault or Derrida. Rather, we are using "postmodernism" to refer to a configuration of cultural and intellectual elements that represents one fairly pervasive type of response to globalization found in a variety of groups, ranging from social theorists to theologians to clothing designers.[2] There are three elements of postmodernism as we are using the term here: an affirmation of radical pluralism, a heightened awareness of the risks attending scientific research and technological innovation, and a highly processive view of life in which identity is constructed repeatedly over the course of life. In our research on adolescents in the United States and Germany, as part of a larger collaborative project, we have found various combinations of these elements in the thinking of a large number of adolescents.[3] As we will argue below, postmodernism in this sense is best viewed as one of several reflexive responses various groups are making to globalization. That postmodernism is not the only response to this phenomenon emerging in recent years can be seen clearly in the resurgence of various forms of fundamentalism and ethnocentricism around the world.

2. David Lyon in *Postmodernity* (Minneapolis: University of Minnesota Press, 1994) makes a helpful distinction between *postmodernity* as a social and institutional phenomena and *postmodernism* as a cultural and intellectual response to the social conditions of postmodernity. The key conditions of postmodernity that cultural postmodernism is responding to, Lyon argues, can best be pointed to by the term "globalization" (see pp. 6-7). Somewhat analogous to Lyon's approach, we see postmodernism as a cultural response to the conditions of globalization.

3. The Princeton Project on Youth, Globalization, and the Church is a research project sponsored by the Princeton Theological Seminary Institute for Youth Ministry. It is exploring the relationship of globalization and adolescent faith in Germany, Japan, the United States, Ghana, South Africa, Paraguay, Argentina, Russia, and India. Both of the authors are participants in this project.

As these initial comments indicate, one of the reasons we have adopted the frameworks of modernization, globalization, and postmodernism has to do with the particular period of time we are examining in this book. The twentieth century represents both the flowering of high modernity and the onset of globalization. Most of the representative figures of religious education examined in Part II may be understood as responding to developments best described by theories of modernization. The analytical framework that modernization theories provide, however, cannot bear the weight of the changes that have taken place in the final decades of the twentieth century. Indeed, it may not capture certain trends beginning to emerge as early as the 1960s, which in retrospect might be viewed as harbingers of globalization and postmodernism.

One of our reasons for adopting all three of these analytical frameworks, thus, has to do with the complexity and rapid social change within the particular period of history we are examining. A second reason is closely related. Theories of modernization and globalization represent the most important tools available, we believe, by which to pursue our basic thesis: the interdependence of religious education and its various social contexts. Our focus is not solely on the *ideas* of the representative figures we are examining. Rather, we are exploring the interrelationship of paradigmatic texts to developments taking place in the social contexts in which they were located. In pursuit of this goal, we are using the tools of sociological analysis, not the history of ideas.

A final reason for our use of these three frameworks is closely related to the constructive thrust of this project. If Germany, the United States, and all countries of the world really are in the midst of a major transition of the sort pointed to in various theories of globalization, then what contribution might religious education make to shaping the institutional and cultural patterns that are only beginning to emerge? Here, in framing our constructive proposals, the attempt to look back, look across, and look ahead proves to be especially helpful. Looking back at prominent figures of religious education of the past century gives us a vantage point from which to better understand our own social context. To what extent are the problems and presuppositions of these figures still ours? Do the challenges of modernization remain with us or has the world changed so significantly as to make the paradigmatic responses of the past of limited usefulness today? Looking across Germany and the United States simultaneously gives us better understanding of those aspects of modernization and globalization that appear to cross national boundaries, which, in turn, helps us discern which dimensions of our contexts are peculiar to the history of one of the nations and which are shared. Looking ahead to the future of religious education challenges us to think in terms of changes in our social context that are currently underway but remain open. If religious education stands in an interdependent relationship to its social contexts, then a better understanding of these contexts enhances the possibility of influencing their development. Looking ahead, we consider the future course of modernization and globalization and religious education's role in shaping this future.

This attempt to look ahead raises one of the more complex issues of cross-disciplinary work we have faced in this project. For the most part, our use of modernization and globalization theories is relatively modest. We are not attempting to construct new theories of our national and global contexts; rather, we are entering into a dialogue with social scientific research that is largely the work of others. Where consensus exists across various theories of modernization and globalization, we have attempted to point to it in the accounts that follow. Inevitably, however, looking toward the future raises critical ethical questions about the kind of future we, as Christian educators, want, in light of the gospel. What sort of national and global communities should we hope for and work toward? At this point, social science inevitably begins to shade into social philosophy and ethics. As will become evident below, a number of contemporary social theories are quite explicit in advocating certain lines of social development as holding out the best prospects for humanity's future. These normative accounts are value-laden and ethically prescriptive. Quite frequently, they are negative, dismissive, or superficial in their understanding of the potential contribution of religion to humanity's future. How is it possible to use these theories to understand the social contexts in which religious education is located without inadvertently allowing them to control our understanding of religious education's possible contributions to the future?

Our response to this question is twofold. Most importantly, we conceptualize our engagement of social scientific theory as a critical dialogue, something noted in the previous chapter. We also explicitly distinguish in what follows the historical-interpretative dimensions of social theory from its normative dimensions; that is, we distinguish social theorists' efforts to analyze human social relationships from their claims about the sort of social relationships that are best for humanity. When social theorists go beyond the descriptive analysis of social developments, and make normative claims, these claims must stand the scrutiny of philosophical, ethical, and theological justification. In our examination of this normative dimension of social theory, we are particularly interested in how various theories view the future of religion. Our concern is not to opt for the most positive and optimistic view of religion currently offered, a kind of wishful thinking. Rather, it is to be sensitive to the undue bias against religion found in many of these normative interpretations of the future and to discern alternatives that are equally plausible projections of religion's possible role in the global community that is beginning to emerge.

Modernization Theory

A Consensus Theory of Modernization

The most important use we are making of the concept of modernization is historical-interpretive. When historians use the term "modernization," they are referring to the various historical processes that have unfolded over roughly the past three hundred years, depending on the country or part of the world that is in mind. In the United States and central Europe, these changes more or less coincide with the eighteenth through the twentieth centuries. Key features of modernization in this historical sense are industrialization, capitalist market economies, urbanization, ongoing technological innovation, and the institutionalization of large-scale systems of education, medicine, and social welfare, to mention only a few.[4]

Social theorists, as well as historians, have constructed many different understandings of modernity and modernization. According to the German sociologist Johannes Berger, however, a "basic consensus" about the core of modernization has gradually emerged among social theorists over the course of the twentieth century.[5] He argues that it is possible to speak of a "single concept of modernity" emerging gradually in the sociological tradition running from Max Weber to Talcott Parsons. Within this tradition, modern societies are portrayed as emerging out of a process of "differentiation." Berger portrays differentiation as operating in four ways: (a) the differentiation and delineation of a society from its past; (b) a social order that is characterized by the emergence of a wide range of subsystems, differentiated functionally

---

4. Examples of a historically descriptive use of "modernization" are found primarily in historical and sociological literature dealing with social change, be it in the West or in so-called developing countries. Authors like Samuel N. Eisenstadt, *Modernization: Protest and Change* (Englewood Cliffs, N.J.: Prentice-Hall, 1966), and James S. Coleman, "Modernization," in *International Encyclopedia of the Social Sciences,* vol. 10 (1968), pp. 395-402, are several of the leading theorists using "modernization" in this sense.

5. Johannes Berger, "Modernitätsbegriffe und Modernitätskritik in der Soziologie," *Soziale Welt* 39 (1988): 224-36.

from one another; (c) the appearance of distinct rationalities and cultures within these subsystems, which operate in relative autonomy from one another; and (d) the fundamentally "dynamic" character of the subsystems in relation to one another and to the future.

To understand the impact of social differentiation, consider the changes in a western Pennsylvania community fifteen miles from downtown Pittsburgh. In 1900 the leadership of the grange (a farmers' association), the leadership of the Lutheran grade school (which almost all the community's children attended), and the leadership in the Lutheran congregation overlapped almost completely. The worlds of work, school, and worship intertwined in ways that allowed children to learn the same values from the same people in all spheres of their lives. Everyone knew everyone else, and everyone farmed, except for the local families that owned and operated the one bar and restaurant in town, the general store, the doctor's office (and perhaps the veterinary clinic), and the feed and seed store. These were the only service jobs available, because families cared for their children and elderly themselves. If people wanted advice they consulted the pastor, the doctor, or each other. Farm work was done by family members or cooperatively with other farmers.

A century later the same area contains two public and three nonpublic grade schools, twelve different churches, seven day care centers, two nursing homes, myriad restaurants, various housecleaning, gutter-clearing, and landscaping services, a multitude of different kinds of medical, dental, legal, and counseling practices, and dozens of specialized businesses, ranging from closet organizing to nightly dinner catering to make-your-own beer stores — the majority of which are owned by national chains. Most adults commute to one of a wide range of specialized jobs. The community's residents live in such widely diverse circles of acquaintance that neighbors who live three houses away commonly never meet unless they happen to see each other carrying out the trash (and even that might be done by a housecleaning service).

What we see in these changes is the reality of differentiation: the emergence of relatively independent social systems in different areas of life. In the example given above, these range from schools to the workplace to religious communities to family life. Each differentiated institution pursues its own goals on the basis of its own media of communication and specialized roles. Many somewhat different accounts of modernization place differentiation at the very heart of their theories. Niklas Luhmann's social systems approach, for example, focuses on the idea of the functional differentiation of systems and subsystems.[6] Functional differentiation refers to (1) specialization of the

6. Niklas Luhmann: *Social Systems*, trans. J. Bednarz (Stanford: Stanford University Press,

functions of various social systems (i.e., various organizations taking on more and more specialized roles, exemplified in, for example, religious education taking place almost exclusively at church), and (2) specialization of roles within these systems (e.g., instead of people working at the wide range of physical, management, and book-keeping tasks farming involves, they are working at highly specialized jobs involving multiple years of graduate school). Portraying functional differentiation as the core characteristic of modern societies, Luhmann describes all areas of modern society in terms of system, environment, and systemic rules. In his extensive work published over the last thirty years he has applied this perspective to a wide variety of different fields — ranging from administration to communication, education, religion, law, aesthetics, and ecology. One of his key explanatory concepts is the "self-referentiality" of systems. By this he means that it is impossible to influence (or "steer") any particular system by means of commands from another system. Every system operates with its own *internal* "binary code" and its own "media." They are not subject to external control, since these internal codes and media cannot be translated into the codes and media of other systems.

While much of the work of Jürgen Habermas during this same period has been directed against Luhmann's exclusive use of systems theory to analyze modern society, he shares with Luhmann an understanding of modernization in terms of differentiation.[7] Building on the work of Talcott Parsons, Habermas describes the functional differentiation of various "spheres of life" across the modern period, giving special attention to those spheres or "institutional domains" that operate according to the distinct rationalities and truth claims of science, art, and morality.[8] As we shall see, his use of the concept of "lifeworld" adds an important dimension that is missing in Luhmann's theory of modernization.

Peter Berger and Thomas Luckmann's collaborative work, as well as their individual writings, also place a type of differentiation at the center of their description of modernization. In *The Social Construction of Reality*, they argue that in the course of their everyday lives, persons move in and out of relatively autonomous systems or "lifeworlds" — systems such as the family,

---

1995) and *The Differentiation of Society*, trans. S. Holmes and C. Larmore (New York: Columbia University Press, 1982).

7. See Jürgen Habermas and Niklas Luhmann, *Theorie der Gesellschaft oder Sozialtechnologie — Was leistet die Systemforschung?* (Frankfurt: Suhrkamp Verlag, 1990).

8. Jürgen Habermas, *The Theory of Communicative Action*, vol. 1, *Reason and the Rationalization of Society*, trans T. McCarthy (Boston: Beacon, 1984), and vol. 2, *Lifeworld and System: A Critique of Functionalist Reason*, trans. T. McCarthy (Boston: Beacon, 1987).

economy, politics, education, religion, and the legal system.[9] Modernization is characterized as involving the "pluralization of lifeworlds." No one institution (such as the family or the workplace) claims the entirety of a person's identity. Modern persons play different roles as they move from one institution to another, roles they hold "at a distance" from their core self.

In *The Heretical Imperative,* Berger makes extensive use of the differentiation thesis to describe the challenges facing modern religion.[10] Individuals, with the freedom to move in and out of the various institutions that give shape to their lives, including religion, now face the task of knitting together a meaningful understanding of life's ultimate meaning and purpose. They confront this as the challenge of going beyond a simple acceptance of the answers of the past, the recipes and life-scripts provided by religious tradition. Hence, Berger proposes the "heretical imperative," the task of sorting out from the diversity of moral and religious positions to which people are exposed those that best help them make sense of their lives. Religious authority in differentiated modern societies must function in a dramatically different way than it did in traditional societies.

Differentiation theory is seen as the key dimension of modern life by most social theorists, even when they focus their attention on only one aspect of modernization. Social theory concerning individualization is a case in point. Many modernization theories view individualization as a consequence of the modern functional differentiation of social systems. As the various subsystems of a modern society become more independent of one another, they also become more independent of individual actors who enter such systems on a part-time basis. Niklas Luhmann describes this relationship as a kind of "interpenetration," by which he means that individuals no longer form permanent parts of systems.[11] Individual persons play certain roles within the various subsystems in which they participate, roles that they do not define for themselves, but that are governed by the rules and functional imperatives of the particular subsystem in which they are participating at any given time. Everyday life, thus, consists of a sequence of such part-time "interpenetrations," revolving around the roles of worker, consumer, family member, learner, and so forth. No one particular role exerts a defining influence on the entirety of an individual's experience. In effect, the individual

9. Peter Berger and Thomas Luckmann, *The Social Construction of Reality: A Treatise on the Sociology of Knowledge* (Garden City, N.Y.: Anchor, 1967).

10. Peter Berger, *The Heretical Imperative: Contemporary Possibilities of Religious Affirmation* (Garden City, N.Y.: Anchor, 1979).

11. Niklas Luhmann, *Gesellschaftsstruktur und Semantik. Studien zur Wissenssoziologie der modernen Gesellschaft,* vol. 2 (Frankfurt: Suhrkamp Verlag, 1981), pp. 276ff.

stands "at a distance" from them all. Both the freedom and burden of making one's way through the various subsystems that make up a modern society thus fall to the individual.

Ulrich Beck describes individualization in a very similar fashion.[12] He argues that the preset bonds of tradition, origin, and belonging, so important in traditional societies, have lost their defining power in differentiated modern societies. The individual has been set free to choose his or her own life, to be responsible for constructing a meaningful "life project," and must endure the "risks" that attend this, at both personal and social levels.

There is little need to continue this survey of recent sociological theories of modernization. Enough has been said to demonstrate the plausibility of Johannes Berger's thesis that much contemporary social theory has reached a consensus about what modernization has meant for human societies. For historical-interpretive purposes, we will follow this thesis and posit institutional and cultural differentiation as standing at the heart of modernization. Since a number of "spin-off" concepts, closely related to modernization, are used by social scientists in somewhat different ways, it may be helpful for us to provide a brief overview of how we are using them in this book.

Differentiation: The emergence of functionally distinct social systems within a particular nation-state. These operate with relative autonomy in their relationships to one another, pursuing their own goals and developing their own means of communication, moral logics, rationalities, and other dimensions of a distinctive "culture."

Pluralization: Differentiation has a pluralizing effect. Persons pass through a variety of lifeworlds as they move from one institutional domain to another in their everyday lives and are exposed to the rationalities and moral logics of each sphere. While not identical, this is closely related to the idea of plurality, which refers to the diversity of experiences and situations characterizing human existence in general. Pluralism refers to a reflexive response to plurality in which its manifold diversity is affirmed.

Individualization: Differentiation and pluralization have an individualizing effect. No single institution or sphere of life is in a position to direct individuals through all of the lifeworlds in which they participate. Consequently, more of the burden falls on individuals to forge meaningful life projects and to negotiate the choices they face in terms of career, family, religion, and so forth. Individualization is not to be

12. Ulrich Beck, *Risk Society: Towards a New Modernity* (London: Sage, 1992).

confused with individuation, a psychological concept pointing to the achievement of personal identity.

Relativization: Together, pluralization and individualization give rise to the awareness that social norms and institutional patterns could be different than they are. "Our way" of doing things is only one of many. This is not to be confused with relativism, a position that affirms all paths to truth, goodness, and beauty as equally valuable.

Public sphere: Among the distinct social systems that emerge in modern societies, some are explicitly oriented toward support of the rights and goods that all members of the community should possess as citizens. This public sphere is typically identified with the political and legal systems of the nation-state and the various associations by which persons come together. For much of the modern period, public life was identified with those things held in common by all members of society. Today, it is described in terms of the interaction of culturally diverse groups, placing the emphasis on difference rather than on commonality.

Private sphere: This term is often viewed as including all institutions falling outside the public sphere and, thus, as including economic systems. We are using it more narrowly to refer to spheres identified with family life, leisure activities, friendships, and personal relations.

Civil society: The sphere of social interaction between the state, the economy, and the private sphere, including voluntary associations, social movements, and forms of public communication. This area of life is "pre-political" in the sense that it does not involve the direct exercise of power by the state. In democratic societies, however, it plays a crucial role in teaching the virtues and practices of democratic culture and in generating cultural values and beliefs that indirectly influence public policy.

Reflexivity: Reflective responses to changes in the social context. These include both scholarly forms of reflection and those found in popular culture.

Differentiation Theory and Religious Education: Four Basic Challenges

Having reviewed the main points of what we may call a "consensus" theory of modernization, it may be helpful to focus our sights once again directly on religious education. Thus, we will briefly describe here four challenges posed to twentieth-century religious education by the various aspects of differentiation, leaving a more detailed discussion of particular individuals and texts to Part II. These challenges are as follows: (1) functional differentiation, the development of specialized social subsystems in modern society; (2) the emergence of religious education as a specialized academic discipline; (3) the emergence of religion as a differentiated social subsystem; (4) the separation of morality, personal identity, and religion. It is important to recall our thesis that religious education and modernization are interdependent, standing in a mutually influential relationship. Obviously, the process of modernization challenges religious education, but it is also the case that religious education challenges modernization, shaping it in some directions and not others. Their relationship is one of interdependence. Our goal here is not to treat the effects of differentiation on religious education exhaustively but to illustrate the importance of viewing religious education as standing in an interdependent relationship to developments taking place in its social context.

Challenge One: Functional Differentiation

Perhaps the most important and comprehensive challenge posed to religious education by the social processes of modernization is that of functional differentiation, which is the emergence of specialized subsystems in modern societies, subsystems that are governed by their own goals, means of communication, and feedback systems. This generalized functional differentiation in society has created two particular forms of differentiation that have had profound effects on religious education: the emergence of religious education as a discipline, and the transformation of religion into a specialized subsystem. Both of these two processes have created their own problems and possibilities, and, if this is not recognized, they can exert great influence on religious education "behind its back," even to the point of subverting its professed intentions.

Challenge Two: Religious Education as a Specialized Discipline

In order for religious education to become a relatively independent field or discipline, three things had to happen. First, religious education as a form of praxis had to separate from education in general. Second, religious education had to be distinguished from other activities of the church and from theological reflection on these activities. Third, religious education had to create its own specialized body of knowledge, both theoretical and practical, by which it could be identified as a field addressing a distinct group of professionals.

41

Looking back at religious education over the course of the twentieth century, we know that all three of these developments necessary for its emergence as a differentiated academic field did in fact take place. To a large degree, these developments have been viewed positively by religious education professionals and members of the academic community. The main reason for this positive appraisal is the high degree of expertise made possible by specialization. No doubt, many gains have followed this emergence of religious education as field, from a greater awareness of developmental differences across the human life cycle to the use of teaching approaches based on a richer understanding of how persons learn. Differentiation and specialization also have a price, however, something that remains out of sight as long as we limit ourselves to the internal self-understanding of the field.

If we widen our perspective to include both the effects of modern general education on religious education and the actual praxis of religious education as carried out in concrete communities, the picture does not look so bright. While expert standards in the field of religious education have led to the construction of a variety of theories and models of religious education praxis, much of the work of this specialized academic field has been counteracted by powerful forces from the outside: forces both within and outside the field of religious education. For example, we can see the force of modern general education. Frequently, especially in the United States, it has influenced religious education with educational theories that are not supportive of religion. We can also see the force of particular congregations and particular theologies that are oblivious to the importance of religious education. Moreover, the very specialization giving rise to religious education's academic status has undercut its ability to reclaim a public role for this field. To a large extent, it has increasingly addressed a specialized audience of professionals, neglecting the wider publics of the congregation, general education, the family, and individuals. In short, the advantages promised by the rise of religious education as a differentiated field of specialized knowledge and professionals have collided with, and even helped to create, a new set of problems.

Challenge Three: The Emergence of Religion
as a Differentiated Subsystem

According to modernization theory, one of the most important effects of differentiation is to displace religion from its role in traditional societies. There, it played the highly important role of social integration and legitimization, serving as the "sacred canopy" under which all spheres of life were bound together into a meaningful whole.[13] Obviously, differentiation creates a very different form of social organization in which various subsystems operate according to their own functional imperatives without any need for overarching integration or legitimization by religion. In effect, modern religion has become merely one subsystem among others, with its own goals, means of communication, and feedback systems. Three trends commonly associated with this transformation of religion have posed important challenges to religious education: (1) privatization, (2) uncertainty over religion's public role, and (3) the need to develop internal means of education in light of diminished support by other educational institutions.

Privatization: Religion, as a specialized subsystem in modern societies, is commonly described as located in the private sphere, the sphere of personal preference and family life. While this is not a fully adequate description of religion's role, it does capture important features of modern religion. Individuals exercise great choice in their affiliation and identification with a religious community. Religious affiliation is no longer attached as closely to ascriptive roles like social class, ethnicity, or parental affiliation. Religious communities, thus, must persuade individuals that they have something to offer, answering existential questions, providing support in raising children, or meeting social needs. Moreover, it is also clear that many individuals who do not affiliate with a religious community still view themselves as religious. Research has consistently revealed, for example, that large numbers of adolescents find their religious and existential questions better addressed by music, literature, movies, art, and social movements than by religion.[14] Thus, the privatization of religion challenges religious educators to ask themselves, How can we address the voluntaristic and individualized expressions of modern religion without losing our integrity?

Role uncertainty: Similar challenges emerge from the uncertainty that has come to be associated with religion's role in the public life of modern societies. Many of the leading intellectuals of religious education in Germany and the United States have been dissatisfied with the confinement of religion to the private sphere, and some have argued that religious communities should be directly involved in social movements seeking to influence public policies. Others have argued that religion's relationship to public life is best construed in terms of its contribution to civil society, where it both provides a network

13. Peter Berger, *The Sacred Canopy: Elements of a Sociological Theory of Religion* (Garden City, N.Y.: Doubleday, 1967).

14. Cf. Friedrich Schweitzer, *Die Suche nach eigenem Glauben. Einführung in die Religionspädagogik des Jugendalters* (Gütersloh: Gütersloher Verlagshaus, 1996).

of social supports and teaches the virtues and practices of democratic culture. Still others have argued that the state should support the goals of religious communities, finding a place for religious education, for example, in state-supported schools. Other perspectives could be added to this list. Enough has been said, however, to make our point: Uncertainty over religion's role in public life has accompanied its emergence as a differentiated subsystem in modern societies, such that it no longer provides integration and legitimation for society as a whole.

An educational ecology with diminished social support: Equally challenging to religious education has been the new set of educational needs characterizing religious communities in modern societies. No doubt, this has been felt more deeply by Protestant communities in the United States and Germany than by Roman Catholics, Jews, and other religious communities, for Protestantism enjoyed a privileged position until the effects of differentiation became evident. Once American and German Protestant communities could no longer rely on the support of the educational systems of public education, universities, denominational colleges, and the family, they were confronted with a distinctly new set of challenges. This leads us to ask, can congregations alone carry out educational tasks that, until recently, were shared by a broader ecology of educational institutions? Even in Germany, where religious education remains an option in state-supported schools, it is unclear whether this education, along with that of congregations, is fully adequate to the internal needs of differentiated religious communities.

In short, the differentiation of religion in modern societies poses a number of challenges to religious education. As religion has become privatized and its public role uncertain, and as the ecology of religious education has shifted, religious education has been faced with a distinctly modern set of issues. Here again, the interdependence of religious education and its social context is evident.

Challenge Four: The Separation of Morality, Personal Identity, and Religion

The emergence of religion as a differentiated subsystem no longer providing integration and legitimization for society as a whole has led to an additional challenge to religious education: the separation of personal identity and morality from any religious grounding. This detachment also can be explained in terms of differentiation.

As society has evolved into a variety of specialized systems and life spheres, which are guided by their own area-specific imperatives and rationalities, the everyday life of individuals has come to be structured by the movement from one subsystem to another. Often, within a few hours, individuals move from the family to work to leisure to church. Since participation in each area of life requires the individual to function according to the rationality, moral logic, and "culture" that each area projects, it becomes more and more difficult for individuals to ground self-identity in their relationship to any one subsystem. In the face of this pluralization, identity becomes multiple or compartmentalized, if not fragmentary and highly contradictory. Religion may play a role in personal identity, but it does not easily serve as the integrative focus of the many "selves" and roles individuals adopt as they move through their everyday lives.

The same is true of morality. Given the different moral logics of the various systems in which individuals live and work, some social theorists insist that it has become exceedingly difficult for religion to provide its members with a unified morality that can guide them in all areas of life.[15] Religious institutions, which in pre-modern America and Germany provided moral guidance and unity for all aspects of life, can now no longer even pretend to speak either from or to a consensus of shared values. Current members of these religious institutions find it difficult to integrate their faith with their behavior in their various life spheres, because each sphere is organized around different moral norms. The challenge this presents to religion in general and religious education in particular is evident in the various strategies that are commonly used in an attempt to reconnect religion and morality in everyday life.

Some religious groups adopt the strategy of reducing morality to interpersonal relations, portraying the link between religion and morality in terms of the way persons are treated — being friendly to the salesclerk or courteous to one's clients. This reduction of morality to personal, face-to-face relations never addresses the complex systemic dimensions of social interaction. This never really touches the moral logic of the marketplace, which is structuring these roles and relationships in terms of a utilitarian calculus of costs and benefits. In the United States, for example, the generally accepted code of business conduct dictates that businesses hire a certain percentage of women and that some of them be placed in high-ranking positions. Employees are also increasingly expected to treat one another with courtesy and respect across gender lines. When, however, the average wages of all female and all male employees with the same amount of education and experience are con-

15. Use of the idea of moral logics as distinctive in different domains is found in Steven Tipton, *Getting Saved from the Sixties* (Berkeley: University of California Press, 1982). See especially chapter 5.

45

trasted in any particular business, it is often the case that the men are making more money. When this is added to the fact that more women than men are heads of single-parent families, and thus have more hands-on parenting responsibilities than their children's fathers, and that more women volunteer in grade schools, nursing homes, and Sunday schools, it becomes clear that no matter how much courtesy these women receive, and how often they are praised for their service, they are bearing an inequitable burden of social responsibilities and receiving less social support.

In contrast to emphasizing personal courteousness, some religious groups use the strategy of commending highly abstract principles that are thought to encompass various areas of life: for example, the imperative to love or to work for reconciliation. Here, too, however, the more concrete rationalities and moral logics of different areas of life are never really engaged. What does love mean in the political sphere, for example? Certainly it means more than considering the personal morals of political leaders. It means considering the claims of justice. Abstract principles alone rarely consider such claims concretely.

Perhaps most common of all is the strategy of reducing morality to the private sphere, the area of lifestyle choice, personal relations, and the family. This strategy of compartmentalization may make it easier for religion to reconnect with morality but it drastically reduces both morality's and religion's role in modern life. Certainly, it is inadequate to put morality in the coat closet when we go to work, yet compartmentalized strategies do just this.

The separation of self-identity and morality from their religious grounding poses a particularly difficult challenge to religious education. Traditionally, securing the grounds of identity and morality was assumed to be one of religious education's foremost tasks — a task it fulfilled on behalf of the whole society, with a broad-based consensus of support. But in today's more pluralistic and differentiated social context, religious education must argue and demonstrate explicitly that self-identity and morality are enriched and deepened when grounded in religion. Religious educators face the complex task of building connections between religion and the multiple moralities and identities of everyday life. They face the challenge of devising an education that supports development toward post-conventional forms of religious identity, a faith stance that can reflect critically on both the diverse moral logics of the various life spheres and the resources of its own religious tradition. We will explore this more fully below.

No doubt other challenges to religious education posed by the differentiation of modernization could be raised. Enough has been said, however, to make our basic point that religious education stands in an interdependent relationship to its social context. If religious educators ignore the kinds of challenges that have been pointed to above, they in effect allow them to take place "behind their backs." Happily, prominent religious education theorists in both Germany and the United States have attempted to address many of the challenges that have just been described, as we hope to demonstrate. We are convinced that religious education has been a shaping force in relation to modernization and not merely a passive participant.

Prospects for the Future

Religions offer alternative visions of what the future can and should be, and religious education therefore can help shape the twenty-first century. To do so, however, it must move beyond attempts to merely describe and interpret the social context *as it currently is*. To influence the future, religious educators must project a theory of what this context *might become*. This can be described as the shift from a historical-interpretive theory of modernization to a normative theory of modernization. To introduce this idea, we will offer an extended discussion of the normative theory offered by the social theorist Jürgen Habermas, focusing on his idea of the unfinished project of modernity. Normative social theories like Habermas's can serve as important dialogue partners for religious educators as they seek to discern possibilities of social transformations that emerge from the symbols and vision of their own faith tradition.

A Normative Concept of Modernization: Jürgen Habermas

We have chosen to explore Jürgen Habermas's normative theory of modernization for two closely related reasons. First, while Habermas offers a particularly important and distinctive vision of what modernity might become, his work represents certain intellectual tendencies that are found more widely than his theory alone. In many ways, he is paradigmatic of social scientists and philosophers who have accepted the basic tenets of the Enlightenment and view modernization and secularization as going hand in hand. Second, Habermas's theory has exerted a particularly important influence on contemporary philosophers of education — extensively in Germany but also in the United States.[16] It represents a long-standing critique of religion mediated to

16. Robert Young, *A Critical Theory of Education: Habermas and Our Children's Future* (New York: Teacher's College Press, 1990); W. Ayers, J. Hunt, and T. Quinn, eds., *Teaching for So-*

modern education by modern philosophy. Since the eighteenth century, education and philosophy have traveled together under the banner of modernity, a trend first evident in the writings of Rousseau, Pestalozzi, and Kant. Both "modern" education and "modern" philosophy have viewed themselves as having a stake in modernization. In the field of education this has gradually led to the virtual identification of general education with "modern" education. A kind of dividing line has been erected between "traditional" forms of education from earlier eras and "modern" education based on the tenets of the Enlightenment and, somewhat later, the social sciences.

From the perspective of religious education, this division has led to an impoverishment of education, seen most clearly in the exclusion of all religiously based answers to the questions of ultimate meaning that commonly emerge in the study of art, history, literature, and even science. Religious ways of framing and approaching such questions are portrayed as belonging either to pre-modern general education or to the private sphere of modern life — the arena of individual preference, the family, and voluntary associations. In either case, possible answers to questions of ultimate meaning couched in religious rather than secular language are viewed as having no place in the public sphere, especially in the praxis of public education. Habermas's normative theory of modernity argues that religion is a part of our evolutionary past, with little to offer humanity's future. His influence on contemporary philosophers of education, thus, is paradigmatic of the influence of "modern" philosophy on "modern" education over the past two hundred years.

The Unfinished Project of Modernity

As noted at an earlier point in this chapter, Habermas accepts the thesis that differentiation lies at the heart of modernization. In a well-known series of debates with Niklas Luhmann,[17] he began developing his vision of "rational discourse" as the promise and aim of modernity, its "unfinished project."

---

cial Justice: A Democracy and Education Reader (New York: Teacher's College Press, 1998). The influence of critical social theory generally is found in the work of Michael Apple and Henry Giroux. Representative texts are Apple, *Teachers and Texts: A Political Economy of Class and Gender Relations in Education* (New York: Routledge, 1986), and Giroux, *Theory and Resistance in Education* (South Hadley, Mass.: Bergin and Garvey, 1983).

17. Habermas and Luhmann, *Theorie der Gesellschaft oder Sozialtechnologie*; Jürgen Habermas, "Modernity: An Unfinished Project," in *Habermas and the Unfinished Project of Modernity*, ed. Maurizio Passerin D'Entrèves and Seyla Benhabib (Cambridge: Polity, 1996), pp. 38-55.

Luhmann relies exclusively on systems theory (which explains human behavior in terms of following agreed-upon rules and striving toward agreed-upon goals) to understand institutional differentiation. In contrast, Habermas argues that systems thinking must be supplemented with an explanation of human interaction that takes the importance of the "lifeworld" more seriously.[18] By "lifeworld" he means the relatively diffuse, shared stock of background knowledge and cultural patterns that is assumed in every act of communication. These convictions about "what life is like" underlie human communication based on a shared lifeworld and cannot be reduced to the rule-governed and goal-oriented behavior captured in systems analysis.

In calling attention to the importance of the lifeworld, Habermas portrays humans as more than goal-seeking beings attempting to maximize their own adaptive competence or the adaptive competence of the systems in which they participate. Humans have a deep drive, he argues, toward achieving "mutual understanding." This is the basis of their ability to live cooperatively and justly and to pursue the higher, noninstrumental goods of life, such as friendship and appreciation of art. Shared understanding lies at the very heart of "communicative action," the ability to communicate through language, affect, and action. It is what makes humans human. In large measure, Habermas describes the unfulfilled project of modernity in terms of the unrealized potentials for communicative action oriented toward understanding in various spheres of modern life.

Drawing on this distinction between system and lifeworld and the closely related distinction between action oriented toward the achievement of goals and action oriented toward the achievement of understanding, Habermas goes on to distinguish between a *descriptive account* of modernization as it has unfolded over the past two hundred years and a *normative account* of what it might become. Differentiation lies at the heart of both of these accounts.

Descriptively, he argues, modernization has resulted in the development of a variety of subsystems in society. This has a twofold effect. First, it has the effect of simultaneously dissolving the taken-for-granted nature of social institutions and reality-interpretations characteristic of traditional societies and opening up the possibility that these might now become subject to critical reflection and open communication. Habermas refers to this as the "linguistification" of beliefs, norms, and values. Second, differentiation allows three distinct forms of communication oriented toward the achievement of understanding to emerge in conjunction with the three most important

---

18. Throughout this section, we will be drawing on Habermas's *Theory of Communicative Action*, vols. 1 and 2, unless otherwise indicated.

spheres of modern life. These are an orientation toward truth found in modern science, an orientation toward the right found in modern legal and political systems, and an orientation toward authentic self-expression found in modern art. As these three orientations and their institutional carriers have gradually become differentiated from one another, the distinctive validity claims of each have become subject to conscious negotiation. They have become open to rational communication, which seeks understanding appropriate to the true, right, and authentic. In modern science, for example, claims about the origin of life are based on empirical research. In contrast, a painting's vision of life cannot be explained through empirical investigation. What is called for is an interpretation that discloses new ways of seeing one's world. Different validity claims are appropriate to each sphere.

The linguistification of beliefs, norms, and values and the emergence of the relatively independent spheres of the true, right, and authentic are both an outgrowth of differentiation. While they are both present in modern societies, Habermas goes on to argue, their potential has not yet been fully realized. Hence, he describes modernity as an "unfinished project" in which new potentials for human life are present but have been stunted and distorted in significant ways. Much of his criticism is directed against the overwhelming — what he calls the "colonizing" — influence of those subsystems of the administrative state and market economy that have come to dominate modern life. These subsystems are characterized by the dominance of instrumental rationality, which seeks to procure goals on the basis of the calculation of the most efficient means. While this form of rationality may be appropriate to economic systems, it becomes pernicious when allowed to eliminate the more fundamental possibilities of communication oriented toward the achievement of understanding, which, as we have seen, takes different forms in the scientific, ethical, and aesthetic spheres of life. The unrealized potential of modernity, thus, lies in putting instrumental rationality "in its place," that is, in limiting its influence to those spheres of life and situations where it is appropriate and, in turn, allowing the communicative rationality of science, ethics, and art to come to the fore in modern life in ways that have not yet been seen.

Habermas's normative understanding of modernity is thus an attempt to describe the latent potentials of modernization and the paths that might be taken to realize these more fully. Of special importance for our purposes is his vision of public life, which he sees as the sphere of communicative action in areas of life having to do with the right,[19] areas of life in which the members of

19. For an introduction see Craig Calhoun, ed., *Habermas and the Public Sphere* (Cambridge: MIT Press, 1992).

a society make decisions about the moral norms that will govern their life together. This sphere of life, then, focuses on society's choices about the sharing of scarce resources and the distribution of "life chances" through social goods like education and health care. Modern democratic societies handle these kinds of decisions institutionally through legal and political systems.

Habermas develops his theory of the "ideal speech situation" to provide a statement of the procedures and rules — the discourse ethic — that ought to govern the institutions and the decision-making processes of public life.[20] This discourse ethic, he argues, cannot be grounded in the moral convictions and practices of any particular community within a pluralistic society. If that were the case, it would not be accepted by the other groups. Rather, it must be grounded in obligations inherent to every act of human communication that seeks to achieve genuine understanding on matters of ethical import.

It is not necessary for us to rehearse Habermas's complex justification of this position at present. More important is gaining a sense of what he proposes as the rules and conditions that should govern the ideal speech situation. How in the face of competing claims by various moral communities can persons who live in pluralistic societies enter into a moral conversation in which the needs and interests of all are given their due? Habermas argues that there are two key conditions: the capacity to engage in general, reciprocal perspective-taking, and the willingness to regard all conversation partners as having equal moral worth.

The first of these points to a long developmental process in which people gradually learn how to construct the point of view of others, commonly referred to in cognitive psychology as *perspective-taking*.[21] Young children are egocentric in their perspective-taking abilities, with little capacity to decenter from their own point of view. Over time, most people in modern societies pass through the stages of simple perspective-taking (taking the point of view of another individual) and mutual interpersonal perspective-taking (the ability to construct another person's perspective and also to take their perspective toward oneself). Eventually, they gain the capacity to construct the point of view of the "generalized other," that is, the conventionalized social perspectives of their primary reference groups. Moral conversation in pluralistic social contexts, however, requires two further steps toward post-conventional perspective-taking. The first step is the ability to reflect on the conventions

20. Jürgen Habermas, *Moral Consciousness and Communicative Action*, trans. C. Lenhardt and S. Nicholsen (Cambridge, Mass.: MIT Press, 1990), chap. 3.

21. In this respect, Habermas refers to the work of developmental psychologists such as Lawrence Kohlberg and Robert Selman. See especially *Moral Consciousness*.

into which one has been socialized, assessing them critically from a variety of theoretical perspectives. For many people, this begins to take place during their college years when they learn to think critically about the norms and roles into which they were socialized. The second step is the ability to set aside one's own point of view temporarily and enter sympathetically, but critically, into those of other individuals and groups. Together, they allow reciprocity in perspective-taking: the ability to articulate one's own point of view as one among many and to enter into the perspectives of individuals and groups whose point of view is different than one's own.

The achievement of general, reciprocal perspective-taking by itself, Habermas goes on to argue, does not constitute "the moral point of view."[22] Such perspective-taking competencies can be used for purposes of manipulation and control. The perspectives of others can be taken into account solely for the achievement of strategic ends. Hence, Habermas argues that a second condition of moral conversation among pluralistic partners is necessary: the universalization of moral regard. This refers to an attitude in which all participants in the conversation are viewed as having moral worth. They are granted equality in the conversation. Their needs and interests are taken seriously, as is their right to influence the course of the conversation. No one person or group has undue power to control the issues raised or the outcomes achieved.

Habermas is quite aware that his description of this discourse ethic represents a "counter-factual" ideal, not to be found in pure form in any of the legal or political institutions of the public sphere in modern societies. But this ideal provides him with a critical norm against which he can measure institutional arrangements and decision-making processes as they actually exist. It also allows him to describe the unfulfilled potential of public life standing at the heart of his normative concept of modernity.

A Critique of Habermas's Theory

Before raising critical questions about Habermas's normative theory of modernization, it is important to acknowledge the continuing importance of his work. We are convinced that his portrayal of modernization as unleashing new potentials for rational communication oriented toward the achievement of understanding in diverse spheres of life remains important. Modernity does indeed represent a challenge to the uncritical force of tradition in all

22. Habermas, *Moral Consciousness*, p. 198.

spheres of life, including religion, and opens up the possibility of new forms of communication in which understanding is achieved in an open and critical fashion. Habermas's description of the conditions making this possible — including his account of both the development of post-conventional forms of moral identity and the procedures of deliberative democracy consistent with his discourse ethic — remains an important, critical vantage point from which to view the actual processes of socialization, education, and democratic governance in modern societies.

Habermas, thus, remains a worthy dialogue partner. We must take issue with him, however, on two fundamental points. First, we do not believe that he adequately conceptualizes the importance of the lifeworld in his normative theory of modernization. On the surface, this criticism might seem odd, for Habermas's affirmation of the importance of the lifeworld was one of the cardinal tenets of his critique of Niklas Luhmann. Nevertheless, he conceptualizes modernity's potential as both the "leaving behind" of particular cultural identities and the "movement toward" cognitive and communicative competencies that are shared by all humans. Both of these tendencies are found in his account of post-conventional moral identity described above. Cultural identity is essentially granted no important role. This is closely related to a second criticism. Habermas does not provide an adequate account of difference in his normative conception of modern public life. In placing a set of procedures at the heart of deliberative democracy, he portrays public life in terms of those things its members can share. Here, Habermas represents a long-standing tendency in social philosophy and social theory since the Enlightenment, a tendency that stretches from Dewey's *A Common Faith*[23] all the way to secularization theory. Cultural and religious differences are portrayed as threatening public life, rather than as enabling tolerance, mutual respect, and fairness. Such differences, thus, are to be left behind when we enter the public square, where a common rationality, a common set of procedures, and universal ethical principles are to hold sway. We will take up each of these criticisms in relation to issues of importance to religious education.

Two questions of special importance to religious education have to do with Habermas's treatment of what might be called "ethos" and "identity." Both of these concepts are highly relevant to each of the four audiences of religious education described earlier (the public, the family, the individual, and the church). Moreover, a number of questions emerge in conjunction with Habermas's treatment of religion, especially the way he portrays its potential contribution to public life. We will start with questions that revolve around

23. John Dewey, *A Common Faith* (New Haven: Yale University Press, 1934).

ethos and identity formation and then return to Habermas's understanding of the role of religion in public life.

In our understanding, "ethos" refers to an ethic that is enacted in life. It is the necessary basis of morality. Morality without ethos may be conceivable, but it will never be able to play a decisive role in shaping moral action. It is the ethos that is the source of moral motives, providing both theoretical and practical answers to the question "Why be moral? Why be moral in a world that is not moral?" Among many theorists of modernization, it is assumed that one of the most important gains of modernity is the possibility (and necessity) of a truly universal morality of the sort we have just seen in Habermas's discourse ethic. This morality must transcend every particular ethos, which, from this universalistic moral point of view, may be no more than a limited forerunner of true morality.

Questions can be raised about this perspective. At the very least, this understanding of morality suffers greatly from its highly abstract nature, which severs it from all motivational resources. Moreover, the justification of this supposedly universalizing moral point of view inevitably must appeal to a set of substantive moral notions and practices that are grounded in the particular ethos of a community or way of life. To borrow Michael Walzer's way of putting this, Habermas's abstract universalism represents a "thin" version of "thick" notions and practices embedded in Western democratic forms of life.[24] Even sympathetic interpreters of Habermas's work such as Seyla Benhabib, David Held, and Thomas McCarthy acknowledge that this is the case.[25] Nevertheless, their various attempts to ground his discourse ethic in a more forthright discussion of the democratic traditions of the modern West seems equally problematic. In a multicultural world, is this way of justifying a supposedly "universal" moral point of view really convincing?

We do not think so. Western liberal democratic ideals represent "essentially contested" concepts in our world today — concepts subject to ongoing debate across different intellectual and cultural communities. It is by no means clear that they can or should be viewed as providing us with the only viable picture of the human future. Indeed, this becomes especially evident

24. Michael Walzer, *Thick and Thin* (Notre Dame: University of Notre Dame Press, 1994).

25. Introduction to Benhabib, *Situating the Self: Gender, Community and Postmodernism in Contemporary Ethics* (New York: Routledge, 1992); David Held, *Democracy and the Global Order: From the Modern State to Cosmopolitan Governance* (Stanford: Stanford University Press, 1995), chap. 8; Thomas McCarthy, "Rationality and Relativism: Habermas's 'Overcoming' of Hermeneutics," in *Habermas: Critical Debates*, ed. J. Thompson and D. Held (Cambridge, Mass.: MIT Press, 1982). See also S. Benhabib and F. Dallmayr, eds., *The Communicative Ethics Controversy* (Cambridge, Mass.: MIT Press, 1991).

when the framework of modernization is replaced by that of globalization, in which the diversity of culture and civilization increases. It will not, we believe, be possible to construct a viable global ethic by attempting to bypass, through an abstract moral universalism, the deeply particular ethoi of different communities, both within societies of one particular nation-state and within communities that cross national boundaries.

This leads to a closely related second dimension of Habermas's normative theory of modernization, his portrayal of the nature of personal identity formation in modern societies. Obviously, this is an issue of major importance to religious education and is closely related to the issue of ethos just discussed. From Habermas's perspective, the promise of modernity lies, in part, in the achievement of a type of ego-identity that, he believes, for the first time in history may truly be called free and humane. This is because it is no longer an identity based on "natural givens" like gender and race or on society's ascription of role and status. According to Habermas and others, this identity is premised on the *detachment* from notions of self that take shape in the ethos of any particular community and on the movement toward a post-conventional identity "beyond" the force of socialization alone. Such identities are critically and freely self-chosen and allow individuals to develop their potentials as humans and not merely as the member of a particular social group. Modern, differentiated societies open up this possibility by loosening the grip of the agencies of socialization through which identity takes shape and by making pluralization and individualization dimensions of everyday life.

Many of the same difficulties attending Habermas's abstract moral universalism are found here. Does the achievement of a post-conventional identity (an identity that is not based on mutually-accepted "conventional" ideas about human roles in society) really reside in development "beyond" all substantive and particularized notions of self and the goods the self prizes? Authors like Paul Ricoeur and Charles Taylor have argued persuasively that this is not the case, pointing to a *narrative* basis of self and identity.[26] Identity, they contend, rests on the ability to knit together past, present, and future into a coherent narrative whole. They argue convincingly that the elimination of the constitutive relationship between self, narrative, and the substantive beliefs and practices of particular moral communities results in an impover-

---

26. Paul Ricoeur, *Time and Narrative*, vol. 1, trans. K. McLaughlin and D. Pellauer (Chicago: University of Chicago Press, 1984), and *Oneself as Another*, trans. K. Blamey (Chicago: University of Chicago Press, 1992); Charles Taylor, *Sources of the Self: The Making of the Modern Identity* (Cambridge, Mass.: Harvard University Press, 1989).

ished conception of the self. Indeed, it portrays the self along the lines of the dehumanizing modernization that Habermas wants to correct.

Is the best way of construing post-conventional identity really along the lines of an "empty" self, an identity "beyond" cultural particularity? While we agree with Habermas that institutional and cultural differentiation pose challenges to the construction of personal identity and that some notion of post-conventional identity development is valuable, we do not follow him in portraying this as a movement "beyond" the narratives and culture-rich notions of identity grounded in the ethoi of particular communities. In spite of the fact that Habermas attempts to reconstruct the neo-Kantian perspective of Lawrence Kohlberg in light of his own theory of communicative action, his picture of post-conventional identity continues to assume the overriding value of autonomy, the ability to choose freely and critically in the construction of a life's project.

A more adequate understanding of post-conventionality, we believe, can be found in the thought of James Fowler and Robert Kegan, who describe post-conventionality as the critical appropriation and reconstruction of particularized cultural and religious identities.[27] These authors describe development *within* and *across* the ethoi of particular communities, not beyond them. Theoretically, their positions do not rule out the possibility of post-conventional religious identities, identities that remain firmly grounded in the beliefs and practices of a particular religious tradition but critically appropriate this tradition in ways that enable openness to perspectives other than their own. Fowler explicitly draws on Ricoeur's understanding of a "second naivete" in his account of post-conventionality, pointing to the continuing importance of the symbolic dimensions of the lifeworld in enabling openness to difference.[28] Post-conventional identity, thus, is not viewed along the lines of an empty, autonomous self but in terms of a narrative-dependent, culture-rich self that critically appropriates the potentials of a particular community or tradition to engage persons and communities holding perspectives other than her or his own.

Our consideration of Habermas's understanding of normative modernity in terms of the achievement of moral universalism and post-conventional identity has pointed toward the difficulties of his portrayal of the potential of modernity as the movement beyond the particularized no-

---

27. James Fowler, *Stages of Faith: The Psychology of Human Development and the Quest for Meaning* (San Francisco: Harper and Row, 1981); Robert Kegan, *The Evolving Self: Problem and Process in Human Development* (Cambridge, Mass.: Harvard University Press, 1982).

28. Fowler, *Stages of Faith*, pp. 187-88.

tions of self and moral meaning that are grounded in different communities. Those who are familiar with the heritage of the Enlightenment will recognize Habermas's view as one of the cardinal tenets of this intellectual movement, and, in fact, Habermas is quite open about his commitment to the Enlightenment. It especially colors the way he views the relationship between religion and modernization and his portrait of a healthy public life, the topics with which we will conclude our discussion.

In his treatment of the place of religion in modern life, Habermas offers his own quite sophisticated version of secularization theory. According to this perspective, modernity comes about through a fundamental break with religious tradition and, indeed, with any religious worldview. Secularization theory postulates that religious worldviews, which base their authority on tradition, have given way to purely rational and experiential types of knowing, which are part and parcel of modernity. Modernization, thus, is viewed as inevitably leading to secularization, a new stage of social development superseding and surpassing an earlier religious stage of social life. The steady decline of religion is interpreted as an inevitable concomitant of modernization, leading either to its privatization (such that it is confined to the spheres of personal lifestyle preference and taste) or to its gradual demise.

This account of religion's relationship to modernization dominated social science across the past century and even influenced theologians such as Dietrich Bonhoeffer and Harvey Cox.[29] On both empirical and normative grounds, however, questions can be raised about the secularization thesis. Scholars in various fields have recently called attention to three social phenomena that challenge secularization theory's analysis of what is happening to religion worldwide: (1) the continuing significance of what has been termed "invisible religion," (2) the continuing significance of religiously motivated social movements, and (3) non-Western critiques of "godless Western secular materialism."

First, as early as the 1970s, Thomas Luckmann pointed to the continuing importance of religion among individuals, what he called "invisible religion."[30] Social scientists have continued to find this to be the case. In research carried

29. Dietrich Bonhoeffer, *Widerstand und Ergebung. Briefe und Aufzeichnungen aus der Haft* (Hamburg: Siebenstern, 1951), p. 132 (letter of 30 April 1944), speaks of a "time completely without religion" ("völlig religionslose Zeit") for which we are headed. See also Harvey Cox, *The Secular City: Secularization and Urbanization in Theological Perspective* (New York: Macmillan, 1965).

30. Thomas Luckmann, *The Invisible Religion: The Problem of Religion in Modern Society* (New York: Macmillan, 1967). For recent discussion cf. Peter L. Berger, ed., *The Desecularization of the World: Resurgent Religion and World Politics* (Grand Rapids: Eerdmans, 1999).

out during the past decade, for example, Robert Wuthnow found a remarkable number of Americans participating in small groups for reasons that included the quest for the sacred.[31] While institutional religion may have declined in the face of modernization, this has not meant that the spiritual dimension has disappeared altogether.

Second, religion has shown itself to be generative of new social movements that have played an important role in public life.[32] The Civil Rights movement in the United States, for example, was largely generated and supported by various religious communities. Contemporary movements that focus on curbing capital punishment, effecting gun control, and ensuring the rights of homosexuals, likewise, have received quite visible support from many sectors of mainline Christianity and Judaism. The religious right's pro-life stance also has been a highly potent force in American politics in recent decades. In central and eastern Europe, moreover, protest movements with strong religious ties played an important role in environmental politics and in bringing about the end of communist rule. It simply is not empirically accurate to portray religion as playing no role in the public life of modern societies. On the contrary, religion has made major contributions to the renewal and transformation of public life in a variety of modern societies.

Third, if our horizon is broadened to include the global community as a whole, it is quite clear that Habermas's picture of public life in terms of secularization is highly Western. To be more specific, it reflects the beliefs of the Enlightenment of Western Europe. Hindu, Muslim, and non-Western Christian intellectuals in many parts of the world have begun to ask why they

31. Robert Wuthnow, *Sharing the Faith: Support Groups and America's New Quest for Community* (New York: Free Press, 1994).

32. See, for example, Luther Gerlach and V. Hine, *People, Power, and Change: Movements of Social Transformation* (Indianapolis: Bobbs-Merrill, 1970); D. McAdam, *Political Process and the Development of Black Insurgency: 1930-1970* (Chicago: University of Chicago Press, 1982); Aldon Morris, *The Origins of the Civil Rights Movement: Black Communities Organizing for Change* (New York: Free Press, 1984); Lawrence Wittner, *Rebels Against the War: The American Peace Movement, 1933-1983* (Philadelphia: Temple University Press, 1984); Troy Perry, *Don't Be Afraid Anymore: The Story of Reverend Troy Perry and the Metropolitan Community Churches* (New York: St. Martin's, 1990); Troy Perry, *The Lord Is My Shepherd and He Knows I'm Gay* (Los Angeles: Nash Publications, 1972); Robert Wuthnow, "World Order and Religious Movements," in *Studies of the Modern World-System,* ed. A. Bergesen (New York: Academic, 1980), pp. 57-75; Mayer Zald and John McCarthy, "Religious Groups as Crucibles of Social Movements," in *Sacred Companies: Organizational Aspects of Religion and Religious Aspects of Organizations,* ed. N. Demerath, P. Hall, T. Schmitt, and R. Williams (New York: Oxford University Press, 1998), pp. 24-50.

should accept this version of humanity's future as their own, especially if it leads to the decline of religious identity.[33] Certainly, modern Western Europe and North America, they often argue, are no paragons of moral goodness. The World Wars, the death camps, the proliferation of weapons of mass destruction, and the crass materialism and hedonism of consumer-oriented economies hardly commend the secularized course of modernization in the West.

Even some of the staunchest supporters of Habermas's theoretical perspective have raised questions about the adequacy of his description of public life. Jean Cohen and Andrew Arato's extensive study of the role of civil society in strengthening the lifeworld against the colonizing influence of the marketplace is a notable case in point.[34] They argue that the associations of civil society, located "between" the state, economy, and private sphere, are crucial to teaching the communicative competencies necessary for participation in the public domain. Unfortunately, like Habermas, they overlook the historically given associations available in modern societies. It does not occur to them that churches and religious communities not only might, but also have, played an important role for civil society. This has been pointed out critically against Habermas by theologians such as Francis Schüssler Fiorenza and Michael Welker and by sociologists including Robert Wuthnow, Daniel Bell, and José Casanova.[35] In Part III of this book, we will take up the potential contribution of the Christian community to civil society more extensively.

In short, religious education and practical theology would do well to engage Habermas's normative theory of modernization critically in forming their own understanding of the future. While there is much to learn from serious dialogue with his work, his account of modernity's future appears to us to be flawed in significant ways. We have examined his work in some depth because he represents in such a powerful way many themes that have been present across modern philosophy and social theory since the Enlightenment. These have exerted an enormous influence on modern education, frequently leading it to adopt a perspective in which the particularized identities of individuals and cultural minorities must be "left behind" in the attempt to affirm what all humans have in common or at least what all Americans, Germans, or

33. For a helpful overview of some of these criticisms, see Peter Beyer, *Religion and Globalization* (London: Sage, 1994).

34. Jean Cohen and Andrew Arato, *Civil Society and Political Theory* (Cambridge: MIT Press, 1992).

35. The criticisms of Fiorenza and Wuthnow are found in Don S. Browning and Francis Schüssler Fiorenza, eds., *Habermas, Modernity, and Public Theology* (New York: Crossroad, 1992); see also Michael Welker, *Kirche im Pluralismus* (Gütersloh: Kaiser, 1995), pp. 11ff.

French have in common. Perhaps especially at this point, we come up against more than the limitations of a single theorist like Habermas. We come up against the limitations of modernization theory itself. Over the course of this project, we have come to the conclusion that modernization theory must be supplemented and, in certain ways, replaced, by globalization theory, a topic to which we now turn.

Globalization Theory: An Overview

It is not possible to offer a consensus perspective on globalization theory, for a wide number of theories on globalization have emerged in recent decades, with markedly different assumptions. While the term "global" is over four hundred years old, the use of closely related terms like "globalization" and "globalizing" was not yet common in the 1960s.[36] Indeed, it was not until the mid 1980s that globalization theory became academically significant in sociology, political science, economics, and communication studies.[37] From that point forward, however, writing on this topic has proliferated, and a number of different theoretical paradigms have emerged.[38] Our task in this section is to locate our own perspective within this emerging discussion.

Two comments of an introductory nature are in order. First, globalization theories differ in their accounts of the relationship between modernization and globalization. Some authors, including, until recently, the sociologist Anthony Giddens, make the latter largely a function of the former. In their view, it is the acceleration of the forces of modernization that leads to globalization.[39] In contrast, others such as Roland Robertson, Malcolm Waters, and Samuel Huntington view globalization as far more than the extension of modernization.[40] Globalization is viewed as a long historical process that pre-

36. Malcolm Waters, *Globalization* (New York: Routledge, 1995), p. 2.

37. Roland Robertson, *Globalization: Social Theory and Global Culture* (Thousand Oaks, Calif.: Sage, 1992), p. 8.

38. See Robertson, *Globalization: Social Theory and Global Culture*, chap. 2; Waters, *Globalization*, chap. 7; and M. Albrow, "Globalization, Knowledge, and Society," in *Globalization, Knowledge, and Society*, ed. M. Albrow and E. King (Thousand Oaks, Calif.: Sage, 1990).

39. Anthony Giddens: *Modernity and Self-Identity: Self and Society in the Late Modern Age* (Stanford, Calif.: Stanford University Press, 1991), and "Living in a Post-Traditional Society," in *Reflexive Modernization: Politics, Tradition and Aesthetics in the Modern Social Order*, by Ulrich Beck, Anthony Giddens, and Scott Lash (Stanford: Stanford University Press, 1994).

40. Robertson, *Globalization: Social Theory and Global Culture*; Waters, *Globalization*; Samuel Huntington, *The Clash of Civilizations and the Remaking of World Order* (New York: Simon and Schuster, 1996).

dates modernity and that both builds on and reconfigures modernizing trends like secularization, individualization, and nationalism, trends particularly prominent in the West.

A second issue of debate in globalization theory is the extent to which civilizational and cultural factors enter into an analysis of globalization. Certain authors portray globalization almost exclusively in terms of the emergence of a global economic system. Rational choice theorists like Gary Becker evaluate the emergence of a global economy positively, while neo-Marxists like Immanuel Wallerstein evaluate it negatively.[41] In contrast, others such as Robertson, Huntington, and Arjun Appadurai view cultural and civilizational responses to the rise of a global economy as an intrinsic dimension of globalization.[42] The Japanese, for example, have developed their own form of capitalism, which is quite different than that found in the United States. The emergence of what we will call "global reflexivity" — a heightened awareness of and reflection on cultural others and diverse images of the global whole — is seen as a key dimension of globalization, giving rise to a wide range of responses to the global economic trends noted by Becker and Wallerstein.

We agree with those who make a clear distinction between modernization and globalization and who see global reflexivity as a key dimension of globalization. Robertson's definition of globalization will provide the organizational principle of our discussion:

> Globalization as a concept refers to both the compression of the world and the intensification of consciousness of the world as a whole . . . its main empirical focus is in line with the increasing acceleration in both concrete global interdependence and consciousness of the global whole in the twentieth century.[43]

Accordingly, our discussion will focus on both the emergence of systems that have compressed the world into "a single place," as Robertson aptly puts it, and the widely divergent consciousness of and responses to this global interconnectedness found in different cultural groups.[44]

The compression of the world into "a single place" is largely the result

41. Gary Becker, *The Economic Approach to Human Behavior* (Chicago: University of Chicago Press, 1976); Immanuel Wallerstein, *The Modern World-System* (New York: Academic, 1974), and *The Modern World-System,* vol. 2 (New York: Academic, 1980).

42. Robertson, *Globalization: Social Theory and Global Culture;* Huntington, *The Clash of Civilizations;* Arjun Appadurai, *Modernity at Large: Cultural Dimensions of Globalization* (Minneapolis: University of Minnesota Press, 1996).

43. Robertson, *Globalization: Social Theory and Global Culture,* p. 8.

44. Robertson, *Globalization: Social Theory and Global Culture,* p. 6.

of the emergence of advanced systems of electronic communication and transportation. The former has the effect of making communication across great distances instantaneous, creating information flows linking virtually every part of the world. Advanced systems of transportation, likewise, link the world more closely, making possible practices like worldwide tourism and global marketing. David Harvey aptly describes the effect of this interconnection of the world as the "annihilation of space by time" and "timespace compression."[45] Space is removed as a barrier to communication, allowing relationships to be formed and maintained in an ongoing fashion across great distances. The effects of these communication and transportation revolutions can be traced briefly in three areas: economics, the polity, and culture.

The Global Economy

Key features of a world economy were largely in place by the middle of the twentieth century. Transportation and communication systems linking the world, the rapid growth of international trade, and the flow of capital around the world were already beginning to occur.[46] Technological advances in electronic communications and air transportation accelerated each of these trends, bringing into being a truly global economy for the first time. As Waters notes, the spread of capitalism has played an important role in the emergence of a global economy "because its particular institutions — financial markets, commodities, contractualized labour, alienable property — facilitate economic exchanges over great distances."[47]

Of particular importance has been the emergence of multinational corporations. These entities have evolved through several phases: corporations oriented toward mass production in national economies, national corporations oriented toward global markets, and multinational corporations organized around the dispersal of production, management, finance, and research to different parts of the world. Some argue that multinational corporations are currently entering a new phase characterized by a hyperdifferentiation of tasks and greater flexibility. The recent spate of partial mergers, joint licensing, cooperative inter-firm ventures, and subcontracting is seen as a sign of new forms of multinational organization in which transnational business al-

45. David Harvey, *The Postmodern Condition* (Oxford: Blackwell, 1989), p. 241.
46. See Waters's discussion in *Globalization,* chap. 4.
47. Waters, *Globalization,* p. 66.

liances and hyperdifferentiation of functions allow greater flexibility in product development, production, and marketing.

The impact of multinational corporations on the global economy is enormous. James Dunning estimates that in 1988, they accounted for 25-30 percent of the GNP of all market economies, 75 percent of international commodity trade, and 80 percent of all international exchanges of technology.[48] Their practices reflect in a particularly powerful way the global economy's shift from a high-volume to a high-value orientation.[49] Financial gain no longer accrues primarily to those corporations that can produce commodities in high volume, through the use of standard assembly line or automation techniques of production. Rather, financial gain accrues to high value, that is, the creation of goods or services that meet the special needs of consumers or businesses and cannot be duplicated by other competitors.[50]

The overall effect of these trends is hotly debated. On the one hand, it is clear that some parts of the world have benefited enormously from the emergence of a global economy. In spite of their recent financial difficulties, Japan, South Korea, Taiwan, and other parts of Asia have become major players in the global marketplace. On the other hand, there is much evidence that many countries have not benefited. An international division of labor appears to have become a relatively stable part of the global economic system. "Core" societies engage in capital-intensive, high-value production of goods and services on the leading edge of technological innovation. "Peripheral" societies engage in labor-intensive, low-value production.[51] Complicating this characterization of the global economy's division of labor in terms of nation-states is the economic stratification within societies. In both newly developing nations and those with advanced economies, an increasingly wide gap has begun to emerge between those with the education and skills needed to participate in the global economy and those stuck in low-paying, menial jobs on its periphery.

When coupled with population demographics, this division of labor is truly frightening. The Yale historian Paul Kennedy estimates that between the 1990s and 2025, 95 percent of all population growth will take place in develop-

---

48. James Dunning, *Multinational Enterprises in a Global Economy* (Workingham, England: Addison-Wesley, 1993), pp. 14-15. See also Waters's discussion, *Globalization*, pp. 76-80.

49. Robert B. Reich, *The Work of Nations: Preparing Ourselves for 21st-Century Capitalism* (New York: Alfred A. Knopf, 1991), chap. 7.

50. Reich, *The Work of Nations*, p. 83.

51. For a more nuanced discussion of the stratification of societies, see Richard Barnet and John Cavanagh, *Global Dreams: Imperial Corporations and the New World Order* (New York: Touchstone, 1994), part III, chap. 2.

ing countries.[52] The erosion of traditional village life based on agriculture is driving more and more of the population of these countries to cities. In the near future, Kennedy notes, there will be twenty megacities of eleven million or more, and seventeen of these will be located in developing countries.[53] It is not difficult to recognize the social unrest and political instability this situation portends. As sociological research has documented repeatedly, increasingly large numbers of young people are leaving their villages to live in overcrowded cities with limited prospects of meaningful participation in the global economy. Matters of economic justice, social instability, and political legitimacy are already matters of grave concern. What role will religion play in addressing this situation? Will it take up these issues? Will it allow its members and nations to ignore them? Will it appeal to the black-and-white answers of religious fundamentalism?[54] It is precisely in giving answer to these questions that religious education will forge its contribution to the rapidly globalizing world.

Globalization and the Polity

The emergence of multinational corporations as key actors in the global economy opens directly to the second general aspect of globalization we will discuss: its effects on the polity or systems of governance. Here, our discussion will be relatively brief and point to the obvious: the changing role of the nation-state. Two basic trends are apparent: the declining power of nation-states, and the growth of international organizations and intergovernmental forms of cooperation to handle matters pertaining to trade, the ecology, human rights, and other issues of a transnational nature.

The rise of the nation-state was an important aspect of modernization and encompassed four basic features: (1) territoriality — sovereignty in a bounded geographical area; (2) control of the means of violence — monopoly of law enforcement and the military within this territory; (3) an impersonal structure of power — a legally circumscribed structure of power with jurisdiction over a territory; and (4) legitimacy — procurement of the alle-

---

52. Paul Kennedy, *Preparing for the Twenty-First Century* (New York: Random House, 1993), pp. 21-25.

53. Kennedy, *Preparing for the Twenty-First Century*, p. 26.

54. For an excellent discussion of this trend on a worldwide basis, see William McNeill, "Fundamentalism and the World of the 1990s," in *Fundamentalisms and Society: Reclaiming the Sciences, the Family, and Education,* ed. M. Marty and S. Appleby (Chicago: University of Chicago Press, 1995).

giance of the population through the perception that the government reflects its interests.[55] The consolidation of these four features during the nineteenth and twentieth centuries went hand in hand with the creation of an interstate system that respected the sovereignty of particular states and forged relationships of various sorts between states.

Accelerated globalization during the last third of the twentieth century altered the role of nation-states considerably, calling into question each of the four features noted above. The emergence of a global economy characterized by a high degree of fluidity across national boundaries through the flow of information, technology, marketing, and investment has made the idea of a national economy anachronistic. States cannot control financial markets, capital investment, and other factors that affect the economic well-being of their citizens. Questions of legitimacy follow. The principles of sovereignty and territoriality, upon which the modern state was based, have become questionable in an economy without borders.

The most important debate about this process among globalization theorists is the role nation-states will continue to play in the emerging global order. Some theorists, including David Held, forecast a continuing decline of nation-states' power and the possibility of new transnational forms of political community.[56] He points to Hedley Bull's image of a "new medievalism" as a seminal way of conceptualizing the emerging political order: one characterized not by a single global state but by a wide diversity of power centers at various levels of political life. According to Held, in this new order nation-states will continue to play a role in national governance but will no longer serve as the primary center of polity. International law, metropolitan government, and regional associations like the European Union will be equally important.

Malcolm Waters and John Gray, in contrast, see nation-states as continuing to play an important role in the emerging global polity.[57] While acknowledging the increased role of international organizations and forums, on the one hand, and decentralized forms of political life, on the other, they point out that the state remains one of the few centers of power strong enough to counterbalance the forces of the global marketplace. Nation-states have been the primary carriers of democratic institutions and rights. National polity represents an alternative to the logic of the marketplace, focusing on the rights of citizens qua citizens, as members of a particular, geographically de-

---

55. Held, *Democracy and the Global Order*, pp. 48-49.
56. Held, *Democracy and the Global Order*.
57. Waters, *Globalization*, chap. 5; John Gray, *False Dawn: The Delusions of Global Capitalism* (New York: New Press, 1998).

fined, localized political community. Do citizens, for example, have the right to a minimal level of health care, not dictated exclusively by their ability to pay? Similar questions can be asked about education, air and water standards, and the safety of foods, as well as fundamental political rights like the free flow of communication and the right to form voluntary associations. More than ever, Waters and Gray argue, nation-states must serve as a buffer against the influences of the global marketplace on local and national communities. An enhancement of national identities in the face of some forms of cosmopolitanism may well be in order.[58]

Globalization, Culture, and Postmodernism

In this final section, we will describe our understanding of postmodernism in relation to the concept of global reflexivity. Postmodernism, we argue, is a concomitant of globalization. It is a configuration of cultural elements that represents one and only one way of responding to the globalization of culture. It is, as we noted earlier, characterized by three elements: an affirmation of radical pluralism, a heightened awareness of the risks attending scientific research and technological innovation, and a highly processive view of life (a sense that the developmental markers of human identity are unstable and that personal identity must be reconstructed repeatedly over the course of the life cycle). In order to explain what we mean by this concept, we must first describe global reflexivity and two of the most important effects of globalization on culture: cultural homogenization and the revitalization of local cultural identities. We will conclude with a brief discussion of the three elements of postmodern global reflexivity pointed to above.

Global reflexivity is a direct result of globalization in the areas of the economy and polity. It can be defined succinctly as follows: a heightened awareness of and reflection on cultural others and the construction of diverse images of the global whole. Recall Robertson's definition of globalization with which we began this section. Globalization, he argues, includes not only the interlocking systems that bring the world closer together but also consciousness of the global whole. This consciousness is shaped in two directions simultaneously. It involves the relativization of local traditions, on the one hand, and a renewed interest in these traditions as providing resources by which to understand and respond to the forces of globalization, on the other.

One of the most important relativizing features of globalization is the

---

58. See Reich's argument in this regard in parts 3 and 4 of *The Work of Nations*.

homogenization of culture it appears to be effecting in many parts of the world. Three aspects of this trend are pertinent: (1) the emergence of a global consumer culture based on appeals to lifestyle, taste, and individual preference; (2) the spread of rational approaches to life in conjunction with the increased administrative needs of modern states and multinational economic organizations; and (3) the communication of idealized, Western lifestyles through the global media, including television, movies, and music. Benjamin Barber aptly refers to these as the spread of "McWorld," pointing not only to the proliferation of fast food chains around the globe but, more fundamentally, to the homogenization of culture that this signifies.[59] Global cultural flows appear to be making cultures more and more alike.

This does not tell the whole story, however. While the various shifts in economics, polity, and culture pointed to above have created a world that is more closely linked, it does not necessarily follow that this leads to a world that is more fully integrated. In many instances, it has led to the reaffirmation of ethnic, religious, national, and civilizational identities that take their shape explicitly in response to cultural homogenization. It is a mistake to view the Western image of globalization — the inexorable movement of humankind toward a secularized, capitalistic, rationalized, and democratic end-state — as the only form global reflexivity can take. Already, the early stages of globalization have seen the emergence of a wide range of cultural and civilizational responses. Moreover, it is possible that a resurgence of religious fundamentalism — a dramatic reassertion (and narrowing) of tradition in the face of global cultural homogenization — will be especially prominent in the future.

It is within this fundamental dynamic of global reflexivity — the pressures toward the homogenization of culture and the counter-pressures reasserting particularized cultural identities — that we locate postmodernism at the level of both popular culture and academic discourse. It represents one fairly pervasive form of global reflexivity, interweaving the three basic elements mentioned above, each of which we will briefly take up in turn.[60]

---

59. Benjamin Barber, *Jihad vs. McWorld: How Globalism and Tribalism Are Reshaping the World* (New York: Ballantine, 1996).

60. The following authors are particularly helpful in describing postmodernism in relation to a set of social and institutional conditions: David Harvey, *The Condition of Postmodernity: An Enquiry into the Origins of Cultural Change* (Oxford: Blackwell, 1980); David Lyon, *Postmodernity;* Mark Poster, *The Mode of Information: Poststructuralism and Social Context* (Chicago: University of Chicago Press, 1990); Zygmunt Bauman, *Postmodernity and Its Discontents* (Washington Square, N.Y.: New York University Press, 1997); Zygmunt Bauman, *Intimations of Postmodernity* (New York: Routledge, 1992).

Affirmation of Radical Pluralism

The first of these is the affirmation of radical pluralism. If the differentiation of modern institutions resulted in pluralization, certain features of globalization have made the experience of pluralism much more pervasive and complex. Our own research on adolescents in Germany and the United States has uncovered a clear affirmation of openness to diversity in its various forms among the majority of those interviewed.[61] This affirmation seems closely related to important aspects of globalization such as firsthand encounters with other cultures through international travel; friendships with persons from other countries, both exchange students and persons who have immigrated from abroad; the study of world cultures in the school curriculum; and the use of computers to communicate with others and to gain access to information.[62] These factors and others have made adolescents much more aware of cultural "others." Moreover, they have led many to affirm the positive value of encounters with these "others." Such encounters are viewed as "expanding" their understanding of life's possibilities — the music, dress, food, and customs that give life its richness and texture. Adolescents also view these encounters as helping them move beyond the limitations and, even, the "destructive blindness" of their own cultures.

These are themes that have been widely developed in the academic discourse of postmodernity, which has given special attention to "otherness." In a much quoted metaphor, for example, Jean-François Lyotard speaks of the "end of all meta-narratives."[63] This implies that it is no longer possible to synthesize all existing stories into a coherent whole. Wolfgang Welsch, likewise, argues that postmodern understandings of plurality are radical in the sense that they involve more than simple variety, more than lack of consensus, and even more than the manifold diversity of reality.[64] Postmodern plurality is radical precisely because it is irreducible. It is not a temporary condition that may be sublated into a higher, unifying order. Any attempt to impose order on plurality is, from a postmodern perspective, considered an act of power

61. This research grows out of our participation in the Princeton Project of Youth, Globalization, and the Church, described above (see note 3).

62. We must qualify the last of these. Comparatively speaking, middle adolescents in the United States were found to use computers with far greater frequency than their counterparts in other parts of the world, including Germany and Japan. Researchers in these contexts speculated that increased use of computers begins to take place upon entry to universities and, thus, the effects would come somewhat later than the age group interviewed in this research.

63. Jean-François Lyotard, *The Postmodern Condition: A Report on Knowledge,* trans. G. Bennington and B. Massumi (Minneapolis: University of Minnesota Press, 1984).

64. Wolfgang Welsch, *Unsere postmoderne Moderne* (Weinheim: VCH, 1988).

and violence. Such an order does not allow "the other" to hold her or his own place and to speak with her or his own voice — a perspective important in contemporary feminism and other liberation movements. The deconstruction of imposed order, thus, is seen as one of the most important tasks of a critical philosophy, a task which strives to uncover the oppressive character of traditional categories of order. In this respect, postmodernism confronts modernization with the issue of power, specifically with those forms of power exerted by modern reason itself.

According to David Harvey, this affirmation of pluralism is one of the decisive contributions of postmodern thinking; in "its concern for difference, for the difficulties of communication, for the complexity and nuances of interests, cultures, places, and the like," he sees a "positive influence."[65] Obviously, the construction of this otherness by adolescents, uncovered in our own research, is far removed from the theoretical perspectives just described; yet both, in part, can be viewed as making sense of the pervasive character of encounters with cultural others that is such an important dimension of the emerging global context. As such, they can be interpreted as a form of global reflexivity.

A Heightened Awareness of Risk

A second element of postmodernism, as we are using the term in this book, is a heightened awareness of the risks attending scientific research and technological innovation. Prominent social theorists such as Ulrich Beck, Anthony Giddens, and Scott Lash have portrayed this as an important dimension of what they call "reflexive modernization."[66] If, they argue, modernity was characterized by great confidence in the use of science and technology to calculate and overcome the "natural" risks facing human communities — risks like crop failure, disease, and poor nutrition — then we now live in a second period of modernity. During this period, persons have become deeply aware that science and technology do not simply overcome risks but create risks of their own, risks that go far beyond those facing the human community in any prior age. The proliferation of weapons of mass destruction, the effects of pollution on the environment, and the altering of the genetic structure of crops, animals, and humans are but a few of the "manufactured risks" that might be pointed to.

Our own research on adolescents in Germany and the United States has led us to view this awareness of "manufactured risk" as a form of global re-

---

65. Harvey, *Condition of Postmodernity*, p. 113.
66. Beck, Giddens, and Lash, *Reflexive Modernization*.

flexivity.[67] It is one of the most important ways persons become aware of the interconnectedness of the world. Problems in one part of the world spill over to other parts of the world. The meltdown of the Chernobyl nuclear plant in the former Soviet Union was a potential disaster not only for the persons located in the immediate vicinity of the plant but also for many parts of Europe. Global warming, the spread of AIDS, the effects of acid rain, the use of genetically altered foods, and many similar problems are of a scale that stretches far beyond any particular national community. They represent global risks and, as such, are particularly potent ways of eliciting consciousness of the global whole.

This skepticism toward modernity's confidence in science and technology takes a variety of forms. In some cases, it modulates skepticism into apocalypticism, a sense that the end of life as we have known it is near and that there is nothing that can be done to alter this impending future. This attitude was found among many Russian youth after the accident at Chernobyl, and it pervades the "darker" forms of youth culture.[68] In other cases, this postmodern sensibility takes the quite different form of a new "primitivism," the attempt to reach behind scientific culture to recover spiritual and cultural resources not yet "polluted" by the modern age. The idealization of Native American culture found in some forms of New Age spirituality is an example of this sort of response. Certain forms of postmodern art, likewise, reflect this sensibility. Different still are the more political forms of this skepticism, ranging from the more established Greens to the anti-corporate activism in full view at recent meetings of the World Trade Organization.[69] What these very diverse movements and cultural trends have in common is their deep, almost visceral distrust of modernity's positive evaluation of science and technology. Awareness of the risks that modern science and technology have unleashed gives rise to a deep-seated skepticism, which is expressed in a variety of cultural forms.

A Processive View of Life

A final element of postmodernism is the adoption of a highly processive view of life. By this is meant a sense that the markers of personal identity formation and movement through the life cycle are no longer stable. Personal identity

67. See the citation above of our research in the Globalization project of the Princeton Theological Seminary Institute for Youth Ministry.

68. Michael Christensen, *The World after Chernobyl: Social Impact and Christian Response* (Wynnewood, Pa.: Evangelicals for Social Action, 1997).

69. For one account of this movement, see Naomi Klein, *No Logo: Taking Aim at the Brand Bullies* (New York: Picador, 1999).

will not be achieved merely one time during late adolescence. It will be constructed and reconstructed over the course of a person's life. Moreover, the path individuals will take cannot be found by looking at the patterns followed by their parents. Change is too rapid for even the near past to serve as a reliable guide. From changes in the structure of the family to those of the economy, unforeseen possibilities and problems make it necessary to negotiate one's way through life like a person on a raft traveling down an unknown river.

A cardinal tenet of modernization theory, we can recall, is the pluralizing and individualizing effects of differentiation, creating social conditions in which individuals must assume greater responsibility for shaping the structure of their own lives over their entire lifespan. On the surface, this account seems to have much in common with the processive understanding of life being pointed to here. There are two features of globalization, however, that press us to move beyond modernization theory in our description of the postmodern life cycle and personal identity formation.

First, the hyperdifferentiation and globalization of the economy has greatly magnified the element of ongoing change and flexibility inherent to the structures of our economic lives. It is no longer a matter of plants closing and relocating in other parts of the world. It is a matter of businesses constantly entering into relatively short-term ventures that are pieced together to take advantage of temporary opportunities in the market. The relatively stable roles that were a part of national, corporate economies have become far more tenuous in the global economy. The need to retool, rethink, and relocate becomes ongoing in ways that were not present even two decades ago. Second, the expansion of the global media and international travel have greatly intensified persons' exposure to cultural values and patterns quite different than those into which they were socialized. Cultural "collaging" — the interpenetration and synthesis of various elements of many cultures — is not merely a possibility for adolescents who use the Internet, watch TV, travel abroad, befriend exchange students, and listen to music from around the world; it is a reality that shapes their experience, making them deeply aware of the many different ways one can move through life.

One of the most important theoretical responses to these new developments has been in the area of psychology. Only a generation ago, the most influential theorist of the life cycle, Erik Erikson, could posit eight stages of "man," through which persons of different genders, classes, and ethnic groups supposedly moved.[70] Advocates of a new, postmodern understanding of the life cycle have begun to portray this as paradigmatic of the sort of master

70. Erik Erikson, *Childhood and Society* (New York: Norton, 1950).

story so common in modernity. Feminist psychologists, in particular, have argued that Erikson's account does not pay attention to the very different ways girls and women grow and develop.[71] They have begun to offer new theories based on gender-specific research. Others have pointed to the variables of class, culture, and race as far more determinative than Erikson's master narrative indicated; when low-income African-American women live lives that are considerably shorter than their white counterparts because of deficiencies in health care and nutrition, it is difficult to see how Erikson's stages of Generativity vs. Stagnation or Integrity vs. Despair really capture their experience.[72] Still others have begun to argue for context- and narrative-dependent understandings of the life cycle, sensitive to the ways individual biography, life history, and cultural circumstances interact.[73]

We will take up this new body of research in Part III of this book in our chapter on the individual. For the present, enough has been said to point to the theoretical foundation of the point being made here: a critical dimension of the postmodern form of global reflexivity at both academic and popular levels is a processive view of life — an awareness that personal identity will be constructed in a wide variety of ways and follow many different paths over the course of a person's life. Again, not all forms of global reflexivity are characterized by this view of life. In some cases, the reassertion of cultural and religious identities leads to the idealization of clearly demarcated roles for children, youth, adults, and elders, as well as those distinguishing men and women. Hence, we will reserve use of the term "postmodern" to indicate those cultural responses to globalization that incorporate a processive understanding of identity and the life cycle.

Conclusion

In this chapter, we have described the three comprehensive conceptual frameworks that will be used in the remainder of this book: modernization, global-

---

71. One of the earliest treatments of this topic is found in Carol Gilligan, *In a Different Voice: Psychological Theory and Women's Development* (Cambridge, Mass.: Harvard University Press, 1982). See also Deborah Tannen, *Gender and Discourse* (Oxford: Oxford University Press, 1994); and Mary Belenky et al., *Women's Ways of Knowing* (New York: Basic, 1986).

72. Jean Spurlock, "Black Women in the Middle Years," in *Women in Midlife*, ed. G. Baruch and J. Brooks-Gunn (New York: Plenum, 1984), chap. 10.

73. Kenneth Gergen, *The Saturated Self: Dilemmas of Identity in Contemporary Life* (New York: Basic, 1991); Theodore R. Sarbin, ed., *Narrative Psychology: The Storied Nature of Human Conduct* (New York: Praeger, 1986).

ization, and postmodernism. As we have indicated, the first two of these are viewed as the most fundamental categories we employ to analyze social contexts, with postmodernism used to denote a special form of global reflexivity. Our use of these frameworks is not uncritical. Nonetheless, they play an important role in our exploration of the interdependence of religious education and its social contexts in Germany and the United States over the course of the twentieth century. It is to this task that we now turn.

II Paradigmatic Figures and Texts in Twentieth-Century Protestant Religious Education

Introduction to Part II

It should be clear from our discussion in Part I that we are interested in a deeper understanding of the difficulties and challenges that Christian religious education faces today. We have analyzed the social and cultural transformations that form the context of these difficulties and challenges in terms which we believe capture the primary features of these transformations — in other words, in terms of the concepts of modernization, postmodernism, and globalization. We may therefore say that we are striving for an understanding of religious education in the context of modernization, postmodernism, and globalization.

Furthermore, we have stated our reasons for assuming that international comparative investigation might turn out to be one of the most promising approaches to the kinds of questions concerning the struggle of religious education. Our primary point is that the standard procedure of comparing different educational approaches within one country will not carry us far in understanding the relationship between Christian religious education and the large-scale social and cultural transformations in which we are interested. The comparative analysis of more or less parallel developments in at least two different countries will put us in a better position to understand these large-scale tendencies.

This kind of comparative international research is already fairly well-established in several fields outside of religious education and theology, such as education, sociology, political science, and cultural studies.[1] Some of the

---

1. To just mention a view examples: Christoph Kodron et al., eds., *Vergleichende Erzie-*

work carried out in these fields actually deals with questions and interests that are quite similar to our own — most notably the work in comparative education that discusses the processes of modernization, internationalization, and globalization in relation to education.[2] The focus in these fields is, however, clearly different from our own concern with religious education. We have not, therefore, attempted to build our methodology on the models existing in other fields, because to do so would require a special investigation into comparative methodology, a time-consuming detour without immediate prospects for our present endeavor. Consequently, we decided to develop our own methodology for the purposes of comparative international research in the field of Christian religious education, in order to increase the likelihood that our methodology will really fit our object of study.

We will trace the development of religious education theory in the twentieth century by offering both parallel accounts of historical developments in the United States and Germany and a critical examination of major religious educators in each country, combining a sociohistorical approach with intellectual history.[3] Major publications that played an important role at the turning points in the development of religious education are given a new reading, connecting them to the background of global social and historical transformations. We hope to do justice to the individual authors' perceptions by asking how they perceived their work in relationship to society and culture at their own time, but we also want to go beyond their own perspective by asking, from our own point of view, how and if they were successful in facing up to the challenges of their particular time and of social modernization in general.

It is clear that a limited study will not be able to cover the entire field of religious education in the twentieth century comprehensively. This is why we will focus on characteristic periods and on the major turning points in

---

hungswissenschaft/Comparative Education, vol. 1 (Köln: Böhlau Verlag, 1997); Dirk Berg-Schlosser and Ferdinand Müller-Rommel, eds., Vergleichende Politikwissenschaft. Ein einführendes Studienhandbuch, third ed. (Opladen: Leske und Budrich, 1997); Gisela Trommsdorff, ed., Kindheit und Jugend in verschiedenen Kulturen. Entwicklung und Sozialisation in kulturvergleichender Sicht (Weinheim: Juventa-Verlag, 1995); Klaus Hurrelmann, ed., International Handbook of Adolescence (Westport, Conn.: Greenwood Press, 1994); Hans-Joachim Klimkeit, ed., Vergleichen und Verstehen in der Religionswissenschaft (Wiesbaden: Harrassowitz Verlag, 1997).

2. For a good summary, see Jürgen Schriewer, "Internationalisierung der Pädagogik und Vergleichende Erziehungswissenschaft," in Pädagogik, Erziehungswissenschaft, Bildung. Eine Einführung in das Studium, ed. D. K. Müller (Köln: Böhlau, 1994), pp. 427-62; Andy Green, Education, Globalization, and the Nation State (London: Macmillan, 1997).

3. For this kind of approach the work of LaCapra has been a helpful model for us. See Dominic LaCapra, History and Criticism (Ithaca, N.Y.: Cornell University Press, 1985).

twentieth-century history. But which periods should we pick? There are at least two competing possibilities to be considered. The standard approach in the literature traces patterns of thought within the field of religious education theory beginning with the religious education reform movements at the beginning of the century, through the theological renewal that followed these movements, up to the restructuring of religious education starting in the 1960s. The periodization is somewhat different for the United States and Germany. While the reform period is thought to have lasted roughly the first three decades of the century in both countries, the influence of dialectical theology or neo-orthodoxy and of neo-Lutheranism is commonly viewed as beginning earlier in Germany, in the 1920s. In the United States the beginning of this new theological influence is often connected to the late 1940s. The 1960s may be considered an important turning point in both countries.

The other approach to periodizing the development of religious education theory (an approach closer to our own) does not isolate religious education from history. Consequently, the different periods of religious education theory are seen from the perspective of the various events and processes that took place during the twentieth century. From this perspective, the end of World War I is the first important marker event. This was particularly important for Germany, as it meant the advent of its first democracy — the Weimar Republic — and also brought about the separation of state and church. The next marker event in German history is the beginning of National Socialism, especially with Hitler coming into power in 1933. This period ends in 1945 — a date that marks a new historical period for both countries. Among all the important trends between 1945 and 1989, the Cold War and the confrontation between East and West were probably the most important in the second half of the twentieth century. Many observers agree that in 1989 a new historical period began — a period that still does not have a definitive name. If we are looking for another marker event between 1945 and 1989, the most likely time is that of the 1960s. In both countries, the social, political, and cultural changes of that era have had long-term effects on general and religious education.

The advantages and disadvantages of both ways of looking at the development of religious education theory in the twentieth century are obvious. Focusing on just the internal structure of the theological or educational theories may yield a much clearer picture of different types of theories or approaches to religious education. But this clearer picture may not be accurate. Religious educators are becoming increasingly aware of the extent to which religious education is intertwined with the larger developments in society and culture. This awareness calls for a historical periodization of the developments in religious education.[4]

Given the need to concentrate on a number of exemplary points in time and hoping to do justice to both traditional accounts and to broader historical developments, we decided to make three periods our primary focal points and to consider them against a wider historical background. We will start with the religious education reform movements (1900-1930), then move to the postwar theological renewal (the time after 1945 through the 1950s), and finally consider the changes starting in the 1960s. This will not give us a comprehensive picture of the twentieth century because we will leave out some important periods. We will omit, for example, the time of National Socialism in Germany, because there is no immediate parallel in the United States.[5] Our concentration on the years after 1900, 1945, and 1960 does, however, put us in a position to look into three of the major periods in the history of the twentieth century.

Having introduced the three periods that are to be our focal points in this part of the book, we face a possible objection concerning our procedure. If we are leaving out certain historical periods such as German National Socialism because there is no parallel to it in the United States, does this not actually prove that the details of history in one particular country or community cannot be replaced by the more abstract understanding to be gained from international comparisons? To some degree this objection is valid. Specific aspects of a particular country's history will be given less emphasis in an international or comparative approach. In the end, however, this objection does not negate the value of this approach. Rather, it helps clarify what we can and cannot realistically expect from international comparative work. We remain convinced that having an eye on other countries will enrich even the particular historical understanding of what has been the case in one's own country. In this sense, different circumstances and different developments may highlight each other. As we argued in Part I, certain historical explanations of a given situation in one country may make sense as long as one does not consider the possible parallels in another country. Once one comes to realize that

4. In their three-volume edition covering the history of religious education in Germany since the Reformation, Karl Ernst Nipkow and Friedrich Schweitzer have tried to establish this kind of broader historical understanding; see K. E. Nipkow and F. Schweitzer, eds., *Religionspädagogik. Texte zur evangelischen Erziehungs- und Bildungsverantwortung seit der Reformation*, 3 vols. (München/Gütersloh: Kaiser/Gütersloher Verlagshaus, 1991-1994).

5. Another reason for not focusing on religious education during National Socialism may be seen in the still insufficient research available on this period. For a critical current summary cf. Folkert Rickers, *Zwischen Kreuz und Hakenkreuz. Untersuchungen zur Religionspädagogik im "Dritten Reich"* (Neukirchen-Vluyn: Neukirchener Verlag, 1995).

practically the same educational ideas have played a comparable role in another country — a country in which the explanatory concepts commonly used to understand one's own country do not apply — the seemingly well-established explanations are called into question.

We do not offer our present study as a comprehensive comparative account of twentieth-century religious education in Germany and the United States. Our more modest goal is to introduce a number of new questions into the standard accounts of religious education in both countries. Successfully raising such questions is reason enough, we think, to establish the usefulness of our comparative procedure and will contribute to a deeper understanding of the challenges that religious education faces as it confronts modernity, globalization, and postmodernism.

Based on these considerations of methodology and of possible periodizations, this part of the book is organized into three main chapters. Each chapter covers roughly three decades — 1900-1930, 1930-1960, and 1960-1990 — with more limited and defined references to special periods or developments within each thirty-year span. Each of the following three chapters follows approximately the same outline:

- a historical overview of educational developments, especially in religious education;
- an interpretation of exemplary texts — i.e., one or two major publications of one or two authors who played a leading role during the period under consideration. Given our interest in restoring a public role for religious education, we will give central attention to the question of the audience being addressed in these publications;
- a discussion of how the respective approach relates to the process of social transformation and modernization.

Within each chapter these points are addressed twice, first for the United States and then for Germany. At the end of each chapter, we add a short section in which the developments in both countries are compared and contrasted.

The introductory section of Part III of this volume will offer a brief summary of what we have gained from the comparative study of twentieth-century religious education in Germany and the United States. There we argue for a more comprehensive approach to religious education in context — an approach that includes an understanding of the relationship between the theological tradition and the cultural and social transformations of modernization, globalization, and postmodernism.

3 Facing Up to Modernity:
Religious Education Reform Movements in the Early Twentieth Century

Social Theory, Religion, and Democracy:
Reform Movements in the United States

During the first three decades of the twentieth century, many Protestant denominations in the United States experienced the impact of a reform movement commonly known as the religious education movement. This movement would reshape the way church leaders and practitioners viewed the
practice of teaching in congregations and the role of religious education in
state-sponsored schools. The public presence of this movement can be identified symbolically with the founding of the Religious Education Association in
1903, an event attended by prominent figures such as John Dewey, the leading
intellectual of progressive education, and William Rainey Harper, the founding president of the University of Chicago.

Leading figures of the religious education movement during this period
were George Albert Coe and William Clayton Bower, and, somewhat later,
Rachel Henderlite, Harrison Elliott, and Sophia Fahs. The movement was
closely identified with both liberal theology (especially its American, Social
Gospel forms) and the educational reforms pursued in public education by
the progressive education movement. Like the progressives, the leading liberal theologians supported the removal of religion from the public schools,
viewing religion as something properly taught by congregations and families.
Much of their attention focused on reforming the education of congregations
in ways that were informed by modern educational theory and developmental psychology.

To achieve this goal, leaders of the reform movement worked to establish a new academic discipline — religious education — with its own disciplinary focus, academic programs, professional guild, and academic journals. They eschewed the rubric of practical theology to describe their work, viewing that rubric as tied to notions of applied theology and as undercutting their interest in emerging fields like psychology, fields to which they made their own contributions. In addition, the leaders of this movement lent support to the emergence of a new profession, the Director of Religious Education.[1] It was hoped that the members of this group might receive the kind of specialized education that would prepare them to lead the reform of education in the church. Lab schools were established in prominent institutions such as Union Theological Seminary in New York, affording seminary students and religious educators the opportunity to experience new approaches to religious education firsthand. New courses and programs in religious education appeared in seminary curriculums, and congregations began to hire the graduates of these programs to direct their educational programs. At the national level, denominations created staff positions designed to produce church school curriculums and to provide support for the educational ministries of congregations.

The various initiatives of the religious education reform movement would have a lasting impact on Protestant religious education over the course of the twentieth century. The movement's heavy reliance on the social sciences, its support of modern approaches to education, and its attempt to shape religious communities responsive to the problems of modernity are a part of its enduring legacy. In the section that follows, we will examine George Albert Coe's *A Social Theory of Religious Education* as representative of this period. We also will examine briefly Sophia Fahs's *Today's Children and Yesterday's Heritage,* which was written in 1952 and is indicative of the continuing influence of the religious education movement in mainline Protestantism over the course of the twentieth century.

George Albert Coe: The Dean of the Religious Education Movement

George Albert Coe was born in 1861 and lived until 1951. His father was a Methodist minister who served churches in upper New York State. He at-

---

1. For a historical overview of the profession of the Director of Religious Education see Dorothy Jean Furnish, "An Historical Analysis of the Work of the Director of Christian Education," Ph.D. dissertation, Northwestern University, 1968, and *DRE/DCE: The History of a Profession* (Nashville: Christian Educators Fellowship, 1976).

tended the University of Rochester and then pursued graduate studies at Boston University School of Theology, where he received both a Bachelor of Divinity and Ph.D. While at the university, he was deeply influenced by the great Boston personalist Borden Parker Bowne. Coe was awarded Boston University's travelling fellowship in 1890 and spent a year in Germany, where he studied theology and philosophy at the University of Berlin. His wife continued to study music in Germany until 1893, leading Coe to join her in Germany during the summers. Following a brief stint as a professor of philosophy at the University of Southern California, Coe joined the faculty of Northwestern University as the Evans Professor of Moral and Intellectual Philosophy. In addition to teaching philosophy, Coe began to pursue his interest in psychology, studying adolescent conversion (the focus of his first book, *The Spiritual Life*, published in 1900) and, then, the challenges of modern science to the religious faith of college undergraduates (the focus of his second book, *The Religion of a Mature Mind*, 1902). Coe moved to Union Theological Seminary in New York in 1909 where he occupied a chair in practical theology for over a decade before taking a position at Teacher's College, Columbia University. He retired in 1927.

Broadly speaking, Coe's intellectual career can be divided into three periods. During the first period, he continued to rely on themes of philosophical personalism to describe the relationship of Protestantism to modern life. In addition to the two books mentioned above, this period included the publication of *Education in Religion and Morals* (1904), in which Coe drew heavily on personalism to conceptualize the relationship between religion and modernity, arguing that "personalizing" impulses could be found in both at their best. Standing at the very heart of Christianity, for example, is the affirmation of the sacredness of the human personality, a core value it shares with modernity's affirmation of the rights of every citizen in a constitutional democracy, its support of the individual's capacity for growth and critical thinking in education, and its valuation of the human quest for truth in modern science. Coe became more critical of modernity during the middle phase of his career, represented in *The Psychology of Religion* (1916) and in the book we are examining in detail, *A Social Theory of Religious Education* (1917). It was during this period that he was most influenced by the thinking of John Dewey and began to develop a sustained critique, informed by the Social Gospel movement, of the problems of urbanization and the industrialization of the economy. Following World War I and the crash of the stock market in 1929, Coe would become even more suspect of a too-close identification of religion with modernity, although he never abandoned his commitment to reconstructing the beliefs and practices of contemporary Protestantism in ways that were supportive of the personalizing trends of modern life. These trends, he now came to believe, were opposed by many counterforces also apparent in modern life. In *The Motives of Men* (1928) and *What Is Christian Education?* (1929), he portrayed the vocation of Protestantism as that of a prophetic, creative minority whose task was to help modernity realize its unfulfilled potential.

A Social Theory of Religious Education was the first major theoretical book in the United States to define religious education as a specialized discipline, locating it in neither the newly emerging social sciences nor theology but in a new disciplinary "space" from which it is free to draw on both. The primary audience of this text is professional leaders of the church responsible for oversight of congregation education. While Coe touches briefly on the potential role of the family, public school, and denominational agencies in religious education, his primary focus is the congregation. He offers a theory of religious education that will allow contemporary Protestant congregations to come to terms with modernity in two basic ways.

First, he advocates a religious education that faces directly the challenges of modern life. From the evolutionary thinking of science to the problems of urbanization and industrialization, modern life presents Protestantism with a new set of challenges. It is precisely these difficult issues that Coe places at the heart of the religious education curriculum. Second, he is interested in reconstructing inherited patterns of congregational education in light of the insights of modern psychology and education. He argues that authoritarian, transmission-oriented models of the past must be replaced by those that support critical thinking and the gradual expansion of social experience. Religious education, as such, is to be a force in the ongoing transformation of the church and society. As Coe puts it in the very first pages of the book, he is attempting to describe a social theory of religious education that follows from a "social interpretation of the Christian message," replacing an individualistic view of salvation with one in which "the redemptive mission of the Christ is nothing less than that of transforming the social order itself into a brotherhood or family of God."[2]

Coe organizes his book around four components that he believes are found in any adequate theory of education:

(1) an indication of the *kind of society* that is regarded as desirable; (2) a conception of the *original nature* of children; (3) a conception of the *sorts of individual experience* that will surely and more economically produce in

2. George Albert Coe, *A Social Theory of Religious Education* (New York: Arno, 1969), pp. viii and 6.

such children the kind of sociality that is desired; and (4) a statement of at least the more general *standards and tests* by which one may judge the degree to which these sorts of experience are being provided by any educational institution or process.[3]

Since Coe employs these categories himself to describe the various parts of this text, they will serve as a convenient way of examining the book.

Chapters two through five focus on the first of these, *the kind of society that is desired*. In these chapters, Coe describes "the social standpoint of modern education" and then draws on this perspective to construct a new set of aims for religious education, openly acknowledging the influence of Dewey on his thought. Two gains of nineteenth-century education, Coe argues, are its attention to the ways the human mind actively constructs the world and its nurture of freedom and critical thinking in order to prepare individuals to participate in popular forms of government.[4] Both have been reconstructed by contemporary forms of progressive education in (1) its attention to the social experiences and interactive processes through which cognition, skills, and motives take shape, and (2) its portrayal of schools as "democracy in miniature" (as Dewey put it), sites in which the young already begin to practice the social skills standing at the heart of popular forms of government. Education along these lines does more than merely transmit a pre-existent cultural heritage or enable students to adjust to society as it currently exists. It allows the young to begin the task of reconstructing society, helping them acquire the capacities to reflect on and share their experiences as they focus on the actual social problems of the present. Coe, like Dewey, places this understanding of education in an evolutionary framework. Education is "evolution becoming conscious," the means by which humans actively direct natural and social forces toward desirable ends.[5]

While Coe accepts this social theory of education, he is not uncritical of the ways it is developed in progressive education. Progressive education has difficulty avoiding "a shallow pragmatism of immediate ends."[6] Moreover, it may unwittingly participate in the creation of a "permanent servile class," failing to include within its scope the democratization of the economic forces of society.[7] Such concerns cannot be avoided in religious education. Accordingly, Coe develops the ideal of the "democracy of God" to describe the type

3. Coe, *A Social Theory*, p. 9.
4. Coe, *A Social Theory*, pp. 26-28.
5. Coe, *A Social Theory*, pp. 32-33.
6. Coe, *A Social Theory*, p. 36.
7. Coe, *A Social Theory*, p. 33.

of society toward which the church should educate its young.[8] Drawing on the insights of liberal theology and the Social Gospel movement, he portrays this educational ideal as a reinterpretation of Jesus' proclamation of the kingdom of God, clarifying the socioethical implications of this ideal for modern life. The aim of Christian education, thus, is defined as follows: "Growth of the young toward and into mature and efficient devotion to the democracy of God, and happy self-realization therein."[9] He leaves no doubt as to what this entails: "the transformation of a social order that is largely unjust into one that shall be wholly just."[10]

Having set forth the educational ideal of religious education, Coe moves to the task of describing *the kinds of educational experiences that will equip persons to pursue this ethical ideal* (the third basic component of a theory of education, noted above) in chapters five through nine. In large measure, he follows the lead of progressive education in his criticisms of the educational practices then dominating American Protestantism. Rather than focusing on the transmission of biblical or dogmatic beliefs, he argues, religious education should promote the gradual expansion of children's social experience of the kind of cooperative thinking, concern, and activity that is consistent with the ethical ideal of the democracy of God. Coe rejects indoctrination of all sorts, especially as found in catechetical instruction. Rather, the Bible is to be introduced in an "expanding series of social activities" by which young people learn to think about and respond to the social issues that actually face modern societies.[11]

Coe is sensitive to the insights of developmental psychology at this point but rejects the notion, espoused by Rousseau, that education merely nurtures the unfolding capacities of the child. Education must shape and direct these unfolding capacities toward an ethical engagement of ever-wider social spheres. As Coe puts it, "The social consciousness of a Sunday-school class must enlarge into a school consciousness, and this into a church consciousness; and the whole must flow outward toward the whole needy world."[12] Religious education, as such, is not merely preparation for future social engagement, it is the process by which such engagement is actively pursued in the present. Knowledge of the Bible and church doctrine will be acquired as they function as instruments in understanding and responding to real social issues. Only in this way does the Christian faith become a living part of young

8. Coe, *A Social Theory*, pp. 54-60.
9. Coe, *A Social Theory*, p. 55.
10. Coe, *A Social Theory*, p. 64.
11. Coe, *A Social Theory*, p. 64.
12. Coe, *A Social Theory*, p. 81.

persons' experience and not an irrelevant compartment of their total personality.

Coe then offers *a conception of the original state of children* (the second component of his theory of education noted above) in chapters ten through thirteen. Here he draws on contemporary functional psychology to portray the psychobiological foundations of human thought and action. While these are the by-product of our evolutionary heritage, they are relatively plastic and can be shaped in remarkably different ways across various cultures. Coe criticizes functional psychology for neglecting the religious capacities of children and the role of religion generally across evolution,[13] a theme he addresses more fully in *The Psychology of Religion.* Children's capacity for consciousness of God and their tendency toward good or evil are an outgrowth of the ways their psychobiological potentials are shaped by their social context. This social interpretation of the original state of children leads Coe to reject the doctrines of original sin and total depravity, which portray sin as an inborn condition of disruption in the individual's relationship with God. In contrast, he argues, "The 'depravity' that the child exhibits . . . is commonly not that of his own heart, but that of remediable faults of adult individuals and of adult society."[14] Moral and religious education can be viewed, in part, as a process of character formation, a process in which social conditions shape the child for better and for worse.

Chapters fifteen through twenty-four of *A Social Theory of Religious Education* provide *a statement of general standards and tests by which to judge the effectiveness of religious education* (the fourth component of his educational theory). Here Coe examines four important sites of religious education: the family, the church, the public school, and denominational agencies. He then scrutinizes five different types of Christianity: Roman Catholicism, dogmatic Protestantism, ritualistic Protestantism, evangelicalism, and liberalism. Throughout this part of his book, Coe draws on his prior description of the aims and processes of religious education oriented toward the democracy of God to evaluate the education offered by these institutions and by different forms of Christianity. In his discussion of the family, for example, he criticizes the ways Protestantism continues to legitimate authoritarian, patriarchal relations, and he calls for an abolishment of the inequality between the sexes and for the establishment of democratic styles of parenting.[15]

Especially important for our purposes is Coe's treatment of the relation-

13. Coe, *A Social Theory,* p. 119.
14. Coe, *A Social Theory,* p. 171.
15. Coe, *A Social Theory,* pp. 211-14

ship between the church and state and of the exclusion of religious education from the public schools, which had begun to take place in the United States during the nineteenth century. Coe would take up this theme more fully in *Educating for Citizenship*.[16] In *A Social Theory*, he applauds the separation of church and state as a positive outgrowth of modern democratic trends.[17] It is the modern state, he argues, not the church, that has been the most important "defender and guarantor of fundamental liberties" across the modern period,[18] and he opposes the use of public funds to support private religious schools. Moreover, he supports the removal of religion as a subject in public education, arguing as follows:

> The interest of a socialized religious education in the public schools is not that they should teach religion in addition to reading, writing, and arithmetic, but that they should teach democracy, and that they should do so thoroughly. To "teach" democracy . . . means to develop intelligent democratic attitudes, activities, habits, and purposes — in short, to make the pupils democrats.[19]

The role of religious education theory in modern societies, thus, is twofold. First, it should lend support to reform movements that are attempting to make public education more democratic. Second, it should attempt to develop educational programs for religious communities (in Coe's case, Protestant communities) that are consistent with the socioethical ideal of the democracy of God. In this way, education in two separate spheres — public schools and religious communities — will work hand in hand toward the achievement of the kind of society to which modernity, at its best, is committed.

Sophia Lyon Fahs: An Early Female Reformer

Sophia Lyon Fahs was born in Hangchow, China, in 1876 to a family of missionaries.[20] She lived in China until she was three, when her father's poor

---

16. George Albert Coe, *Educating for Citizenship: The Sovereign State as Ruler and as Teacher* (New York: Charles Scribner's Sons, 1932).

17. Coe, *A Social Theory*, p. 248.

18. Coe, *A Social Theory*, p. 249.

19. Coe, *A Social Theory*, p. 263.

20. Biographical information on Fahs is found in Edith Hunter, *Sophia Lyon Fahs* (Boston: Beacon, 1966); Dorothy Fahs Beck (her daughter), "Sophia Lyon Fahs: Militant Liberal and Lover of Children," *Religious Education* 73 (Nov.-Dec. 1978, pp. 714-20; Daniel Chandler, "Sophia Lyon Fahs (Religious Educator, 1876-1978)," *Religious Education* 84 (Fall 1989), pp. 538-52.

health forced him to return to the United States.[21] She graduated from Wooster College in 1897 and over a decade later earned a master's degree at Teacher's College, Columbia University, studying under John Dewey. In 1923, at age forty-seven, she enrolled in the Bachelors of Divinity program of Union Theological Seminary, studying under Harrison Elliott and George Coe, who was then teaching at Teacher's College. After graduation from Union, she became the principal of the seminary's School of Religion, a lab school for children, and a lecturer in its department of religious education.[22] During this period, Fahs became increasingly disenchanted with Protestantism and, eventually, joined the Unitarian Universalist Church. In 1937 at age sixty-one she became the chief editor of this denomination's publishing house for children's curriculum and was ordained as a minister at age eighty-two. Until her death at the age of nearly 102, she remained an active speaker, lecturer, and author, leaving a huge body of books, articles, poetry, and curriculum that includes the widely read *Beginnings: Earth, Sky, Life, Death; Consider the Children: How They Grow;* and *The Old Story of Salvation.*

Today's Children and Yesterday's Heritage was published in 1952, long after the period we are examining in this section. It is included at this point to indicate the continuing influence of the ideas of the early religious education movement long after the first three decades of the twentieth century. Even as new trajectories of Protestant religious education emerged in later decades, this movement's synthesis of liberal theology, progressive education, and Social Gospel remained a potent force. Fahs's book, written at the midpoint of the century, reflects each of these elements. Her primary audience in this text is the professional leaders of congregational education, although her style is clear and nontechnical to the point of being accessible to lay teachers in the congregation's educational program. While she does not extensively address the family, public education, or the individual in this particular text, she does take up these topics in other writings. Indeed, of all the persons from the United States examined in Part II of this volume, Fahs comes the closest to addressing parents directly, writing in ways that cross over to a nonspecialist audience.

The opening words of the preface set the tone for the entire book: "In this attempt to set forth an emerging philosophy of religious education, we have

21. Although her father returned to China when she was ten, Fahs remained in the United States with her mother and siblings, settling in Ohio.

22. Fahs describes the school in a book coauthored with Helen Firman Sweet, *Exploring Religion with Eight-Year-Olds* (New York: Henry Holt, 1930). For a description of this school, see also Harris Parker, "The Union School of Religion, 1910-1929: Embers from the Fires," *Religious Education* 86, no. 4 (Fall 1991), pp. 597-607.

dwelt especially on those points where the natural approach to religious development stands in marked contrast to the traditional approach of authority and indoctrination."[23] The book is structured around a series of contrasts between traditional and natural religious education. In the opening two chapters, Fahs brings this contrast into focus by comparing the two types of education's very different attitudes toward religious belief. She begins by arguing that religious beliefs continue to be important in modern society, drawing special attention to the challenges of religious pluralism and the "disconnect" between the inherited beliefs of traditional religion and those plausible to modern persons who have come to terms with scientific thinking. She argues that it is crucial to realize the important role religious beliefs play in the personality: "One's faith is the philosophy of life that gathers up into one emotional whole — sometimes, although rarely, into a reasoned whole — all the specific beliefs one holds about many kinds of things in many areas of life."[24] It is at this "deeper level where universal truth and universal human need are found" that religion plays its proper role, not in the ability to espouse the conventional beliefs of the past which have lost their ability to address the modern situation.[25]

Accordingly, Fahs argues in the second chapter, it is extremely important to pay close attention to *how* persons acquire their beliefs. Traditional religious education has approached this issue by presenting the beliefs of a religion as something "given to an individual by an authority other than himself, by an authority coming from the past — from revelation, from an inspired book, from a divine person, or from a divinely ordained church."[26] In contrast, the natural approach she is advocating views the acquisition of religious beliefs as something that emerges organically out of an individual's total experience. Above all, such beliefs emerge gradually over the course of human development, growing out of the child's various attempts to build "his own religion."[27] Fahs is not advocating here a Rousseauistic approach to religious education in which religious impulses unfold naturally without substantial guidance from the social world. Rather, like Dewey, Coe, and Elliott, she is advocating an approach that takes the developing child's needs and interests seriously and guides the child toward a wider circle of social experience and richer, more complex forms of thinking.

23. Sophia Lyon Fahs, *Today's Children and Yesterday's Heritage: A Philosophy of Creative Religious Development* (Boson: Beacon, 1952), p. vii.
24. Fahs, *Today's Children*, p. 8.
25. Fahs, *Today's Children*, p. 9.
26. Fahs, *Today's Children*, p. 15.
27. Fahs, *Today's Children*, p. 16.

Fahs describes in greater detail how religious education can guide the naturally emerging religious beliefs of the child in chapters three and four. She relies heavily on contemporary research in psychology to frame her understanding of children's emotional and cognitive development, correcting certain beliefs of orthodox Christianity in the process. Following modern psychology, for example, she argues that infants are active organisms whose search for love and mastery should not be curbed in the name of original sin.[28] Rather, a "scientifically based confidence in the potential goodness of human nature" should undergird approaches to parenting that follow the "natural schedule by which all children seem to grow" and that are more "permissive" in their approach to discipline.[29] All forms of moralism, as such, should be ruled out. Similarly, religious education should build on children's curiosity and desire to play, for these represent the first, "natural" steps in the human search for truth and the formation of moral relationships with others. Fahs provides numerous examples of how this might be done, pointing the reader to the fuller accounts in her book *Consider the Children: How They Grow* and her other writings. She draws a parallel between the natural development of religion in children and the development of religion across human evolution.

Fahs then describes the differences between traditional and natural religious education through four contrasts: the old Bible and the new, the old cosmologies and the new, the old morality and the new, and the old world-brotherhood and the new (chapters five through ten). In each case, she explores the various ways cultural modernity has challenged the beliefs of traditional religion and she poses "new" ways of thinking about these topics that might help religious education assist modern persons in forging new constellations of belief. Her treatment of the old Bible and the new illustrates her approach throughout this section.

The old Bible of orthodox Christianity and Judaism, she argues, is portrayed as the "record of God's divine plan for mankind's destiny — it is 'The Great Story of Salvation.'"[30] Here, the Bible is viewed as a narrative of salvation history, beginning in eternity and ending in eternity. Fahs provides a summary of this story, drawing on Augustine. She then contrasts this with the new picture of the Bible emerging out of modern biblical scholarship. Here, the Bible is portrayed as a diverse literature that reflects the conditions and experiences of a community across many centuries. It does not contain a single, unified message. Indeed, some biblical perspectives are less desirable than others.

28. Fahs, *Today's Children*, pp. 39-40.
29. Fahs, *Today's Children*, p. 40.
30. Fahs, *Today's Children*, p. 62.

As an example, Fahs points to the "nationalistic point of view" inherent in Israel's understanding of itself as a chosen people.[31] The whole story of salvation, she argues, was woven around this idea and was taken over by the Christian church, injecting "an exclusiveness and a self-righteousness that have poisoned Western civilization ever since."[32] Similarly, she contends that Israel was not the first and only monotheistic religion and that its ethical standards are "conflicting," teaching justice and mercy before God at one moment and justifying "slavery, national exclusiveness, race hatred, cruelty, stealing, murder and war" in God's name at the next.[33] In light of these sorts of contradictions, she believes, religious education should approach the Bible historically, helping students place its various stories and ethical codes in their original contexts. In this way, children will learn to use the Bible as a valuable cultural resource, like other great literature, with the capacity to address enduring human questions and issues, including those of modern persons. But religious education should not grant it special intrinsic authority on the basis of inherited church teaching or ecclesiastical custom, as in traditional Christian education.

In similar fashion, Fahs contrasts traditional and natural religious education in the areas of cosmology, morality, and world-brotherhood. In each case, she advocates the abandonment of traditional beliefs and practices in order to allow contemporary people to construct new ones consistent with modern life. She concludes the book by attending to three practical issues: the art of leading groups, the subject matter of religious education, and the role of worship.

Coe and Fahs in Context

It is illuminating to place the rhetoric of Coe and Fahs in the context of processes of modernization that were reshaping the United States during the end of the nineteenth century and opening decades of the twentieth. This period marks the transition of the United States to an industrialized, urban society, a process that began in earnest in the last three decades of the nineteenth century, following the American Civil War (1861-1865).[34] Although the war had left all parts of the country depleted, it served as a spur to manufacturing, especially in the North. By the late 1870s, the postwar economy had entered a

---

31. Fahs, *Today's Children*, p. 77.
32. Fahs, *Today's Children*, p. 78.
33. Fahs, *Today's Children*, p. 80.
34. The various statistics in this paragraph are taken from the following sources, unless otherwise noted: Cornel West, *Race Matters* (New York: Vintage, 1994); and *The New Encyclopedia Britannica*, Macropaedia, vol. 18 (Chicago: William Benton, 1974), pp. 975-77.

period of growth. During the final two decades of the century, the volume of industrial production, the number of workers employed in industry, and the number of manufacturing plants all doubled. The aggregate annual value of all manufactured goods increased from $5.4 billion in 1879 to $13 billion in 1899. A series of inventions during this period — the telephone, typewriter, linotype, phonograph, electric light, cash register, air brake, refrigerator car, and automobile — became the basis of new industries. Corporate forms of business organization also began to emerge, marking the shift to a national economy based on large-scale financing and the marketing of goods across regional lines. The woeful conditions of many workers led to the formation of labor unions, such as the Knights of Labor in 1869 and the American Federation of Labor in 1881. Accompanying these developments was a steady process of urbanization. Most plants were located in or near urban areas and agriculture in general became less important. In 1860, it represented 50 percent of the total national wealth; in 1900, it represented only 20 percent.

All of these trends would have an enormous impact on education. The public school movement during the first half of the nineteenth century had largely focused on the establishment of compulsory, state-supported elementary education. It was only during the last decade of this century that it began to turn its attention to the high school. In large measure, this was a response to increased automation of farm and factory work, which removed large numbers of adolescents from the workforce. The emergence of a new managerial and professional class likewise led to a precipitous rise in high school and university education. In 1875, fewer than 25,000 persons attended high school. By 1900, over 500,000 did. Between 1870 and 1900, the number of college students jumped nearly fivefold, from 52,000 to 238,000.[35] One of the most important reasons higher education grew during this period was a shift in its financial benefactors from religious denominations to private donors and the federal government. The Morrill Act of 1862 made millions of acres of land and millions of dollars available for the establishment or expansion of colleges and universities. Increases in the size of faculties and enrollment in graduate schools soon followed.[36]

By the dawn of the twentieth century, thus, the United States was well on its way to becoming an industrial, urban society. When Coe and Fahs are viewed against this backdrop, their rhetoric can be seen as responding to four central facets of modernization: (1) the cognitive challenges of modern scien-

---

35. James Davison Hunter, *Evangelicalism: The Coming Generation* (Chicago: University of Chicago Press, 1987), p. 166.

36. Hunter, *Evangelicalism*, p. 166.

tific thinking, (2) the socioethical challenges of urbanization and industrialization to democratic culture and political society, (3) the institutional differentiation of religion from other institutions, especially from public education, and (4) the emergence of religious education as a specialized discipline with its own academic program, professional audience, journals, and guild. Coe and Fahs address each of these trends in the issues they take up and the rhetorical strategies they adopt. Indeed, permeating their arguments is both a challenge and a warning: Contemporary religion must come to terms with modernity; otherwise, it will play no role in the lives of contemporary people and have little influence on the forces shaping modern life.

The cognitive challenges of modern scientific thinking to the church and to modern people of faith is a consistent theme running throughout Coe's and Fahs's writings. It appears both as an explicit issue to be addressed and as a methodological problem for scholars in religious education. We will take up the latter in our treatment of the emergence of religious education as a specialized discipline. As an issue, the cognitive challenges of modern science are described primarily as a crisis of belief, creating the need to reconstruct the inherited beliefs of traditional Christianity. The expansion of higher education exposed an increasingly large segment of the population to modern scholarship, from evolutionary theory to historical-critical approaches to the Bible. Coe experienced firsthand the crisis this posed to Christian youth and carried out research on this issue while teaching at Northwestern University. The church, he argued, was faced with a choice: It could stick its head in the sand and pretend this cognitive crisis did not exist or it could revise its beliefs in dialogue with modern scientific thinking. From the beginning to the end of his writing, he opted for the latter. In *A Social Theory of Religious Education,* for example, he reconstructed central Christian beliefs like the kingdom of God (now the democracy of God) and original sin (now concrete social disorders) to make them more plausible to modern persons. Likewise, the basic thrust of Fahs's rhetoric in *Today's Children and Yesterday's Heritage* is to contrast the old religion and the new. She is attempting to show congregational teachers how they can help their students come to terms with critical perspectives on the Bible, new cosmologies, and other facets of modern scientific thinking.

Just as important as their attempt to address the cognitive challenges of modern science is Coe's and Fahs's attempt to construct an approach to education that both moves beyond the unquestioned affirmation of tradition that characterized education in pre-modern societies, and grants much greater freedom to the individual in constructing a personal faith stance. Here they are responsive to two of the most important dimensions of modernization: rationalization and individualization. They portray religious education as a process in which the entire Christian community is engaged in the ongoing reconstruction of Christian beliefs, rather than scholars (e.g., dogmatic theologians) alone engaging in such activity on the people's behalf. They adopt a form of the experimentalism of progressive education. Religious beliefs, they argue, must be tested against a gradually expanding field of social experience, including the intellectual findings of science. Only those beliefs that prove useful in helping persons live religiously in modern life are to be accepted and, even then, only tentatively. Religious education, as such, does not focus on handing on a fixed, authoritative tradition. Nor does the community dictate to the individual what beliefs and values should be most plausible. A post-traditional, individualized faith stance is accommodated; indeed, it is readily embraced as holding the key to Protestantism's ability to adapt to the challenges of modern science.

A second dimension of modernization prominent in the rhetoric of Coe and Fahs is the socioethical challenges of urbanization and industrialization. Both were deeply aware of the social dislocation and economic disparities that characterized American life in the early twentieth century. They viewed these realities as challenges to democratic culture and political community and were closely aligned with progressive reform movements in politics and education. Their agenda for religious education in Protestant communities paralleled that of Dewey in public education. Religious education was to embody the practices of democratic life, serving as "democracy in miniature," and was to teach the members of religious communities how to think critically and communicate respectfully in situations of conflict. Coe's goal in *A Social Theory* was to project a form of education consistent with the "democracy of God." Likewise, Fahs frames her discussion of group leadership and teaching in *Today's Children* in explicitly democratic terms.

Coe and Fahs broke with Dewey and progressive education generally, however, in projecting an important role for contemporary religious communities in responding to the challenges of modern democratic life. As we have seen, Coe criticized progressive education as too easily falling prey to a "shallow pragmatism of immediate ends." Religious education, he argued, has the unique task of holding up ideals like the democracy of God, which unify modern persons' disparate aspirations and serve as a source of social criticism. Protestant communities, as such, should align themselves with those groups and movements that are struggling to reshape the forces of modernity toward democratic and personalizing ideals. This is reflected in Coe's use of the term "social" in the title of his book. This term was a standard part of the rhetoric of persons and groups calling for new, more organic forms of community that might overcome the problems of overcrowded cities, assembly line work, and the concentration of wealth in the hands of a few industrialists. Its use was widespread in a number of important practical and intellectual movements of this period: social settlement, social service, Social Gospel, and social philosophy.[37] In aligning himself with the rhetoric of these movements, Coe was challenging American Protestantism to join the ranks of those seeking to "socialize" a wide variety of contemporary institutions, from the modern family to the industrial economy, toward more democratic ends.

A third facet of modernization to which Coe and Fahs responded is the changing role of religion in an institutionally differentiated social context. Differentiation was described in the first part of this book and points, in part, to the separation of public institutions such as education from the influence of religion. One of the most important goals of the American public school movement was the removal of religion from state-supported education and the creation of a curriculum based on modern (i.e., scientific and nonreligious) conceptions of the arts and sciences. Coe, in particular, addresses this trend in *A Social Theory,* advocating the removal of religion from public schools. Religious education was to focus on the education of religious communities and their families. Its task vis-à-vis public education was to support reform movements pressing for more democratic education. As we have noted, the advocacy of the separation of religious education from public education did not lead Coe or Fahs to abandon religion's role in public life. Indeed, they explicitly portrayed religious education as public in the sense of addressing matters of the common good and as making an important part of its own agenda preparing persons for participation in public life.

A fourth facet of modernization to which Coe and Fahs responded is the emergence of religious education as a specialized discipline, differentiated from general education, on the one hand, and from theology, on the other. In part, this is closely related to their understanding of the role of science in modern life. Methodologically, they raised the following question: How might scholars focusing on the education of religious communities both learn from and contribute to the natural and social sciences that were increasingly prominent in academic communities? Their response was to form a new discipline, religious education, which was independent of theology and was committed methodologically to cross-disciplinary dialogue and empirical research. Both Coe and Fahs eschewed practical theology as a rubric by which to understand their work. Coe explicitly rejected the "dogmatic method" of theology at the very outset of his career, for he believed it attempted to bypass the insights of modern science and merely reassert the authority of traditional religious be-

37. Hunter, *Evangelicalism,* p. 76.

liefs. No doubt, the common perception of practical theology as "applied dogmatics" made this field doubly undesirable. Accordingly, Coe attempted to chart a new "disciplinary space" for religious education as an academic discipline, a "space" in which theoretical proposals for the education of religious communities were formed through ongoing empirical research and a dialogue with modern psychology, education, biology, and other scientific fields, on the one hand, and with theology — at a safe distance — on the other.

The target audience of this specialized knowledge was focused largely on the emergence of a new role in congregational life: the Director of Religious Education. It was hoped that Directors of Religious Education might move the church beyond the "amateurism" of the traditional Sunday school. They were to serve as "experts" in churches, comparable to the professionals already found in social work, psychotherapy, and public education.[38] These professionals were the target audience of many of the specialized writings, professional organizations, and educational programs that the religious education movement spawned. It was hoped that they might spearhead the reform of religious education in the local church in ways that would allow this community to respond intelligently and ethically to the modern world.

From the vantage point of a new century, how might we evaluate the relative strengths and weaknesses of Coe's and Fahs's positions? On the positive side, both were self-consciously engaged in the task of trying to find a new place for religion in modernity. Intellectually, they were open to the cultural resources of modernity, forming theories of religious education through a dialogue with developmental psychology, modern education, and the newly emerging social sciences. In Coe's case, this dialogue included modern philosophy and was informed by his own empirical research. Their forthright engagement of the intellectual resources of modern life is something that religious education cannot afford to lose.

On the positive side, also, is their attempt to help the church think its way beyond older patterns of education and religious life, to come to terms with the changed role of religion in a modernized society. While supporting the removal of religion from public education, for example, they did not advocate the removal of religion from public life. The commitment of their educational models to democratic ideals was a clear attempt to describe religious communities' new role in teaching their members the habits of thought and action necessary for modern democracies to flourish. Similarly, the ethical ideals toward which their theories of religious education pointed kept before the church its prophetic, transformational role in democratic societies.

38. Hunter, *Evangelicalism*, p. 126.

We must also view positively their acknowledgement of the multiple audiences that religious education is to address in a differentiated social context. Standing at the end of the twentieth century, we have the advantage of hindsight; the secularization, pluralization, and individualization that have become so prominent over the past one hundred years are social processes that Coe and Fahs did not have before them. Despite this, both recognized that the church must make greater room for the individual in religious education and advocated models that supported exploration of the faith and did not merely hand on a fixed, authoritative tradition. Both attempted to address the *paideia* of modern, democratic America. And both attempted to address the congregation, especially its professional leaders. If the importance of the family is less evident in Coe's writings, Fahs certainly must be seen as addressing parents in both the substance of her proposals and her writing style.

In short, when we locate Coe and Fahs in the context of modernization, many positive dimensions of their work become apparent. Nevertheless, the limitations of their responses to modernity also become apparent. Indeed, their strengths and weakness seem to go hand in hand along three lines. First, while both were concerned to help religion come to terms with modernity, they were overly confident that modernization was a positive development with which religion should make common cause. Their evaluations of modern science and democratic political governance in particular look naive after a century of death camps, nuclear proliferation, industrial pollution, and economic and racial inequality. Coe and Fahs write on the near side of Risk Society, to recall Ulrich Beck's term, unaware of the manufactured risks that modernization would bring into being. Second, while both were open to the cultural resources of modernity in their attempt to map out the new disciplinary "space" of religious education, Coe and Fahs were also both exceptionally weak theologically. It is not just that they have bad theology, but that they virtually have no theology. The complex cross-disciplinary work of bringing theology into dialogue with the social and natural sciences is absent from their research programs. Religious education today cannot afford to follow Coe and Fahs down this path, which in effect ignores the distinctive religious convictions of different religious communities in pluralistic societies. Third, while both attempt to address the multiple audiences emerging in a differentiated social context, they severely underestimate the difficulties this presents to both religious education and religion generally. It is almost as if Coe and Fahs still assume that the core Protestant culture is in place and that modernization would not unleash forces hostile toward religion. In hindsight, however, it is evident that the hedonism of the media, the profit motive driving much scientific research and development, the uncoupling of the economy from democratic governance through the emergence of multinational corporations, and the anti-religious bias of much public and university education represent contextual forces that are not benign and do not share the same values as many religious communities. Rather, they are actively hostile to the values and beliefs that many religious communities hold most dear. Coming to terms with modernity is not as easy or as pleasant as Coe and Fahs seemed to think.

Psychology, Religion, and Modern Culture: Reform Movements in Germany

In ways that are strikingly similar to the situation in the United States, the first three decades of the twentieth century were a time of special efforts toward a new shape of religious education in Germany. These parallels indicate that the reform movement in general education at that time, and the influence of leading figures like John Dewey and Maria Montessori, had international effects that went beyond general education. Many German philosophers of education were involved in international cooperation or, like Peter Petersen, became themselves influential at an international level.[39]

The German religious education reform movement (which sometimes is mistakenly identified as "liberal religious education") was rooted not only in current theology but also in the new ideas and developments specific to the field of religious education. Practical theologians and religious educators including Richard Kabisch, Otto Eberhard, and Friedrich Niebergall worked toward a new understanding of the tasks of religious education, attempting to reconstruct the relationship of religious education to modern culture by grounding their new understanding in current work in general education and psychology, including the psychology of religion. This new understanding emphasized active learning and a more experiential approach.

Although these reformers worked from a variety of theological backgrounds, sometimes liberal but sometimes also conservative (what then was called "positive"), the leading figures were in agreement that religious education should continue to be taught in public schools. Some of the innovations they suggest in their writings may even be seen as a response to the ongoing opposition to religious education in the public schools voiced in the political

---

39. The international character of the reform movement has been a major topic of Hermann Röhrs. See, for example, *Die Reformpädagogik, Ursprung und Verlauf unter internationalem Aspekt*, fifth ed. (Weinheim: Deutscher Studien-Verlag, 1998), and *Die Reform des Erziehungswesens als internationale Aufgabe. Entwicklung und Zielstellung des Weltbundes für Erneuerung der Erziehung* (Rheinstetten: Schindele-Verlag, 1977).

process and by public school educators, philosophers of education, and certain teacher associations. This opposition was often based on the claim that religion is a private matter and therefore should not be taught in public schools. Opposition to public school religious education was also directed against the frequently outdated methods of instruction.[40]

It is no coincidence that a new term came into use at this time: "religious education" *(Religionspädagogik)*, as opposed to "catechetics." The intention behind the new terminology was to indicate that this "religious education" was supposed to be based on current educational and psychological theories, not just on the catechetical tradition in the church or theology. Nevertheless, religious education was not supposed to lose its ties to theology. In many cases, the theory of religious education was treated as a theological discipline; Friedrich Niebergall, for example, whose work will be addressed in more detail below, taught it as part of practical theology.

The ideas of the reform movement, including its new terminology, later met with much suspicion in Germany. Starting in the 1920s and 1930s, a new theological movement emphasizing revelation eclipsed the insights from the fields of education, psychology, and modern culture in setting the agenda for religious education. But the work of the earlier reformers ultimately prevailed in the second half of the twentieth century, even if people were not aware of the continuity between the reforms in religious education at the turn of the century and those in the 1960s.

It is fair to say that in the German reform movement, there was no single leading figure who stood out so much that we automatically have to turn to him or her. Our decision to take up Friedrich Niebergall is based on the influence he exerted at least within the liberal camp of the reformers, and also on the fact that his influence lasted for almost forty years, from before the turn of the century into the 1930s.

Friedrich Niebergall: A Liberal Reformer

Niebergall was a first-rate religious educator and practical theologian in Germany, one of the foremost representatives of the modern turn in religious education, and was considered a leading figure in his field. He was born in 1866

---

40. For an overview cf. Ralf Koerrenz and Norbert Collmar, eds., *Die Religion der Reformpädagogen. Ein Arbeitsbuch* (Weinheim: Deutscher Studien-Verlag, 1994); Karl Ernst Nipkow and Friedrich Schweitzer, eds., *Religionspädagogik. Texte zur evangelischen Erziehungs- und Bildungsverantwortung seit der Reformation* (Gütersloh: Gütersloher Verlagshaus, 1994), vol. 2/1, pp. 30-43, and vol. 2/2, pp. 19-34.

in Kirn, not too far from Mainz or Frankfurt am Main.[41] After studying theology in Tübingen, Berlin, and Bonn and working as a pastor, he became lecturer (1903) and professor of practical theology in Heidelberg (1908-1922), then held a chair of practical theology in Marburg where he lived until his death in 1932, the year before Hitler came to power. Niebergall was quite influential, not only through his academic work but also through his active involvement with the reform movement, involvement which included his service as chairperson of the (liberal) reform association *(Bund für Reform des Religionsunterrichts/Bund für Religionsunterricht und religiöse Erziehung)*. Especially after World War I, this association worked toward a middle way between, on the one hand, the new (socialist) left which aimed for purely "objective" information about religion rather than education in religion in public schools, and, on the other, the conservatives who hoped to reestablish a precritical type of (catechetical) instruction.

Niebergall's bibliography is enormous, with close to six hundred titles, including major monographs on religious education, homiletics, and practical theology.[42] From early on, he was interested in questions of reforming or modernizing religious education. His interest in changing theology and religious education in such a way that they would reach what Niebergall calls "modern man" is most visible in his influential publications on "how to preach for modern man."[43] His writings also focus on systematic theology, liturgics, and pastoral theology, thus testifying to the breadth and influence of his work in practical theology.

Because of National Socialism as well as the later dominance of Barthian and Neo-Lutheran theology, Niebergall did not play a major role in the German discussion for a long time after the 1930s. Over the last decades, however, there has been a marked renewal of interest in Niebergall, leading to several monographs on him.[44] He is now considered a classic figure in the history of religious education.

41. For his biography see Friedrich Wintzer, "Niebergall, Friedrich," in *Theologische Realenzyklopädie*, vol. 24 (Berlin: de Gruyter, 1994), pp. 464-68.

42. The bibliography of Niebergall is compiled in Henning Luther, *Religion, Subjekt, Erziehung. Grundbegriffe der Erwachsenenbildung am Beispiel der Praktischen Theologie Friedrich Niebergalls* (München: Chr. Kaiser, 1984), pp. 379-93.

43. Friedrich Niebergall, *Wie predigen wir dem modernen Menschen? I. Eine Untersuchung über Motive und Quietive* (Leipzig: Mohr, 1902).

44. Cf. Jörg Viktor Sandberger, *Pädagogische Theologie. Friedrich Niebergalls Praktische Theologie als Erziehungslehre* (Göttingen: Vandenhoeck und Ruprecht, 1972); Luther, *Religion, Subjekt, Erziehung;* Wolfgang Steck, *Das homiletische Verfahren* (Göttingen: Vandenhoeck und Ruprecht, 1974).

It has often been observed that Niebergall's work shows great continuity through the three or four decades of his academic life. A number of key ideas remain characteristic of most of his writings, especially those in religious education but also those in practical theology in general. Most of these ideas are connected to the general tendencies in German theological liberalism of the time. Niebergall considered Julius Kaftan his academic teacher, and, through Kaftan, Niebergall became part of the famous Ritschl-School, that is, the liberal tradition going back to Albrecht Ritschl.

Niebergall's theology is geared toward modernity and modern culture. He argues for a realistic turn in church and theology, which are to be open not only to ideal conceptualizations but also to the actual situation of religion and society. Both culture and religion are seen by him as involving values. Human development is to lead from selfish materialism to the higher stages of ethical ideals that are incorporated and supported by the Christian religion. The educational meaning of religion is therefore an important aspect of Niebergall's work, not only when he refers to the context of religious education but also in reference to church or culture. Education is needed wherever higher values are to be achieved. In a certain sense, all practical theology is to be an educational theory.

Given the enormous number of books and articles written by Niebergall and given the fact that no single book among them has ever been considered his magnum opus, it is difficult in his case to follow our procedure of singling out one book for closer scrutiny. Since some of Niebergall's articles may be considered his most condensed programmatic statements, we will first turn to two of these and then turn to his book on the *New Religious Education (Der neue Religionsunterricht)*, published in the early 1920s.

As one part of their reform efforts, Niebergall and his friends started their own journal, which was to focus on new ideas of religious education.[45] The first issue of this journal, published in 1908, contains a foundational article by Niebergall on the teaching of religion. Here he addresses two issues which for him are closely related: the effect of historical criticism of the Bible on religious education, and the question of whether religion can really be taught. Let us first turn to this article.[46]

Niebergall was very much aware of the problems the scientific study of the Bible caused for many contemporary pastors and teachers of religion. For

---

45. *Monatsblätter für den Evangelischen Religionsunterricht.*
46. Friedrich Niebergall, "Die Lehrbarkeit der Religion und die Kritik im Religionsunterricht," *Monatsblätter für den Evangelischen Religionsunterricht* 1 (1908): 238-43, 321-35, 353-59.

them, the new ways of studying religion created enormous obstacles for the praxis of religious education and preaching. While it is true, Niebergall tells these people, that the modern ways of doing research on religion work against traditional religion, they may also be of help in finding new perspectives for religious education. In this vein, Niebergall introduces the idea of a psychological and experiential interpretation of the Bible. He suggests looking not merely at the surface of words and historical reports that can indeed be questioned by critical research, but rather looking at the religiöse personalities presented in the Bible. The inner life and the experience of these personalities cannot be questioned. And it is these personalities giving testimony to certain intellectual and spiritual values which, even in the present, remain the foundation of the further development of values. For Niebergall, the uncovering of these biblical personalities was the primary focus of religious education.

At a later time, Niebergall called his approach "psychological theology," making it clear that he did not want psychology to replace theology.[47] Without question, however, we can say that Niebergall's whole theology found a new basis in these emerging sciences — the psychology and sociology of religion which later on came to be called the social sciences. As we will see, Niebergall argued that the social sciences would replace history as the main reference of religious education. There are practical reasons for this point of view, but even more there are cultural and theological reasons. People of early-twentieth-century Germany would accept only the faith of "religious personalities," Niebergall believed, or they would accept no faith at all.

The term "social sciences" was not in existence in Germany in Niebergall's time. There were, however, several equivalents, which are to be found throughout his work. His *Practical Theology* even carries the subtitle "based on the scientific study of religion."[48] This includes the psychology of religion and what we would call today the sociology of religion — *Religiöse Seelen- und Volkskunde* (empirical sociology or anthropology of religion).

Niebergall wrote extensively on questions such as the "meaning of the psychology of religion" for religious education and practical theology. The core idea is always the same. The ultimate aim of religious education is values education, in the sense of those values that Niebergall considers as Christian values and as higher values in general. *Religionswissenschaft*, the scientific

---

47. Friedrich Niebergall, "Fortschritte in der Religionspädagogik," *Christliche Welt* 37 (1923): 652-56.

48. Friedrich Niebergall, *Praktische Theologie. Lehre von der kirchlichen Gemeindeerziehung auf religionswissenschaftlicher Grundlage*, vol. 1: *Grundlagen* (Tübingen: Mohr/Siebeck, 1918).

study of religion, gives the basis for this theory of values in two ways. First, as a philosophy of religion, it furnishes a philosophical and historical understanding of how higher values have emerged and developed over time. Second, as a psychology of religion, it may tell us how the individual soul may incorporate such higher intellectual and spiritual values. The central image by which Niebergall's work is guided is always the ascent from nature to culture. In this respect, Niebergall distinguishes between the "person" as an expression of nature, and "personality" as an expression of higher culture.[49] All education and church work is to support the transformation of persons into personalities.

In Niebergall's 1908 article on teaching religion, his reference to "religious personalities" is intended to safeguard both elements, religion and personality. It is intended to provide a positive answer to the question of whether religion can really be taught, and to uphold the continuing value of the Bible for religious education, now as an important possibility for the encounter with such personalities. In his own words, "That which criticism has removed, devalued, or contested, is, generally speaking, not apt to transmit religion; it is teachable, possibly even very much so, but what is so nice to teach, must not yet be religion." And "the other way round, again speaking generally, what the criticism has identified as the best — the contents referring to the personal life of faith, purity, and love — is the best means for awakening religion."[50]

The second article we want to take up here was published a few years later in 1911 in the same journal.[51] It describes what Niebergall calls the "transformation of catechetics into religious education" *(Entwicklung der Katechetik zur Religionspädagogik)*. Niebergall believed that religious education in the state schools should be clearly distinguished from catechetical instruction in the congregation, and the article contains a systematic summary of the characteristics of the new religious education. Five key points covered are as follows:[52]

1. The emphasis on history is replaced by an emphasis on psychology.
2. The psychology of choice is no longer one of the intellect but one of feelings; it is a psychology of life, not of dogma.
3. The personal life of the teacher, his or her personality, becomes of central importance.

---

49. Friedrich Niebergall, *Person und Persönlichkeit* (Leipzig: Quelle und Meyer, 1911).
50. Niebergall, "Die Lehrbarkeit," p. 353.
51. Friedrich Niebergall, "Die Entwicklung der Katechetik zur Religionspädagogik," *Monatsblätter für den Evangelischen Religionsunterricht* 4 (1911): 1-10, 33-43.
52. Niebergall, "Die Etwicklung," pp. 41-43.

4. The child is to be respected in her or his own right.
5. The theories for state school religious education and for religious education within the church are to be separate.

The emphasis on psychology and on the needs of the child is especially characteristic of the new religious education. The older catechetics was seen as violating the principles of modern psychology and as opposed to the insights of the psychology of the child. But Niebergall's considerations concerning the relationship between the public school and the congregation are also noteworthy, particularly since he comes back to them in later publications.

In 1912 Niebergall published an entire book on the relationship between religious education in the public school and confirmation, one of the main education activities of the church.[53] In this book he argues for a clear distinction between these two types of instruction. While religious education in the school works toward "education and the cultural life of the time," confirmation classes work toward an active and personal "religious life and participation in the life of the church congregation."[54] The dividing line between the two would thus be the difference between culture in general as the horizon of all school-based education, and church or congregation as the aim of all church-based instruction.

Nevertheless, according to Niebergall the public school may not neglect Christian religion. This religion is part of the culture that the state has to cultivate. Christian religion has been the source of the very values that are indispensable for the well-being of the individual and the maintenance of society. Here Niebergall again thinks of those higher values that are central to all of his thinking: spirituality and idealism, social feelings, courage.

For Niebergall, the educational motives of the church are different from those of the state. Religious education in the context of the church is based on the church's need to continue to gain new members. Niebergall puts it quite bluntly: "The congregation wants to have offspring."[55] At the same time, the church's teaching is more personal than religious education in a school context. As a result, it can be directed to the soul of the students.

It is important to note that this plea for a clear distinction between religious education in the state school and in the congregation was written before the separation of church and state, which in Germany took place only af-

53. Friedrich Niebergall, *Der Schulreligions- und der Konfirmandenunterricht* (Leipzig: J. Klinkhardt, 1912).
54. Niebergall, *Der Schulreligions*, p. 12.
55. Niebergall, *Der Schulreligions*, p. 14.

ter the end of the old monarchy in 1918. Niebergall's ideas in 1912 have to be seen in connection with certain educational tendencies that, as mentioned before, were popular among schoolteachers even before the separation of church and state. More and more, religion teachers wanted to be independent of the church — a wish that obviously was affirmed by Niebergall's argument. At the same time, we need to be aware of something else in the background of Niebergall's thinking: According to his evaluation, the cultural and religious situation of the time no longer allowed the church to have a monopoly on Christian religion. Other spokesmen — from among the teachers or within academic pedagogics, for instance — now also acted as representatives of a Christian faith that was viewed as broader than the church. In this situation it became necessary to find a new basis for religious education in the state school. The church could no longer warrant the acceptance of this school subject on theological grounds alone. It had to be justified on educational grounds as well.

From this point of view, we may say that Niebergall's way out of the difficulties that arise with modernity's religious pluralism is a strategy of differentiation and specialization in the sense of modern systems theory. In order to accommodate the changes in the religious environment, he considers an internal differentiation within religious education to be necessary. What up to then had been the single field of Christian religious education administered partly within the congregation and partly within the state school was now to be transformed into two parallel yet independent and distinct fields of religious education. The advantage Niebergall hoped to gain from this differentiation was the possibility of maintaining religious education as a school subject even under the conditions of religious pluralism.

When Niebergall addressed the same question in his later writings after the separation of church and state, for example in his *Practical Theology* of 1919, he did not change his basic argument.[56] The new ideas in this later statement all point toward an even clearer dividing line between the two types of religious education. But the differentiation between the two still follows the same general concept.

It should also be mentioned that Niebergall is somewhat ambiguous about the relationship of the two types of religious education to the reform movement. At times he seems to presuppose that the reform movement is only active in the context of the school, while religious education in the church follows the traditional ideas of religious instruction or catechetics. At

---

56. Friedrich Niebergall, *Praktische Theologie*, vol. 2: *Die Arbeitszweige* (Tübingen: Mohr/Siebeck, 1919), pp. 262-65.

other times, he argues for a comprehensive reform of all types of religious education, be it in the state school or in the congregation. This may mean that Niebergall perceived a certain catechetical traditionalism within the church which he hoped to overcome by including the new educational reform ideas within his practical theology.

This inclusion of religious education within practical theology again shows that, for Niebergall, the distinction between congregation and school does not mean isolating the new religious education from theology. While it is based on psychology and on the scientific study of religion, it still may be treated as part of practical theology alongside religious education in the church. Unfortunately, Niebergall is not explicit about why he wants to include both in his practical theology. He merely points out that both belong to the field of "religious instruction and education," which he considers "reason enough."[57] With respect to Niebergall himself, we should keep in mind that he held a chair of practical theology on a theological faculty. Thus, for him personally, there was no contradiction between being a theologian and acting as a representative of the religious education reform movement.

Looking back at Niebergall's 1911 programmatic statement, we may say that Niebergall was less concerned about religious education theory becoming a discipline of its own than with making sure that the distinct character and needs of the church and state school were given sufficient attention and that both contexts became equally open to the new educational impulses of the reform movement.

The book on the *New Religious Education,* which Niebergall published after World War I in 1922, and to which we will now turn, is in many ways a summary and outgrowth of the ideas Niebergall developed earlier.[58] The book is organized in three parts. It begins by stating the "task" of religious education, then presents what Niebergall considers the presuppositions of religious education (among others, child psychology), while the main body of the book is devoted to the "means and ways" of religious education.

The first chapter of the book is clearly addressed to a general public. It states the "need for religious education" by referring to "religion as the basis of the moral orientation of the nation and of its renewal." Moreover, Niebergall points out that religion is an important part of the "intellectual possessions" of a nation, which are to be protected and to be handed on to the next generation.[59] The next chapter deals with the relationship between

---

57. Niebergall, *Praktische Theologie,* vol. 2, p. 326.
58. Friedrich Niebergall, *Der neue Religionsunterricht* (Langensalza: J. Beltz, 1922).
59. Niebergall, *Der neue Religionsunterricht,* p. 6.

church, state, and public school. Here we must remember that the separation of church and state in Germany had just been achieved a few years earlier in 1918 to 1919. Niebergall affirms the right of the state to take over the leadership of the schools, and, for him, this leadership includes religious education. Niebergall's only stipulation is that the state must not be allowed to functionalize religion for political purposes. The content of religious education is then determined as values education in the broad sense of an introduction to higher cultural values. Finally, the aim of this religious education is identified not as "inheriting heaven," not as becoming a "church member," and not as being "converted," but, much more modestly, as becoming an "able person."[60] Or, to take one of Niebergall's statements referring to values education, "to lift up our students to that higher stage of religion with the kind of valuing mentioned before, will turn out as our most important task in religious education."[61]

The second part of the book describes the situation from which religious education has to work — the "reality" that religious education must address. Rather than starting out with the contents of religious education, Niebergall wants to start out "inductively from the child."[62] He does not, however, see the child in isolation; rather, he aims for a "more comprehensive rendering of the Christian religion" in terms of psychology. Consequently, this is the place where Niebergall develops his understanding of values, the development toward higher values, and the education that is needed to foster this development. Additional chapters are devoted to the emerging discipline of child psychology, including the religion of the child and contemporary empirical studies on religion in childhood. All these considerations are summed up in the understanding that lifting up the child's religion toward ideal rather than materialist forms is the main task of religious education.

The remainder of the book, which we will not render in detail here, is concerned with practical questions of teaching methods, of textbooks, and of how to become or be a good teacher.

The audience for which Niebergall wrote *New Religious Education* was primarily teachers working in state schools. In addition, Niebergall was aware of the public debates about the legitimacy of religious education in these schools, so he made sure that the book included arguments that might be convincing to a wider audience. But even in this book, with its exclusive focus on religious education in the schools, Niebergall also speaks as a theologian.

60. Niebergall, *Der neue Religionsunterricht*, p. 26.
61. Niebergall, *Der neue Religionsunterricht*, p. 28.
62. Niebergall, *Der neue Religionsunterricht*, p. 47.

All his main theological points are present — as much as in his *Practical Theology* published only a few years earlier.

Niebergall in Context

To understand Niebergall's approach to religious education in context means understanding it against the backdrop of modernization. And to do so is actually very much in line with Niebergall's own thinking. As mentioned above, he wanted to reach "modern man" with new and convincing ways of educating and preaching. Before we look into Niebergall's own understanding of modernization, however, we need to consider the historical and social changes occurring in Germany before and after the beginning of the twentieth century.

The time between 1870-1871 and 1918 — the era of the *Kaiserreich* — is often described as a period of rapid social change and of dramatic movement toward modernization.[63] It was during this time that the last steps in the process of transforming an agricultural society into an industrial society occurred, and along with that transformation came the effects typically considered as modern: urbanization, a higher rate of mobility, and rapid growth of the population (from about forty million in 1870 to almost sixty-five million in 1910). In 1882, for example, a little more than 7 percent of the population lived in cities, while in 1907 the comparative figure was up to more than 19 percent. In 1910, almost 35 percent of the population lived in cities with more than twenty thousand inhabitants. The figures concerning mobility within Germany are telling: In Frankfurt, more than 50 percent of the population was exchanged in the year 1900; that is, the numbers of those leaving the city, and of those moving into the city, together amounted to more than half of the total population.[64] During the time between 1873 and 1913, the German road system doubled in length and the railway tracks tripled.

---

63. For differing perspectives cf. Christa Berg, ed., *Handbuch der deutschen Bildungsgeschichte*, vol. 4: *1870-1918: Von der Reichsgründung bis zum Ende des Ersten Weltkriegs* (München: Beck-Verlag, 1991); Heinz-Elmar Tenorth, *Geschichte der Erziehung. Einführung in die Grundzüge ihrer neuzeitlichen Entwicklung* (Weinheim/München: Juventa Verlag, 1988), pp. 177ff.; Thomas Nipperdey, *Religion im Umbruch. Deutschland 1870-1918* (München: Beck-Verlag, 1988); Friedrich Wilhelm Graf, ed., *Profile des neuzeitlichen Protestantismus*, vol. 2: *Kaiserreich: Teil 1* (Gütersloh: Gütersloher Verlagshaus, 1992); Kurt Nowak, *Geschichte des Christentums in Deutschland. Religion, Politik und Gesellschaft vom Ende der Aufklärung bis zur Mitte des 20. Jahrhunderts* (München: Beck-Verlag, 1995), pp. 149ff.

64. Cf. Tenorth, *Geschichte der Erziehung*, pp. 186f.

Schooling was also affected by these changes. By the year 1900, for the first time in history, mandatory school attendance was no longer just a legal requirement but was a reality for all children. Even with all these changes, however, the Germany of the *Kaiserreich* remained a country with major social divisions, especially with respect to the working class. The workers at the time did not profit much from industrialization.

Speaking of general education, it has become common knowledge that the educational ideas of the reformers in the early twentieth century have to be seen against the backdrop of the historical situation and of the rapid and far-reaching changes this situation implied. There is some controversy over the question of whether the educational reform movement should be considered conservative, in that it tried to escape the pressures of modernization by returning to pre-modern forms of life (back to nature, withdrawal from the cities, focus on small communities, etc.), or if it should be seen as expressive of modernizing impulses (ideals of modern education, modernizing schools and teaching methods, and so on).[65] Beyond this question, however, there is much agreement about the close relationship between social change (in the sense of modernization) and the new education.

For religious education, we also need to be aware of the changing religious landscape. The Protestant church was closely identified with the *Kaiserreich* and, accordingly, supported German nationalism. In this sense, the church had a very official status. At the same time, the population became more pluralized, and active participation in the church was on the decline.[66] According to the judgment of today's historians, the church had not been able to keep pace with the rapid social and cultural changes of the time.[67] For example, urbanization turned the traditional congregations in the cities into enormous anonymous bodies of thirty thousand or more members. So it is no surprise that the numbers of the unchurched were increasing rapidly during the *Kaiserreich*. While the separation of church and state in 1918-1919 cannot be explained by such developments, it certainly was influenced by them.

As mentioned in Part I, there are few historical accounts of religious education in Germany that really take the influence of the social and cultural changes into consideration. The majority of the textbooks focus exclusively

65. From this discussion cf. Jürgen Oelkers, *Reformpädagogik. Eine kritische Dogmengeschichte* (Weinheim: Juventa-Verlag, 1989).

66. As a contemporary witness see Friedrich Niebergall, *Die evangelische Kirche und ihre Reformen* (Leipzig: Quelle und Meyer, 1908).

67. Cf. Nowak, *Geschichte des Christentums in Deutschland;* Graf, *Profile des neuzeitlichen Protestantismus,* vol. 2.

on intellectual history. It is easy, however, to identify at least four ways in which Niebergall and his contemporaries responded to the challenges of modernization: (1) by overcoming a traditionalist understanding of religious education as catechetics, (2) by establishing a modern type of religious education based on the insights of education and psychology, (3) by coming to terms with the modern (critical) study of the Bible and the challenges of modern sciences, and, (4) by addressing the changing reality of church and Christianity in modern culture.

All four of these challenges are interconnected. In some ways, the academic questions of catechetics, religious education, and modern science gained their actual weight only on the basis of the cultural, social, and religious changes that increasingly made themselves felt around the turn of the century. As Niebergall himself observes,[68] even within the church there was no longer any creedal identity of the various members but only a variety of individual religious outlooks. And beyond the church, there were other worldviews that were more and more influential — such as, for example, the Monism of evolutionary thinking which was adopted by some of the well-known representatives of the reform movement in general education.[69] In addition, some of the teachers associations in Germany picked up the claim that religion was to be considered a private matter and that, consequently, there should be no confessional religious education in the public school.

It is easy to see why traditional catechetics had no answers to offer such questions. Obviously, Niebergall and his friends came to the conclusion that this kind of catechetics was altogether related to a different time and to different cultural and religious presuppositions. If the church no longer worked as a stable institutional basis for this catechetics, there was a need for a new and different grounding of religious education, especially in the state schools. The turn toward psychology, modern culture, and general education may be explained against this background. It is here that Niebergall hoped to find a new basis for school religious education, one which could claim plausibility for a modern public audience.

It also makes sense that the new religious education would have to include not only the insights of psychology and education but also critical perspectives on the Bible as well as on the relationship between faith and modern science. Once religious education was taken out of the church-defined con-

---

68. Niebergall, *Die evangelische Kirche.*

69. For more details see Friedrich Schweitzer, *Die Religion des Kindes. Zur Problemgeschichte einer religionspädagogischen Grundfrage* (Gütersloh: Gütersloher Verlagshaus, 1992), pp. 252ff.

text of catechetics, there was no longer a chance to exclude the critical under-standings held by the representatives of modern culture.

Niebergall formulated most of his ideas on religious education well be-fore World War I, which, for Germany, would eventually lead to a new consti-tution with the separation of church and state. Once this separation was real-ized with the Weimar Republic beginning in 1918 to 1919, his ideas made even more sense. Religious education in state schools had to find its own legiti-macy, which could not be derived from the authority of the church. If the Weimar constitution, after a number of severe conflicts around this matter, eventually contained the legal guarantee that, with very limited and narrowly defined exceptions, religious education was to be a subject in all public schools, this result was first of all due to the political influence of the church and of the political parties which identified themselves with the Christian tradition.[70] It may also be hypothesized, however, that it would not have been possible to maintain this subject in the curriculum without the modernizing influence of the reform movement in religious education.

As far as this hypothesis concerning the contribution of the reform movement to the constitutional provision for religious education in German schools holds true, the turn to the new and modern understanding of reli-gious education certainly has to be appreciated as successful. And saying this, we also have to keep in mind that the legal provision for school religious edu-cation in the Weimar constitution still plays an important role in Germany today, in that this provision was taken over by the constitution of the Federal Republic of Germany in 1949, the constitution that still is in force today. In addition to this, many of the elements that are characteristic of Niebergall's new religious education have also been adopted by German religious educa-tion in the second half of the twentieth century, most notably the attempt to interpret the Christian tradition in the context of contemporary culture and to include the perspectives of modern science.

In this sense, the harsh refusal that Niebergall's understanding of reli-gious education received in the 1920s from the representatives of Barthian and Neo-Lutheran theology was certainly not justified or fair. As is often the case with a new movement trying to establish itself against the background of its precursor, there was no attempt at evaluating the possible merits of

70. Important background information may be found in Ernst C. Helmreich, *Religious Ed-ucation in German Schools: A Historical Approach* (Cambridge: Harvard University Press, 1959); Peter C. Bloth, *Religion in den Schulen Preußens. Der Gegenstand des evangelischen Religions-unterrichts von der Reaktionszeit bis zum Nationalsozialismus* (Heidelberg: Quelle und Meyer, 1968); Sebastian Müller-Rolli, ed., *Evangelische Schulpolitik in Deutschland 1918-1958. Doku-mente und Darstellung* (Göttingen: Vandenhoeck und Ruprecht, 1999).

Niebergall's views. Consequently, there is a need to defend Niebergall against the later wholesale criticism of his work. Nevertheless, some of the more specific criticisms launched against Niebergall and his friends were not without basis.

The main critique was directed against Niebergall's lack of theological grounding and against his optimistic attitude toward modern culture. While the first criticism overlooks the fact that Niebergall's understanding of religious education was not without theological basis — it just happened to be based on a different theology than either Barthian or Neo-Lutheran theology — the synthesis of Christianity and modern culture advocated by Niebergall and his friends turned out to be all too tenuous and fragile once it was put to the test of the crisis experienced in the aftermath of World War I. The extreme destructiveness of this war, which was the first war in history to use enormous amounts of technical weapons and equipment, made the appeal to the higher values of idealism sound powerless and stale to many people. With the new German republic, the traditional association of God and *Kaiserreich* was gone, and the republic did not seem to offer anything reliable in its place. Rather, the many far-reaching political and economic crises terminating in the worldwide crisis in 1929 ushered in a basic feeling of insecurity and of general crisis. It seems that Niebergall's theology and religious education had nothing to offer to deal with this kind of experience. His ideas did not include enough critical distance toward modernization to be able to theologically deal with what may be called the dark side of modernization.

Another problem with Niebergall's writings concerns the relationship between religious education in the congregation and religious education in state schools. Niebergall makes a clear distinction between the religious education of the state schools and the traditional catechetics of the congregation; at times, however, he seems to indicate that the reform movement applies only to the context of the school, while at other times he argues for a comprehensive reform of all types of religious education, whether in the school or in the congregation. He never resolves the tension between these two concepts of reform — broad or limited — and consequently, he does not address the severe problems that might result from a dual system of traditional catechetics and modern religious education, which, in many ways, must contradict each other.

So this account of the German reform movement must end on an ambivalent note. The successes of this movement remain with us, and, without even knowing it, many religious educators still profit from this movement. At the same time, it may well have been too optimistic about school religious education while neglecting the needs and possibilities of the congregation.

Comparative Aspects

In the final section of this chapter we will not offer a detailed one-to-one comparison of the reform movements in the United States and in Germany. The parallel accounts of their views above make such comparisons an easy task, which may be left for the reader. The focus of our own conclusions will be a number of general questions that refer back to the first part of the book — primarily the question of how the developments in religious education described in this chapter are related to modernization and how it may help to see the emergence of modern religious education against this background.

Before we go into such questions we also want to mention that the early twentieth century was the period in the history of religious education when, possibly for the first time, the international dimension became important for this field. At the beginning of this chapter we mentioned Coe's studies and his regular visits to Germany. For American scholars of the time this was not exceptional. In fact, many American students of theology and philosophy went to Germany for graduate education. In addition, translations played an important role in making the discussion more international — less in the field of religious education in the narrow sense but certainly in practical theology. A variety of European books became available in English, for example the works of A. Vinet and J. J. van Osterzee.[71] The same can be said about the psychology of religion, where the pioneering works of scholars from the United States (those of W. James and E. D. Starbuck, for example) were quickly made available in German. In addition, German practical theologians and religious educators such as Carl Clemen traveled to the United States and, upon their return to Germany, published academic reports on the situation of religious education there.[72] The increasing number of international conferences — whether on moral education, general education, or, with the emerging worldwide ecumenical movement, on religious education in an ecumenical perspective — also point to the growth of international awareness within the field of religious education. As a result, Otto Eberhard was able to publish a book on the *World Education Movement* in 1930 — probably the first book to cover religious education in all parts of the world.[73] As a related example

71. A. Vinet, *Pastoral Theology; or, The Theory of the Evangelical Ministry* (New York: Ivison and Phinney, 1853); J. J. van Osterzee, *Practical Theology. A Manual for Theological Students* (London: Hodder and Stoughton, 1878).

72. Carl Clemen, *Der Religions- und Moralunterricht in den Vereinigten Staaten von Nordamerika* (Gießen: Töpelmann, 1909).

73. Otto Eberhard, *Welterziehungsbewegung. Kräfte und Gegenkräfte in der Völkerpädagogik* (Berlin: Furche, 1930).

from the United States we may point to Coe's 1911 article on "Religious Education" in *Monroe's Cyclopedia of Education*.[74] Coe's focus in this article is on the future of religious education in the United States, yet it is fascinating to see how his arguments, at least in part, grow out of comparative considerations on state school religious education in Germany and in the United Kingdom. Given these signs of an incipient internationalization of religious education it seems especially appropriate to consider the religious education reform movements in Germany and in the United States in comparative perspective.

The first and, perhaps, most important point has to do with the fact that we find a religious education reform movement in both the United States and in Germany. What is commonly viewed as a distinct part of each country's national heritage turns out to be, at least in part, a past that each shares with at least one other national context. Of course, it has also become clear that there are many differences between the reform movements in Germany and the United States. Nevertheless, the common interests and the parallels are striking, and this fact itself is a persuasive argument for the value of looking at the history of religious education from an international-comparative perspective. When applied, this perspective helps us discover new aspects and horizons, because it forces us to go beyond the standard accounts of the development of religious education in both countries.

More specifically, it is easy to see that there are a number of striking parallels to be found in Coe's and Niebergall's understanding of religious education. Both are reflecting on a situation in which the connection between church and state or between the congregation and the state school has become problematic. For Coe and Niebergall, the overriding question is how religious education will continue after the separation of church and state. Their answers to this question are different because religious education remains part of the state school in Germany but not in the United States. Niebergall seeks to legitimize state school religious education by separating it from church-based education in the sense of catechetics. Coe hopes to establish a modern approach to religious education in congregations, giving only secondary attention to the public dimensions of education.

Both are informed by the social sciences and, to a certain extent, find their identity in this field. This shift from theology to the social sciences is reflective of the academic specialization of the modern research university and especially of the growing influence of the new social scientific disciplines

---

74. George Albert Coe, "Religious Education," in *A Cyclopedia of Education*, ed. Paul Monroe, vol. 5 (Detroit: Gale Research Co., 1968 [reprint of 1911 Macmillan edition]), pp. 452-62.

within the academic world. It also shows how both authors consider the social sciences and the new educational philosophies of the reform movements in their countries to be important sources for the future improvement of religious education as well as for legitimizing this field to a broader public. Like the general educational reform movements of the time, for example, they refer to the child as a new focus of religious education. The criteria by which this child-oriented character is to be discerned are taken from the new psychology of the child.

Both men are at least guardedly optimistic about the prospects of modernity. They view the break with traditional forms of religious thinking and practice as irreversible. In many ways, they adopt the language of "progress," identifying God's work and guidance with historical developments and trends including personalization and (in the United States) democratization. In spite of their different outlooks on democracy, both are very interested in the individual person. Both are looking at historical and cultural processes that are moving away from traditional religious authority, and both of them clearly affirm this tendency. They see religion as part of an evolutionary process to which it has to respond — by, for example, finding a new language like the language of values instead of the more traditional language of theology.

The parallels of Coe's and Niebergall's work point to modernization and the social and cultural changes that went along with it as a common background. Industrialization, urbanization, the increased role of science, the expansion of education — the reformers and their movements in both countries were responding to all these changes. In addition, the differentiations in religious education, catechetics, and practical theology, which may be observed in different ways in both countries, clearly are reflective of differentiations in society. For example, such theories reflect the separation of church and state and the growing distance between school-based general education and church-based religious education. The increasing degree of professionalization in the field is seen in the parallel between the Director of Religious Education in the United States and the religious education schoolteacher in Germany. This, too, must be seen in this context of educational specialization.

The strong interest of Coe, Fahs, and Niebergall in the social sciences corresponds to the modern situation in several respects. First, it is indicative of the fact that modernity challenges and erodes reasoning based on tradition. Second, it shows how the model of scientific research, especially of the natural sciences, affects religious education. While traditional theological doctrines receive little or no attention, the category of religion, based on the philosophy of religion or the social scientific study of religion, becomes central. This is indicative of the need to communicate in a manner acceptable to a plural audience. The kind of discourse used by the representatives of the reform movements is interdisciplinary. It may be seen as an attempt at what today is often called the "correlation" of the Christian tradition and the present situation.

These shifts within the theoretical approach to religious education may be considered part of a new (modern) form of rationality beginning to make its way into religious education and practical theology. It would, however, be wrong to view this process as turning religious education into a form of technical rationality. The process is clearly more complex. For example, Coe and Niebergall are not naively importing social scientific theories into their field. Rather, both are appropriating their dialogue partners in the social sciences critically and selectively. Even if it is obvious that the model of the natural sciences becomes influential for religious education theory, it also must be noted that the inclusion of new educational and psychological insights in religious education helped educators and teachers do justice to the needs of the child. The traditional methods of catechetical instruction were no longer acceptable in light of modern child psychology. The children and youth who came to know different methods of education in other fields also became more critical of traditional forms of religious education or catechetics. In sum, the modern turn in religious education brought about by the reform movements in Germany and the United States in the early twentieth century was two-sided, bringing about both educational progress and the danger of religious education being overwhelmed by technical rationality.

Taking these observations together it makes sense to see the religious education reform movements of the early twentieth century against the backdrop of modernization. This leads to further insights emerging from an international comparison. Two standard assumptions concerning the reform movements are called into question. The first refers to the political implications of the reform movements, the second to their theological implications.

It is interesting to see that the political implications of the reform movements in the United States and in Germany were quite different. In the United States, especially with Dewey and Coe, it is assumed that there is an intrinsic, almost natural, tie between the (religious) educational reform movement and democracy. In Germany, especially with certain representatives like Otto Eberhard or Hermann Tögel, it is often said that the reform movement must be counted among the precursors of National Socialism. Eberhard, for example, sometimes attacks the American reform movement's democratic tendencies: "The kingdom of God evaporates into a social program"; it is "even perverted into the 'democracy of God.'"[75]

75. Eberhard, *Welterziehungsbewegung*, p. 192.

What are we to conclude from the contrary political outlooks within the reform movements on either side of the Atlantic? Obviously, the standard accounts are accurate *historically* in that the political characterizations offered by them hold true for the reform movements in the first decades of the twentieth century. Yet whether they also hold true *systematically* is a question that deserves additional consideration. In any case, it is not legitimate to claim, as is often done in Germany, that the educational ideas of the reform movements per se are anti-democratic. Rather, it seems to be the German tradition in general that is responsible for the anti-democratic turn the German reform took in later years, adopting National Socialism as its political ally. For the United States, the parallel question may be raised with regard to the strategies developed by Coe and his colleagues in addressing the separation of church or religion and the state school. Are these the only strategies compatible with democracy? Again, the historical connection between the reform movement and democracy should not be confused with systematic considerations. As we will argue in the third part of this volume, other ways of supporting democracy through a public role for religious education that includes the state school may not be excluded simply because different solutions were preferred in the past.

Parallel to the need for a reevaluation of the political implications of the religious education reform movements, there also is a need to look anew at certain theological issues. In Germany, the reforms of religious education in the early twentieth century are often identified with theological liberalism, but this identification does not take account of the conservative ("positive") influence of leading reformers like Eberhard. In the United States, it was the Social Gospel that served as an important basis of the reform movement, and the theology of the Social Gospel may be called "liberal." Clearly, there are parallels between Coe's, Fahs's, and Niebergall's liberalism; yet theological liberalism in Germany and liberalism in the United States are definitely not the same. There are, for example, important differences related to the influence of American pragmatism, which at that time was literally detested by all serious German theologians and philosophers, even if they were liberals.

The question that arises from such observations concerning differing theological influences within the religious education reform movements has to do with the relationship between theology and education. Can the educational ideas cherished by the reform movement actually be combined with different theological perspectives? How are these ideas affected by different theological backgrounds? Is it the case that different theologies also lead to different forms of education, or is it more accurate to say that the same educational approach may be appropriated in different theological frameworks?

We do not want to answer these complex questions here. Our present interest is focused on the question of how to understand the history of religious education in Germany and in the United States historically and systematically. Again, the standard assumptions concerning the supposedly natural proximity of certain educational approaches and certain theological positions turns out to be in need of reexamination — a conclusion to which we will come again in later sections of this part of the book. International-comparative perspectives are apt to challenge what is taken for granted at a national level.

4 Modernity Reconsidered: The Reaffirmation of Theological Identity in Protestant Religious Education after 1945

A Theological Critique of Modernity: Christian Education in the United States

The period spanning 1945 to 1960 is generally viewed as a time of theological renewal in Protestant religious education in the United States. The theological, social scientific, and educational assumptions of liberal theology and the religious education movement came under sharp attack. They were portrayed by prominent theologians as embedded in a liberal culture that had disintegrated under the impact of the two world wars, the Great Depression, the advent of nuclear weapons, and the appearance of Communism as a major force in world politics. Many leading figures in American Protestant religious education marked their break with the recent past by dropping the term "religious education" altogether, using the terms "Christian education" and "the teaching ministry" in its stead. This language captured more adequately, they believed, the unique nature of education by and for the church, a community whose nature and purpose can be grasped only theologically.

The theological influence of the European crisis theologians was great. Karl Barth's early writings had first appeared in English in 1919 (*The Epistle to the Romans,* first edition), and by the thirties and forties were being translated into English at a rapid pace, along with those of Brunner and Bultmann. Moreover, the first English translation of a selection of Soren Kierkegaard's writings appeared in 1923; by the middle of the 1940s, three to four of his books were being translated every year. Shelton Smith threw down the Barthian gauntlet to the religious education movement in his famous 1934 address to the Religious Education Association: "Let Religious Educators

Reckon with the Barthians."[1] Elmer Homrighausen and James Smart would take up the challenge of forming a theory of Christian education on the basis of Barth's theology.[2] We will examine Smart's *The Teaching Ministry of the Church* as representative of this perspective.

It is important to recognize, however, that Barthian Christian education remained a minority position during this period. Many leading Protestant religious educators remained firmly committed to the synthesis of liberal theology and progressive education standing at the heart of the religious education movement. Harrison Elliott and Sophia Fahs, for example, wrote widely influential books from that perspective during this period.[3] Others, like Randolph Crump Miller in his important *The Clue to Christian Education,* would acknowledge the need for greater attention to theology in Protestant religious education but were more interested in philosophical sources like process thought than in European crisis theology.[4] Moreover, the majority of Protestant religious educators participating in the theological turn were far more dependent on the thinking of Tillich, Brunner, and the Niebuhr brothers than on Barth. Lewis Sherrill, Campbell Wyckoff, and Hulda Niebuhr, for example, and, somewhat later, William Kennedy, Robert Lynn, and Sara Little followed these figures in their portrayal of the task of Christian education as one of bringing neo-Reformation theology into dialogue with the cultural resources of modernity.[5] A careful reading of Shelton Smith's programmatic statement of Christian education, *Faith and Nurture* (written in 1948), finds him much closer to the theologies of Reinhold Niebuhr and Emil Brunner than to Karl Barth.[6] It is no accident, thus, that the report of a committee of the International Council of Religious Education on the place of theology in Christian education pointed a range of positions.[7]

1. Shelton H. Smith, "Let Religious Educators Reckon with the Barthians," *Religious Education* 24 (1934): 45-51. McMurry Richey, "Toward the Renewal of Faith and Nurture," *Duke Divinity School Bulletin,* 28 May 1963, pp. 127-41.

2. Elmer Homrighausen: "Barthianism and the Kingdom," *Christian Century* 48 (1931): 922-25; "Christian Theology and Christian Education," *Religious Education* 44 (1949): 353-63; "Theology and Christian Education," in the same issue of *Religious Education,* pp. 415-21. Smart's writings are cited below.

3. Harrison Elliott, *Can Religious Education Be Christian?* (New York: Macmillan, 1940); Sophia Lyon Fahs, *Today's Children and Yesterday's Heritage* (Boston: Beacon, 1952).

4. Randolph Crump Miller, *The Clue to Christian Education* (New York: Charles Scribner's Sons, 1950).

5. See the section on Chapter 4 in the bibliography at the end of this volume. For references on Little, Lynn, and Kennedy, see the section on Chapter 5.

6. Shelton Smith, *Faith and Nurture* (New York: Charles Scribner's Sons, 1941).

7. P. Vieth, ed., *The Church and Christian Education* (St. Louis: Bethany, 1947).

We will examine Sherrill's *The Gift of Power* as representative of those religious educators who were interested in a more dialogical position. Not only did Sherrill explicitly adopt Tillich's method of correlation in this book, but he also followed Tillich in drawing on the resources of depth psychology to describe the dynamics of Christian education. Not only, thus, was his theology post-liberal, but his psychology was post-Freudian. This move toward forms of psychological and social analysis that were more critical was a hallmark of the period. Tillich's ongoing dialogue with psychoanalysis and his early engagement of socialism, H. Richard Niebuhr's use of class analysis in *The Social Sources of Denominationalism,* and Reinhold Niebuhr's frequent portrayal of reason as serving the hidden "interests" of group power all represented a turn to what we would call today a hermeneutic of suspicion. Such tools of analysis were thought to be necessary to understand the crisis of modernity. They went hand in hand with neo-Reformation themes like the transcendence of God, the pervasiveness of sin, the "otherness" of grace, and the uniqueness of the church as a community of reconciliation.

These theological themes began to take a distinctly American cast prior to the Second World War in an intellectual movement that has come to be known as Christian realism.[8] This movement was closely identified with important texts of prominent American theologians of this period: Reinhold Niebuhr's *Moral Man and Immoral Society* (1932), Walter Horton's *Realistic Theology* (1934), John Bennett's *Christian Realism* (1941), and H. Richard Niebuhr's contribution to *The Church Against the World* (1935).[9] Permeating the rhetoric of this group was a mood of impending crisis, readily apparent to all who were "realistic" about the massive problems facing modernity. This was coupled with the promise of a new beginning for American Protestantism and society if they would abandon the illusions of liberalism. H. Richard Niebuhr's famous assessment of liberal theology captures well the realists' critique: "A God without wrath brought men without sin into a kingdom without judgment through the ministrations of a Christ without a cross."[10] This sort of theology, they argued, was incapable of discerning the plight of modernity or pointing the way ahead.

---

8. The term was first used in a symposium on *Religious Realism* by a group of thinkers from Chicago and Yale. See Martin Marty, *Modern American Religion,* vol. 2: *The Noise of Conflict 1919-1941* (Chicago: University of Chicago Press, 1941), p. 306.

9. Reinhold Niebuhr, *Moral Man and Immoral Society* (New York: Scribner's, 1932); Walter Horton, *Realistic Theology* (New York: Harper and Brothers, 1934); John Bennett, *Christian Realism* (New York: Charles Scribner's Sons, 1941); Richard Niebuhr, Wilhelm Pauck, and Francis Miller, *The Church Against the World* (Chicago: Willett, Clark, and Company, 1935).

10. H. Richard Niebuhr, *The Kingdom of God in America* (New York: Harper and Brothers, 1937), p. 191.

In his assessment of Christian realism, Martin Marty reminds us that Tillich, Horton, Bennett, and the Niebuhrs were "public theologians," seeking to interpret ancient texts and traditions in ways that address not only the church but also various publics in American society.[11] We would be hard-pressed to find theologians in subsequent years with the popular and intellectual influence of Paul Tillich and Reinhold Niebuhr. An important question for us to consider is whether prominent theorists of Protestant religious education like Smart and Sherrill maintained this public emphasis in their work.

James Smart: Taking Up the Barthian Gauntlet

James Smart was born in Canada in 1906. Upon the completion of his undergraduate and Bachelor of Divinity degrees, he served churches in Canada for a number of years and then pursued a Ph.D. in Semitics. Subsequently, he was appointed as the Jesup Professor of Biblical Interpretation at Union Theological Seminary, New York, and was closely identified with the biblical theology movement in the United States. He wrote nineteen books and numerous articles, the best known of which are *The Strange Silence of the Bible in the Church; The Rebirth of Ministry; The Past, Present, and Future of Biblical Theology; The Cultural Subversion of the Biblical Faith;* and *The Teaching Ministry of the Church,* the book we will be examining in this section.[12] Smart was highly influential in the Presbyterian church in the United States, serving as editor-in-chief of the *Christian Faith and Life* curriculum (1944-1950), generally considered one of the best Protestant church school curriculums produced in the United States during the twentieth century. He also served on the denominational committee of the northern Presbyterian church that composed *The Confession of 1967.* This document would become a part of the confessional standards of this denomination and, subsequently, of the Presbyterian church body formed through the reuniting of the southern and northern Presbyterian branches in the 1980s.

In the foreword to *The Teaching Ministry of the Church,* Smart provides insight into the programmatic intent of his book. He was prompted to write the book as a result of his decision to become the editor-in-chief of the *Faith and Life* curriculum of the Presbyterian Church (U.S.A.) in 1944, a position which allowed him to focus on "the theological foundations of the Church's

11. Marty, *Modern American Religion,* vol. 2, p. 306.
12. See the bibliography.

educational program."[13] Throughout the book, Smart describes the church as standing "at the beginning of a new period of development, the period of theological recovery."[14] The theology of Karl Barth was to exert great influence on Smart's thinking in *The Teaching Ministry,* although Smart also draws on Emil Brunner and H. Richard Niebuhr at points and explicitly points to the diversity of the new theological currents.[15] His task is to tap these theological currents to project a new program of Christian education for postwar Protestant congregations. While the 1946 Vieth report to the International Council of Religious Education *(The Church and Christian Education)* and Randolph Miller's *The Clue to Christian Education* marked first steps toward theological renewal in Christian education, Smart argues that neither went far enough in criticizing the theological and educational assumptions of the recent past.[16] To correct that error is his programmatic task.

In the first two chapters of *The Teaching Ministry,* he sets forth the material and methodological assumptions that guide his work. He begins with a brief discussion of Israel and the church as covenant communities, called into being and sustained across the centuries by God's word. Their education, as such, is an outgrowth of their unique nature and mission as God's people. This leads Smart to drop the widely used term "religious education," adopting in its stead the terms "teaching ministry" and "Christian education" to make it clear that education in the church must be portrayed theologically. The branch of theology most directly related to this task, according to Smart, is practical theology, "the study of the Church in action, the critique of its practices in the past, the determination on principle of what should be its practices in the present, and the training of its ministry to be guides into right fulfillment of its nature in response to God in the future."[17]

Within practical theology, Smart makes an important distinction between preaching and teaching. Both are portrayed as ministries of proclamation and distinguished from those parts of practical theology that focus on liturgics, pastoral theology, missiology, and evangelism; but while the content of preaching and teaching are the same, he argues, preaching "essentially is the proclamation of this Word of God to man in his unbelief" and teaching "essentially addresses itself to the situation of the man who has repented and turned to God and to the situation of children of believers who through the

13. James Smart, *The Teaching Ministry of the Church* (Philadelphia: Westminster, 1954), p. 9.

14. Smart, *Teaching Ministry,* p. 67. See also pp. 62 and 64 for similar statements.

15. Smart, *Teaching Ministry,* p. 64.

16. Smart, *Teaching Ministry,* pp. 65-67.

17. Smart, *Teaching Ministry,* p. 38.

influence of their parents have in them a measure of faith."[18] Smart portrays the relationship of these two ministries as dialectical. Christians live in the tension of belief and unbelief and, as such, always stand in need of preaching by which they encounter anew God's word of judgment and grace. At the same time, they have some measure of faith in them and must be helped by the church through its teaching ministry to grow in their understanding of God's word.

On the basis of this distinction between preaching and teaching, Smart goes on to describe three interrelated purposes of Christian education: (1) proclamation of the gospel in an intimate person-to-person situation; (2) teaching that challenges the members of the church to understand more fully the truth of the gospel, leaving behind inadequate understandings of God, themselves, and the world in relation to God; and (3) training in ministry, equipping the members of congregations to participate in the redemptive mission of Jesus Christ to the world in their own time and place.[19] Smart develops these goals in explicit opposition to those of character development, growth of the personality, and an expanded sense of social responsibility, all of which figured prominently in the religious education movement. Such goals, he argues, reflect the moralism of an older liberal theology and contemporary humanism. Not only are they shallow in their understanding of the crisis of modern life but they confuse cultural values and achievements with God's word of judgment and grace, the most important gift the church has to offer the modern world. Smart puts it like this:

> Liberal optimism about human nature was shattered by the outbreak of startling forms of inhumanity within Western civilization. Modern man, confronted by evil in its naked reality, began to find the Biblical description of it once more believable. The idea of an inevitable progress of the human race no longer carried conviction, and the corollary belief, that divinity is to be identified with the natural process by which man moves toward the fulfillment of his destiny, seemed hard to distinguish from a humanism in which all belief in God is abandoned.[20]

Accordingly, Smart projects a new program for Christian education on the basis of his theologically defined goals. His primary audience throughout this text is the leaders of congregations, both ministers and directors of Christian education. He describes his theory of congregational education as

---

18. Smart, *Teaching Ministry*, pp. 19-20.
19. Smart, *Teaching Ministry*, pp. 84-88.
20. Smart, *Teaching Ministry*, p. 63.

consisting of five basic points. First, the entire congregation must be seen as the primary educator. Children and youth will not learn to be disciples through an hour or two per week in the Sunday school but only if they encounter adults who are enacting the mission of the church in their corporate and individual lives. Second, worship plays a crucial role in teaching the Christian life, for here the movement of God to congregations in the word and their response in faith and obedience is enacted paradigmatically; worship must include all age groups, and the young must be instructed in its meaning. Third, the congregation in its common fellowship teaches its members how to bear one another's joys and sorrows. Bible studies, church school classes, and other educational groups, thus, must seek to foster a climate of mutual caring, not least between teachers and students. Fourth, the church must teach its members the story of God's people as found in the Bible and church history that they might learn to discern God's call to the church today. Fifth, the teaching ministry should seek to equip the members of the church to carry out concrete forms of ministry that are suitable to their particular gifts and to the needs of the present moment.

It is not surprising in light of Smart's education as a biblical scholar and his Reformed (especially Barthian) theological commitments that he would place the Bible at the center of the congregation's teaching ministry. He offers relatively little in this text on the complex heremeneutical issues involved in teaching Scripture to modern persons, a topic he would take up more extensively in *The Strange Silence of the Bible in the Church.*[21] His desire to place the Bible at the heart of Christian education stands in stark contrast to the emphasis on contemporary issues and the expansion of social experience found in the writings of Coe and Fahs.

Of special interest to us are the audiences Smart seeks to address in this text. Eight of ten chapters are devoted to congregational education and seek to address those leading and teaching in this part of the church's life. In the final two chapters of the book, however, he takes up the family and public education. Even here, it is clear that the implied audience of these chapters con-

---

21. James Smart, *The Strange Silence of the Bible in the Church: A Study in Hermeneutics* (Philadelphia: Westminster, 1970). In this book, Smart argues that the interpretation of Scripture in Christian communities should be based on a special theological hermeneutic that is not derived directly from either philosophical hermeneutics or the interpretive strategies of other nontheological disciplines. While it should incorporate the insights of historical and literary criticism (something he criticizes Barth as failing to do), such an approach would be based on a more comprehensive "hermeneutic of revelation" that does justice to Scripture's function as the medium through which God addresses the church from age to age (here, following Barth's actualism).

tinues to be the leaders of congregations. His primary concern is how they might support families and raise critical questions about the direction of public education. Nonetheless, these chapters indicate awareness on Smart's part that congregations interact with education in other settings that support, complement, or undercut the congregation's teaching ministry.

As editor of the *Christian Faith and Life* curriculum, Smart was well aware that involving the family in Christian education was a difficult proposition. This curriculum was structured around ongoing cooperation between families and the church school and, in large measure, fell out of use because of the failure of families to offer the sort of teaching that the curriculum presupposed. In *The Teaching Ministry*, Smart traces the decline of the family as a site of Protestant education and outlines theological foundations for the recovery of the teaching ministry of the family, grounded in infant baptism and the "divine order" of the Christian home.[22] Here, as in the book as a whole, Smart offers no empirical data or social scientific analysis of the changing form of the family in modern life. He points to such changes anecdotally and, then, focuses his attention on providing a theological framework by which congregational leaders might assist parents in recovering a clearer understanding of their role as teachers in the Christian home.

Smart's chapter on public education explores the church's relationship to public life, drawing on H. Richard Niebuhr's *Christ and Culture* to describe the range of ways the church might relate to culture in general and to public education in particular. He describes public education as an area of "mounting tension" in the church, due to increasing alarm among Christians that their children are beginning to receive an education in the public schools that is hostile to religion. Smart shares this alarm and points to examples of an anti-religious bias in the writings of prominent educational theorists. There is an irresolvable element of tension between the church and culture, he argues. While the church must maintain a stance of openness to culture, on the one hand ("We must be open to receive God's good gifts to us, not only through Greece, but from countless other sources"), it must not attempt "to harmonize and unite the Christian and the non-Christian forces in culture into an eclectic religion."[23] He calls on the church to take more seriously the vocation of the Christian teacher in public education. In *The Cultural Subversion of the Biblical Faith*, he would later draw the lines between the church and culture more strongly, mounting a critique of American civil religion and

22. Smart, *Teaching Ministry*, pp. 179, 182-86.
23. Smart, *Teaching Ministry*, pp. 196-97.

portraying its decline as a positive development in American life.[24] As he put it in this book:

> In fact, nothing would do more to release and promote a genuine, healthy patriotism than the vanishing of that false patriotism which feeds on self-justification. Christians are released to be good cooperative members of a pluralistic community when they remember that they share a sinfulness and a responsibility for the sins of their society with all the non-Christians. In the same way, a nation is released to be a good cooperative member of a world society of nations when within its citizenship there is willingness to drop all pretensions of moral superiority and to be just one among the many nations in which wisdom and folly, virtue and vice, humanity and inhumanity are constantly struggling for the mastery.[25]

While Smart is aware, thus, that the American church must take on a new, more critical role in American public life, he does not provide in *The Teaching Ministry of the Church* or in other writings an extensive discussion of the ways the education of congregations can equip their members to contribute to this domain. Gone is the concern with educating persons in the habits of democratic thinking and acting so central to Coe's and Fahs's work.

Lewis Joseph Sherrill: The Tillichian Alternative

Lewis Sherrill was born in 1892 in Haskell, Texas. He remained in Texas throughout his childhood and young adult years, receiving his undergraduate degree from Austin College in 1916. His theological education began at Presbyterian Theological Seminary of Kentucky but was interrupted by his enlistment in the army during World War I. Following the war, he enrolled in Louisville Seminary in 1921 and upon graduation served as the pastor of the First Presbyterian Church in Covington, Tennessee. Louisville Seminary called him to serve on its faculty as professor of "Religious Education and Young People's Work" in 1925. After one year of teaching, he took a leave from Louis-

---

24. James Smart, *The Cultural Subversion of the Biblical Faith: Life in the 20th Century under the Sign of the Cross* (Philadelphia: Westminster, 1977). Arguing against Robert Bellah, Robert Handy, and others, Smart contends that the American church would do well to view the breakdown of this civic faith as an opportunity to repent of its long-standing legitimization of America's sense of special destiny, an ideological position that was proving to be quite dangerous as it assumed the status of a world power.

25. Smart, *Cultural Subversion*, p. 33.

ville to begin a doctoral program at Yale University, where he completed his Ph.D. under Luther Weigle. He returned to Louisville where he taught courses in Christian education and served as the Dean of Faculty for twenty years. During the final seven years of his life (1950-1957), he taught at Union Theological Seminary of New York, succeeding Harrison Elliott. He wrote numerous books and articles, some of which are cited in the bibliography at the end of this volume.

Sherrill's most important text on Protestant religious education is *The Gift of Power*, and it will be the focus of this section. Like Smart's *Teaching Ministry*, this volume focuses on the education offered by Christian congregations. Far more than Smart, however, Sherrill gives extensive attention to the individual, the family, and, to a lesser extent, public *paideia* in his writings. In *The Struggle of the Soul*, for example, he pays special attention to the developmental dimensions of the individual's achievement of maturity in the life of faith, acknowledging the increased freedom and burden placed on the self in modern societies.[26] In *Family and Church*, he shares empirical research on the changing nature of the family and calls on congregations to support families as they attempt to negotiate these changes.[27] He highlights both the formal and the informal ways parents hand on the faith to their children. In his dissertation at Yale University, *Presbyterian Parochial Schools, 1846-1870*, he explores the American Presbyterian church's early response to the shifting *paideia* of public life as it was being reshaped by the public school movement.[28]

In the complete body of Sherrill's work, thus, we find a rich understanding of the changing ecology of Protestant religious education in the face of modernization and of the need for religious education theory to address the increasingly differentiated audiences of the individual, congregation, family, and public *paideia*. It is helpful to keep Sherrill's writings as a whole before us for another reason. When *The Gift of Power* is viewed alongside these other writings, three prominent themes found in this book can be seen as permeating Sherrill's rhetoric as a whole: (1) a note of crisis, (2) a call for theological renewal, and (3) an exploration of the depths of modern life. These themes were found extensively in the rhetoric of Christian realism and neo-Reformation theology, a point we touched on in the first part of this chapter.

From his earliest writing to his last, Sherrill consistently employs a rhetoric of crisis. In *Family and Church* (1937), this is described as the crisis of the

---

26. Lewis Joseph Sherrill, *The Struggle of the Soul* (New York: Macmillan, 1953).

27. Lewis Joseph Sherrill, *Family and Church* (New York: Abingdon, 1937).

28. Lewis Joseph Sherrill, *Presbyterian Parochial Schools, 1846-1870* (New Haven: Yale University Press, 1932).

modern family, documented in rising divorce rates and the internal strains of family life found in various empirical studies.[29] In *Guilt and Redemption* (1945), this crisis is portrayed more broadly as the widespread experience of anxiety in modern life, manifested in widespread "feelings of guilt."[30] In *The Struggle of the Soul* (1961), Sherrill strikes a note of crisis at the very beginning of the book, arguing that a realistic appraisal of the modern situation makes it obvious that "we live in a time of trouble; harassed by uncertainty, heartbreak, and despair."[31] Far from the optimistic appraisals of modernity found in liberal culture and theology, he argues, many modern people are now asking if the twentieth century marks the "night of western civilization." The church's response to this crisis, he contends, must be one of theological renewal. This represents a second pervasive theme in Sherrill's writings.

Throughout his writings, Sherrill draws on the theology of the Niebuhr brothers, Paul Tillich, Emil Brunner, and Soren Kierkegaard to recover central themes of the Reformation. Unlike Smart, however, he portrays this retrieval as necessarily engaged in a dialogue with the resources of cultural modernity, especially those resources that articulate the profoundest questions with which modern persons are struggling. He follows Paul Tillich in using the method of correlation in theology, an approach that explores the "depth dimension" of culture to discern the "questions" with which a particular era is struggling and to determine the "answers" that the Christian tradition has to offer. Like Tillich, moreover, Sherrill's preferred dialogue partner in the engagement of culture is depth psychology, especially as formulated in the work of neo-Freudians like Karen Horney, Harry Stack Sullivan, and others. His comments at the beginning of *Guilt and Redemption* give insight into why he believes Christianity needs to engage culture in this way:

> Christianity has the most penetrating and the most constructive solution ever offered for the tremendous problems arising out of human guilt. . . . But . . . Christians of our own day commonly are trying to use the resources of the Christian gospel and the Christian church without facing the depths of the guilt from which that gospel promises to redeem us. The redemption that is then realized among us is superficial and often even trivial . . . the vocabulary of religion serves to help us hide our faces from an understanding of the deeper meanings of sin. . . . Because of such convictions I have sought . . . to draw not only upon the Bible and theology,

29. Sherrill, *Family and Church*, p. 7. Various empirical studies are cited throughout the first chapters of the book.

30. Lewis Joseph Sherrill, *Guilt and Redemption* (Richmond: John Knox Press, 1945), p. 61.

31. Sherrill, *The Struggle of the Soul*, p. 2.

but also upon psychology and psychiatry. The latter . . . hold promise of aiding us in utilizing more fully certain religious resources that, at the present, lie almost dormant within Christianity.[32]

Sherrill's use of terms like "penetrating" and "depths" in this paragraph is no accident. They reflect his ongoing engagement of cultural resources like depth psychology to penetrate the surface of modernity's present crisis. Only in this way, he believes, can the church find the questions to which it must respond.

All of these themes — a note of crisis, a call for theological renewal, and an engagement of cultural resources that explore the "depth" dimension of modern life — are found in *The Gift of Power* (1955), Sherrill's most comprehensive treatment of Christian education.[33] In his preface, Sherrill describes three questions that guide his thinking in the book: "Why is man so profoundly disturbed today? In what way is the Christian religion relevant to this condition? If the Christian religion is really relevant to the deeper needs of our own time, how can the church's educational work be made equally relevant?"[34] The first question sets the problematic for the book. Modernity has unlocked the secrets of the universe through science and technology and taken hold of tremendous power, yet it is not ready for the gift of power that has been put in its keeping. Sherrill explores this theme in greater depth in the first two chapters of the book, treating the "threats to the self" which foster a profound sense of anxiety among modern persons. He draws on Tillich's distinction between normal and neurotic anxiety to make the point that anxiety is not present only among persons with some form of psychological pathology. Rather, it is pervasive in modern life and, indeed, is an existential dimension of human selfhood. The burden of this part of Sherrill's book is to explicate the depth dimension of the crisis of modernity.

In the third and fourth chapters, he takes up the question of the relevance of the Christian message and community to this crisis. Drawing extensively on H. Richard Niebuhr's *The Meaning of Revelation,* he describes revelation as a transforming "encounter" between God as self and persons as selves who are profoundly threatened by the existential and social anxieties described in the first part of the book. Revelation, Sherrill argues, always is characterized by the fact that "the disclosure fits the need."[35] As such, it is portrayed as possessing two basic characteristics: (1) it is redemptive in nature, addressing the

32. Sherrill, *Guilt and Redemption,* p. 7.
33. Lewis Joseph Sherrill, *The Gift of Power* (New York: Macmillan, 1955).
34. Sherrill, *The Gift of Power,* p. x.
35. Sherrill, *The Gift of Power,* p. 105.

self in its depths and bringing healing and insight; and (2) it normally takes place through the fellowship of the Christian community, in the communication and interaction by which God as Person encounters humans as persons.[36] The church, as such, is to be a "revelatory fellowship."

In the remainder of the book, Sherrill takes up the third question raised in the preface, describing the sort of Christian education that follows from this understanding of the church as a "revelatory fellowship." The great weakness of the religious education movement, he argues, was its failure to recognize the unique nature of the church as a redemptive community, which led it to underestimate the depths of the problems with which modern persons struggle and which undercut its ability to bring the Christian message to bear upon these problems. The alternative he proposes is structured around two elements: *predicament* and *theme*. In place of the problem-solving or needs-based education of the recent past, Christian education should focus on various aspects of the human predicament. Sherrill unpacks this concept as follows:

> it is becoming common now to use the term "predicament" in preference to such terms as "need" and "problem" when the more profound aspects of the human situation are under view, as they are when one speaks of anxiety, estrangement, helplessness, and the like. . . . The sense of predicament arises out of the profound anxiety which we carry as human creatures in an existence where every form of security tends to be threatened sooner or later.[37]

Different aspects of the human predicament are to be addressed in Christian education by bringing them into a meaningful dialogue with corresponding biblical themes. Sherrill explains what he means by "theme":

> We propose that the analysis of the Bible and the selection of materials from it for the purpose of teaching in the Christian community can be made in terms of themes that are found in the Bible. The concept "theme" refers to some aspect of God's Self-disclosure to man which persists more or less prominently throughout the Bible.[38]

Sherrill's indebtedness to Tillich's method of correlation for the basic structure of his theory of Christian education is obvious. He describes his ap-

---

36. Sherrill, *The Gift of Power*, p. 78.
37. Sherrill, *The Gift of Power*, p. 107.
38. Sherrill, *The Gift of Power*, p. 109.

proach, however, as based on a "principle of correspondence" to give primacy to the "personal mutuality" at the heart of the divine-human encounter in the revelatory fellowship of the church. This emphasis on the *personal* element of the divine-human encounter is lost in Tillich's theology, he believes.[39]

Sherrill provides an overview of the biblical themes of creation, lordship, vocation, judgment, redemption, re-creation, providence, and faith, all of which he correlates to various predicaments of modern life. This opens out to a discussion of the symbolic character of religious language and the ways that teaching, which seeks to facilitate revelatory encounter of selves with God, must attempt to honor the capacity of symbols to address persons in their depths. The most important learning fostered by the church, he argues, does not take place at the level of conditioned responses (as in the behaviorism of American academic psychology) or in trial-and-error learning (as in progressive education) but at the level of personal insight and the deeper changes of the self that characterize personal healing and the transformation of personal relations.[40] Such learning goes far beyond the transmission of information and the cultivation of problem-solving reasoning to address persons in their depths. Its closest analogy is therapy. Sherrill concludes his book with a discussion of how the correspondence of predicament and theme might take place along different lines at different ages and stages. He would later expand the developmental perspective offered here in *The Struggle of the Soul.*

Smart and Sherrill in Context

The rhetoric of both Smart and Sherrill is responsive to certain aspects of modernization in American life between 1930 and 1960. These years fall into two distinct periods: the years following the crash of the stock market in 1929 through the end of World War II, and the years following the Second World War, largely characterized by the expansion of the American economy and America's new status as a world power in the Cold War era.

The most significant marker of the first period is the crash of the stock market in 1929. Stocks lost 40 percent of their value virtually overnight and continued a downward spiral through 1932. This began what is commonly known as the Great Depression, which colored all aspects of American life until the end of World War II. By 1932, hundreds of banks had failed. Large numbers

---

39. Sherrill, *The Gift of Power,* p. 105. His comments on Tillich are found in footnote 1 of chapter V, p. 198.

40. Sherrill, *The Gift of Power,* pp. 147-62.

of mills and factories had shut down or were working on a part-time basis. Estimates of unemployment range as high as thirteen million, representing one in every four workers. Family farmers were also hit hard during this period by a series of droughts and an inability to procure loans from banks to keep their farms afloat. With the election of Roosevelt in 1932, the federal government inaugurated a program of recovery, commonly known as the New Deal. While ameliorating some of the harsher effects of the Depression, it had limited success in moving the country out of a state of economic decline and stagnation.

This period of social and economic turbulence affected religion profoundly. It diminished the financial resources available to religion and also set in motion what Martin Marty has called a rhetorical civil war between and within religions.[41] At the heart of this war was the continued hegemony of Anglo-Saxon Protestantism in American life. The 1920s already had seen an increased public presence of Judaism and Roman Catholicism in American society. Anti-Jewish and anti-Catholic prejudices were high, symbolized by a resurgence of the Ku Klux Klan in many parts of the country. Within Protestantism, conflict between fundamentalists and modernists received national attention in the Scopes trial, in which a schoolteacher was put on trial for teaching evolution in the public schools of Tennessee. The Depression exacerbated the sense of crisis in the Protestant community. Not only was the country at risk, many believed, but also the place of Protestantism within American society was imperiled. Many people turned nostalgic, longing for a time in which "all" Americans agreed with one another on faith and morals.

When viewed through the lens of modernization theory, this rhetorical "civil war" can be viewed as a response to the increased reality of institutional differentiation and cultural pluralism. Institutions that in the recent past had been under the influence of Protestantism were now largely secularized and operating according to the inner "logics" of their own functional imperatives. Educational institutions, for example, were increasingly under pressure to use textbooks and to establish curriculums that reflected the values and knowledge of disciplines operating in accordance with the norms of modern scholarship. The increased reality of cultural pluralism stretched the older forms of civic and political discourse — largely dominated by the core Protestant culture — to the breaking point. Robert Handy and others have described this period as the second disestablishment of American Protestantism.[42] It is im-

---

41. Martin Marty, *Modern American Religion*, Vol. 2: *The Noise of Conflict 1919-1941* (Chicago: University of Chicago Press, 1991), ch. 1.

42. Robert Handy, *The Protestant Quest for a Christian America* (Philadelphia: Fortress, 1967).

possible to understand the rhetorical appeal of neo-orthodoxy and Christian realism among Protestant intellectuals during this period without taking this social context into account.

This appeal was threefold. First, Christian realism and neo-orthodoxy seemed to chart a way beyond the fundamentalist/modernist controversy, pointing to the recovery of central themes of the Reformation and Bible while rejecting the anti-intellectualism of fundamentalism. They appeared to offer a theological position that allowed the church to come to terms with modern scientific thinking, on the one hand, without following the modernists in capitulating to its autonomous frames of reference, on the other. Second, neo-orthodoxy and Christian realism appeared to possess the resources needed to address the sense of crisis permeating American life. Indeed, they portrayed the collapse of Protestant hegemony as God's judgment on this community, a sign of its over-accommodation to American culture. The rhetorical war for the soul of America was seen as a form of idolatry, one more example of American Protestantism's confusion of the American way of life with the Christian way of life. Third, they appeared to point the way ahead, describing a new role for Protestant churches within an increasingly secular and pluralistic context. Freed from their cultural captivity, they argued, Protestant congregations might finally be the church, in a new, less domesticated fashion.

Following World War II, these themes continued to have widespread rhetorical appeal. The world had entered the nuclear age. Millions of Americans had experienced the horrors of war firsthand. Communism loomed as a threat in world politics, leading to the bipolar structuring of interstate relations that would characterize global politics until the final decade of the twentieth century. McCarthyism would soon rear its ugly head, making dissent increasingly risky and pressuring Americans to hold a single, anti-Communist point of view. The memory of economic depression was still fresh in the minds of adults who had grown up during the Great Depression. All of these lent plausibility to the rhetoric of crisis that neo-orthodoxy and Christian realism had forged between the wars and to their call for Protestant churches to shed their over-accommodation to American culture. In retrospect, however, it is clear that American society and religion were changing in ways that would make it increasingly difficult for Protestant churches to heed this call.

The end of the war marked both a period of growth in the American economy and the increased stature of America as a world power. The public school system grew rapidly to accommodate the influx of children born in the years immediately following the war. Higher education expanded as well, absorbing large numbers of men and women returning from the war whose education was subsidized by the federal government. For the moment, all seemed well in

American Protestantism. Membership and financial support were on the rise. Between 1941 and 1945, for example, expenditures on personal consumption grew from $80 billion to $120 billion — in other words, by 50 percent. During this same period, religious contributions grew from $1.06 billion to $1.74 billion, a 64 percent increase.[43] New churches were being built at a rapid pace, mirroring the relocation of the middle class to the suburbs.[44] Denominational identity continued to be important, symbolized by an expansion of national bureaucracies and the publication of new denominational curriculums. Barth, Tillich, and the Niebuhrs dominated theological education.

When we place the writings of Smart and Sherrill in this broader social context, it is obvious that both relied heavily on theological currents first entering American life during the 1930s. Even in the 1950s, when Smart and Sherrill wrote their programmatic books on Christian education, these currents continued to provide the dominant interpretive frames by which to understand the social and historical processes of modernization that were reshaping American life. Four prominent themes characterized their understanding of these forces and their portrayal of the church's response.

First, both called attention to the crisis of modernity. Sherrill spent a great deal of time describing this crisis in terms of new cultural resources such as psychoanalysis, following the lead of Paul Tillich. As he frequently put it, if the church was going to play a significant role in a context of pervasive anxiety and uncertainty, then it must grasp and respond to this crisis in its "depths." Smart sounded this note but offered little in the way of analysis. How are we to interpret this note of crisis? Obviously, the historical events of this period had a sobering effect on the American psyche. It had now experienced two world wars, a major economic depression, and the dropping of the first atomic bomb. There are structural features, moreover, that also can be noted. A differentiated social context had allowed modern art to emerge as a relatively independent sphere of life, affording it the freedom to serve as a center of values and insights standing in tension with those of the business world and popular culture. It is here that the first notes of caution about modernity's overconfidence in human reason were sounded. Freud's influence on the literature, painting, and drama of this period was profound, pointing to a pessimistic understanding of the ego's captivity to the forces of the un-

43. Robert Wuthnow, *The Restructuring of American Religion: Society and Faith Since World War II* (Princeton, N.J.: Princeton University Press, 1988), p. 26.

44. Wuthnow, *Restructuring of American Religion*, pp. 27-28. Three-quarters of all Protestant churches were located in rural areas or small towns of fewer than 2,500. By some estimates, as many as 1,000 rural churches would have needed to close every year in the postwar decades simply to keep pace with the population's relocation to cities and suburbs.

conscious. A shift had taken place, at least among the cultural elites, to a perspective more critical of modernity and the confidence it placed in scientific research and technological innovation. In retrospect, this note of crisis can be viewed as anticipating the far broader sense of risk that has come to permeate popular consciousness in the United States and Europe. Indeed, Sherrill's *The Gift of Power* seems almost prophetic in its articulation of this sense of risk. In forging a rhetoric of crisis, thus, Sherrill and Smart can be viewed as joining a chorus of voices across the spheres of art and culture who were becoming more reflective and critical about modernity, but doing so from the perspective of their reworking of classical Protestantism.

A second prominent theme in the writings of Smart and Sherrill was their criticism of the cultural accommodation of American Protestantism. This theme is readily apparent in their call for Protestant churches to recover a clearer sense of their own theological identity. The churches, they argued, were ill-equipped to respond to the crisis of modernity because they had come to be so closely identified with the intellectual resources and social currents of the modern period. They had become little more than forms of "culture Protestantism," a theme featured prominently in Smart's *The Cultural Subversion of the Biblical Faith* but already evident in *The Teaching Ministry of the Church*. The religious education movement, he argued, had led the way toward cultural accommodation through its optimistic assessment of modernity, its moralism, its abandonment of beliefs central to biblical and Reformation faith, and its wholesale adoption of the experimental orientation of progressive education. Sherrill was more measured in his critique of the religious education movement, but he was equally adamant that it was incapable of projecting a model of congregational education that would enable American Protestantism to recover its distinctive identity. Both relied heavily on the new theological currents coming out of Europe and American Christian realism to project an understanding of the church that was in tension with American culture, less apt to bless America's special sense of destiny or the economic and familial mores of the middle class.

While there is no question that certain substantive theological understandings of the church lay behind their call for a renewal of theological identity, it is also possible to view this call as a reflexive response to the continuing disestablishment of American Protestantism and the emerging pluralism of American religious life. The Protestant church was, in fact, already becoming less dominant in American life. Not only were the major institutions of public life increasingly free of the influence of Protestantism, but other religious traditions were also making their presence felt in public life. Smart, in particular, viewed these developments positively. In theological terms, he in effect gave expression to an idea later articulated by Niklas Luhmann in terms of general systems theory.[45] In a highly differentiated society, religion becomes free to pursue its own goals (which Luhmann describes in terms of contingency) and is no longer forced to play the roles of legitimization and integration vis-à-vis other social systems (as in traditional societies). While Smart would describe this in terms of the freedom of the word of God and the need for the church to heed this word and not the words of its cultural context, it is not difficult to perceive the parallels between this position and the institutional differentiation and cultural pluralism that were reshaping American life. This accounts, moreover, for the "loss of audience" characterizing Smart and Sherrill, something we will take up below.

This emphasis on the recovery of theological identity had important methodological implications for Smart and Sherrill, a third emphasis of their writings. Both viewed the task of constructing a theory of Christian education as theological from beginning to end. Smart described his work as a form of practical theology. While he pointed in passing to the importance of nontheological cultural resources, his primary focus was on the discipline's dialogue with dogmatic and biblical theology. These fields, he argued, provide important insights into the nature and purpose of the church, the methodological starting point of an adequate understanding of this community's teaching ministry. Sherrill, likewise, portrayed his work as a form of theological reflection. His reliance on Tillich's method of correlation, however, led him to bring theology into dialogue with the social sciences. His correlation of predicament and theme in his theory of Christian education represents an alternative to Smart's exclusive preoccupation with theological and biblical resources. In many ways, Sherrill's approach is more representative of the methodological commitments of prominent theorists of Protestant religious education throughout this period, most of whom continued to view dialogue with the social sciences as an important part of their work. A recovery of theological identity, they believed, did not preclude engagement of the resources of cultural modernity.

This reassertion of the importance of theology for Protestant religious education points to one of the most perplexing issues that plagued this field over the course of the twentieth century. On the one hand, the reform movement described in the previous chapter was fully committed to the emergence of religious education as a specialized field of knowledge that operated with relative independence from theology and patterned its research programs along the lines of the social sciences and modern education. On the other hand, the dif-

---

45. Niklas Luhmann, *Funktion der Religion* (Frankfurt: Suhrkamp, 1977) and *Religious Dogmatics and the Evolution of Society* (New York: E. Mellon 1984).

ferentiation of religion in general and the disestablishment of Protestantism in particular created new demands on the Protestant churches to develop their own forms of education, since they could no longer depend on the family, higher education, or public schools to assist them in this task. This put pressure on Protestant religious education theory to move closer to the church, to provide theological reasons for the positions it commended that made sense within the religious convictions of this particular community. American religious education has not been able to resolve this tension and has aptly been described as undergoing a permanent identity crisis.[46] The way beyond this crisis, however, depends in part on recognizing contextual developments beyond the field itself that have created this tension. In other words, it involves acknowledging religious education's interdependent relationship to its social context.

A fourth prominent characteristic of the rhetoric of Smart and Sherrill was a narrowing of the audience addressed by their writings. They took the differentiation and secularization of other institutions as a given and focused their attention almost exclusively on the Protestant Christian community. Both wrote primarily for the professional leaders of this community, and both made the congregation the center of their educational programs, although Sherrill continued to acknowledge the importance of the family and the new place of individualized dimensions of faith. Even when drawing on social scientific analysis of broader trends in modern American life, however, Sherrill cast these trends primarily in terms of their influence on contemporary Protestantism, pointing to ways congregational education might respond to the predicaments of modern life. He and Smart give virtually no sustained attention to the church's role in the education of the public — its preparation of persons for participation in pluralistic, democratic communities or the ethical ideals that should inform education in other public institutions. In narrowing their audience to the leaders of congregational education, they followed a trend already evident in the religious education movement. Indeed, they intensified this trend in their preoccupation with the recovery of the theological identity of the Protestant community.

Much of our evaluation of the strengths and weaknesses of Smart and Sherrill has been offered already in these final comments. On the positive side, their call for a recovery of theological identity in Protestant religious education and Protestantism generally was a much-needed corrective to the religious education movement. Sherrill, moreover, kept alive the importance of theology's dialogue with the cultural resources of modernity, following the

46. J. Westerhoff, ed., *Who Are We? The Quest for a Religious Education* (Birmingham, Ala.: Religious Education Press, 1978). See Westerhoff's introductory essay.

lead of Paul Tillich. Their theological critique of modernity, moreover, represented a (religiously based) reconsideration of this period that was also taking place in art and the academy and, later, in popular culture. Long before "risk society" became a common way of describing the heightened awareness of the risks of modern science and technology, Sherrill called attention to the pervasive sense of anxiety attending the modern "gift of power."

On the negative side, neither Smart nor Sherrill drew on sociological forms of analysis to understand the changing place of the church in American society or in modern life generally. In Smart's case, this seems to have been a methodological decision not to allow the resources of culture to determine his theological stance. In Sherrill's, it seems to have more to do with his preference for psychology than with a desire to rule out social analysis on methodological grounds. Indeed, unlike Tillich, who moves from psychology to existentialism in ways that confuse contextual issues with ontological claims, Sherrill keeps his focus on the historical context of modern anxiety. His primary focus, however, is on psychological understandings of these issues. A closely related second area of weakness is their failure to articulate a clear vision of the public role of Protestant Christianity. Unlike in Coe and Fahs, there is no real attention to the importance of teaching the virtues of democratic thinking and acting, for example. While both in their own way affirmed a culture-shaping and -transforming vision of Protestantism, they did not give sustained attention to how this might play out in the sort of religious education offered in congregations.

Evangelical Instruction and Proclamation: The Christian Renewal of Education in Postwar Germany

In this section, we will focus on the development of religious education after the end of World War II in Germany. In doing so, we will again encounter interesting parallels between the situation in Germany and in the United States, although these postwar parallels are sometimes more remote than those between the religious education movements in both countries earlier in the twentieth century. In both the United States and Germany, the postwar period has been perceived as a time of theological renewal, so our comparisons will look not only at the effects of social modernization on religious education in both countries but also at the effects of theological change.

The German situation in 1945 was of course very different from the situation in the United States. Germany had not only lost the war but was suffering greatly in its aftermath. Most of Germany's cities were in ruins, with no infrastructure for meeting even the most basic needs. There was sometimes not even enough food. In addition, the breakdown of the political system of National Socialism released all kinds of political questions concerning the past, present, and future of Germany as well as existential questions concerning guilt and an unknown future.

In 1949, the Federal Republic of Germany in the West and the German Democratic Republic in the East were founded. This new development was closely connected to the beginning of the Cold War, a situation that strongly influenced these two German states during the 1950s. Because of the socialist system in East Germany, religious education there developed in different ways than it did in West Germany, with its Western political system.[47] West Germany, which will be our focus in this chapter, became a member of NATO and developed especially strong connections to the United States. The political and economic support from West Germany's new allies made it possible for this country to reach a comparatively stable and economically strong position by the end of the 1950s, the decade that is often seen as the time of the economic reconstruction of Germany.

One of the decisive issues for Germans in 1945 was finding the foundations for a new and different political system. Both the Western allies and parts of the German population saw the churches as being one of the few institutions in German society whose credibility had not been disqualified by its actions during National Socialism (giving the church more credibility than its historical actions really warranted). The military government's circulars and directives demonstrate that the Americans, especially, trusted the churches.[48] In actuality, the churches had been divided — with different camps siding for and against Hitler's government. The best-known group that opposed Hitler was the Confessing Church, associated with theologians like Dietrich Bonhoeffer and Karl Barth.[49] Understandably, after 1945

---

47. Cf., with additional references, Comenius-Institut, ed., *Christenlehre und Religionsunterricht. Interpretationen zu ihrer Entwicklung 1945-1990* (Weinheim: Deutscher Studien-Verlag, 1998).

48. See the documents in Oskar Anweiler et al., eds., *Bildungspolitik in Deutschland 1945-1990. Ein historisch-vergleichender Quellenband* (Bonn: Bundeszentrale für politische Bildung, 1992), pp. 63ff.; Sebastian Müller-Rolli, ed., *Evangelische Schulpolitik in Deutschland 1918-1958. Dokumente und Darstellung* (Göttingen: Vandenhoeck und Ruprecht, 1999). For a discussion cf. Jochen-Christoph Kaiser and Anselm Doering-Manteuffel, eds., *Christentum und politische Verantwortung. Kirchen im Nachkriegsdeutschland* (Stuttgart: Kohlhammer Verlag, 1990).

49. For an introduction cf. Kurt Nowak, *Geschichte des Christentums in Deutschland. Religion, Politik und Gesellschaft vom Ende der Aufklärung bis zur Mitte des 20. Jahrhunderts* (München: Beck Verlag, 1995), pp. 243ff.

religious educators were looking in that direction for a new basis for their work.

If we look at the theological renewal after 1945 from the perspective of the historical situation, we can see it as an immediate outgrowth of World War II. But the attempt to renew religious education along the lines of a different theology began before the war, and has been dated by some as beginning with the publication of Gerhard Bohne's *The Word of God and Instruction. Foundations for an Evangelical Pedagogics* in 1929.[50] This monograph, drawing on the new theology of the 1920s (Karl Barth, Neo-Lutheranism), is based on a theology of "crisis" that is opposed to all attempts to synthesize faith and culture or religion and personality — efforts that were so characteristic of the earlier German religious education reform movement. Several years prior to Bohne's book Eduard Thurneysen (a close friend of Karl Barth) published an influential article on confirmation that contains similar arguments.[51] In pointing to these publications of the 1920s it is important to note that the writings of Bohne and Thurneysen were not isolated pieces but should be considered the beginning of a whole movement that was of growing importance and considerable influence during the 1930s.[52] This group of authors chose the name "evangelical instruction" *(Evangelische Unterweisung)* to characterize what they saw as the goal of the church's teaching — in contrast to the religious education reform movement's stated goal of "religious education." The phrase "religious education" came to be perceived as growing out of a theological liberalism which the new theology of the 1920s wanted to overcome. The new theologians did not want to speak in terms of "religion." They preferred to speak of the "word of God" and "revelation."

For a long time, it was assumed that this movement of theological renewal not only possessed a sound theological basis but also was legitimized by the role that it played during National Socialism. It is true that some of the main representatives of this group belonged to the Confessing Church. Most notably Oskar Hammelsbeck played a leading role in the oppositional church, serving as its main resource in the field of catechetics and Christian education. It has been recently discovered, however, that others, like the influ-

---

50. Gerhard Bohne, *Das Wort Gottes und der Unterricht,* third printing (Berlin: Verlag "Die Spur" Herbert Dorbandt, 1964).

51. Eduard Thurneysen, "Konfirmandenunterricht. Ein Kapitel aus der Praktischen Theologie," in *Das Wort Gottes und die Kirche,* by Eduard Thurneysen (München: Kaiser, 1927), pp. 136-64. Cf., for example, Karl Ernst Nipkow and Friedrich Schweitzer, eds., *Religionspädagogik. Texte zur evangelischen Erziehungs- und Bildungsverantwortung seit der Reformation,* vol. 2/2: 20. *Jahrhundert* (Gütersloh: Gütersloher Verlagshaus, 1994).

ential Helmuth Kittel, made their peace with National Socialism.[53] One of the rationales given by such theologians for their lack of strong opposition to National Socialism was a distorted version of the Lutheran teaching of the two kingdoms — a dualistic approach that dichotomizes the "worldly reign" from the "spiritual reign." From this perspective, even Hitler's government could be considered legitimate as long as it did not attempt to make National Socialism a religion. Not only did some of these new theologians accept the political regime uncritically, they also showed clear signs of a theological anti-Semitism. This is seen in their negative attitude toward the Old Testament, which they referred to as the "Jewish Bible."

Given the many problems and tensions that dominated the situation in Germany after 1945, the compromising relationships with National Socialism were soon forgotten. This was partly because people like Kittel actively covered them up in their writings, and partly because their publications after 1945 are indeed free of such problematic political allegiance and, instead, give undivided attention to the main orientations of this postwar theological renewal.

What are the main characteristics of the evangelical instruction movement? Its primary aim is to take the revelatory character of the word of God seriously. Revelation is seen as opposed to all human possibilities of knowing and acting. Therefore revelation may be received only through proclamation, not through experience or experiential ways of teaching and learning. Consequently, most of the aims of the reform movement in religious education described in the previous chapter are seen as theologically questionable. Any synthesis of theology with psychology or social theory is rejected because it seemed to contradict the character of revelation as the free word of God that could never be bound to the laws of the human psyche or to cultural achievements. Revelation is also seen as standing in tension with modern education. The contemporary philosophy of education was accused of striving for human autonomy and self-perfection, which, from the perspective of evangelical instruction, denied human dependence on God for the redemption from sin and evil. For those in the evangelical instruction movement, God's revelation could only mean judgment on — or even "annihilation" of — the idea of education. The proponents of evangelical instruction insisted that the emphasis on method in religious education be abandoned. In his oft-quoted explanation, Theodor Heckel maintained that the Holy Spirit was much more important than any method of instruction.[54]

---

53. Cf. Folkert Rickers, *Zwischen Kreuz und Hakenkreuz. Untersuchungen zur Religionspädagogik im "Dritten Reich"* (Neukirchen-Vluyn: Neukirchener Verlag, 1995).

54. Theodor Heckel, *Zur Methodik des evangelischen Religionsunterrichtes* (München: Kaiser Verlag, 1928), p. 29.

The proponents of evangelical instruction agreed with the proponents of the religious education movement that both the congregation and the state school were the proper focus of their efforts. National Socialism's attempts to control all of education led to the repression of any traditional Christian forms of religious education in the school curriculum, or to their removal altogether. In response to this repression, the church tried to strengthen Christian education in the congregation. Special classes for Christian instruction were established in congregations in order to replace the religious education that had formerly been offered in the state schools. Later on, these congregational classes became the basic model for religious education in Eastern Germany after 1945, because the socialist government did not allow religious education in the schools.[55] In West Germany, Christian education in the congregation also continued in the form of Christian youth work and Sunday school, but there it went along with a strong emphasis on evangelical instruction in the state school. West German schools allowed — and still allow — denominational religious education as part of the curriculum.

The issue of whether or not the state schools should be reconstituted as Christian (denominational) schools was hotly debated during this period.[56] Although many Catholic and some Protestant church leaders recommended turning the state schools into Protestant or Christian schools, the primary spokespersons of the evangelical instruction movement did not advocate this goal. The main reason for not supporting the general establishment of Christian schools was not that the adherents of evangelical instruction would have been opposed to a stronger Christian influence in school. Rather, they considered the majority of the German population to be lacking a Christian commitment strong enough to support such schools.[57] Consequently, they settled for two things: having "religious instruction" in the sense of evangelical instruction (or Catholic religion classes) included in the school curriculum, and giving the schools a general Christian basis that was to combine the Protestant and the Catholic traditions, rather than having denominational schools. Drawing on the teaching of the two kingdoms, representatives of evangelical instruction understood the relationship between religious education as a school subject and the other subjects of the curriculum according to the distinction between Law and gospel or between revelation and secular science. Religious education classes were the place for revelation and proclama-

---

55. Cf. Comenius-Institut, *Christenlehre und Religionsunterricht.*

56. Cf. Müller-Rolli, ed., *Evangelische Schulpolitik in Deutschland*, pp. 347ff.

57. As a document from the Confessing Church (1943), cf. "Kirche und Schule," in *Bildung und Erziehung. Die Denkschriften der Evangelischen Kirche in Deutschland*, vol. 4/1, ed. Evangelische Kirche in Deutschland (Gütersloh: Gütersloher Verlagshaus, 1987), pp. 19-25.

tion while other subjects of the curriculum were to be based on human reason and were to respect the limitations of human knowledge concerning all matters of revealed faith.

Since the field of religious education in Germany between 1945 and 1960 was certainly not monolithic, it has been difficult to pick one piece of writing and call it representative. The proponents of evangelical instruction proposed many different ways of understanding this instruction. There also was diversity in the scope of their publications. Some focused only on religious education while others were geared to more general issues of education, addressing them from a Christian point of view.

We have decided to use Helmuth Kittel's 1947 monograph on evangelical instruction as our primary example. This choice is easy to justify. If any book was a programmatic statement of the evangelical instruction movement's perspective over the past half-century, it is this monograph. In order to avoid any impression that religious education theory could be reduced to the views developed by Kittel in this book, however, we will also look at some of Oskar Hammelsbeck's publications on general education and schooling from the time after 1945.

As mentioned earlier, our focus in this chapter is the time between 1945 and the late 1950s. Since the evangelical instruction movement has its roots in an earlier time, we will look first at a representative figure from the 1920s and 1930s, Magdalene von Tiling, before we move to Kittel and Hammelsbeck. Von Tiling can be called with some justification the most influential woman in twentieth-century German religious education.

Magdalene von Tiling: A Neo-Lutheran Philosophy of Education

Magdalene von Tiling, born in 1877, was very influential in the Protestant women's movement during the 1920s.[58] Her political views, however, were rather conservative. In 1918 she became one of the founders of the German National People's Party (DNVP), a party that stood for monarchism, anti-Semitism, and what was perceived as championing Christian values. Becoming a member of the Prussian parliament in 1921, she wielded not only academic but political influence. Starting in the mid 1920s, her theology became

58. For biographical information on Magdalene von Tiling cf. Liese-Lotte Herkenrath, *Politik, Theologie und Erziehung. Untersuchungen zu Magdalene von Tilings Pädagogik* (Heidelberg: Quelle und Meyer, 1972); Gury Schneider-Ludorff, "Magdalene von Tiling (1877-1974) — Pädagogik und Geschlechterbeziehungen," in *Religionspädagoginnen des 20. Jahrhunderts,* ed. Annebelle Pithan (Göttingen: Vandenhoeck und Ruprecht, 1997), pp. 20-39.

closely linked to that of Friedrich Gogarten and to the Neo-Lutheranism of the time. Her main interests concerned the education of girls and the relationship between the sexes. Her many writings include influential publications on the Christian philosophy of education, on educational approaches for different age levels, and on religious education in the sense of evangelical instruction.

Von Tiling's *Foundations of Educational Thinking (Grundlagen pädagogischen Denkens)*, published in 1932, is her major theoretical statement.[59] It shows how German Neo-Lutheran theology was to be applied to education in general as well as to religious education in particular. Although the book's broad scope leads one to assume that von Tiling was intending to address a wide audience in general education, her style makes it clear that she is writing primarily for an audience that feels close to Neo-Lutheranism.

In the foreword, von Tiling emphasizes that she does not have a "system" to offer.[60] This is no coincidence. For her, the "consideration of reality" she is striving for does not allow for any system. Nevertheless, her intentions are surely systematic. She wants to determine anew the "basis and starting point" of educational thinking. The first step toward this goal is the identification of the parent-child relationship as the most basic relationship for education. Consequently, education in school must be relativized. For her, there is a "law of the reality of human existence in the likeness of God," which she attempts to explain by examining the relationship between "lordship" and "service."[61]

All five parts of *Foundations of Educational Thinking* clearly show that theological anthropology should operate as the basis of general education and should provide the framework for all education. The first part focuses upon the "human person" while the next two parts offer an anthropological account of the "sexes" and of the relationship between "the adult and the child." The fourth part is on "education." Only the fifth and last part directly addresses the "question of education in the light of faith." This breakdown of the book is indicative of von Tiling's Lutheran theology. According to the teaching of the two kingdoms (as it was interpreted at that time), education wholly and fully belongs to the worldly realm. Consequently, it is the Law rather than the gospel that is to determine the shape of education. The distinction between Law and gospel is one of the foundations on which Luther's theology rests.[62] It means that we have to be aware of the fundamental difference between God's promises, for which Luther reserves the term "gospel,"

---

59. Magdalene von Tiling, *Grundlagen pädagogischen Denkens* (Stuttgart: Steinkopf, 1932).

60. Von Tiling, *Grundlagen*, p. 5.

61. Von Tiling, *Grundlagen*, p. 6.

62. One of the best introductions is still Gerhard Ebeling, *Luther: Einführung in sein Denken* (Tübingen: Mohr, 1964).

and God's demands, which in Luther's terminology is the Law. The Law is theologically important in that it shows humans their sinful nature. They break the Law rather than obeying it, which is why their justification can come only from God, through the gospel. But the Law also has a political function in that it gives order to the world — for example, in the shape of the Ten Commandments. From a different perspective, Luther can say that God is active against the evil in the world in a twofold manner or with two kingdoms. One of these kingdoms works through the gospel on the side of faith; the other, through the Law, which establishes peace, justice, and order. Peace, justice, and order are not dependent on faith but are accessible to human reason, and education is viewed as necessary for their establishment. Or, to put it differently, education is an issue of human reason, not of faith. Since human beings are sinful, they cannot be educated according to the gospel, which, in turn, must be proclaimed to them but may not be used as a guideline for the aims and methods of education.

Education as a "worldly affair" is a phrase that is often used in Neo-Lutheran writings on education.[63] As may be seen in von Tiling's book, this does not mean that theology is not of importance for general education. There are at least two decisive ways in which theological thinking shapes her understanding of education, both of which are connected with her use of the term "reality." The first way she refers to "reality" in education is a way of insisting upon a new realism, a realism that makes a thorough critique of all the idealism that she perceives in the approaches to education and religious education since the nineteenth century. The second way she uses the term "reality" is to indicate clearly the reality of God's creation. For her, reality means order — the different types of order that are given for human life in accordance with God's will for creation.

The foundations of von Tiling's educational thinking in this book, thus, are a critique of educational idealism and a rendering of the order of creation. This order applies to the human person in general but also to the sexes and to the relationship between adults and children. In her view, the family is understood as a "basic order" through which parents and children belong to each other in authority and obedience.[64] Von Tiling compares the authority of the parents to the authority of God: The parents are to give "order and law" to the life of the child.[65]

---

63. This phrase actually goes back to Martin Luther, but it did not play a central role for him.

64. Von Tiling, *Grundlagen*, p. 101.

65. Von Tiling, *Grundlagen*, p. 105.

The understanding of education that is offered by von Tiling is strongly influenced by her understanding of the order of creation. This order determines what the child should be, and education that is realistic, according to von Tiling's use of the term, must help the child to live according to this order. The God-given nature of this order, which von Tiling and other Neo-Lutheran educators and theologians favored so much, sometimes makes this type of educational thinking appear authoritarian. To some degree this critical assessment holds true. There is not much emphasis on individual autonomy in general or on the autonomous development of the child. It should not be overlooked, however, that in spite of her rejection of the way in which the earlier religious education reform movement used child psychology, von Tiling is remarkably sensitive to the developmental stages of childhood and adolescence. In her chapter on education she relies heavily on a developmental framework to describe the aims and methods of education — an approach that becomes even more central in her later publications.[66]

The last part of *Foundations of Educational Thinking* considers education from the perspective of faith. Here von Tiling acknowledges that her anthropology is not neutral but is based on the Christian faith. And according to this faith, the intended order of creation for human beings is not fulfilled. It is disturbed by human resistance to it. This view once more distinguishes von Tiling's realism from an educational idealism that hopes for the self-perfection and divinization of the human person.[67] Moreover, seeing the human person as sinful and as up against God's order also defines the task of the church. Von Tiling argues that the church fulfills God's will by preaching the divine Law and by confronting humans with their violation of God's will. Lutheran theology describes this process by insisting that preaching the Law is the necessary precondition for preaching the gospel. As von Tiling puts it, this is so "Because the Gospel is only accepted by that human being who, in view of his reality, is judged by his own conscience."[68]

The final section of the last part of the book outlines the "meaning of proclamation in education" with a condensed summary of von Tiling's views of religious education in terms of proclamation. All proclamation, she says, is based on preaching Law and gospel. In this sense, there is no difference between proclamation for adults and for children. Yet von Tiling also points out that the reality of the child's life is different from the reality of adult life. The

---

66. Especially Magdalene von Tiling, *Wir und unsere Kinder. Eine Pädagogik der Altersstufen für evangelische Erzieher in Familie, Heim und Schule* (Stuttgart: Steinkopf, 1955).

67. Von Tiling, *Grundlagen,* p. 204.

68. Von Tiling, *Grundlagen,* p. 211.

child's life is always intertwined with the life of the parents. Until the first school years, the child's relationship to God does not go beyond the child's relationship to the parents. Before that time, the relationship to the parents defines the relationship to God. It is not before adolescence and adulthood that the question "Do you believe?" may receive an answer that truly goes beyond the faith of childhood.

It is worth noting that von Tiling's approach to education in the name of a new realism is exclusively based on theology and that she is convinced that theories derived from psychology, from other social sciences, or from the philosophy of general education should no longer play any decisive role in determining Christian thinking on education. This is clearly one of the main differences between evangelical instruction and the earlier reform movement in Germany and in the United States. At the same time, von Tiling's publications clearly show the continuing interest in questions of general education, sometimes to the degree that her interest in religious education, even in the sense of evangelical instruction, appears rather limited. This limitation corresponds with her deep conviction that the Christian faith is the aim of proclamation and that it can "never be the aim of education."[69] Education is a "worldly matter."

Von Tiling's approach is not the only type of evangelical instruction. In later years, especially after World War II, others like Helmuth Kittel became much more influential. This is why we now turn to Kittel's understanding of religious education.

From Religious Education to Evangelical Instruction: Helmuth Kittel's Programmatic Statement

Having examined von Tiling's pre-war evangelical instruction, we are now ready to turn to the main period we are considering in this chapter, the time between 1945 and 1960, and look at the work of Helmuth Kittel. As will become clear later in this section, Kittel actively participated in the discussion on religious education in the 1930s, building upon the work of Magdalene von Tiling and others; yet his main influence clearly was later, during the time after 1945 and well into the 1960s and 1970s.[70]

---

69. Von Tiling, *Grundlagen*, p. 232.

70. For biographical information cf. Helmuth Kittel, "Helmuth Kittel," in *Religionspädagogik in Selbstdarstellungen,* vol. I, ed. Bernhard Albers (Aachen: Religionspädagogik heute, 1980), pp. 91-117; Johannes Lähnemann, "Helmuth Kittel (1902-1984)," in *Klassiker der Religions-*

Kittel was born in 1902. He studied theology in different places, especially in Berlin under Adolf Holl, the influential Lutheran theologian. Holl introduced Kittel to the theology that remained decisive for him all of his life. In the 1930s, after he had finished his theological dissertation, Kittel took a teaching position at a new teacher's college in Hamburg. Kittel's role during National Socialism is still under debate.[71] Contrary to earlier assumptions — and contrary to Kittel's own later self-descriptions — it has been established in recent historical research that Kittel was not opposed to National Socialism in any public way and that some of his publications from that time are strongly influenced by the language, images, and ideas of National Socialist politics and ideologies. Kittel's political tendencies were the reason why, at first, it was impossible for him to get a chair on a theological faculty after 1945. Instead, he became involved again in teacher training, especially in religious education. From 1954 to 1959 he was the president of a teacher's college in Osnabrück, finally becoming a professor of religious education on the theological faculty of the university of Münster in 1962. He died in 1984, after a long and successful career in religious education.

Kittel's 1947 monograph on evangelical instruction,[72] which is often quoted as a prime example of this approach to religious education, can be read from at least three different perspectives. The text is, most ostensibly, an educational treatise in which Kittel argues that religious education must change in fundamental ways — that it should become more expressly Christian. At the same time, the book reflects a turning point in Kittel's life. Due to his cooperation with National Socialism, Kittel had been denied a professorship in New Testament studies in Münster immediately prior to the publication of this book. Since *Evangelical Instruction* was his first major postwar publication, he could not escape addressing the question of his theological and political credibility. A third possible reading of this book places the question of Kittel's cooperation with National Socialism in the context of German history or, since most of this happened under the military government of the Allies, the context of international political history. We will focus on the primary, educational meaning of the text itself and refer to biographical, political, and historical matters as secondary concerns.

The title of Kittel's book — *From Religious Education to Evangelical Instruc-*

---

pädagogik, ed. Henning Schröer and Dietrich Zillessen (Frankfurt am Main: Moritz Diesterweg Verlag, 1989), pp. 250-66.

71. Folkert Rickers, *Zwischen Kreuz und Hakenkreuz*, pp. 37ff.; Lähnemann, "Helmuth Kittel (1902-1984)."

72. Helmuth Kittel, *Vom Religionsunterricht zur Evangelischen Unterweisung* (Wolfenbüttel: Wolfenbütteler Verlagsanstalt, 1947).

tion — indicates that he is writing a programmatic statement. Simply glancing through the book's contents page makes it clear that Kittel has shaped the volume in accordance with this program. The first part of the book contains a description of the "situation and task" of evangelical instruction, which begins with a rejection of the idea of "religious education." It continues with chapters on the content of evangelical instruction: the meaning and educational use of the Bible, the hymnal, and the catechism; church history; school worship services; and the question of sanctification. Almost half of the book's one hundred pages are devoted to selections from Martin Luther on theology, Holy Scripture, justification, the sacraments, and so on. The chapters on teaching methods and on school and church as the contexts of evangelical instruction are clearly of secondary importance. This structure of the book indicates Kittel's intention of basing the new evangelical instruction exclusively on theology, or rather, more specifically, on the theology of the Lutheran Reformation.

In the text itself, the focus on Luther's theology is widened in order to include "theological approaches . . . which we owe to a renewal, in our generation, to the ideas of the Danish thinker Søren Kierkegaard and the German reformer Martin Luther. Karl Barth and Friedrich Gogarten are the most important names which characterize this new evangelical theology."[73] The main thrust of the theological renewal as Kittel sees it is a rejection of the concept of religion implied in the term "religious education." Since the Enlightenment, the term "religion" had, under the influence of the philosophy, psychology, and the history of religion, evolved from a concrete term referring to Christianity into an abstract term, detached from Christianity, that denotes all religions. According to Kittel, the religious education reform movement had viewed the nurturing of a "general religious consciousness" and of a "religious-moral personality" as the prime tasks of religious education, in contrast to introducing children and youth to the Christian faith. Against this background, Kittel formulates his first critical summary of his own position:

> Evangelical Instruction — this is the name of the new task that is set before us — never again religious education. We now know that all instruction beyond the confessions will in truth be less than confessional, all instruction beyond Christianity less than Christian. "Religion in general" has been found out as without content — in spite of its many feelings and words. Determinedly we turn to the tasks that are set before us since the Gospel of Jesus Christ has again become the word of God to us.[74]

73. Kittel, *Vom Religionsunterricht,* p. 6.
74. Kittel, *Vom Religionsunterricht,* p. 8.

This statement of Kittel's is not only a summary of the new task but is also indicative of Kittel's rhetoric. His style breathes authority — the authority not of an academic writer who masters empirical or theoretical evidence on which his argument is based, but of the preacher and, more specifically, of that preacher who wants to proclaim the word of God as God's revelation.[75] It is the gospel itself that is to be the very center of this approach. "Prayer for the gift of God's Spirit" is the starting point. The Bible is expected to speak to the individual person, not religiously or morally, but strictly as the "revelation of the holy."[76] Hymns and the use of the catechism are to support this kind of instruction.

Is there any room for the ideas of modern education in this "evangelical instruction"? The chapter on methods entails an answer to this question. For Kittel, what is most crucial is the inner attitude of the teacher who wants the "word of God to be heard in Holy Scripture." Consequently, "all problems of method" are "secondary."[77] There is no "Christian or evangelical method," so all educational methods may be used. But all methods have to conform to the content of evangelical instruction; they are never to be allowed to dominate the content.

It is also of interest here to consider the chapter on the relationship between "Evangelical Instruction and the other subjects" in school.[78] Like von Tiling, Kittel bases his argument on the Lutheran teaching of the two kingdoms or reigns — the understanding explained above that God governs the world in a twofold manner, through the proclamation of his word and will (spiritual reign) and through the political order based on human reason (worldly reign). From the perspective of the two kingdoms or reigns, evangelical instruction has the task of proclamation while the other school subjects are to be strictly worldly. The worldly character of those subjects is actually to be guaranteed by the presence of evangelical instruction, which watches over them so that they may not become ideologized or become expressions of a certain worldview *(Weltanschauung)*.

In summary, Kittel's 1947 monograph has a dual purpose. It is, first of all, a programmatic statement intended to both summarize and establish the model of evangelical instruction as the replacement of the theory and praxis of the religious education reform movement prior to the 1930s. It is, second, an attempt to support teachers in giving a new shape to their religious in-

75. From a later point of view, Kittel's style has been characterized as "authoritarian"; see Rickers, *Zwischen Kreuz und Hakenkreuz*, pp. 60ff.

76. Kittel, *Vom Religionsunterricht*, p. 9.

77. Kittel, *Vom Religionsunterricht*, p. 20.

78. Kittel, *Vom Religionsunterricht*, pp. 22ff.

struction, a shape that is in strict accord with a theology of revelation and the word of God.

Today's readers may mistakenly assume that, with this dual purpose, Kittel was addressing religion teachers alone. On the contrary, he was speaking primarily to the teachers of the non–college-bound lower track of schooling, which at that time comprised approximately 90 percent of the students. The teachers in this type of school had not been trained to teach only one subject; they had to teach all subjects. Religion classes were either Protestant or Catholic, and the teacher had (and still has) to belong to the same denomination as her or his students. So a teacher taught religion to the students who were in the same denomination as the teacher. Kittel, thus, was not writing just for teachers who taught religion alone, because there were no specialized religion teachers in this type of school. He was writing for all Protestant teachers. Nevertheless, in this book Kittel speaks to them only with respect to their religion classes and not about their work in general. Only some years later, in 1951, did he publish a book on the *Educator as a Christian* that clearly addresses the whole person and professional life of teachers beyond religious instruction.[79]

The exclusive focus on religious education seen in Kittel's programmatic statement on evangelical instruction is not necessarily typical of religious education theory or of theological approaches to education at this time. Two examples of a broader focus are Kittel's own book on the educator, mentioned above, and the work of Kittel's colleague Oskar Hammelsbeck, who addresses a general public even more clearly from the outset. In this respect, Hammelsbeck's interest in general education stands in continuity with the work of Magdalene von Tiling.

On Weal and Woe in Public Life: Oskar Hammelsbeck

Oskar Hammelsbeck was another highly influential postwar Protestant educator. His influence was closely related to his biography and to the political stance that he took during the time of National Socialism. He was the central catechetical figure in the Confessing Church, which opposed Hitler. In addition, his *The Instruction of the Church*, published in 1939, was one of the foundational documents for the type of church-based Christian instruction organized in response to the Hitler state's ideological and indoctrinary takeover of the state school and to the suppression and marginalization of religion classes

---

79. Helmuth Kittel, *Der Erzieher als Christ* (Göttingen: Vandenhoeck und Ruprecht, 1951).

in this setting.[80] This explains why, after 1945, Hammelsbeck was in a position to address the German public with the authority and legitimacy of not having been compromised by his actions before 1945.

Hammelsbeck was born in 1899.[81] The first thirty years of his life did not bring him into contact with religious education or theology. He studied history, the social sciences, and philosophy at Heidelberg. After his studies, he became involved in the new movement of adult education and founded his own institute of adult education in Saarbrücken. With the advent of National Socialism, Hammelsbeck was forced to give up his work in this field. For a while he worked as a schoolteacher, teaching, among other subjects, religion. In 1936, he accepted the offer to become the director of the catechetical seminary of the Confessing Church — a task that forced him into an illegal position when this kind of work was outlawed by the Hitler government. After the end of World War II, Hammelsbeck was offered a chair in practical theology in Göttingen, but he preferred to become the president of a teacher's college in Wuppertal, where he also taught catechetics at the seminary nearby. He retired in 1964 and died in 1975.

In 1946 Hammelsbeck edited three small books which contain his own and others' work. Their titles indicate the broad scope of his concerns: *The Cultural and Political Responsibility of the Church; Church, School, Teachers: Lectures on the Reconstruction of the German School in the Christian Spirit;* and *On Weal and Woe in Public Life.*[82] All three books address questions that go well beyond religious education, such as public life, politics, and the task of political parties as seen from a Christian point of view. It is in light of these concerns that he addresses questions of schooling and education in general.

The book on which we will now focus, *On Weal and Woe in Public Life,* is only fifty pages long. Its main chapter is an "Address to the Chairmen of the Political Parties in Germany" — an address which, because of the political situation, he never actually delivered. From today's perspective, this situation and the need for an address on democratic politics or communication may

---

80. Oskar Hammelsbeck, *Der kirchliche Unterricht. Aufgabe — Umfang — Einheit* (München: Kaiser, 1939).

81. For biographical information cf. Gottfried Adam, "Oskar Hammelsbeck (1899-1975)," in *Klassiker,* ed. Schröer and Zillessen, pp. 236-49; bibliography in Bernhard Albers, *Lehrerbild und Lehrerbildung. Eine historisch-systematische Untersuchung zum Werk Oskar Hammelsbecks* (Aachen: Rimbaud, 1988), pp. 108ff.

82. Oskar Hammelsbeck: *Die kulturpolitische Verantwortung der Kirche* (München: Kaiser, 1946); *Kirche — Schule — Lehrerschaft. Vorträge zum Wiederaufbau der deutschen Schule im christlichen Geiste* (Gütersloh: Bertelsmann, 1946); *Um Heil oder Unheil im öffentlichen Leben* (München: Kaiser, 1946).

look absurd, but we have to keep in mind that Germany had a lot to learn in order to become a democratic country. Open communication was a new and challenging experience for the political parties after 1945, which is why Hammelsbeck was unable to deliver this address. The politicians had refused to accept the church's invitation to a conference because, according to their understanding, the presence of the other political parties made open dialogue impossible.[83] Hammelsbeck then chose to publish his statement and make his address available at least to those who were willing to read it.

Hammelsbeck's purpose in writing this lecture was to help the political parties in Germany "become conscious of the political responsibility of the church."[84] They should, he argues, respect the "willingness of the Protestant church to be involved with the public." Obviously, this message is addressed to the German people in general and to their politicians in particular. At the same time, it should be noted that Hammelsbeck was writing out of his involvement in the Confessing Church and that his message was addressed to those groups within the church that wanted to stay out of politics and that aimed at a clear separation between the church and political life. So Hammelsbeck's address must also be read as a plea for a politically active church.

Hammelsbeck sees the special reason for his convictions in the unprecedented situation in which he speaks and writes. After 1945, the question of the "guilt" of the German nation was a pressing concern for Hammelsbeck, and, in solidarity with the German people who shared this guilt, the church also was to be aware of what it failed to do during National Socialism. At the same time, Hammelsbeck's views and explanations remain fairly abstract and are not focused on National Socialism. For him — and in this respect he is very close to Kittel — the real reasons for what happened during National Socialism have to be seen in the developments of the nineteenth century — in other words, in how "Reformation theology was given up during the Enlightenment and was overrun by the philosophy of idealism."[85] In effect, religion had come to be seen as a purely private matter. It was against philosophical idealism's transformation of theology that, according to Hammelsbeck, the theological renewal since the 1920s and 1930s was directed. Now, after 1945, everything depended on if and how the consequences of this renewal were realized, on whether a critical view of idealism was accepted and on whether religion was given back its public role. It is in this sense that Hammelsbeck maintains his understanding of the relationship between church and politics. The deci-

---

83. Hammelsbeck, *Um Heil oder Unheil*, p. 5.
84. Hammelsbeck, *Um Heil oder Unheil*, p. 9.
85. Hammelsbeck, *Um Heil oder Unheil*, p. 12.

sion over "weal and woe in the public life of the German future may depend" on the question of whether or not the "political powers" become aware of the "special historical opportunity which is given through the church's responsibility in politics."[86]

Hammelsbeck's message to the "political powers" certainly sounds surprising. In what ways does he think the future of the German people and public life depend on the church? Hammelsbeck is very clear that he is quite opposed to any attempt to allow the church to dominate politics. The church should neither rival the political parties in order to gain influence nor strive for "Christian politics" in the sense of blending the Christian faith with a particular political program or political party. The church is not "of this world" and must not give up its special character by claiming political power.[87] Hammelsbeck is highly critical of all attempts to base politics on a worldview, or *weltanschauung*, even if it is a Christian one. For him, the combination of politics and worldviews produces a dangerous "totalizing tendency." Moreover, the commonweal gets lost in the conflict between different worldviews. Consequently, the critique of any amalgamation of politics and worldview is to be the core message of the church — "to the Marxists and to the liberals, to the conservatives and to the religious." Then follows what may be called the center of Hammelsbeck's address: "The detoxification of the sphere of politics and worldviews is only possible in Christian freedom."[88] In other words, Christian faith liberates politics from having to cling to a worldview with its woeful consequences. This understanding presupposes that the Christian faith is not a worldview — a presupposition that has been contested at other times. For many German theologians after 1945, however, it seemed natural and necessary to insist on the distinct nature of the Christian faith, which makes it different from all philosophical and political worldviews.

In sum, "Christian renewal" is Hammelsbeck's answer to the question of how the German nation might become once again healthy.[89] This does not mean that he expected everyone to become a deeply convinced Christian. As we have seen from his writings, Hammelsbeck was much too realistic to harbor this kind of expectation for postwar Germany. But for Hammelsbeck, the "Christian renewal" of Germany does mean that the Ten Commandments are to be acknowledged as the basis of the common life. Not everyone in Ger-

---

86. Hammelsbeck, *Um Heil oder Unheil*, pp. 15f.
87. Hammelsbeck, *Um Heil oder Unheil*, pp. 16f.
88. Hammelsbeck, *Um Heil oder Unheil*, p. 19.
89. Hammelsbeck, *Um Heil oder Unheil*, p. 22.

many should be expected to base their behavior on the Sermon on the Mount, but they should be expected to accept these Commandments as the basis of the commonweal and law. This includes the political parties, which are to "watch over the respect for the Ten Commandments in our people."[90]

In short, this is Hammelsbeck's main argument, which is also his foundation for the reconstruction of general education and schooling in Germany. The church's proclamation is to free politics — and to liberate the people — from the undue influence of totalizing worldviews that make life together impossible. In this sense, the "weal and woe" of public life depend on the Christian church. In addition to this, the Ten Commandments are seen as a basis for living together peacefully and responsibly, not in a Christian society — which Hammelsbeck does not consider a realistic possibility — but with respect for the Creator as well as for each other.

Evangelical Instruction in Context

Before we look at Christian education in Germany during the period of evangelical instruction in light of international processes like social modernization, it is important to remember the uniqueness of Germany's historical situation in this prewar-postwar period — and the limits of any generalizing concept of modernization. We need to remain aware of the concreteness of history. Having affirmed this point, however, it is obvious that some of the events and developments mentioned in the parallel section on the United States also shaped the general situation in Germany. The 1929 crash of the United States stock market strongly affected Germany's economy and thus its politics; the ensuing economic depression was one of the most important reasons for the rise of National Socialism in Germany. After Hitler came to power in 1933, the church experienced increasing pressure from the National Socialist government's attempts to minimize the influence of the church whenever this influence was not in support of the government. As mentioned earlier, the church was divided into several different camps.[91] First, there were those who hoped to be able to maintain the church by avoiding open conflict with the state. Second, there was the Confessing Church, which, in part, played the role of an illegal opposition. And third, a substantial number of church members turned to National Socialism — seeking to blend it with the Christian faith or even transforming the Christian faith itself into a national-

---

90. Hammelsbeck, *Um Heil oder Unheil*, pp. 24f.
91. For an introduction cf. Nowak, *Geschichte des Christentums in Deutschland*, pp. 243ff.

ist worldview ("German faith"). While the government never succeeded in excluding religious education from the school curriculum altogether, National Socialism did continuously attempt to limit the church's influence on this school subject and to make teachers adapt their instruction to the ideologies of National Socialism.[92]

All this must be kept in mind when the situation after 1945 is addressed. The political, cultural, educational, and religious dimensions of postwar life need to be counted among the most important parameters of German religious education during the whole period between 1945 and 1960. It must also be realized, however, that the general development of West Germany during the 1950s and 1960s clearly followed the pattern of further industrialization and economic growth. For example, the per capita income in Germany more than doubled between 1950 and 1960.[93] Although this increase partly reflects postwar reconstruction, it should be noted that the per capita income in 1960 was more than three times higher than the per capita income in 1900, a trend that may be partially explained by social modernization theory.

The understanding that social modernization deeply influenced German Protestant religious education during this period finds support when we examine the origins of the evangelical instruction movement. As we have seen in this chapter, the approaches and positions that exerted a decisive influence after 1945 have their roots in the crisis experiences of the 1920s. They are related to the crisis of the cultural synthesis of Christianity and modernity that some German religious educators had developed before World War I. In Germany, the 1920s were a time of enormous political and cultural struggle. After the end of the German monarchy in 1918-1919, the new democracy needed to be established. This was a difficult process, which, as the rise of National Socialism shows, finally failed. The church faced a new situation of religious plurality. The separation of church and state mandated in 1918-1919 made it easy, for the first time in German history, to drop out of the church. And

92. Cf. Rickers, *Zwischen Kreuz und Hakenkreuz;* Friedhelm Kraft, *Religionsdidaktik zwischen Kreuz und Hakenkreuz. Versuche zur Bestimmung von Aufgaben, Zielen und Inhalten des evangelischen Religionsunterrichts, dargestellt an den Richtlinien und Entwürfen zwischen 1933 und 1939* (Berlin: de Gruyter, 1996); Müller-Rolli, ed., *Evangelische Schulpolitik in Deutschland.*

93. Cf. Heinz-Elmar Tenorth, *Geschichte der Erziehung. Einführung in die Grundzüge ihrer neuzeitlichen Entwicklung* (Weinheim: Juventa, 1988); Christoph Führ and Carl-Ludwig Furck, eds., *Handbuch der deutschen Bildungsgeschichte,* vol. 6: *1945 bis zur Gegenwart. Teilband 1* (München: Beck, 1997); Helmut Fend, *Sozialgeschichte des Aufwachsens. Bedingungen des Aufwachsens und Jugendgestalten im 20. Jahrhundert* (Frankfurt am Main: Suhrkamp, 1988); Max-Planck-Institut für Bildungsforschung [Max Planck Institute for Human Development], ed., *Bildung in der Bundesrepublik Deutschland. Daten und Analysen,* vol. I: *Entwicklungen seit 1950* (Reinbek: Rowohlt, 1980).

many did so. Between 1918 and 1920, the number of dropouts multiplied from 8,724 to 313,995.[94]

In many ways, then, the development of evangelical instruction is closely related to Germany's political, social, and cultural crises between the 1920s and the 1950s. The aftermath of World War I brought the crises of the new German democracy and international economic catastrophe. Hitler's rise to power in 1933 was a crisis that ended democratic politics, and it caused a nonconformist Christian church. The postwar period brought the crises of setting up an educational system and of determining the role of the church in the new state. All these experiences of crisis were addressed by evangelical instruction even if the concept of "crisis" played a central role only in the beginnings of this movement.

The leading figures of the evangelical instruction movement saw the establishment, or the reestablishment, of a clear theological identity for religious education as their primary focus. What they actually wanted was the establishment of a particular theological identity — that of dialectical theology and of Neo-Lutheranism — as opposed to the theological liberalism of the religious education reform movement at the beginning of the century. According to von Tiling, Kittel, Hammelsbeck, and many others, the new theological identity of evangelical instruction was to stand in critical contrast to modernization, especially to modern philosophy. They wanted to counteract what they saw as the Enlightenment's reduction of Christian faith to a matter of personal inner feelings and moral motivations. They often identified modern philosophy with idealism, and they confronted this idealism with what von Tiling and others called the "new realism." They did not ask the question, "To what extent is this new theological identity a product of modernization?"[95] One of the evangelical instruction movement's basic tendencies, for example, was to dichotomize religion and culture and set them over against each other — a separation that seems to mirror the increased division be-

---

94. Andreas Feige, *Kirchenmitgliedschaft in der Bundesrepublik Deutschland. Zentrale Perspektiven empirischer Forschungsarbeit im problemgeschichtlichen Kontext der deutschen Religions- und Kirchensoziologie nach 1945* (Gütersloh: Gütersloher Verlagshaus, 1990), p. 132. For further background information see Dieter Langewiesche and Heinz-Elmar Tenorth, eds., *Handbuch der deutschen Bildungsgeschichte*, vol. 5: *1918-1945. Die Weimarer Republik und die nationalsozialistische Diktatur* (München: Beck, 1989).

95. For a general discussion of the relationship between dialectic theology and modernization see Trutz Rendtorff, *Theorie des Christentums. Historisch-theologische Studien zu seiner neuzeitlichen Verfassung* (Gütersloh: Gütersloher Verlagshaus, 1972); Trutz Rendtorff, ed., *Die Realisierung der Freiheit. Beiträge zur Kritik der Theologie Karl Barths* (Gütersloh: Gütersloher Verlagshaus, 1975).

tween religion and culture portrayed by modernization theory as part of the process of social differentiation. But this sort of modernization theory, based in the social sciences, was mostly unknown to the theorists of evangelical instruction and clearly was neglected by them. They were convinced that the social sciences were an aspect of modern culture and, as such, should not influence theology and the church.

In this context, the relationship between religious education and modern education theory, including sociological and psychological theories of education, should be mentioned. As we have seen, the theological renewal after 1945 (and even prior to this period) developed hand in hand with a critical withdrawal from the attempt to base religious education on modern educational and psychological theories. Evangelical instruction implies that it is the gospel and the Christian tradition that are to determine the content as well as the form of religious education. Other disciplines may, at best, play the role of subordinate "handmaidens" *(ancillae theologiae)*, not of partners in dialogue.[96] Yet this is not the whole picture. What is often overlooked is the openness of people like von Tiling, Kittel, and Hammelsbeck to the use of modern educational theory and practice, as long as these were utilized outside the field of religious education. In addressing questions of education and schooling in society, these figures advocate an important role for modern educational theory. In this sense, they were striving to connect the church and modern educational theory as partners wherever questions of general education — that did not involve religious education — were under discussion.

Another aspect of modernization these individuals (especially Hammelsbeck) addressed is the meaning of totalizing ideologies in modern society. Here they suggest that theology might have an important role to play in democracy by critically purifying political discourse from totalitarian claims. At the same time, it is clear that Kittel and Hammelsbeck do not envision pluralistic democracy as the ideal political future. Nowhere do we find an effort in their work to strengthen pluralism, nor do they seem to be aware of the social and religious plurality that existed both within and outside the church. The question of plurality does not enter the picture for them because they make no place for a thorough and realistic analysis of the social and cultural situation within their program. As a consequence, in creating its model of religious and general education, evangelical instruction theory assumes much

96. For an overview on the German discussion cf. Friedrich Schweitzer, "Practical Theology, Contemporary Culture, and Social Sciences: Interdisciplinary Relationships and the Unity of Practical Theology as a Discipline," in *Practical Theology: International Perspectives*, ed. Friedrich Schweitzer and Johannes A. van der Ven (Frankfurt am Main: Peter Lang, 1999), pp. 307-21.

more theological and cultural consensus than actually existed after 1945. Obviously, we have the hindsight of history to make this evaluation, an advantage that was not possible at the time.

Given the complexities of the historical changes related to the German *Kaiserreich,* the Weimar Republic, National Socialism, the postwar situation after 1945, the establishment of two German states in 1949, and the parallel yet different reconstruction in West Germany and in East Germany during the 1950s, it is easy to understand why we do not yet have a full understanding of how religious education theory and the changing social context interacted between 1945 and 1960 — or even between the 1920s and the 1950s. It has become clear, however, that the new approach of evangelical instruction, even if it was conceived by its proponents as being a purely theological approach, was in fact a response to modernization and to the crises modernization produced during this period. Evangelical instruction addressed these crises and was successful in speaking to many religious educators at that time. If this movement was not successful in the long run this may be due, in large measure, to its refusal to make use of nontheological interpretations of the situation. Evangelical instruction was never able to base its theory and practice on a realistic picture of the social and cultural situation. During the 1950s and 1960s, Germans proved to be increasingly unreceptive to the social and cultural disconnectedness of this kind of theological and educational thinking.

Comparative Aspects

The first two sections of this chapter, which describe the development of religious education in Germany and in the United States during the period from 1945 to 1960, again reveal several striking similarities and parallels. We take this as further support for our thesis about the importance of international comparative perspectives on religious education. Obviously, what we see in these similarities and parallels has to do not simply with the national histories of these two countries but also with international phenomena. At the same time, these commonalities must be seen against the backdrop of important historical and cultural differences that distinguish the two countries. The countries' respective experiences of World War II, for example, were very different. The continuing role of religious education in German state-supported schools, likewise, has no parallel in the United States. Even when these differences are taken into account, however, certain similarities are apparent. Viewing them through the lens of modernization and globalization theories provides insight into common institutional and social changes that were taking place in both countries. No claim is made here that these theories "explain" the ideas of the individuals we discussed in any reductive sense. Rather, they point to social processes to which these figures were responsive, processes that obviously were mediated through the different historical experiences of each country. As will become clear, the concept of modernization adds an important dimension to our understanding of parallel calls for theological renewal in religious education in both Germany and the United States.

As far as international contacts and cooperation are concerned, the first point to be made is that the initial steps taken in the first decades of the twentieth century toward the internationalization of religious education and practical theology did not continue. In the 1920s, the "turn" taking place in theology did not focus its attention primarily on ecumenical or international topics. From the 1930s through 1945, National Socialism in Germany and, then, the war itself discouraged and in part outlawed international cooperation. Even after 1945, there was no real international awareness in religious education, much less German-American cooperation. Nevertheless, it should not be forgotten that there was a great deal of American influence in postwar Germany through the Allies' various efforts to re-educate the Germans. In addition, a number of people (including Hammelsbeck) traveled to the United States and visited churches there. Such visits also entailed coming into contact with colleagues in the field of religious education. Smart, likewise, studied in Europe. There were several conferences of the World Council of Christian Education during this period, and in 1957 the World Council of Churches produced a statement concerning the essential importance of education for the future of *ecumene*. It would certainly be worthwhile to study these ecumenical developments in detail — a task that has not yet been undertaken, to our knowledge.[97]

While the various publications in religious education during this period do not reveal much international awareness, they nevertheless all draw on a common pool of ideas in German dialectical theology and, to some degree, in the new Christian realism, which represents a somewhat different theological tradition in the United States. The degree of theological consensus among von Tiling, Smart, Sherrill, Hammelsbeck, and Kittel is noteworthy. Their theologies share a common interest in the recovery of themes from the Reformation as these were being recast by contemporary theologians in Germany and in the United States. They are all committed to a theological renewal of religious education, which, again in both countries, leads to a new terminol-

---

97. For a beginning cf. Ulrich Becker, "The History of Education in the World Council of Churches: A Brief Survey," *Education Newsletter. Unit II, WCC* no. 2 (1998): 3-5.

ogy that is to reflect this new theological identity: "Christian education" and "evangelical instruction." Given the considerable overlap in the theological sources that were prominent on each side of the Atlantic, it is interesting to note that the term "Christian education," so important in the United States, is explicitly rejected by religious educators like Hammelsbeck. He believed it would ideologize education in ways that were similar to the creation of a "Marxist" or "Socialist" education.

Obviously, theological texts and intellectual trends have always flowed across geographical boundaries. What is remarkable about this period is the speed and pervasiveness of this exchange of ideas across the Atlantic, an indicator of processes associated with both modernization and early forms of globalization: (1) advances in the speed of publication, translation, and dissemination of texts, (2) expansion of international travel and trade, and (3) increase in transnational academic exchange. Even if National Socialism and World War II put a damper on the exchange of students, professors, and lecturers, the overall pattern continued. The very fact that Hammelsbeck and Kittel, on one side of the Atlantic, and Smart and Sherrill, on the other — working in isolation from one another — are influenced by the same, relatively recent set of intellectual sources is striking. Of course, international exchange and influences were not new in the 1920s or 1940s. But the fast pace of the international reception of European theology in these years shows the acceleration and intensification of these processes. The transnational, theological consensus among the figures examined in this section, thus, can be viewed as an early result of the increasingly rapid and widespread exchange of ideas across national boundaries — what globalization theory today describes as "global cultural flows."[98]

A common theme in the figures we have examined in this section is the note of crisis in their writings. Here, historical differences are immediately evident. In Germany, for example, this note of crisis is largely cast in terms of the devastating experience of the two world wars and their shattering consequences for German society and culture. In addition, after 1945, the German church had to deal with its former relationship to National Socialism. Hammelsbeck featured the issue of "German guilt" prominently in *On Weal and Woe in Public Life* and raised the issue of the church's failure to resist the totalitarian tendencies of Nazism. In the United States, Sherrill introduced this note of crisis in more general terms, describing it in *The Gift of Power* as the crisis of modern life. In spite of these kinds of differences, however, all of

---

98. Robert Schreiter, *The New Catholicity: Theology Between the Global and the Local* (Maryknoll, N.Y.: Orbis, 1997).

the figures examined in this section appear to be responding at some level to a common set of issues: (1) a sense that the early promise of modernity had failed in the face of two world wars, global economic depression, the spread of nuclear arms, and various totalitarian threats to democracy, and (2) a sense that the church and religious education had been over-accommodating to modernity, both culturally and intellectually, and needed to recover their own theological identity.

Both of these issues are intertwined in the critique of liberalism, featured prominently in the writings of all the figures examined in this chapter as well as in the writings of many of their contemporaries. Liberalism in its various forms is now perceived — not always very objectively — as the example par excellence of cultural modernity's optimistic overconfidence in the capacity of autonomous human reason to guide the processes of modernization toward the Enlightenment's ideals of liberty, equality, and fraternity. In reality, these figures argue, the various forces unleashed by modernization — from cruel wars and the Holocaust to the social-economic inequalities of industrialization to totalitarianism — are closer to a living nightmare than to the humanity "come of age" promised by liberalism. Theological liberalism, in particular, is subject to criticism. It is portrayed as the clearest example of the contemporary church's over-accommodation to cultural modernity — a view that certainly is also due to the need to find a new theological identity after the catastrophe of the two world wars.

This leads to a final theme found in all of the figures examined above: a deep and abiding affirmation of the church's theological identity. In somewhat different ways, all of them attempt to place the church's evangelical instruction, teaching ministry, or Christian education on a new foundation, described variously as Law and gospel, the word of God, or God's self-revelation. The church's teaching and education, they argue, is unique in kind. It cannot be reduced to or closely identified with education, socialization, or any other process that can be described in purely human terms. This is the practical implication, they argue, of the affirmation that the church finds its identity primarily in God's work of reconciliation in Jesus Christ and the continuing activity of word and Spirit by which this community is constituted ever anew. It is here that the church finds the grounds of its identity and the source of its own distinctive type of teaching and education.

While all this may be said about the new type of religious education in both Germany and the United States, there also are important differences. One of the most important of these has to do with the relationship of religious education to general education. In the United States, a kind of loss of audience may be observed in that the representatives of the new Christian education are not addressing the general public and are not interested in the reconstruction of schooling and education in general. This is clearly not the case with regard to their German counterparts. In part, the interest of the German writers in the general public as an audience and in the general field of education is due to the German legal and political situation, with its much weaker separation of church and state. Nevertheless, this comparison makes it clear that it is not enough to look exclusively at the theological foundations of a given approach in religious education. Similar theological foundations may have very different institutional consequences, not only in different countries but even within the same country.

A similar point can also be made with regard to the relationship between religious education and modern theories of education. The clear distinction between the two found on the German side — with strong formulations like the "annihilation of the idea of education" through the gospel — is unparalleled in the United States. Also, the negligent attitude toward all questions of teaching method and toward an engagement of the resources of psychology and the social sciences generally is more extreme in German evangelical instruction than among representatives of Christian education in the United States, although James Smart reveals some tendencies in this direction.

As we reflect on religious education during this period from a contextual perspective, we must be aware that the main arguments characteristic of the figures examined above are theological arguments. It would be reductionistic to portray their understanding of education and the church as "nothing but" a reflexive response to modernization or globalization. It is fair to ask, however, two types of questions of this way of describing the church's identity: (1) How do these figures describe the relationship of the church and its education to the resources of modern culture? (2) In retrospect, can we discern ways that their theological rhetoric about the church's unique identity is shaped by social forces operative "behind their backs," that is, outside of their awareness?

In giving answer to the first of these questions, we are focusing on the constructive counterpart of these figures' theological critique of cultural modernity. If theological liberalism got it wrong, leading the church to an overaccommodation to modernity, then what is the alternative that von Tiling, Hammelsbeck, Kittel, Smart, and Sherrill propose? Once more, similarities and differences can be seen. Let us first point to certain similarities. As noted above, all five of these figures hold in common the belief that the teaching of the Christian community is unique because of its foundation in the activity of God. This leads them to portray theology as the only discipline adequate to the task of describing evangelical instruction or Christian education. For von

Tiling, Smart, Hammelsbeck, and Kittel, this has a further implication: a rejection of any straightforward reliance on the social sciences in Protestant religious education. No synthesis of theology and the resources of cultural modernity should take place. The social sciences have a role in their thinking only insofar as general education is concerned. The alternative, of course, would have been to pursue a full-blown program of cross-disciplinary dialogue in which theology plays a critical, even constitutive, role in its relationship to the social sciences. Of the figures examined in this chapter, Sherrill alone undertakes such a program in an explicit fashion. Even he, however, places theology in a privileged position in its dialogue with psychology, determining the answers to the questions it raises.

All five figures, thus, portray the church as finding its identity and as defining its educational ministry on theological grounds. At this point, however, real differences between these figures can be discerned. The two Americans focus on the congregation, describing the teaching ministry almost exclusively in terms of this setting. In contrast, von Tiling, Kittel, and Hammelsbeck have in mind a much wider audience and are addressing educators and teachers even within the state school. It would not occur to the Americans to think of offering Protestant religious education, explicitly based on the teaching and proclamation of the gospel, in state-supported education. Their audience is narrower than that of their German counterparts, and they work with a much stronger sense of the boundaries separating church and state.

This brings us to the second question raised above vis-à-vis these figures' preoccupation with the theological identity of the church: Can we discern ways that their rhetoric is shaped by social forces operative "behind their backs," that is, outside of their awareness? Here, we speak from the vantage point of fifty additional years of history. Looking back at this period, can we discern social conditions and trends that would lead von Tiling, Hammelsbeck, Kittel, Smart, and Sherrill to place so much emphasis on the church's theological identity? Modernization theory's understanding of institutional differentiation and social pluralism seem particularly helpful at this point. In both Germany and the United States, these forces gathered new momentum after World War II. The churches found themselves in a social context that appeared increasingly secularized, with important spheres of life like the state, the economy, the media, and the family operating outside the influence of the church. It may well be that the individuals examined in this section were all struggling to find a new foundation for the church in this context. Certainly, viewing them from this perspective throws light on their various attempts to define the church's identity over against modern culture.[99] If the culture is no longer ostensibly Protestant or even Christian, then where does the church find the resources by which to determine its identity and mission?

Again at this point, we have to keep in mind the differences between the United States and Germany. While the new theological approach to religious education in the 1920s and 1930s was somewhat "countercultural" in both countries, the German situation after 1945 allowed Kittel and Hammelsbeck to have a much more dominant influence than Smart and Sherrill had in the United States. After the breakdown of National Socialism, there was a strong drift toward the church. Due to the prevailing views of the time, the representatives of the Confessing Church enjoyed a great deal of political and theological respect, which afforded them great influence. Looking back at religious education in postwar Germany, however, from today's point of view, it probably was less the emphasis on theology and on theological identity that made figures like Kittel and Hammelsbeck attractive to a wider audience and more that their insistence on a clear theological identity fit very well with the political needs of a society and state under reconstruction. Most Germans needed to find a new basis for their lives, one that had to be different from National Socialism. The new German government, also, was looking for support for its future. The ostensibly Christian character of the evangelical instruction movement certainly looked promising to both — a government searching for legitimization and individuals who wanted to escape the past. So in this sense, evangelical instruction may be said to have served political and cultural functions that were not explicitly addressed in its program and could also not be admitted by politicians or by former adherents of National Socialism.

While the situation in the United States was certainly quite different than that of Germany during this period, it is interesting to note that the proposals of those Christian educators most influenced by Barth, Tillich, and the Niebuhr brothers flourished in the conservative ethos of postwar America, a period in which the Cold War began to take shape, McCarthyism emerged, and Dwight Eisenhower was president. Such proposals seemed to capture nicely the chastened but confident mood of the time. Here too, thus, certain contextual factors seem to have influenced the role these theories played in American Protestantism, even if the factors were largely not taken into account by the theories themselves. Here, Sherrill remains the exception that proves the rule.

---

99. For a discussion of the theology of this period in relation to these kinds of issues, see David Tracy, *Blessed Rage for Order: The New Pluralism in Theology* (New York: Seabury, 1975), and Rendtorff, *Theorie des Christentums*.

It is important to note that the full implications of social modernization are not yet evident in the forties and fifties. The kind of social plurality and secularization that will further "disestablish" Protestantism in both countries during the sixties has not emerged. On the surface, Protestantism appears to continue as a major cultural force in both Germany and the United States. The church's important role in the social reconstruction of postwar Germany and its rapid growth in the suburbs in the United States prevent the individuals examined in this section from coming to terms with the kind of plurality that will emerge full-force in only a few years. There is little reflection in the writings of these figures on the church's role in a culturally diverse, secular public life or on the theological and ethical foundations of this sort of national community. Hammelsbeck describes the church's role as the ongoing critique of totalitarian ideologies in this sphere, a theme that is mirrored in Smart's criticism of American civil religion. But he goes no further than commending the Ten Commandments as the ethical basis of public life in Germany. As limited as this treatment might be, it is more than is found in either Smart or Sherrill. Institutional differentiation and social pluralism will proceed in both countries, but they will do so largely outside the awareness of the figures examined here.

At the end of Chapter 3, our first comparative chapter, we stated a number of issues that arise from our comparative work, issues that standard accounts of the religious education movements in the United States and Germany do not raise. Similarly, in concluding the present chapter, we want to point to a number of critical issues that may be of interest for future work.

First, it must be noted that similar or even identical backgrounds in theology do not always have the same consequences for religious education. The similarities between the theological foundations introduced in Germany and the United States during the period examined in this chapter are striking, yet the differences between the understandings of religious education are also very visible, especially with respect to the methods of education and to the relationship of religious education to the philosophy of general education. Consequently, the relationship between a certain type of theology and a certain type of religious education appears to be much more flexible than is commonly assumed.

Second, this flexibility implies that there may be space for alternative combinations of theology and religious education, combinations that are different from those that have already been realized in history. This leads to a closely related question. Is the relationship between different theologies and different theories of religious education fully *contingent* or are there *limits* to the ways they might be combined, speaking systematically? In any case, there is a need to re-examine the possible and actual relationship between theology and education beyond the historical givens.

Third, since social, political, and ecclesial contexts play such important roles in how theology and education do and do not come together in Germany and in the United States during this period, it is necessary to go beyond a bipolar way of thinking about the relationship between education and theology. A more realistic picture presupposes that more than these two factors (theology and education) need to be taken into account. Indeed, there are always at least *three* factors in play — context, theology, and education. Consequently, the new emphasis on the theological (theology vs. education) character of religious education, championed so strongly during this period, can no longer be taken at face value. Today, it is not adequate to simply accept the question these individuals posed, "How can religious education become more theological?" In hindsight, it is apparent that, at least in part, these individuals' emphasis on the renewal of theological identity in religious education was responsive to certain contextual factors. Today, thus, we must think in terms of the interplay of theology, education, and context, an insight that informs not only our reconstruction of the history of religious education but also our own constructive proposals.

5 Beyond Modernity? Protestant Religious Education after the 1960s

Diversity and Ecumenicity: Protestant Religious Education in the United States

Historians and sociologists generally portray the 1960s as a watershed in American society. It was not only a time of political and cultural turmoil but also one of transformation of long-standing institutional patterns of work, family life, education, and the state. Together, these forces would alter the religious landscape of American life in dramatic fashion, leading to what some have called the third disestablishment of American Protestantism.[1] While Protestantism was legally disestablished by the framers of the American constitution, the white Anglo-Saxon Protestant culture of mainline Protestantism dominated American religion and society throughout the nineteenth century and into the early decades of the twentieth. As we have seen, the second disestablishment took place during the 1920s and 30s following World War I, as Protestant cultural hegemony gave way to a more pluralistic religious culture including Roman Catholicism and Judaism. As late as 1955, Will Herberg could describe American religion in terms of the tripartite scheme of *Protestant, Catholic, Jew,* the title of his influential book on American religion.[2] He went so far as to write, "Not to be — that is, not to be a Protestant, a Catholic, or a Jew — is somehow not to be an American. It may imply being foreign, as is the case when one professes oneself a Buddhist, a Muslim, or

---

1. Wade Clark Roof and William McKinney, *American Mainline Religion: Its Changing Shape and Future* (New Brunswick, N.J.: Rutgers University Press, 1987), pp. 33-39.
2. Will Herberg, *Protestant, Catholic, Jew* (Garden City, N.Y.: Doubleday Anchor, 1955).

anything but a Protestant, Catholic or Jew, even when one's Americanness is beyond question."[3] Only a decade later this assessment would seem hopelessly out of date, with the expanded presence of Eastern-based religions like Hare Krishna and Meher Baba and various expressions of the human potential movement like est (Erhard Seminars Training) and transcendental meditation. The religious landscape changed dramatically during the 1960s. As Robert Wuthnow aptly puts it, "It was as if the bits of mosaic that had given shape to the religious topography had been thrown into the air, never to land in exactly the same positions as before."[4]

One of the most important effects of these changes on Protestant religious education was the appearance of much greater diversity in the field. If neo-orthodoxy and Christian realism dominated the previous period, no single theological paradigm would do so after the 1960s. It is no accident that virtually every book attempting to provide an overview of religious education in the decades following the 1960s was forced to rely on the language of models or approaches to chart the field.[5] Moreover, a spirit of ecumenicity permeated religious education, blurring sharp distinctions between denominations and religious traditions. Protestant religious educators learned much from Roman Catholics like Gabe Moran, Michael Warren, James Michael Lee, Maria Harris, Thomas Groome, Berard Marthaler, and Gloria Durka.[6] Conversely, Protestants like James Fowler, Ellis Nelson, Charles Foster, Mary Elizabeth Moore, John Westerhoff, Sara Little, James Loder, and Daniel Schipani influenced Catholic religious educators.[7] Four different trajectories of religious education can be identified during this period, each of which influenced religious educators across a variety of religious traditions and continues to exert an important influence on American religious education to the present. As we will see, the diversity and ecumenicity of this period reflect important aspects of modernization that were reshaping American religion during the final decades of the twentieth century.

One of the most important trajectories during this period was a developmental model of religious and moral education influenced by Lawrence Kohlberg, James Fowler, and Robert Kegan.[8] Drawing on the structural devel-

3. Herberg, *Protestant, Catholic, Jew,* pp. 257-58.

4. Robert Wuthnow, *The Restructuring of American Religion: Society and Faith Since World War II* (Princeton, N.J.: Princeton University Press, 1988), p. 152.

5. See, for example, Jack Seymour and Donald Miller, eds., *Contemporary Approaches to Christian Education* (Nashville: Abingdon, 1982).

6. See the bibliography for works by these individuals.

7. See the bibliography for works by these individuals.

8. See the bibliography for works by these individuals.

opmental approach to human cognition established by Jean Piaget, these individuals portrayed growth in moral reasoning and faithing (the verb form was commonly used) as passing through an invariant sequence of stages. Particularly important was this trajectory's distinction between the contents of a person's morality or faith and the cognitive operations by which these contents are structured. This provided a critical lens by which to examine the ways a given community supports or impedes growth toward higher stages, what Fowler would call its modal level of development.[9] Particularly important in this regard was the developmental norm of post-conventional moral and religious identity, the ability to accommodate a variety of moral and religious perspectives on the basis of higher-order principles. This understanding of post-conventionality, in its Kohlbergian form, would be taken up and reconstructed by the critical social theorist Jürgen Habermas. A somewhat different understanding of post-conventionality is found in Fowler's theory and informs his understanding of the public church. Kegan, likewise, has portrayed cognitive development in relation to his understanding of the challenges of postmodernity.[10]

A second trajectory is found in the faith enculturation models of Ellis Nelson and John Westerhoff. We will examine in some detail Westerhoff's *Will Our Children Have Faith?* as representative of this understanding of religious education. Ellis Nelson first articulated this trajectory in *Where Faith Begins,* drawing on the insights of anthropology to describe the ways the cultures of religious communities shape the identities, values, and perceptions of their members.[11] His discussion of revelation and his portrayal of the church as a community of interpretation show lines of continuity with the theological renewal of the previous period. This approach anticipated the increased interest in congregational studies emerging during the 1980s and, more generally, the accent on the distinctive identity and practices of religious communities found in the writings of communitarians like Alasdair MacIntyre and Stanley Hauerwas.[12] More than Nelson, Westerhoff would describe the church as a

9. James Fowler, *Stages of Faith: The Psychology of Human Development and the Quest for Meaning* (San Francisco: Harper and Row, 1981), p. 294.

10. James Fowler, *Faithful Change: The Personal and Public Challenges of Postmodern Life* (Nashville: Abingdon, 1996); Robert Kegan, *In Over Our Heads: The Mental Demands of Modern Life* (Cambridge, Mass.: Harvard University Press, 1994).

11. Ellis Nelson, *Where Faith Begins* (Richmond: John Knox Press, 1967).

12. Alasdair MacIntyre, *After Virtue* (Notre Dame: University of Notre Dame Press, 1984); Alasdair MacIntyre, *Whose Justice? Which Rationality?* (Notre Dame: University of Notre Dame Press, 1988); Stanley Hauerwas, *Character and the Christian Life: A Study in Theological Ethics* (San Antonio: Trinity University Press, 1975).

"countercultural" community, one which enculturates its members into beliefs and practices in tension with the dominant culture.

A third trajectory reflects the increased influence of liberation and feminist theologies during this period. Drawing on the liberationist pedagogy of Paulo Freire and the transformational paradigm of James Loder, Daniel Schipani is, perhaps, the most articulate representative of this trajectory among Protestants.[13] Here, however, the cross-fertilization of Protestant and Catholic educators is particularly evident. The writings of Michael Warren on youth, Maria Harris on feminist pedagogy, and Thomas Groome on shared praxis were to have enormous influence on Protestant educators interested in liberationist and feminist perspectives throughout this period.

A fourth trajectory continues the religious education movement's emphasis on education as a distinctive function within religious communities and society generally. Among Protestants, Sara Little and Charles Melchert are, perhaps, the foremost representatives of this trajectory.[14] Both are far more sensitive to the importance of theology than their predecessors in the religious education movement, and both brought theology into dialogue with philosophy, psychology, and education in their writings. While realizing that education cannot be reduced to teaching, they gave special attention to the ways teaching can foster deeper understanding of religious beliefs and practices, drawing on the insights of contemporary pedagogical theory to describe various models of teaching that might be used in Protestant religious education.

As this brief overview makes clear, no one approach to Protestant religious education is dominant during the period we are considering. Many Protestant educators drew from some combination of the trajectories outlined above. The decision to focus on John Westerhoff's *Will Our Children Have Faith?* should not be construed as a judgment on our part that this text is paradigmatic of the field as a whole. The diversity and ecumenicity of this period makes it impossible to identify one such paradigmatic text. Westerhoff, however, was widely influential in Protestantism during this period and offers a unique perspective on each of the four trajectories that have just been described.

13. References on all of the persons mentioned here are found in the bibliography.
14. See the bibliography.

John Westerhoff

John Westerhoff was born in Paterson, New Jersey, in 1933 and educated at Ursinus College, graduating in 1955. He attended Harvard Divinity School, receiving a Master of Divinity in 1958, and Columbia University, receiving an Ed.D. in 1974. He was ordained in the United Church of Christ in 1958 and served as a pastor of churches in Maine and Massachusetts for the next eight years. He then served as editor for the United Church Board of Homeland Ministries, leaving this position to become a professor of religious education at Duke Divinity School in 1974. From 1977 to 1987, he served as the editor of *Religious Education,* one of the most influential journals in the field in the United States. He left the United Church of Christ in 1978, when he was ordained as a priest of the Episcopal church. He retired from his teaching position at Duke in 1994 and currently lives in Atlanta, Georgia.

Perhaps no Protestant religious educator exerted more influence on the field during the seventies and eighties than John Westerhoff. His writings were cast in a popular style accessible to a wide reading audience, including pastors, Christian educators, and laypersons. He drew extensively on and popularized others' ideas, including those of Ellis Nelson, Lawrence Cremin, James Fowler, and Urban Holmes, to name but a few. His primary audience was "reflective practitioners," persons actively involved in the leadership of the educational ministry of congregations and denominational agencies.[15]

It would be a mistake, however, to view Westerhoff as merely a popularizer. He was a highly creative, even prophetic voice during the period under discussion. He had his finger on the pulse of American culture and religion and consistently challenged American Protestantism to reform its inherited patterns of education. If his writing as a whole is taken into account, three overarching themes emerge: (1) the importance of reclaiming and strengthening Christian identity in the face of increased cultural pluralism, secularization, and a dominant consumer culture; (2) the special importance of congregations as communities of religious socialization and faith enculturation; and (3) an accent on particularity in Protestant religious education theory and practice. We will examine each of these themes briefly in his various writings and, then, describe how they come to expression in *Will Our Children Have Faith?*

---

15. Typical of Westerhoff's construction of his audience are comments found in a letter to the "reader" in his first book, *Values for Tomorrow's Children: An Alternative Future for Education in the Church* (Philadelphia: Pilgrim, 1970): "This is a personal statement. . . . [It is] neither meant to be a lecture nor an academic thesis to be debated by scholars. I want my opinion to be the basis for a conversation with those adults who are concerned about tomorrow's children" (p. xi).

The first of these themes reflects Westerhoff's persistent call for American mainline Protestantism to view its "disestablishment" in American culture as an opportunity to claim a much clearer sense of its identity and mission as the church. His comments in *Values for Tomorrow's Children* (1970) almost echo those of James Smart: "For too long Christianity has been a favored 'official religion' in our society. . . . I sense, however, that something very important is occurring. The church may for the first time since the third century be free from the bondage of cultural acceptance and state support."[16] In his early writings, Westerhoff casts this theme with the rhetoric of "counterculture," describing authentic Christian community in terms of small groups, house churches, and highly committed congregations, which eschew the patterns of middle-class religion.[17] By the late seventies, he adopts a more "confessional" stance, using the language of revelation, catechesis, conversion, and Christian nurture to describe the unique identity and mission of the Christian community in relation to the surrounding culture.[18] Moreover, he begins to emphasize consensus in faith communities — their common memory and practice — as the key to the maintenance of Christian identity in a pluralistic society.[19]

The second theme — the special importance of congregations as communities of religious socialization and faith enculturation — captures two closely related aspects of Westerhoff's work: his emphasis on congregations as unique contexts in which persons acquire the beliefs and practices of the Christian faith, and his critique of the schooling-instructional paradigm of Protestant religious education and advocacy of a religious socialization and faith enculturation paradigm. The first of these points to the special emphasis

16. Westerhoff, *Values for Tomorrow's Children*, p. 11.

17. This is especially evident in *Values for Tomorrow's Children*. Half a decade later, in *Building God's People in a Materialistic Society*, Westerhoff would continue to describe the church as a countercultural community. See p. 52.

18. In *Learning through Liturgy*, written with Gwen Kennedy Neville, for example, Westerhoff explicitly casts his description of Christian liturgy as "confessional" (p. viii), something he had already begun to explore in "Risking an Answer: A Conclusion," his contribution to the volume *Who Are We? The Quest for a Religious Education* (Birmingham, Ala.: Religious Education Press, 1978), pp. 268-69.

19. The shift in Westerhoff's thinking at this point is evident in comments like the following: "The days of improvisation and change need to end, for in our secular, alien world, a community of renewed, reformed faith needs to establish new structured rituals. . . . Only an identity-conscious, tradition-bearing community, rich in meaningful ritual, can help us to know and remember who we are. Life is fragmented and compartmentalized. . . . Vital community rituals alone can prevent us from spiritual dislocation and lostness" (*Learning through Liturgy*, pp. 102-3).

Westerhoff places on congregational life over the course of his career. While he frequently draws on Lawrence Cremin's understanding of an ecology of education (i.e., a network of institutions that work together to educate persons toward a common cultural ideal) to describe the historical importance of families, public schools, the media, and congregations in Protestant religious education, he gives little sustained attention to any institution but the congregation.[20] With a few notable exceptions, his focus from the beginning of his career until his retirement was on the congregation. His collaboration with the cultural anthropologist Gwen Kennedy Neville in *Generation to Generation* (1974) and *Learning through Liturgy* (1978) anticipates by almost a decade the interest in congregational studies that emerged in American practical theology during the 1980s.[21]

Westerhoff does not, however, merely focus on the importance of congregations amid a broken ecology of Protestant religious education. He advocates a paradigm shift within congregational education, calling for the elimination of the schooling-instructional paradigm and its replacement by a religious socialization and faith enculturation paradigm. As we shall see, this is the heart of *Will Our Children Have Faith?* In his later writings, Westerhoff would become more theological in his description of his "new paradigm" of Protestant religious education, describing it as catechesis and faith formation or transformation. The sociological and anthropological presuppositions of his earlier work are still present, but his primary interest now is in describing the ways congregations create contexts of Christian nurture and conversion. This "theological turn" in Westerhoff's thinking is informed by H. Richard Niebuhr, Urban Holmes, and, somewhat later, Stanley Hauerwas.[22]

The third theme — an emphasis on particularity in Protestant Christian education theory and practice — points to Westerhoff's response to religious

---

20. His attention to the educational ecology of Protestant education is found in *Values for Tomorrow's Children*, chap. 2; *Who Are We?* p. 66; and in *Will Our Children Have Faith?*, treated below. Attention to the Christian family is found in *Values for Tomorrow's Children*, chap. 8; and *Generation to Generation*, pp. 45-47, 119, and chap. 7. Brief discussion of Christian responsibility for public education and its advocacy of religious education in this setting is found in *Values for Tomorrow's Children*, pp. 107-8; and *Who Are We?* pp. 264-65. Exploration of Christian parochial schools is found in his contribution to a book co-edited with Stanley Hauerwas, *Schooling Christians: "Holy Experiments" in American education* (Grand Rapids: Eerdmans, 1992), pp. 262-81.

21. See the bibliography for details. Neville's fieldwork on folk liturgies in *Learning through Liturgy* remains some of the best and most interesting work in this area.

22. Explicit references to these individuals are found in *Learning through Liturgy*, pp. 120 and 150, and are scattered throughout *Building God's People*.

and cultural pluralism. He grants methodological priority to the different beliefs and practices of particular religious communities. As early as 1978,
Westerhoff began to distinguish religious education from church or synagogue education, pointing to the very different ways particular religious communities conceptualize the nature and purpose of their education in light of
their distinctive convictions and practices.[23] He also began to employ the language of catechesis to describe the educational ministry of the Christian
community, explicitly disavowing the claim that this confessional frame
would be appropriate for Jewish, Muslim, or other non-Christian, religious
communities.

The methodological implications of this affirmation of religious particularity are found in Westerhoff's adoption of practical theology as the disciplinary frame for *Building God's People in a Materialistic Society*. He describes
this discipline as continuously moving "back and forth between our life experience and the church's fundamental and constructive theology," locating
catechesis in relation to the liturgical, moral, spiritual, and pastoral dimensions of the Christian life.[24] Moreover, he explicitly claims the vantage point
of his own denominational heritage (now, the Anglican-Episcopalian tradition) as the starting point of his practical theological perspective. As he puts
it, "I have written this book from what I intend to be an Anglican perspective. . . . It is, therefore, *The Book of Common Prayer* (1979) that provides me
with a starting point for engaging in practical theology. *Lex orandi, lex
credendi,* 'the law of praying is the law of believing.'"[25]

Each of these three themes is found in *Will Our Children Have Faith?*,
Westerhoff's most influential text on Protestant religious education. The
first chapter, "The Shaking of the Foundations," begins by exploring the broken ecology of Protestant religious education and the problem of continuing
to think of this ministry in terms of the Sunday school. This leaves the
church trapped in a schooling-instructional paradigm, Westerhoff argues.
As he puts it,

> Since the turn of the century, in spite of nods to other possibilities, Chris-
> tian educators and local churches have functioned according to a
> *schooling-instructional paradigm.* That is, our image of education has been

23. This is laid out most clearly in "Risking an Answer: A Conclusion," in *Who Are We?*
This turn toward the particularity of the education of different religious communities also begins to take shape in *Learning through Liturgy,* in which the confessional and pastoral nature of
catechesis is explored.

24. Westerhoff, *Building God's People,* p. 8.

25. Westerhoff, *Building God's People,* p. 140.

founded upon some sort of a "school" as the context *and* some form of instruction as the means.[26]

The problematic nature of this paradigm, Westerhoff goes on to argue, is evident in five areas: (1) an inability to account for education in small churches, the most important context, demographically, of American Protestantism; (2) an inability to account for education in ethnic congregations, most of which have not relied heavily on the Sunday school pattern of Christian education; (3) lack of recognition of the breakdown of the ecology of Protestant education in which the church school had support from other institutions; (4) failure to attend to the "hidden curriculum" in congregational life, perhaps the most important influence on persons' actual beliefs and values; and (5) an inability to account for the ways faith is actually formed, not through instruction "about" Christianity but through the living interaction of persons in community. What is needed, Westerhoff argues, is a paradigm shift, not merely improved curriculum, teaching, or administration within the dominant schooling-instructional approach.

This opens out to discussion of the theological foundations of contemporary Protestant religious education in Chapter Two, "Beginning and Ending in Faith." Westerhoff treats this theme along two lines. The pluralism of contemporary theology, ranging from evangelical to feminist to process theologies, makes it impossible for congregations to agree on "theological essentials."[27] This is accompanied by weaknesses in the theological perspectives undergirding Protestant religious education over the course of the twentieth century, which bifurcate concern for the social order (liberal/Social Gospel theology) and the tradition (neo-orthodoxy). Westerhoff argues that liberation theology represents a way beyond both contemporary theological pluralism and the false dichotomies of the immediate past, and he offers a summary of this perspective's understanding of God, persons, and the church's relationship to society. He draws on liberation theology to ground his understanding of the church as a "countercultural," prophetic community, standing in tension with the surrounding culture and sharing God's "bias" toward the oppressed.[28]

What kind of community can make this sort of liberating witness? This is the question Westerhoff takes up in Chapter Three, "In Search of Community." His answer represents a clear alternative to more recent understandings

---

26. John Westerhoff, *Will Our Children Have Faith?* (New York: Seabury, 1976), p. 6.
27. Westerhoff, *Will Our Children Have Faith?* p. 27.
28. Westerhoff, *Will Our Children Have Faith?* p. 41.

of liberation pedagogy growing out of the work of Paulo Freire.[29] He argues that only congregations with a clear sense of their identity and mission will be able to witness to and work toward God's liberating activity on behalf of the poor. Such communities must have three characteristics: unity in theological essentials, meaningful face-to-face interaction across three generations, and practices that call forth the diverse gifts of their members. Westerhoff relates the first of these to the increased reality of cultural pluralism in American life. As he puts it, "A community possesses a clear identity. Pluralism is only possible or healthy when persons have an identity and are open to others. A faith community must agree on what it believes."[30]

For the remainder of this chapter and in the final two ("Life Together" and "Hope for the Future"), Westerhoff explores how faith communities with a clear sense of their identity and a mission grounded in liberation theology can form and transform the faith of their members. Rather than focusing on teaching within the church school, he argues, they should give explicit attention to the rituals, shared experiences, and interactive patterns of the community. It is here that persons actually learn the story and practices of the Christian life. In his description of what this implies concretely, Westerhoff is long on example and creative suggestion and short on theoretical guidelines. "It is easier to name the context for Christian education than it is to name the means," he writes.[31] He offers a creative (though nontechnical) discussion of faith development theory as providing some broad educational guidelines for persons as they move through the experienced, affiliative, searching, and owned phases of faith.

Of special importance is Westerhoff's discussion of the reasons for his shift from the language of religious socialization to that of faith enculturation. The former, he has come to believe, is too heavy-handed: "Intentional socialization implies that someone does something to someone else."[32] In contrast, the language of enculturation, which he now prefers, "emphasizes the process of interaction between and among persons of all ages. . . . One person is not understood as the actor and another acted upon, but rather both act, both initiate action, and both react."[33] Within the overall socialization of a religious community, therefore, faith enculturation represents its systematic and intentional efforts to shape the knowledge, skills, and attitudes of its members.[34]

---

29. See particularly *Pedagogy of the Oppressed* (New York: Seabury, 1974).
30. Westerhoff, *Will Our Children Have Faith?* p. 52.
31. Westerhoff, *Will Our Children Have Faith?* p. 79.
32. Westerhoff, *Will Our Children Have Faith?* p. 79.
33. Westerhoff, *Will Our Children Have Faith?* p. 80.
34. Westerhoff, *Will Our Children Have Faith?* pp. 49, 80.

The context and means of such education are the interactions of faithful persons, which may occur in classrooms but are not to be conceptualized primarily in terms of this setting.

In this language shift, Westerhoff is responding to the charge that his use of socialization theory traps him in an approach to education that ultimately is conservative, accentuating the inculcation of persons into the pre-existent norms of a community.[35] If true, this charge would appear to contradict his commitment to liberationist themes. A careful reading of Westerhoff's work as a whole, however, allows us to discern three important qualifications of his socialization/enculturation theory. First, even in his early work, when he was most dependent on socialization theory, he portrays the one being socialized as an active respondent to the forces of socialization, one who shapes as well is shaped by these forces.[36] Second, Westerhoff consistently locates socialization and enculturation theory in relation to psychological theories of development, making it clear that adolescents and adults play a far more active role than children in appropriating selectively knowledge, values, and skills. He emphasizes the importance of supporting this sort of critical appropriation.[37] Third, Westerhoff consistently attends to the variety of cultural norms that may be present in a community. Some communities do, indeed, socialize toward unthinking obedience. But others do not, creating a culture of thinking and democratic interaction. Such norms, he argues, are the "hidden curriculum" of group life, and they must be subject to the critical scrutiny of religious education.[38] Accordingly, in his early work, he posits an important distinction between religious socialization and religious education.[39] Only the latter — on the far side of the critical assessment of cultural norms — allows communities to hand on knowledge, skills, and dispositions consistent with their educational ends, those ideals toward which education is "leading persons out."

Westerhoff in Context

Historians and social analysts of the 1960s to 1990s point to two sources of social transformation during this period: new social movements and alterations

35. See, for example, Thomas Groome's discussion of religious socialization in *Christian Religious Education: Sharing Our Story and Vision* (San Francisco: Harper and Row, 1980).

36. See, for example, his comments in *Generation to Generation,* pp. 47-48.

37. Westerhoff, *Generation to Generation,* pp. 39-41.

38. Westerhoff, *Generation to Generation,* pp. 39-41.

39. Westerhoff, *Generation to Generation,* pp. 39-41.

in the institutional patterns of work, family, education, and the state. Together, they would intensify certain aspects of modernization that had already begun to reshape American life over the course of the twentieth century.

Institutional changes of significance during this period are closely related to the expansion and restructuring of the American economy that began immediately after World War II. The war had demonstrated the importance of science and technology to the nation's defense, something that continued to be a national priority during the Cold War era. The launching of Sputnik by the Soviet Union in 1957 led to an intensification of the American government's interest in expanding research and development in science and technology. By 1965, the United States had 500,000 scientists engaged in research and development, the highest proportion relative to the total labor force of any nation in the world.[40] It was spending 2.9 percent of its gross national product on research and development, nearly twice the proportion spent only ten years earlier. Accompanying this investment in science and technology was an expansion in higher education, a trend that accelerated enormously between 1950 and 1970. In 1950, 2.6 million persons were enrolled in colleges and universities; by 1970, 8.6 million were enrolled. This represents an enormous increase in the percentage of young people going to college — from 22.3 percent in 1960 to 35.2 percent in 1970. Expenditures on higher education by federal, state, and local governments rose from $2.2 billion in 1950 to $23.4 billion in 1970.

Accompanying these investments in research and higher education were changes of major importance in the structure of the American economy — referred to variously as the advent of a "post-industrial," "globalized," or "high value" economic system.[41] At the heart of this transformation of the economy was the shift away from manufacturing as the driving force of economic growth to technologically based knowledge and service industries. Throughout this period, national corporations became multinational in every sense of the word, exporting manufacturing, decentralizing management and product development, and marketing goods and services around the world. The net result was a destabilization of the standard pattern of work that had existed through much of the twentieth century: one job with one company located in one place for the duration of the adult life. Job obsolescence, managerial downsizing, plant closings, corporate mergers, inter-firm

40. Wuthnow, *Restructuring of American Religion*, p. 155. The statistics given throughout this section are drawn from Wuthnow's analysis.

41. Daniel Bell, *The Coming of Post-Industrial Society* (New York: Basic, 1976); Malcolm Waters, *Globalization* (London: Routledge, 1995); Robert Reich, *The Work of Nations* (New York: Vintage, 1991).

short-term ventures, and regional relocation became common features of the workplace during this period.

Equally important during this period was a wide range of new social movements. These movements mobilized around a specific set of issues that called into question and reshaped some aspect of American culture. It is impossible to understand the sixties and seventies without pointing to the importance of the Civil Rights movement, the anti-war movement, the women's movement, the ecological movement, the nuclear disarmament movement, and the more diffuse cultural expressions of the "counterculture." All of these movements had both political and cultural agendas, and they extended far beyond the specific legal and legislative victories they won. They brought about changes in long-standing patterns of moral meaning by which Americans viewed their lives.[42] The long-established ideal of the Puritan work ethic and its association with a life trajectory of high achievement in school, entry into a stable career, and establishment of long-term family commitments now seemed repugnant to many young persons. The search for expanded consciousness and a personally satisfying way of life that did not "sell out to the system" led many young persons to "tune in, turn on, and drop out," if only for a short period of their lives.

It is important to remember that the new social movements of the sixties and seventies do not tell the whole story of this period. The seventies saw the reemergence of evangelical Protestantism as both a cultural and a political force. The sheer diversity of this movement cautions us against portraying it as merely a conservative reaction to the social turmoil of the sixties. Nevertheless, it was the rise of the Religious Right as a political force that received the greatest attention in the national media and had the most visible impact on American culture. Groups like the Moral Majority began to use highly sophisticated political tactics to support candidates who held their views on hot-button issues like abortion, school prayer, and homosexual rights. The ensuing polarization between religious liberals and conservatives would prove to be one of the most important factors shaping American denominationalism during this period. This polarization not only distinguished different denominations but also ran right through the middle of many. As Wuthnow points out, the rise of "special purpose" groups with specific moral and political agendas became a prominent feature of denominational life during this period.[43] Affiliation with such groups was an important way of

42. See Steven Tipton's discussion of the moral style of the counterculture in *Getting Saved from the Sixties* (Berkeley: University of California Press, 1982).

43. Robert Wuthnow, *Restructuring of American Religion*, chap. 6. By this term, Wuthnow

mobilizing religious conviction for public activity, far surpassing identification with denominational social teachings on public issues.

Together, these social movements and institutional changes represent an intensification of four aspects of modernization that were to reshape American religion over the course of this period: (1) the expansion of moral and religious pluralism; (2) increased emphasis on the individual as the "anchor" of religion, commonly known as the "new voluntarism" in American religion; (3) the polarization of conservatives and liberals within and across different denominations, noted above; and (4) the rise of congregationalism in American religion. Each of the broad themes we have identified in John Westerhoff's work as a whole — coming to expression in *Will Our Children Have Faith?* — can be viewed as responsive to these trends.

The first trend, the expansion of moral and religious pluralism, is easily documented. Between 1952 and 1985, Protestantism declined from 67 percent of the total population to 57 percent.[44] As has been frequently documented, this includes shifts within Protestantism as well, with large declines in membership taking place in the historic mainline denominations (Presbyterian, United Methodist, Lutheran, Episcopalian, and Congregational) and rapid growth in the Southern Baptist Convention, Assemblies of God, and other forms of conservative Protestantism. During this same period, Roman Catholicism grew from 25 percent to 28 percent of the population, other religions from 1 percent to 4 percent, and the unaffiliated sector of the population from 2 percent to 9 percent.[45] Polling data throughout this period consistently began to reveal far greater interdenominational and interfaith tolerance among all religious groups than in earlier decades, including increased acceptance of those not belonging to any religious community.[46]

Westerhoff's entire program of religious education takes as its starting point the collapse of the Protestant ecology of education and the increased reality of religious and cultural pluralism. He challenges congregations to become countercultural communities, tightening the boundaries that set them

---

means a wide range of groups that are present within, between, and outside of specific religious communities. Not all are politically motivated (for example, neighborhood Bible studies, holistic health ministries, and the Cursillo movement). Our point here is more limited than Wuthnow's, focusing specifically on the way some special purpose groups have taken shape in response to public policy issues and seek to foster a particular version of the common good.

44. Roof and McKinney, *American Mainline Religion*, p. 16. See also their discussion in "Denominational America and the New Religious Pluralism," *The Annals*, AAPSS (American Academy of Political and Social Science) 480 (July 1985): pp. 24-38.

45. Roof and McKinney, *American Mainline Religion*, p. 16.

46. Wuthnow, *Restructuring of American Religion*, pp. 91-95.

off from the surrounding culture and thereby heightening the enculturation of their members into a distinctive Christian identity. His critique of the schooling-instructional paradigm and his advocacy of a faith enculturation paradigm is in service to this fundamental commitment. In the face of the new cultural and religious pluralism, he argues, incremental improvements in the church school are not enough. Only congregations that project a clear sense of their Christian identity will be in a position to enculturate their members into their distinctive beliefs and practices. This is essentially a *communitarian* response to the pluralism of late modernity. As it gradually emerged in academic circles across this period, this communitarian perspective abandons the idea that human rationality or a common set of human characteristics can serve as the basis of the public sphere, maintaining instead that such characteristics are inherently narrative and practice-dependent. Public life becomes a dialogue across incommensurable moral positions, each grounded in the distinctive beliefs and practices of various religious and moral communities.[47]

Westerhoff's faith enculturation model can also be seen as responsive to the second trend characterizing American religion during this period: the increased importance of the individual as the "anchor" of religion, the so-called new voluntarism of American religion. We have discussed certain aspects of this dimension of modernization in earlier parts of this book. What is significant about the present period is the intensification of this trend, pointed to in major sociological studies such as *Habits of the Heart,* by Robert Bellah and his colleagues; Roof and McKinney's *American Mainline Religion;* and Phillip Hammond's *Religion and Personal Autonomy.*[48] Each of these studies points to new forms of individualism in American religion characterized by two elements: (1) the diminished importance of denominational identity, leading to greater choice by the individual in determining religious affiliation, and (2) an increased emphasis on the personal dimensions of religiosity, the perceived "fit" between a religious community and the felt needs of individuals and families. The latter is sometimes referred to as an "individual-expressive" style of attachment to religious institutions.[49]

47. For a discussion and critique of this perspective, particularly focusing on MacIntyre, see D. Fergusson, ed., *Community, Liberalism, and Christian Ethics* (New York: Cambridge University Press, 1998).

48. Robert Bellah et al., *Habits of the Heart* (Berkeley: University of California Press, 1985); Roof and McKinney, *American Mainline Religion;* Phillip Hammond, *Religion and Personal Autonomy: The Third Disestablishment in America* (Columbia: University of South Carolina Press, 1992).

49. Hammond, *Religion and Personal Autonomy.*

Historically, denominational affiliation in the United States had mirrored social, ethnic, and class distinctions, as noted in H. Richard Niebuhr's influential *The Social Sources of Denominationalism*.[50] The expansion of higher education and restructuring of the American economy following World War II eroded many of the socioeconomic distinctions separating denominations.[51] Higher education also contributed to the increased prevalence of denominational "switching," the shift from one denomination or religion to another.[52] In 1955, a Gallup poll indicated that only 4 percent of the adult population had "switched" from the faith of their childhood; in 1985, this was true of 33 percent.[53] Switching was especially prevalent in mainline Protestant denominations, now increasingly described as "old-line." Data gathered in the 1970s and early '80s found that 45 percent of persons raised in the Presbyterian church, 40 percent in the Methodist church, and 38 percent in the Episcopal church now belonged to another denomination, religion, or the unaffiliated sector of the population.[54] Religious affiliation, therefore, was no longer rooted primarily in ascriptive factors like class, national origin, and ethnicity.[55] A much higher degree of individual choice was involved in religious affiliation, the "new voluntarism" of American religion.

Westerhoff's increased emphasis on denominational identity (in his case, Episcopal-Anglican) can be interpreted as directly responsive to this trend. Congregations could no longer take it for granted that members had grown up in their denomination and had any sense of its distinctive beliefs and practices. An important part of their educational efforts, therefore, must be helping members learn what it means to think and live out of a particular Christian tradition. In Westerhoff's view, this focus on denominational identity

50. H. Richard Niebuhr, *The Social Sources of Denominationalism* (New York: World, 1929).

51. Wuthnow, *Restructuring of American Religion*, pp. 83-88. See also Roof and McKinney's discussion of the decline of ascriptive loyalty in *American Mainline Religion*, pp. 63ff.

52. Wuthnow, *Restructuring of American Religion*, p. 89.

53. Wuthnow, *Restructuring of American Religion*, p. 88.

54. Wuthnow, *Restructuring of American Religion*, p. 88.

55. The one major exception to this trend is the affiliation patterns of racial and ethnic groups. African and Asian Americans overwhelmingly continue to affiliate with religious communities composed of their own racial and ethnic group. Even here, however, shifts have occurred, as many of the young are not affiliating with any religious community at all, the so-called "silent exodus" from the church. For a discussion of some facets of this issue, see David Daniels, "Chatham and Greater Grand Crossing: The Dominance of Religion and Race," *Religious Report of the Religion and Urban America Program* (Chicago: Office of Social Science Research, University of Illinois at Chicago), pp. 204-20; and Stephen Warner and Judith Wittner, *Congregations as Cultural Spaces: Immigration, Ethnicity, and Religion in the United States* (Philadelphia: Temple University Press, 1997).

was not an end in itself, however. It was in the service of a renewed emphasis on the processes of conversion and catechesis, which gradually were given greater prominence over the course of his writing. In the face of the increased individualism and denominational switching of American religion, many congregations were beginning to market religious education programs explicitly designed to meet the felt needs of prospective members. Westerhoff projected a real alternative to this approach, challenging congregations to develop new, more demanding practices of faith formation by which individuals are invited to take the claims of Christian discipleship more seriously. If individuals do, in fact, have more freedom in choosing their faith in late modernity, congregations should respond by using this as an opportunity to help them become clearer about what it means to choose to be a follower of Jesus and to enter a way of life standing in tension with the dominant mores of the American middle class.

This points to the third trend to which Westerhoff's proposals can be viewed as responsive: the polarization of religious liberals and conservatives and the rise of "special purpose" groups focusing on controversial moral issues like abortion and the ordination of homosexuals. Westerhoff's use of the rhetoric of counterculture to describe congregations and his explicit adoption of theological themes of liberation theology portray Protestant communities as strongly identified with the advocacy stances of the political left. Moreover, he argues that congregations must have unity in theological essentials if they are to possess a sufficiently strong Christian identity to stand in tension with the dominant American culture. Rather than calling for communities to embrace political diversity and to teach their members the virtues of reasoned debate and civility, he challenges them to identify closely with groups who are most vulnerable in society, taking up their cause in the political sphere. Congregations are, in effect, to become one large special purpose group, in Wuthnow's sense of the term, holding in common a particular socioethical stance in relation to the controversial issues of the day.

Finally, the new emphasis on congregationalism is a fourth trend in American religion of this period that is closely related to Westerhoff's proposals. Recent empirical research on congregations by Nancy Tatom Ammerman, Penny Edgell Becker, Stephen Warner, and many others has noted that the so-called new voluntarism or individual-expressive mode of attachment to religious communities has not resulted in a decline of congregational affiliation, if American religion as a whole is taken into account.[56] Rather, what has resulted

---

56. Nancy Tatom Ammerman, *Congregation and Community* (New Brunswick, N.J.: Rutgers University Press, 1997); Penny Edgell Becker, *Congregations in Conflict: Cultural Models*

is a lessening of the authority of denominations and pastors, the decline of membership in some denominations and growth in others, and, most germane to the point being made here, *an increased emphasis on congregations as the center of the religious life.* Social interpreters like Ammerman and Becker are cautious in their interpretation of this trend, for American religion has been characterized by a strong element of voluntarism and congregationalism from the beginning.[57] What is important about the post-sixties expressions of these elements, however, is the increased importance of the congregation as the center of religious identification and affiliation. In a pluralistic moral and cultural context in which individuals experience more freedom to affiliate (or not) with a particular religious community, congregations have become more important in the decision to affiliate and remain involved. Moreover, this research has begun to uncover a wide range of models of congregational life in American religion. Almost all of these communities view worship and religious education as core tasks;[58] many view participation in public life as an important part of the congregation's mission.[59] In short, the "restructuring" of American religion in the post-sixties era has led to a renewed accent on congregations, rather than denominations, as the central focus of the religious life.

Clearly, Westerhoff's overwhelming emphasis on the congregation is responsive to this trend. In retrospect, he can be viewed as advocating one primary model of congregational life — strongly countercultural, left-leaning politically, and conservative-parochial liturgically. Numerous alternatives to this model have been identified empirically and, obviously, many alternatives have been advocated in the normative proposals of religious education theorists and practical theologians. The point being made here, however, is the way Westerhoff's emphasis on the congregation both mirrored and anticipated the new emphasis on congregationalism that has come to characterize American religion in the period between 1960 and 1990.

How are we to evaluate Westerhoff's proposals for Protestant religious education? It is important to recall the diversity and ecumenicity pointed to

---

of Local Religious Life (Cambridge: Cambridge University Press, 1999); Stephen Warner, *New Wine in Old Wineskins: Evangelicals and Liberals in a Small-Town Church* (Berkeley: University of California Press, 1988); Stephen Warner, "Toward a New Paradigm for the Sociological Study of Religion in the United States," *American Journal of Sociology* 98, no. 5, pp. 1044-93.

57. For a helpful discussion, see Brooks Holifield, "Toward a History of American Congregations," in *American Congregations,* vol. 2, ed. J. Wind and J. Lewis (Chicago: University of Chicago Press), pp. 23-53.

58. See Becker's discussion of core tasks in *Congregations in Conflict,* chap. 8.

59. David Roozen, William McKinney, and Jackson Carroll, *Varieties of Religious Presence: Mission in Life* (New York: Pilgrim, 1984).

in the initial part of this chapter. Westerhoff represents only one trajectory that emerged during this period, and our evaluation of his positions should not be construed as applying to the field as a whole. On the positive side, his recognition of the importance of the quality of congregational life in the face of a pluralistic social context has much to commend it. Congregations remain the heart of American Protestant Christianity. It is here that faith takes hold through the quality of the models, shared experiences, and practices a community offers its members. Westerhoff's collaboration with Neville anticipated by over a decade the renewed interest in congregational studies that has become such an important part of practical theology and religious education in recent years. Likewise, Westerhoff's plea for Protestant congregations to resist the lure of the new voluntarism and to develop forms of ministry that take seriously the need for conversion, catechesis, and discipleship must be viewed positively. In the face of the spiritual supermarket that has come to characterize American religion over the past decades, these are issues with which Protestant religious education should continue to grapple.

As is the case with all of the persons and texts examined in this part of our book, however, these strengths go hand in hand with certain weaknesses. Westerhoff's insistence on close-knit, tightly bound communities can be viewed as a defensive response to religious pluralism, precisely at a moment when the members of religious communities needed help in maturing toward a more dialectical faith stance in which conviction and openness are held in tension. His preoccupation with the congregation also limited the attention he gave to other sites of Protestant religious education — the family, Christian schools, and the church's contribution to public *paideia* — and his call for agreement in theological essentials seems to preclude leaving space for individuals to hold theological and ethical positions that are genuinely different. Moreover, his criticism of the schooling-instructional paradigm offered a false alternative — either schooling or enculturation — when in fact it is apparent that those Protestant congregations doing best in the pluralistic context emerging since the 1960s find ways of attending to both of these tasks. Not only do they offer substantive programs of Bible study, catechesis, and critical reflection on contemporary issues, but they also offer meaningful experiences of community and service in small groups, spiritual direction, retreats, fellowship meals, and congregational worship. Finally, for all of his talk of liberation, Westerhoff offers no sustained analysis of the political and ethical conflicts of our time. Where is the class analysis, dependency theory, or ideology critique we would associate with a liberation perspective?

Each of these points of criticism is subject to debate. Thus it is important to recall the diversity that has come to characterize this field since the 1960s.

No one model dominates the discipline of religious education or congregational life. The criticisms offered here reflect our commitment to what is sometimes described as the public church and to forms of Protestant religious education that intentionally seek to prepare persons for participation in pluralistic, democratic forms of public life. But this is to get ahead of ourselves, and must wait for the final part of this book.

Secularization, the Social Sciences, Ecumenical Cooperation: Protestant Religious Education in Germany

During the thirty years between 1960 and 1990 West Germany experienced a thorough restructuring that clearly separates this important period of social, cultural, and political change from the earlier period of postwar reconstruction. This restructuring took place at several different levels, changing the situation politically as well as socially, culturally as well as religiously and educationally. This period, which is often considered to have been important in the modernization of German society, was a time when modern science and technology came to have increased influence. Particularly in the 1960s and early 1970s education was expected to help society and individuals come to terms with the changing situation.

One of the main concerns for the German churches was the growing effect of secularization, which many believed was an automatic and inevitable result of the increasing influence of science. Drop-out rates, especially for the Protestant church, increased dramatically during the 1960s.[60] High school students refused to participate in religious education classes offered by their schools and exercised their constitutional right to elect out of such classes.

Given the general climate of change and of educational renewal, it is no surprise that the 1960s also brought about major changes in the field of religious education. The pressures against religious education experienced in society as a whole as well as in the schools made it clear that new approaches were needed. Moreover, new developments in theology and religious education theory also called for far-reaching changes. The model of evangelical instruction that had appeared so promising after World War II was now considered traditionalist, dated, and incapable of facing up to the new challenges.

60. For a good overview see Andreas Feige, *Kirchenmitgliedschaft in der Bundesrepublik Deutschland. Zentrale Perspektiven empirischer Forschungsarbeit im problemgeschichtlichen Kontext der deutschen Religions- und Kirchensoziologie nach 1945* (Gütersloh: Gütersloher Verlagshaus, 1990).

Giving a precise date for the beginning of these changes is difficult. Clearly, even during the 1950s the evangelical instruction approach was more and more rivaled by the growing influence of the so-called hermeneutical approach. At that time, hermeneutics referred to the theology of exegetes and systematicians like Rudolf Bultmann and Gerhard Ebeling, who, moving beyond the word of God theology, pointed out the connection between the historical study of the Bible and the situation of modernity. According to these individuals, modern people encounter biblical texts first of all as historical texts and not as expressions of revelation. Only by studying these texts historically and critically will they gain access to the deeper existential meaning of the Bible. Applying this kind of thinking to the religious education of young people led to classroom teachers' presenting biblical texts historically — that is, as primary sources for the Christian tradition — an approach that was developed by authors like Martin Stallmann and Hans Stock.[61] Students also were expected to be taught the principal insights derived from the historical and critical study of the Bible undertaken by academic theologians. Clearly, this hermeneutical turn was a first step toward opening up religious education to the challenges of modernity and "modern man," as it was often put.

It is important to note that the Bible, even when studied in this more historical manner, remained the center of religious education. Religious education remained biblical instruction. This changed drastically in the 1960s, when religious educators started to ask the question, "Does the Bible have to be the center of religious education?"[62] Some religious educators began to see the true task of religious education not so much as teaching the Bible but as making sense of contemporary reality. The Bible was to be used as a source or as a tool in this process of understanding and interpreting reality. The new approach based on this idea was called *"problem-oriented" religious education*. The Bible was not to disappear from the classroom, according to this approach, but it was to be viewed as one perspective among others. It was to be brought into dialogue with contemporary experience and to prove itself through its ability to solve contemporary problems.

This correlation approach has remained the basic model of religious education in Germany since the 1960s. The Bible has, since then, become a more independent focus for religious education again, and further refinements of

---

61. Martin Stallmann, *Die biblische Geschichte im Unterricht. Katechetische Beiträge* (Göttingen: Vandenhoeck und Ruprecht, 1963); Hans Stock, *Studien zur Auslegung der synoptischen Evangelien im Unterricht* (Gütersloh: Gütersloher Verlagshaus, 1959).

62. This is the title of a famous essay by Hans Bernhard Kaufmann, "Muß die Bibel im Mittelpunkt des Religionsunterrichts stehen? Thesen zur Diskussion um eine zeitgemäße Didaktik des Religionsunterrichts," *Loccumer Protokolle* 12 (1966): 37-39.

the problem-solving approach, such as the critique of ideology, have been introduced.[63] One of the characteristics of the period between 1960 and 1980 was that no single approach could really reach a dominant position. After the introduction of problem-oriented religious education in the late 1960s, a whole array of different approaches came into the picture.[64] They were often heralded as ground-breaking, and they often proved to be short-lived. Some educators favored a focus on religion in general rather than on Christianity in particular. Others argued for a critical approach in the sense of the Frankfurt school of social theory by making the critique of religious and nonreligious ideologies the main task of religious education. Still others thought that religious education should attempt to liberate students from the oppressive influence of bourgeois religion. By the late 1970s, the fast pace of change in religious education slowed down. In the early 1980s some religious educators attempted to integrate teaching the Bible with the more contemporary problem orientation. German religious education since the late 1970s has also been characterized by a new openness toward developmental psychology (Eriksonian as well as Piagetian) and by a new awareness of the meaning of symbols and metaphors for religious education.[65] This new appreciation of symbolism reflects an awareness of the aesthetic dimensions of religious education that is in line with the postmodern reappreciation of symbol, myth, and aesthetics.[66]

While German religious education theory/praxis in the 1980s shows the influence of postmodernism, it also is characterized by a return to some of the ideas of the religious education reform movement of the early twentieth century. This is especially true in the turn toward the social sciences as a main reference point for religious education, a turn that was already beginning to take place in the 1960s and that parallels the influence of psychology in the early twentieth century. Another parallel of this kind is the extensive use of general education research by religious educators. At the same time, it is important to note that genuine mutual dialogue between general education and religious education was a rare phenomenon during this period. Instead, religious education theory tended to draw on general education and the social sciences while these disciplines

---

63. A good example is Gottfried Adam and Rainer Lachmann, eds., *Religionspädagogisches Kompendium*, new ed. (Göttingen: Vandenhoeck und Ruprecht, 1997).

64. These approaches are described at length by Godwin Lämmermann, *Religionspädagogik im 20. Jahrhundert* (Gütersloh: Gütersloher Verlagshaus, 1994).

65. Cf. Friedrich Schweitzer, *Lebensgeschichte und Religion. Religiöse Entwicklung und Erziehung im Kindes- und Jugendalter* (München: Kaiser, 1987).

66. This is true especially for the work of Peter Biehl. See *Symbole geben zu lernen. Einführung in die Symboldidaktik anhand der Symbole Hand, Haus und Weg* (Neukirchen-Vluyn: Neukirchener Verlag, 1989), and his later books on this topic.

tended to become more and more secular both in their orientation and in their expressed self-understanding. Given the insecure status of religious education within the state schools, much energy was devoted to modernizing this subject and to legitimizing its place in the curriculum of the school.

One other important new characteristic of religious education during this period is its increasing ecumenical openness. Since the 1960s, Protestant and Catholic religious education in Germany have not only taken parallel paths in the development of new ideas and approaches, they have also entered a dialogical and cooperative relationship with each other. Catholic publications have included Protestant authors and vice versa, and a major handbook was published under joint denominational editorship.[67] Even if Germany had long been influenced by a Catholic as well as a Protestant population, this was clearly the first time that this kind of cooperation had taken place. Quite obviously, this was due to the new ecumenical openness that had been achieved through the ecumenical movement and through the Second Vatican Council. This increased ecumenical openness mirrors demographic changes that blurred the formerly clear-cut boundaries between denominational subgroups. Mobility and intermarriage, to mention only two factors, made it increasingly difficult to maintain the former cultural and religious barriers between the denominations.

Looking for an exemplary statement from this period, with all its variations, we are again confronted with a hard choice, and a choice not only among different authors but also among any given author's various phases across the thirty years from 1960 to 1990. It obviously is impossible to capture all of this variety within a single publication. Since the programmatic statements of the mid 1960s on a "problem orientation" in religious education played a major role in defining this period, it seems appropriate to select one of these texts for closer scrutiny.

"Christian Faith Instruction in a Secular World": *Karl Ernst Nipkow's Introduction to the Problem-Oriented Approach*

Karl Ernst Nipkow is not a figure from the past. As we write this chapter, he is retired but still plays a very active and influential role in German religious

---

67. Erich Feifel, Robert Leuenberger, Günter Stachel, and Klaus Wegenast, eds., *Handbuch der Religionspädagogik,* 3 vols. (Gütersloh: Gütersloher Verlagshaus, 1973-1975). For a documentation of the parallel paths of Protestant and Catholic religious education cf. Klaus Wegenast, ed., *Religionspädagogik,* 2 vols. (Darmstadt: Wissenschaftliche Buchgesellschaft, 1981/1983).

education and beyond.[68] Nipkow was born in 1928 in Bielefeld.[69] He studied theology and education at Heidelberg and Marburg, taught religious education classes in various high schools, and earned his doctorate in education. He taught in the field of general education in the universities of Marburg and Hannover. In 1968 he became professor of religious education and practical theology at the University of Tübingen, where he worked until his retirement in 1995. His impressive bibliography includes several hundred articles and chapters in books. Since 1975, he has authored several major books on religious education, including three volumes on foundational questions of religious education, a major volume on education in evangelical perspective, and two volumes on moral and religious education in the context of pluralism.[70]

Even if it is impossible to make objective historical statements about one's own present, there can be no doubt concerning Nipkow's leading role in Protestant religious education since the 1970s. This includes not only teaching and publishing but also active leadership in the most important educational institutions of the Evangelical Church in Germany. In many cases it was Nipkow who drafted what later became the official statements of the church.

Following the procedure we have chosen for this part of the book, we will, for the most part, limit ourselves to one central piece of Nipkow's many writings, "Christian Faith Instruction in a Secular World: Two Basic Didactic Types of Evangelical Religious Education."[71] This seminal article is one of the important texts of the 1960s that documents certain changes and helps bring these changes about. Although this article clearly contains some of the central ideas found in Nipkow's earlier and later writings, it certainly does not contain all the ideas that characterize his later publications in the 1980s and 1990s.

---

68. It must also be mentioned that Nipkow supervised the doctoral work of the German author of this book.

69. For biographical information cf. Karl Ernst Nipkow, "Religionspädagogik zwischen Theologie und Pädagogik, Kirche und Gesellschaft," in *Lebensweg und religiöse Erziehung. Religionspädagogik als Autobiographie*, vol. 2, ed. Rainer Lachmann and Horst F. Rupp (Weinheim: Deutscher Studie-Verlag, 1989), pp. 215-34.

70. Karl Ernst Nipkow: *Grundfragen der Religionspädagogik*, 3 vols. (Gütersloh: Gütersloher Verlagshaus, 1975-1982); *Bildung als Lebensbegleitung und Erneuerung. Kirchliche Bildungsverantwortung in Gemeinde, Schule und Gesellschaft* (Gütersloh: Gütersloher Verlagshaus, 1990); *Bildung in einer pluralen Welt*, 2 vols. (Gütersloh: Gütersloher Verlagshaus, 1998).

71. Karl Ernst Nipkow, "Christlicher Glaubensunterricht in der Säkularität — Die zwei didaktischen Grundtypen des evangelischen Religionsunterrichts," in *Schule und Religionsunterricht im Wandel. Ausgewählte Studien zur Pädagogik und Religionspädagogik,* by Karl Ernst Nipkow (Heidelberg: Quelle und Meyer, 1971), pp. 236-63.

As mentioned in the preceding section, one of the controversial issues of religious education in the 1960s concerned the Bible and its position in teaching religion. The most widespread assumption at the time, derived from evangelical instruction, was that the Bible should be the center of religious education and that the contents of religious education should be taken directly from the Bible. The new approach, which was seen as an alternative to that kind of biblical instruction, was called a "problem" or "theme" centered approach. With this approach, problems or themes taken from contemporary experience became the main source for content. In problem-oriented religious education the Bible was not expelled from religious education, but it was turned to only after a current issue or contemporary problem had been scrutinized quite independently from theological or biblical perspectives. Within this scrutiny, teachers and students were expected to search for solutions to the problem and then find them in, among other places, the Bible.

Nipkow's position on the role of the Bible in religious education is more cautious than the radical problem-centered approach advocated by some of his colleagues. While affirming adamantly the need for a new approach to religious education, he also wants religious educators to teach the content of the Bible. So, in the subtitle of his seminal 1968 article, he describes "two basic didactic types of evangelical religious education" — teaching the Bible, and what he calls "instruction about being Christian and human in the contemporary world," which is his more sophisticated version of the problem-oriented approach.[72] It is important to note that Nipkow's recommendation to continue teaching the content of the Bible does not represent a return to theological conservatism, a point that is apparent when one considers that he wants this instruction about the Bible to be based on both modern theology and modern educational theory.

Nipkow's article begins with his criteria of how biblical teaching should be shaped, that is, how it should both meet the "challenge of the rationality of our time and of the scientific results of theology" and be presented "in a modern educational style."[73] Nipkow is arguing here for a threefold modernization of religious education — vis-à-vis modern culture and its rationality; vis-à-vis modern theology, which he calls "scientific" and therefore regards as expressing modern rationality; and vis-à-vis modern education, which means that religious education should be open to the helpful insights of social scientific theories of teaching and learning. Both kinds of religious instruction — teaching the content of the Bible and teaching how one can be

---

72. Nipkow, "Christlicher Glaubensunterricht in der Säkularität," p. 252.
73. Nipkow, "Christlicher Glaubensunterricht in der Säkularität," p. 236.

"Christian and human in the contemporary world" — should face up to this threefold challenge of modernization in culture, theology, and education. In other words, the biblical instruction recommended here is supposed to do justice to the demands of modern society.

Nipkow argues that religious educators should acknowledge that, in modernity, biblical instruction must be "interpretive."[74] It should, therefore, include the insights of modern hermeneutics in general and of hermeneutical theology in particular. In this way, Nipkow draws upon the insights of the hermeneutical turn in religious education mentioned above. Why is this so important to Nipkow? In stating his reasons, Nipkow points to the influence of the sciences in contemporary culture. Quoting German sociologist H. Schelsky, he maintains that "contemporary civilization . . . has become a 'scientific civilization.'" It is "determined by the sciences and it depends on the sciences." And this is not the result of any particular scientific discoveries but of a general scientific consciousness. The social sciences and the natural sciences — and their technological applications — have brought about "a far-reaching change of consciousness," and this change affects "the human relationship to religion at its roots."[75]

The main consequence of the changes in culture, theology, and education is then identified as the demand of "rationality" confronting church and religion. But how is the church to respond to this demand? Not via a religious "flight" from rationality and history or via a new religious ideology. Nipkow argues that contemporary religious education should teach toward a "thinking faith," that is, a faith informed by thinking, a faith that is willing and able to account for itself by means of modern theology.[76] For Nipkow, this type of intellectual responsibility for one's own faith is not opposed to the Christian tradition but has its roots in the theology found in the Bible itself. At the same time, a rational theological approach is not enough. Theology needs to become aware of the limits of its knowledge. It should become self-critical and "self-enlightening," not just by including the scientific approaches promoted by the Enlightenment but by moving on toward an "Enlightenment of this Enlightenment."[77] By this Nipkow means that critical thinking must be self-critical if it is not to become contradictory by being applied uncritically to everything in the world. One important aspect of modern theology is, according to Nipkow, its attempt to investigate the processes of religious tradition.

74. Nipkow, "Christlicher Glaubensunterricht in der Säkularität," p. 236.
75. Nipkow, "Christlicher Glaubensunterricht in der Säkularität," p. 237.
76. Nipkow, "Christlicher Glaubensunterricht in der Säkularität," p. 239.
77. Nipkow, "Christlicher Glaubensunterricht in der Säkularität," p. 241.

Yet theology must remain aware of the difference between academic discourse and a living relationship with God, which may never be fully translated into scientific language.

All this is said with reference to biblical instruction. What then about the *second type* of religious instruction, the problem-oriented approach, or "instruction about being Christian and human in the contemporary world," as Nipkow calls it? The section on this type of religious education begins with the following statement, indicating the importance of the concept of secularization and secularity for justifying the introduction of this new approach:

> The secularity of our time finds its expression not only in the self-sufficient worldliness of thinking which demonstrates no need for religion. . . . It also finds expression in a similarly self-sufficient worldliness of behavior that also shows no need for religion. Not only thinking one does not need a God anymore; one in fact acts as if there is no God. Isn't it therefore necessary to talk about God in this god-empty world in a new way?[78]

It is clear, then, that one of the foundations of Nipkow's approach is his conviction that religious education needs to face up to the fact that the culture in which it teaches sees the world as essentially godless and secular, as a world that has emptied itself of all references to God or religion in thinking and acting. The emphasis with which Nipkow sets forth this interpretation of the contemporary situation shows that he wants to convince others in school or church that the world has indeed become as remote from the Christian tradition as he says and that there is no point in denying this. Nipkow is not suggesting changes in praxis because he and his theological friends in religious education want to revolutionize religious education but because the world out there makes these far-reaching changes mandatory and inevitable.

In these arguments based on secularization theory Nipkow is clearly addressing church and theology. He is also, however, trying to gain a hearing with a second audience: his colleagues in general education. From the beginning of the article, Nipkow advocates the acceptance of modern educational theory and praxis. His call for religious education to change its praxis in light of the world's secularity may be interpreted as being partly motivated by this advocacy — that is, it may be seen as an attempt to gain more legitimacy for religious education praxis in the eyes of general educators by changing this praxis in light of an educational critique of its traditionalism and the mono-

---

78. Nipkow, "Christlicher Glaubensunterricht in der Säkularität," p. 252.

lithic nature of its didactics. While talking to religious educators in churches and schools, he is also, therefore, implicitly addressing his colleagues in general education who are critical of the way in which religious education is done.

It is interesting to see how Nipkow continues his argument by pointing out that the "alienation of the human from the religious" is also due to certain trends in Protestant theology itself, most of all in the dialectical theology of Barth. With its critical distinction between religion, seen as an inescapably human and sinful phenomenon, and Christian faith, seen as being based on the divine revelation of the only true word of God, this theology, according to Nipkow, left no room for any positive appreciation of religion, not even for children or youth who are not yet able to understand the concept of sin.[79] Consequently, the reappreciation of Christian religion demands a different theological basis as well.

The consequence of all this may be seen in the demand for a type of religious instruction that takes the contemporary world as its starting point, educationally as well as theologically — a type of instruction that takes the secular character of this world as seriously as possible. If Nipkow still uses the term "faith instruction" as opposed to "religious education," this may be interpreted as his way of highlighting the tension and conflict between the Christian tradition and the secular world. At the same time, it may be taken as an attempt at inviting dialogue with the adherents of evangelical instruction, who, as described in the preceding chapter, widely refused to speak of "religion."

This openness to modern theology, to modern education, and to the challenges posed by modern rationality is characteristic of all of Nipkow's publications. In this sense, his 1968 article on "faith instruction" is indicative of some important ideas found in his later publications between the 1960s and the 1990s and also of some major tendencies in German religious education as a whole at that time. Nipkow's later works do also include, however, some different characteristics, which is why, in concluding this section, some of these must be at least mentioned.

What in 1968 Nipkow refers to as modern education was, for the most part, the philosophy of education which, at that time in Germany, was based on hermeneutics and not on the empirical approaches of the social sciences. After the late 1960s German general education made a major turn toward the social sciences, especially by including sociological and psychological insights. Parallel to these changes in general education Nipkow's later publications include a strong reliance on the social sciences and developmental psy-

---

79. Nipkow, "Christlicher Glaubensunterricht in der Säkularität," p. 253.

chology. In many places, he draws on pyschological and sociological research about youth, including survey data. Jean Piaget's and, later on, James Fowler's theories of faith development play a major role in his accounts of religious development and education in childhood, adolescence, and adulthood. At the same time, his focus on secularization is replaced more and more by references to religious and cultural pluralism, especially in his writings of the 1990s.[80] Even though we are not aiming at a comprehensive overview of Nipkow's work, we must mention his continued effort to stay in dialogue not only with the field of religious education but also with education in general — and with the philosophy of education. In one of his major books, published in 1990, Nipkow sets forth a theory of the church's responsibility for all of education.[81] This responsibility includes religious education but clearly goes beyond it. Church and theology should claim a voice in the public debates on all types of education: youth work, adult education, education within the public schools, and education within the family. With this comprehensive theory Nipkow has made an important contribution to what we have called *paideia.*

Religious Education in Germany between the 1960s and 1990s in the Context of Modernization

In this section, we will broaden our scope and go beyond developments in the 1960s in order to include the entire period between the 1960s and the 1990s. Nipkow's approach, outlined in his 1968 article, will be merely our starting point for a discussion that leads us into a wider field of pertinent changes. As the preceding section made clear, it is easy to see why the context of social modernization is an important background for understanding the new problem-oriented approach. Nipkow makes it clear that he is responding to *modern theology, modern rationality,* and *modern education.* Religious education, he argues, should face up to modernization by becoming open to the various challenges emerging from the three sources of modernization he identifies (theology, science, and education). For Nipkow, the social and cultural context in which religious education takes place in school and society evidences social modernization. Nipkow sees rationality as challenging all traditions and science as having conquered the world, even to the point that it has come to shape individual consciousness.

---

80. See especially Karl Ernst Nipkow, *Bildung in einer pluralen Welt.*
81. Karl Ernst Nipkow, *Bildung als Lebensbegleitung und Erneuerung.*

Nipkow considers the position of religion in this modern world to be precarious. The decisive parameters of rationality — scientific thinking, moral action, and modern education — do not stop short of religion. Far from this, they define the grounds on which religion has to defend its claims and has to maintain a place for itself, Nipkow is convinced. This raises for him serious questions about the theology on which religious education should be based. In Nipkow's 1968 article, we found a slight criticism of how a certain type of theology maintains a view of revealed faith that sets it apart from human religion rather than appreciating human religion. At least in the 1960s, however, a more positive view of religion presupposing a different theological understanding did not really exist in Germany. Theologians and sociologists alike saw religion as being on the wane. They did not expect a recovery of religion, be it through changes in society or through conscious efforts to strengthen religion by supporting and defending it. Obviously, the concept of secularization worked as an obstacle against even thinking of this possibility. If religion does not have a future because the future will be secular, there is no point in appreciating religion or fighting for it. It was not until the 1970s and 1980s that the concept of secularization came under critical scrutiny in religious education and that new and constructive ways of coming into dialogue with the religion of children and youth could be introduced.[82] This attempt to reconceptualize religious education in relation to modernization, especially the challenges of secularization, was not an isolated tendency. Rather, it points to a broader context of changes taking place in Germany at this time, including changes in the political situation, the educational system, and also the position of the church in society.

In Germany, the 1960s are often associated with the political movements emerging during this period, especially the student movement that had its peak in Germany in the year 1968. It has become customary to speak of the "1968 generation," meaning those people who were young or old enough to become involved in the politicization and the new lifestyles emerging during this period. Another important change in Germany in the 1960s involved the party coalition on which the German government was based. For the first time, it included the Social Democratic Party. This put an end to a long postwar conservative Christian Democratic government tradition founded by chancellor Adenauer, and it finally led, in the 1970s, to the Social Democratic governments of chancellors Brandt and Schmidt. While the Social Democrats, with

---

82. To mention just one example, Volker Drehsen, *Wie religionsfähig ist die Volkskirche? Sozialisationstheoretische Erkundungen neuzeitlicher Christentumspraxis* (Gütersloh: Gütersloher Verlagshaus, 1994).

their emphasis on equality and justice, were closer to the new ideals of the 1960s, political conflict was nevertheless a matter of daily concern for Germans because of public political rallies and, in the late 1970s, because of the perverted politics of terrorism in the name of liberation.

The various governments between the 1960s and 1989 maintained the course of what has come to be called Germany's orientation toward the West in international politics.[83] More and more, Germany became a well-established partner in NATO and also, with increasingly important implications, of the western European market and economic community, which since 1999 has been unified by a single currency. At the same time, the Social Democratic governments and, most notably, chancellor Brandt, achieved a major detente with the neighboring East Bloc countries. Brandt negotiated Germany's official acceptance of the territorial claims allotted to Poland in 1945. (That is to say, Germany permanently relinquished claims to those territories that had been part of Germany before World War II.) Consequently, the road was paved for more peaceful relationships with neighboring communist countries, a development that was one of the factors leading to the German unification of 1990 and to the political reconstruction of Eastern Europe in the 1990s.

In the 1960s a new era of prosperity dawned in Germany. Postwar reconstruction, which had used up many resources in the 1940s and 1950s, had come to an end. Between 1960 and 1975 the gross national product increased by 100 percent.[84] This increase was accompanied by an important shift away from the agricultural sector, while the economic importance of services and also of government spending grew steadily.[85] Another indicator of the economic growth of this period is the growing need for non-German workers. Starting in the 1960s, many were lured to Germany with financial incentives. Between 1955 and 1965 their number increased from eighty thousand to over one million, and by 1975 the figure had gone up to two million.[86] This immigration of so-called "guest workers" from southern Europe and, later on, from Turkey was the beginning of a more multicultural Germany, as it has been called since the 1980s.

83. Jürgen Habermas, *Die Normalität einer Berliner Republik. Kleine Politische Schriften VIII* (Frankfurt: Suhrkamp, 1995), offers philosophical observations on the political traditions of West Germany.

84. Cf. Max-Planck-Institut für Bildungsforschung (The Max Planck Institute for Human Development), ed., *Bildung in der Bundesrepublik Deutschland. Daten und Analysen*, vol. 1: *Entwicklungen seit 1950* (Reinbek: Rowohlt, 1980), p. 25.

85. Max-Planck-Institut, ed., *Bildung in der Bundesrepublik Deutschland*, pp. 27f.

86. Max-Planck-Institut, ed., *Bildung in der Bundesrepublik Deutschland*, p. 26.

Starting in the 1960s, the German government made a new effort to provide a much larger segment of the population with access to public resources than had been the case before. This effort can be seen in reforms in health and welfare policies, programs for special groups in society, and in educational programs. Government spending in the area of social policy doubled and that in education tripled between 1960 and 1975.[87] By the late 1960s major reforms in education were under way. To some extent, these were spurred by international economic competition, but they also included an emphasis on educational equality and education as a right of all citizens.[88] To mention just one example, the percentage of students in university-track secondary schools tripled between 1960 and the 1980s, from approximately 10 percent to more than 30 percent. In 1950, the figure had been 3 percent![89]

These quantitative changes within education were accompanied by important qualitative changes in the understanding of education and its contents or aims. More and more, modern science became the leading model for education. Some traditional educational ideals, such as valuing obedience over autonomy, were rejected as ill-suited for the future. One important indicator of this change is that research data suggests that from the 1960s to the 1980s the importance placed on obedience in Germany dropped from 25 percent to less than 10 percent, while the importance placed on autonomy increased from less than 10 percent to almost 50 percent.[90]

The idea of liberation (or "emancipation," as it was then called) played a major role in the culture of the 1960s and 1970s. It should be added that this development had important implications for the church and for religion in general in Germany. Before 1945, the various territories that together made up Germany had been close to uniform in their denominational character. This uniformity was based on the Peace of Westphalia, a treaty of 1648 dictating the principle of *cuius regio eius religio*, which meant that the ruler's religion determined the religion of those living in his territory. Within predominantly Protestant Germany, there had been denominational subcultures that sepa-

---

87. Max-Planck-Institut, ed., *Bildung in der Bundesrepublik Deutschland*, p. 51.

88. For an overview cf. Ludwig von Friedeburg, *Bildungsreform in Deutschland. Geschichte und gesellschaftlicher Widerspruch* (Frankfurt: Suhrkamp, 1989).

89. Max-Planck-Institut, ed., *Bildung in der Bundesrepublik Deutschland*, p. 67; Heinz-Elmar Tenorth, *Geschichte der Erziehung. Einführung in die Grundzüge ihrer neuzeitlichen Entwicklung* (Weinheim: Juventa Verlag, 1988), p. 274. For additional information see Christoph Führ and Carl-Ludwig Furck, eds., *Handbuch der deutschen Bildungsgeschichte*, vol. 6: *1945 bis zur Gegenwart* (München: Beck, 1997).

90. Fend, *Sozialgeschichte des Aufwachsens. Bedingungen des Aufwachsens und Jugendgestalten im zwanzigsten Jahrhundert* (Frankfurt am Main: Suhrkamp, 1988), p. 114.

rated the people, not only religiously but also socially. Roman Catholics formed the most important subculture of this type.[91] After the 1950s, however, the Catholic subculture (as well as the other subcultures) gradually ceased to exist, because, as mentioned at the beginning of this chapter, people started to socialize across denominational dividing lines and intermarry without regard to their churches' advice to find a partner within their own denomination. In part, the erosion of the Catholic subculture may also be attributed to the new ecumenical openness that resulted from the Second Vatican Council in the 1960s.

After saying all this, we have to keep in mind that the major issue for the churches themselves during this period was secularization.[92] A visible decline in church attendance and a sharp increase in drop-out rates from church membership were probably the signs of change that most alarmed German church boards and leaders.[93] This drop-out rate in church attendance was mirrored by a high drop-out rate in the religious education classes of the public schools. More students than ever made use of their constitutional right to opt out of the religious education program. Student groups drafted fliers urging other students to drop out en masse. This overt crisis in religious education in the schools must be taken into account when analyzing the developments in religious education theory after the mid 1960s in Germany.

Although the developments of the 1960s were a watershed for German religious education and the church, they were not the only determinants of the marked changes that took place from 1950 to 1980. New developments in the 1970s and 1980s also exerted an influence on religious education. The oil crisis of the early 1970s, for example, put ecology on the agenda not only of politics but also of religious education. The peace movement of the early 1980s and, somewhat later, what came to be called the ecumenical process for justice, peace, and the integrity of the creation also became major factors influencing religious education.

The rapid and far-reaching changes in religious education in Germany between the 1960s and the 1990s may be considered another clear example of the way in which the pressures of modernization — seen not only in science, rationality, religion, and modern education, but in the overall social mindset —

91. Cf. Franz-Xaver Kaufmann and Bernhard Schäfers, eds., *Religion, Kirchen und Gesellschaft in Deutschland. Gegenwartskunde Sonderheft 5* (Opladen: Leske und Budrich, 1989).

92. Feige, *Kirchenmitgliedschaft in der Bundesrepublik Deutschland.*

93. Cf. Jürgen Henkys and Friedrich Schweitzer, "Atheism, Religion and Indifference in the Two Parts of Germany: Before and After 1989," in *Religion and the Social Order: Leaving Religion and Religious Life,* ed. Mordechai Bar-Lev and William Shaffir (Greenwich, Conn.: Jai, 1997), pp. 117-37.

have affected religious education. Many of the new approaches ushered in by the turn to problem-oriented religious education in the 1960s may be regarded as responses to this modernization — as attempts to face up to modernization and to make use of whatever positive forces could be seen in the social changes.

Looking back at the 1960s and 1970s, it is an open question how much progress in terms of liberation and autonomy the new educational ideas of that period really brought about. Many of these ideas now appear one-sided and prone to rationalism. By the late 1970s, many conservative educators and politicians expressed their fear that the educational reforms of the 1960s had a detrimental effect on character education and that a more conservative type of education was needed again. Neither the conservatives nor the liberals really understood that their debates fell short of the actual problems facing society and that they should not only set forth educational ideals but also address the changing cultural and religious situation.

One of the topics that is surprisingly absent from the educational literature of the 1960s and 1970s is the plurality of the social and cultural situation. Quite often, the situation encountered by religious education was interpreted in terms of clear-cut alternatives: religious or secular, the church or the world, and so on. There exist, in fact, many different outlooks along the spectrum between religious and secular and between ecclesiastical and worldly. There also exist several outlooks that consider these sorts of dichotomies as false. The increasingly multicultural and multireligious nature of contemporary societies makes it mandatory to work with more precise and differentiated terminology and interpretations by including consideration of other pertinent concepts such as pluralization and individualization.

Obviously, the year 1990 by no means marks an end to the process of religious education responding to modernization and struggling with it. During the 1980s and 1990s postmodernism and globalization entered the picture and are now claiming much attention in religious education along with other new challenges. We will come back to these challenges in the last part of this book.

Comparative Aspects

The time between the 1960s and 1990 was different from the earlier periods examined in this book in that it was a period of much greater international awareness and cooperation in religious education. Several aspects and developments can be mentioned in this regard, and they often involve German-

American cooperation and exchange. In both countries during the 1960s, common themes were emphasized in education, and psychological theories from Erik H. Erikson, Lawrence Kohlberg, and, somewhat later, James W. Fowler and Carol Gilligan strongly influenced religious education theory and praxis in both Germany and the United States and worked as another common background. In addition, with the introduction of international seminars and associations, personal contacts across national boundaries also became more frequent. The activities of the World Council of Churches should also be mentioned here. The increasingly visible role that educational questions were allowed to play at the WCC meetings at all levels during this period certainly helped to create a climate in which international interest in religious education could flourish. International student exchange programs began to include religious education, and, in contrast to the nineteenth century, more and more Germans came to the United States rather than Americans going to Germany.[94]

In light of this backdrop of growing international cooperation and exchange, comparative considerations gain additional weight. If the field of religious education has become international, theoretical approaches must also come to be international in scope. International comparative research clearly is an outgrowth of the "internationalization of the field," as we will call it below. In this sense, our own study builds on, and carries forward, the developments described in this chapter.

As we look back at religious education in Germany and the United States during the period spanning 1960 to 1990, a number of similarities are apparent. Our discussion will focus on general trends in religious education in both countries as well as the particular ideas found in the works of Westerhoff and Nipkow. In spite of the very important historical and contextual differences characterizing these two countries, it is remarkable that similarities in the field of religious education can be discerned along at least five lines.

First, religious education in both countries after the 1960s came to be characterized by a high degree of pluralism. As our discussion of Westerhoff and Nipkow noted, it is virtually impossible to identify a *single* dominant figure or approach to religious education during this period. Rather, the field in both countries increasingly put forward a wide variety of approaches and models. These were characterized by important theological differences, as

---

94. The German author of this book came to the United States as a student at Harvard in the late 1970s. One purpose of his time at Harvard was to work on a dissertation in the field of religious education.

well as differences in the overarching conceptualization of the purpose, sites, and methods of religious education.

Second, religious education in both countries was characterized by a new spirit of ecumenicity. The sharp divisions that had existed between Protestants and Roman Catholics and between Christians and other religious communities increasingly were blurred. Interdenominational and interreligious dialogue became an important feature of the discourse of religious education. Influence and mutual learning flowed much more easily and without suspicion across ecumenical lines. Prominent Roman Catholic religious education theorists influenced Protestants and vice versa.

A third common trend was the internationalization of the field in both countries. This was driven, in part, by the increased involvement of religious education scholars in a wide range of international organizations and consultations. The educational work of Paulo Freire, William Kennedy, and Ulrich Becker at the World Council of Churches in Geneva is only the tip of the iceberg. Numerous scholars in both countries participated in ISREV (International Seminar on Religious Education and Values) and the newly formed International Academy of Practical Theology. International consultations took place on faith development theory in Tübingen, on church development in the Netherlands, on religious education and pluralism in England, and on practical theology and ethics in Heidelberg.[95] The translation of prominent religious education texts originally written in other national contexts into German and English increased in scope and pace (even if the availability of book-length publications in translation is still a problem in this field). Nipkow and Westerhoff, for example, had numerous international contacts and exchanges and are well-known by their counterparts in other countries.

A fourth point of similarity is the prominence of a note of transformation/change in the rhetoric of religious education theorists in both countries. Not only is this apparent in the writings of Nipkow and Westerhoff, it is found across a variety of writings by scholars holding perspectives quite different than theirs. Two things are being pointed to here: on the one hand, a sense that the approaches to religion, church life, and religious education developed in the postwar period were no longer working and that new forms of religious education were needed to take their place; on the other hand, a sense that

95. To mention some of the publications: James W. Fowler, Karl Ernst Nipkow, and Friedrich Schweitzer, eds., *Stages of Faith and Religious Development: Implications for Church, Education and Society* (New York: Crossroad, 1991); M. C. Felderhof, ed., *Religious Education in a Pluralistic Society* (London: Hodder and Stoughton, 1985); Wilhelm Gräb et al., eds., *Christentum und Spätmoderne. Ein internationaler Diskurs über Praktische Theologie und Ethik* (Stuttgart: Kohlhammer, 2000).

changes both inside and outside of the church posed new challenges to religious education. The perception of the increased pace of secularization, for example — a process which led many youth to refuse to take religious education courses in the school or to drop out of organized religion altogether during adolescence (a pattern evident in both countries) — led many religious educators to point to the need for new forms of religious education. Both Nipkow and Westerhoff pointed to something like this trend. Likewise, the influence of liberation and feminist social movements during this period led many to argue that new forms of religious education were needed. In short, the rhetoric of a wide range of religious education scholars during this period was characterized by a note of transformation and change, both denoting a break with the recent past, especially postwar forms of religious education, and pointing to new social problems and possibilities that needed to be addressed.

A fifth trend is the widespread recognition of the need for religious education to engage in a sustained dialogue with the social sciences. Especially prominent during this period was the influence of various life-cycle and structural developmental psychological theories. The influence of Erik Erikson, Jean Piaget, Lawrence Kohlberg, James Fowler, and, somewhat later, Carol Gilligan was widespread. Moreover, the socialization approaches to religious education championed by Ellis Nelson and Westerhoff led many in the United States to discover the importance of cultural anthropology and sociology as dialogue partners. In Germany, the critical social theory of the Frankfurt School, especially of Jürgen Habermas, became important, and, more recently, the writings of Niklas Luhmann have been influential. In some instances, religious education theories began to reach behind the models of the postwar period to the religious education reform movements of the early twentieth century. Here they found a history of dialogue with the social sciences that seemed worth recovering. In Germany, particularly, the strong tradition of academic practical theology led many prominent scholars to view this dialogue as one in which theology figured prominently, that is, as a dialogue between theology and the social sciences.[96] This perspective was not as well developed in the United States, although it became increasingly important across this period in the writings of James Fowler, Thomas Groome, Don Browning, and Westerhoff. While the Barthian models of the recent past seemed to offer little help in conceptualizing the conversation between theology and the social sciences, the

---

96. See, for example, Karl Ernst Nipkow, Dietrich Rössler, and Friedrich Schweitzer, eds., *Praktische Theologie und Kultur der Gegenwart. Ein internationaler Dialog* (Gütersloh: Gütersloher Verlagshaus, 1991); Norbert Mette and Hermann Steinkamp, *Sozialwissenschaften und Praktische Theologie* (Düsseldorf: Patmos, 1983).

tradition of this sort of conversation in the thinking of the Niebuhr brothers and Paul Tillich and the emerging models of liberation, feminist, revisionist, and process thought were important in the United States. Indeed, the variety of ways theology and the social sciences were viewed as related was one of the hallmarks of the pluralism, pointed to above.

As we stand back from these five trends that are evident in both countries, how do the frameworks of modernization and globalization help us make sense of these commonalties? Modernization theory is helpful, but it takes us only so far. It draws attention to the rapid expansion of higher education in both countries and the advances in pluralization, individualization, and secularization in a variety of institutions (such as higher education) and the culture generally. It also calls attention to the emergence of numerous social movements during this period, movements that sought to actualize the critical potential of values that had been a part of the Western political tradition since the Enlightenment. The Civil Rights movement, the human rights movement, and contemporary feminism, at least in part, drew on the long traditions of emancipation and civil/political rights that were a part of the cultural heritage of both countries. These contextual factors played an important role in the changing shape of religious education during this period. They fostered a sense that a new social context was emerging — filled with challenges and possibilities — and that new forms of religious education were needed to respond to this context.

At the same time, however, we can also see from the perspective of hindsight that modernization, by itself, cannot account for many of the most important characteristics of this period. The perspective of globalization is more helpful. The 1960s marked the acceleration of the emergence of a global economy, driven by advances in electronic communication, international trade, and the emergence of multinational corporations (factors pointed to in Part I of this book). Moreover, this decade saw the beginning of the flow of new immigrant populations to both Germany and the United States, something that continued in the decades that followed. While secularization describes some facets of this period, it does not really capture the new forms of religiosity emerging in both countries. Eastern forms of spirituality became more prominent among the young; Muslim communities became a presence in both countries. Religiously motivated political action by both the Right and the Left were a part of national political life. Surely this pluralistic religious mix in society accounts in part for the pluralism within the field of religious education. It also accounts for an increased spirit of openness and ecumenicity across denominational and religious lines. In addition to this, a high degree of religious individualization and a spirituality that is not connected to religious institutions and formal membership account for the challenges religious education had to face in both countries.

The internationalization of religious education during this period, likewise, is best viewed in terms of globalization. Not only was international travel easier and less expensive, but also academic texts disseminated across cultural boundaries more quickly and electronic communication between scholars living in different parts of the world was now possible. But these changes alone do not tell the whole story. What seems to be emerging during this period is a much greater awareness of the global whole, the interconnectedness of the human community across national boundaries. An important part of this was an increased awareness of the diversity of cultures and religions. The celebration of secularization, found in the 1960s in prominent texts like Harvey Cox's *The Secular City*, gradually gave way to a sense that religious education faced the daunting task of preparing persons for participation in a multicultural and multireligious world. The older social boundaries of nationality, religion, ethnicity, and race were now being refigured in ways that were yet to be determined.

In hindsight, we may even be able to venture the idea that it was the perspective of modernization itself that was beginning to be questioned in religious education during this period, the perspective — largely based on the experience of the West — that secular, liberal democratic, and capitalistic forms of social organization inevitably form the wave of the future. In ways that were only dimly perceived initially, religious educators in both countries were beginning to rethink many of the inherited categories of the past to better respond to the challenges of an emerging global context. In this context, the pluralism, internationalization, spirit of ecumenicity, and sense that something new was on the horizon — prominent characteristics in religious education in both Germany and the United States during this period — can, perhaps, best be interpreted as the first steps to a much larger rethinking of religious education in the face of globalization.

If this interpretation has merit, then it allows us to grasp the important differences distinguishing Nipkow and Westerhoff in a new light. When both are viewed as offering early forms of response in religious education to the emergence of a global context, their proposals represent stark alternatives, alternatives that remain before the field. In terms of their relationship to national and global publics, Westerhoff represents a communitarian form of response; Nipkow, a public church response. By the former is meant the belief that Christian congregations, in the face of national pluralism and global multiculturalism, must tighten their communal boundaries in order to hand on a clear sense of Christian identity. If children, youth, and adults are bombarded by a range of cultural possibilities and values, the church must clear its own space in this cultural mix in order to help persons construct a Christian identity, enabling them to internalize a meaningful sense of the Christian story and virtues. By a "public church" approach is meant the belief that the church has a stake in national and global public life and that its task is to teach its members the kinds of communicative competencies and values that are needed for participation in these publics. Moreover, the congregation is not viewed as the exclusive locus of God's concern for the world. The church, by definition, is seen as a church for the world. It finds its reason for being not apart from the world in a kind of countercultural community, but in its participation in the historical and social transformations by which the human community builds a common life together or tears itself apart.

Obviously, this characterization of Westerhoff and Nipkow goes beyond the particular writings that we examined. But it does indicate the sort of interpretive perspective that begins to emerge when these figures are located in the context of globalization theory. They represent early forms of response to globalizing trends, much as Coe and Niebergall responded to the acceleration of modernization in the industrialization of the economy, urbanization, and other factors at the beginning of this century. While the problems of modernization remain with us, it is also the case that a distinctly new set of issues has emerged over the past decades. In the final part of this book, we will examine some of these issues, pointing to the challenges they pose to religious education as it enters the twenty-first century.

In concluding this part of the book it can again be pointed out in what respect our international comparative approach leads us beyond the standard account of religious education theory in the twentieth century. As mentioned above, the standard account tends to focus on the internal structuring of different theoretical positions in order to arrive at a typology of religious education approaches. In this view, different types of religious education are understood as combinations of particular theologies and corresponding educational perspectives. While this kind of analysis and interpretation clearly has its value, it runs the risk of overlooking the more comprehensive contextual challenges to which religious education theory and praxis are always responding. By viewing religious education more contextually, we are trying to overcome these limitations and to widen the understanding of the task of religious education. As will become clear in the last part of the book, this is more than an academic question. What is at stake is the future of religious education itself, and with it the future of our children — as Christians and also as human beings whose life prospects must be supported by today's adult generation.

III The Challenges of Protestant Religious Education in the Twenty-First Century

Introduction to Part III

In the final part of this book, we turn to the task of pointing to issues that face Christian religious education as it moves into the twenty-first century. Before taking up this task, it may be helpful to look back at the first two parts of this book. Our guiding thesis, described at the outset, has been that Protestant religious education stands in an interdependent relationship to the social contexts in which it is located and that these contexts are best understood today on the basis of international, comparative analysis. Using the frameworks of modernization, globalization, and postmodernism, we have examined key texts of prominent figures in Germany and the United States, locating them in relation to certain sociohistorical transformations within their respective national contexts and to broader social transformations that cross national boundaries. This approach varies in two ways from standard accounts of religious education in the German and American literatures.

First, it does not focus exclusively on the *ideas* of representative figures, locating their thinking in relation to the ideas of others in the field. Rather, we have focused primarily on the relationship of texts to contexts, exploring the possible relationship of ideas to social-historical transformations taking place at different points across the twentieth century. We have attempted to identify both the challenges that are explicitly addressed within the writings of these figures and the possible influence of social transformations taking place "behind their backs," which are more clearly evident in hindsight. Increasingly, social history has drawn on rhetorical modes of analysis to highlight the relationship of ideas and audience, texts and contexts. This has been a kind of subtheme of this book, and something explored in the chapter on the family below.

Second, rather than focusing on the ideas of prominent figures within a specific national context, our international-comparative approach has explored similarities and differences across Germany and the United States. Increasingly, we have come to believe this sort of research should be an important dimension of the historical investigation of religious education. Not only is new light thrown on standard accounts of national literatures but social and institutional forces that increasingly cross national boundaries are brought into focus. As became evident over the course of Part II, we have discovered a number of remarkable similarities in our comparison of representative figures in Germany and the United States.

That said, we are well aware of the limited scope of these comparisons. Even within our respective national contexts, we have focused primarily on "mainline" Protestant figures. No doubt, an examination of the writings of prominent Pentecostals or Baptists in these contexts, for example, would have yielded a very different set of findings. Moreover, we are quite clear that our decision to compare mainline Protestant religious education within two countries located in the North and West, which participated in a range of social transformations at roughly the same time, is an important factor in the similarities that have been discovered. It is quite possible that future comparative research will reveal massive dissimilarities between Christian religious education in the United States and Korea, for example, or Germany and Ghana. No claim is made here that the patterns discovered in our comparison of Germany and the United States are generalizable.

What is claimed, however, is that such international-comparative research throws important light on the ways religious traditions in different national contexts respond to social forces and patterns that increasingly have a transnational character. It may well be that religious education in the mainline Protestantism of Korea will pass through a phase comparable to the increased ecumenicity and pluralism found in both Germany and the United States after the 1960s. Then again, it may not. Only international-comparative research can discover these sorts of commonalities and differences, bringing into focus the ways different religious traditions respond to the forces of modernization, globalization, and postmodernism.

From the vantage point of our international-comparative research on Germany and the United States, what are some of the general trends that stand out? Especially as we turn to the constructive portion of this book, what have we learned about our past that throws light on our future? Four trends, in particular, are evident.

First, we can identify a trend that we have gradually come to call the "loss of audience." In both Germany and the United States, Protestant religious education theory has increasingly been addressed to leaders and teachers of religious education in congregations and, in Germany, religious education in state schools. This reflects two far-reaching developments pointed to repeatedly over the course of the first two parts of this book: (1) Protestantism has been displaced as the "core" religious culture of both national contexts and, under the impact of institutional and cultural differentiation, has become one subsystem among many; (2) simultaneously, religious education as an academic discipline has emerged, with its own professional audience, journals, guilds, and technical forms of discourse, much like other academic disciplines and professional fields. Together, these changes have led most of the representative figures examined in Part II to focus their attention on addressing professional leaders and teachers who are responsible for religious education in the primary "sites" of this activity: the congregation and, in Germany, the school. What disappears in this "loss of audience" is concern for the family and for the *paideia* of society generally. We do not want to overstate the point being made here. Some of the individuals examined in Part II, as well as many not examined, do continue to write about the family and address broader social concerns. On the whole, however, the discourse of religious education has tended to be addressed primarily to professionals providing leadership or teaching courses on religious education in congregations or schools.

A second trend follows closely. As Protestantism has become one religious community among many in a differentiated and pluralistic social context, it has been forced to rethink its relationship to public life generally. For much of the twentieth century, Protestants focused on the contributions of their religious communities to the common good of national communities. With the intensification of globalization, they have begun reflecting on their contribution to the global "commons." By focusing primarily on congregational life or religious education in schools, however, much of the discourse of religious education has left these kinds of issues in the background, if they are treated at all. There are many exceptions to this generalization. When viewed historically and cross-culturally, however, these exceptions prove the rule. Few scholars have taken up the daunting challenge of arguing for an important role for religious communities in public life. Little attention has been given to the virtues and communicative competencies these communities should teach their members if they are to participate in national and global publics. Nor has the argument often been made that the *paideia* of national communities must include attention to religion. In a world in which multiculturalism is increasingly prominent, this is deeply problematic. Is it

211

really possible to understand our Muslim neighbor, much less the challenges of the Middle East, without education that teaches us the history and contemporary expressions of Islam? And can we teach about other religions without also being given the opportunity to learn about our own religion and the ways it provides ethical resources for coming to terms with the other? For a wide variety of reasons, it is no longer adequate to conceptualize religious education in ways that do not give sustained attention to its contribution to public life.

Third, one of the most important trends to emerge in our examination of representative figures in Germany and the United States across the twentieth century is the struggle to articulate for religious education the relationship between theology and the cultural resources of modernity. As we have noted repeatedly, the emergence of the natural and social sciences posed an important challenge. On the one hand, the reformers of the religious education movement, especially in the United States, virtually defined their field in terms of modern science. On the other hand, the theological renewal found in both countries reacted against this use of modern science and reasserted the primacy of theological discourse in Protestant religious education theory. In retrospect, both tendencies can be viewed as reflexive responses to the differentiation of modern America and Germany, including their secularization, and the emergence of autonomous, scientific forms of scholarship in modern academic life. Neither provided an entirely adequate response. In religiously plural social contexts, it is evident that the religious self-understanding of different communities will play a role in the ways they think about religious education. Hence, attention to theological reflection is important and necessary — and, from a Christian perspective, religious education must always be related to such reflection because of its content and because of the educational consequences of theological anthropology. It is equally the case, however, that modern forms of scholarship in psychology, anthropology, sociology, gender studies, and education — to name but a few — are important resources that religious education ignores at its peril. What seems needed is further reflection on the variety of ways that religious education theory can bring theology and the cultural resources of its social context into dialogue. In recent decades, a range of possibilities has emerged.

A fourth trend focuses on the pluralism in religious education since the 1960s. If the first two historical periods were characterized by the dominance of a limited range of paradigms in religious education, this was no longer the case after the sixties. Increasingly, religious education in both Germany and the United States has been characterized by a high degree of diversity, including cross-fertilization across ecumenical and religious lines. In recent decades, moreover, this has been heightened by international exchange of various sorts. No doubt, this trend toward greater diversity within religious education reflects the increased reality of cultural pluralism and multiculturalism, both within and across national communities. It is no longer the case that one model fits all. Religious educators have begun to appropriate this insight at a methodological level, taking over one of the most important insights of intellectual postmodernism. The search for a "master narrative" that comprehends all cases can be a covert form of intellectual hegemony that is quite different from today's understanding of biblical or Christian narrative. Accordingly, religious educators have increasingly become more aware that they are developing particular models on the basis of specific theological and cross-disciplinary commitments.

In the remainder of this book, we attempt to point to some of the ways that religious education in the twenty-first century might respond to each of these trends. Most importantly, we address the "loss of audience" thesis by attempting to examine in the following chapters four important audiences of religious education. Religious education must take into account its contribution to the *paideia* of society, the church, the family, and the individual self. In a sense, we are proposing a "recovery of audience" for the religious education of the future.

Each chapter, moreover, seeks to take up one of the pressing issues that have been identified above, pointing to possible ways practical theology and religious education theory might address that particular issue. Chapter Six, "Christianity's Contribution to *Paideia* and to Society," gives special attention to the public task of practical theology and religious education theory. Here, the importance of conceptualizing religious education's contribution to the common good is addressed in the face of the tendency to limit it to congregations or to special courses of religious education. Chapter Seven, "Congregational Education and the Challenge of Cross-Disciplinary Thinking," examines the ongoing struggle to define the relationship of theology and the scholarly resources of contemporary culture. Different types of cross-disciplinary thinking are identified, and religious educators are encouraged to be clear about what is at stake in each type. Chapter Eight, "The Religious Dimension of the Self," focuses on the importance of acknowledging diversity in our accounts of the postmodern self. The "master narratives" of recent psychological theories are called into question, and the importance of acknowledging in religious education the wide variety of patterns of the individual religious journey is pointed to. Chapter Nine, "The Family: The Rhetoric of Practical Theology and the Engagement of Audience," points to a rhetorical model of rationality. It seeks to articulate a model of rational communication that makes it possible for scholars to see themselves as addressing a wide range of publics, including the nonspecialist audience of parents and families.

In the final part of the book, we have written from our own perspectives as individual scholars. Schweitzer wrote the chapters on *paideia* and the self; Osmer, on congregations and the family. While we have read and responded to one another's chapters, each reflects the author's own particular point of view. This is reflected in the use of "I" at various points in this part of the book. Our purpose in signaling this at the outset is not so much to indicate major areas of disagreement between us but to make it clear that each of these chapters represents one attempt to address complex issues that could be addressed very differently by others. As we turn to the future, our task is not so much to reach consensus in the field — something we no longer believe is possible or desirable — but to work in a methodologically self-conscious fashion, articulating the commitments we hold and our reading of the social context being addressed. By allowing our own voices to come to the fore in the constructive part of this book, we hope to make it clear that this sort of "situated," pluralistic conversation is how we see the future of our field.

6 Christianity's Contribution to Paideia and to Society

This section on perspectives for the future of Christian religious education begins with a chapter on the *public* role of practical theology and religious education. We will consider this public role first because we believe that it is important and that it has been neglected. We are not arguing that the public is a more important audience for us than the congregation or other sites of Christian religious education treated in subsequent chapters, but we do think that the sparse attention typically given to the public role of practical theology (often in short paragraphs or at the ends of books) certainly misses the central importance of the public as an audience.

This chapter begins with a section examining the question, What is the public task of practical theology in general and of religious education in particular? The chapter's second part will review and analyze social and theological developments during the twentieth century (described in Part II of this book) in order to provide societal and theological rationales for a public role for religious education. Based on this analysis, the final section of this chapter will offer some perspectives on the future role of religious education in society.

The Public Task of Practical Theology and of Religious Education Theory

When I speak of the public task of practical theology or of a public practical theology, I am referring to a specific task or dimension of this discipline. The claim is not that all practical theology ought to be public in the sense of addressing and making sense to a general audience. Practical theology also has to play a role within the church and consequently must address a Christian audience. Yet practical theology will not be able to live up to its tasks fully if it does not include the public dimension in its work.

The understanding of practical theology we are presenting needs an explanation because this discipline has quite often been understood exclusively in terms of clerical or congregational tasks. In this view the proper role of practical theology is merely to inform pastors and congregations about their various tasks and functions that are *not* seen in relationship to a wider context. In contrast to this narrow view, a public practical theology takes quite seriously the public's role as an audience of its work, both by addressing issues of the common life — local, national, and global public concerns — and by bringing theology into dialogue with contemporary culture. In order to explain the possibilities of a public practical theology more clearly, we will briefly review recent scholarship on two related concepts: public theology and the public church.

Public practical theology may be seen as a particular branch of public theology. The term "public theology" came into use only a few decades ago and is connected specifically to the work of authors like David Tracy and Ronald Thiemann who have developed models of public theology.[1] Although there are philosophical and theological differences between Tracy's and Thiemann's models, they agree that public theology refers to theology's responsibility to address the general public beyond congregation and church by critically relating the Christian tradition to contemporary social and political issues. Furthermore, this implies a commitment to a dialogue between theology and the public that is considered necessary for the common good, as well as for a theology that does not reduce its role to internal questions of the church. Although they have not used the term "public theology" to describe their work, theologians like Johann Baptist Metz, Matthew Lamb, and Rebecca Chopp have expressed similar reasons for the necessity of dialogue between theology and the public. They have developed liberation theologies that publicly and critically address issues of oppression, discrimination, and injustice.[2]

---

1. Cf. David Tracy, *Blessed Rage for Order: The New Pluralism in Theology* (Chicago: University of Chicago Press, 1996 [1975]); Ronald F. Thiemann, *Constructing a Public Theology: The Church in a Pluralistic Culture* (Louisville: Westminster/John Knox, 1991).

2. Johann Baptist Metz, *Faith in History and Society* (New York: Crossroad, 1980); Matthew Lamb, *Solidarity with Victims* (New York: Crossroad, 1982); Rebecca S. Chopp, "Practical Theology and Liberations," in *Formation and Reflection: The Promise of Practical Theology*, ed. Lewis S. Mudge and James N. Poling (Philadelphia: Fortress, 1987), pp. 120-38.

Public practical theology shares the concerns of public theology and extends them by relating them to praxis and to the church. This is why the notion of a "public church" is of special interest to practical theology. Martin E. Marty coined the term "public church" in 1981 to describe ecumenical cooperation between different churches, a type of cooperation he calls a "communion of communions."[3] Marty envisions this "communion of communions" as a vehicle for bringing together different Christian denominations so that they can "contribute out of their separate resources to public virtue and the common weal."[4] At various points Marty emphasizes that, while morality and ethics are concerns of the public church, its chief concern is the Christian faith. But the primary focus of his vision of the public church is for it to contribute to the stimulation of "public and social morale" and a "public ethic" — an understanding that is in line with other pleas for a Christian contribution to the "renewal of America's public life."[5] The American discussion of the public church therefore has as its primary emphasis the moral effects the public church should exert upon society.

Wolfgang Huber has been the primary contributor to the German discussion of the need for a "public church" and a "public theology."[6] Huber uses the term "public church" to indicate the position the church should assume in society after the separation of church and state. The church should maintain a clearly Christian character that, to a certain degree, separates it from the rest of society. At the same time, the church should be, in Dietrich Bonhoeffer's words, a "church for others," and must therefore be committed to society as a whole. As in the American discussion around public theology, Huber places a strong emphasis on general ethical issues. At the same time, he advocates that the church maintain a public presence as a distinct community that holds a distinct faith. This public presence is not based upon "general or universal discourse," to use the terminology of Habermas. Instead, this public presence, as Huber envisions it, presupposes the dialogical coexistence of different communities and institutions within society. Consequently, Huber sees an important place for the public church in civil society — a civil society made up of such communities and institutions.

James W. Fowler was the first practical theologian to include the idea of

---

3. Martin E. Marty, *The Public Church: Mainline, Evangelical, Catholic* (New York: Crossroad, 1981).

4. Marty, *The Public Church*, p. 16.

5. Marty, *The Public Church*, p. 152. Cf. Parker J. Palmer, *The Company of Strangers: Christians and the Renewal of America's Public Life* (New York: Crossroad, 1981).

6. Wolfgang Huber, *Kirche in der Zeitenwende. Gesellschaftlicher Wandel und Erneuerung der Kirche* (Gütersloh: Bertelsmann Stiftung, 1998). Also see his *Kirche* (Stuttgart: Kreuz, 1979).

the public church in his work.[7] His focus is on practical theology's contribution toward an ecclesial community committed to the common good on a personal as well as on a structural-societal level. In similar ways, Don Browning suggests a broader basis for practical theology in what he calls "fundamental practical theology." Browning argues that practical theology should be based on "critical reflection on the church's dialogue with Christian sources and other communities of experience and interpretation with the aim of guiding its action toward social and individual transformation" — a view that draws upon Tracy's understanding of public theology mentioned above.[8]

This brief overview of the recent discussion of public theology and the public church shows the renewed interest in the public role of theology and the church. It also confirms the understanding of the threefold task of a public practical theology: to take the public seriously as an audience, to address issues of common concern, and to bring theology into dialogue with contemporary culture.

It is easy to recognize why this line of thinking should see Christian religious education as having the potential of making a special contribution to the common good and to responsible citizenship. The term *paideia* is used by some American Christian religious educators to point toward an understanding of the task of Christian religious education as education for discipleship as well as for citizenship. In the German discussion, the term *kirchliche Bildungsverantwortung* (educational responsibility of the church) is sometimes used in a similar way. I will discuss what this sort of Christian religious education might look like after considering what needs for a Christian contribution to *paideia* were generated by the social developments of the twentieth century that were discussed in Part II. By taking account of these social developments we will have a much fuller understanding of what is at stake for Christian religious education vis-à-vis the public.

In sum, while practical theology should have a clear ecclesial focus, its task also includes a public dimension and a broader responsibility to society as a whole. Practical theology must take into account the social, cultural, and political situation — a situation it must analyze, and must also address.

---

7. James W. Fowler, *Faith Development and Pastoral Care* (Philadelphia: Fortress, 1987); see esp. pp. 22ff. See also his *Weaving the New Creation: Stages of Faith and the Public Church* (San Francisco: Harper, 1991).

8. Don Browning, *A Fundamental Practical Theology: Descriptive and Strategic Proposals* (Minneapolis: Fortress, 1991), p. 36.

Why Christian Religious Education Should Contribute to the Education of the Public: Lessons from the Twentieth Century

The developments in Christian religious education through the twentieth century in the United States and Germany, which we traced in Part II, follow a general pattern that we have described as *specialization*. Over the course of the twentieth century, publications in the field of Christian education came to treat religious education as a separate and specialized field of education. As religious topics increasingly became the only focus, issues of general education began to be disregarded. Christian educators in the United States focused almost exclusively on the educational needs of the congregation, while in Germany the primary focus became religious education in state schools. In both cases religious education became a highly professional and specialized endeavor that, with few exceptions, was not considered in the context of an overall perspective on education as a whole.

The development of a very specialized type of religious education did have some positive effects. It allowed for a higher degree of professionalization by producing expert knowledge as religious education theory was developed in accordance with the academic standards in related fields like developmental psychology or the philosophy of education. But this specialization also had some negative effects, which have since become obvious. Treating religious education as a specialized field, isolated from general education, often lent unknowing support to the growing popular assumption that religion is a purely private matter. This assumption weakens the position of religious communities in public life, and it robs society of the potential contribution of religious education toward the common good.

The understanding of religious education as a separate and specialized field goes hand in hand with parallel developments in general education. Most of the pre–twentieth-century classic philosophers of education such as Pestalozzi, Herbart, or Fröbel included religion as part of education. They assumed that without reference to religion, education would not be complete, and that any philosophy of education that fails to account for the place of religion would not do justice to the child or to the person in general. During the twentieth century, this understanding changed. Especially in the second half of the century, references to religious education or even to religion in general became sparse. This was due, in part, to a change within the field of the philosophy of education, which came to see itself as secularized and independent from all worldviews.[9] This is not the place for a critical evaluation of this new

9. For a recent discussion cf. Friedrich Schweitzer, "Bildung und Wahrheit," in *Befreiende*

conception of the philosophy of education, although such an evaluation is indeed an important task. But it is necessary to point out that this new perspective can be partially attributed to the ways in which religious education developed during the twentieth century. The more religious education came to be considered a specialized field, the more general education was able to neglect it because it became a topic for specialists alone. Curiously enough, this relationship also worked the other way around; the more general education neglected religious education, the more specialists were needed to take care of this neglected field. Together, both movements created a dynamic that intensified the tendencies toward secular education, on the one hand, and specialized religious education, on the other. A new and different approach is obviously needed at present if we are to overcome the results of this dynamic.

Another way to analyze the development of religious education as a specialized field during the twentieth century is by looking at the changing relationship between church and state. In both the United States and Germany one can distinguish three phases in the development of the relationship between religion and public life during the twentieth century:

The first phase is characterized by the legal separation between church and state. In the United States, church/state separation goes back to the American Constitution; in Germany, it was achieved during the Weimar Republic after World War I. In both countries, this separation, however, still allowed for a strong influence of the church in all matters of education. In the United States this influence lasted at least until the beginning of the twentieth century, and in Germany it continued after World War II, well into the 1960s and even beyond.

The second phase is characterized by the dominance of Protestantism giving way to a co-presence of Protestants, Catholics, and Jews or, in Germany, other groups in society. This process was more visible in the United States than in Germany and was summarized by American Will Herberg's famous book *Protestant, Catholic, Jew*, published in the 1950s.[10] During this period many Americans were still confident that a common religious and moral basis could unite the American public and serve as a guiding ideal for public education. In many ways, John Dewey's 1934 plea for *A Common Faith* is indicative of this search, because Dewey argued that it was possible for a common moral-religious faith not only to transcend all particular religious communities but also to include them as well.[11]

Wahrheit. Festschrift für Eilert Herms zum 60. Geburtstag, ed. Wilfred Härle et. al. (Marburg: Elwert Verlag, 2000), pp. 563-75.

10. Will Herberg, *Protestant, Catholic, Jew* (Garden City, N.Y.: Doubleday, 1955).

11. John Dewey, *A Common Faith* (New Haven: Yale University Press, 1934).

A third phase began in the 1960s, which were characterized by a more radical plurality of views on the relationship of religion and public life. This was due in part to the increasing number of religious groups and also to the increasing opposition of some people to the church or religion having any influence on public education. Supreme Court rulings during the 1960s put a definite end to all religious instruction in public schools in the United States.[12] In Germany, religious education did not disappear from the school curriculum, but it had to shed its catechetical format in order to become a more general educational subject in line with other subjects in the school curriculum. At the same time, the difference between religious education in the state school and in the congregation was made greater and greater.

The application of the separation of church and state to public schools in the twentieth century has encouraged the privatization of religious education, especially in its congregational forms. The professionalization of religious educators has, to some degree, counteracted this tendency as professional religious educators have become aware of this trend and have intentionally included topics of public importance in their curricula. By itself, however, this kind of religious education cannot reclaim the public role of religious education.

At the end of the twentieth century, certain counter-movements against the privatization of religious education emerged. One counter-movement within the church is the emerging discussion about public theology and the public church. The ecclesiology behind this discussion clearly runs counter to tendencies to limit the scope of religious education to the private sphere. Advocacy for a public church with a public theology is based not only on arguments put forward by theologians but also on observations made by those outside the church. Since the 1980s, conservatives and liberals have increasingly come to agree that democratic societies need a strong public life, that is, a civil society with vigorous associations and communities to serve as "mediating structures" between the state and the individual.[13] The most influential statement on this is probably still *Habits of the Heart*,[14] by Robert Bellah and his colleagues.

Communitarianism can be interpreted as another more general counter-

12. Cf. Warren A. Nord, *Religion and American Education: Rethinking a National Dilemma* (Chapel Hill: University of North Carolina Press, 1995).

13. Peter L. Berger and Richard J. Neuhaus, *To Empower People: The Role of Mediating Structures in Public Policy* (Washington, D.C.: American Enterprise Institute of Public Policy Research, 1977).

14. Robert N. Bellah et al., *Habits of the Heart: Individualism and Commitment in American Life* (New York: Harper and Row, 1985).

movement against the privatization of life. The more conservative versions of communitarianism can been seen as self-centered structures focused primarily on the maintenance of a group's own social enclave.[15] Other communitarian groups have introduced the notion of an international civil society to ensure that the values supported by community structures do not fall short of the global challenges in today's world.[16] One of the fundamental concerns these groups are addressing, out of a desire to strengthen some sort of communal solidarity that extends beyond national boundaries, is the role of international solidarity vis-à-vis economic globalization. They oppose leaving the future to the relentless forces of international competition.

The vision of civil society advocated by groups of this second type clearly involves more than volunteer work in the interest of one's own community. It is, rather, based on the vision of a democratic society that will not be achieved by the government and the economy alone. Jean L. Cohen and Andrew Arato's "working definition" of civil society in some ways summarizes this viewpoint: "We understand 'civil society' as a sphere of social interaction between economy and state, composed above all of the intimate sphere (especially the family), the sphere of associations (especially voluntary associations), social movements, and forms of public communication."[17] According to Cohen and Arato, it would be "misleading to identify civil society with all of social life outside the administrative state and economic processes." Therefore they exclude political parties and economic organizations, on the one hand, and the general "sociocultural lifeworld," on the other. Their focus is on institutionalized forms of communication.[18] Such institutions are needed for the reproduction of traditions, solidarities, identities, and so on.[19]

Cohen and Arato do not foresee a central role for religion in their theory. In many ways, they follow Jürgen Habermas's views (discussed in Part I) by assuming a general process of rationalization or secularization. In this process "the sacred core of traditions, norms, and authority" is replaced by a consensus that is based on communication.[20] Others like Robert Wuthnow, how-

15. For a critical discussion cf. Micha Brumlik and Hauke Brunkhorst, eds., *Gemeinschaft und Gerechtigkeit* (Frankfurt: Fischer, 1993).

16. Cf. Michael Walzer, ed., *Toward a Global Civil Society* (Providence: Berghahn, 1995), and Reinhart Kössler and Henning Melber, *Chancen internationaler Zivilgesellschaft* (Frankfurt: Suhrkamp, 1993).

17. Jean L. Cohen and Andrew Arato, *Civil Society and Political Theory* (London: Cambridge University Press, 1992), p. ix.

18. Cohen and Arato, *Civil Society and Political Theory*, p. x.

19. Cohen and Arato, *Civil Society and Political Theory*, p. 429.

20. Cohen and Arato, *Civil Society and Political Theory*, p. 435.

ever, have pointed out that Christianity can play a crucial role in civil society.[21] This is in line with the observation of other scholars that religions continue to play a public role in the modern world.[22]

From what has been said above about the need for an international civil society, it is clear that Christianity's contribution to civil society must be in line with the demands of international solidarity and global ethics. This is increasingly recognized at least by some theologians who are looking for a Christian ethics of globalization.[23]

Although some of the discussions on civil society and globalization include references to general education as well as to religious education, there has been no serious attempt to articulate a theoretical model for the role of religious education within a civil society adhering both to the separation of church and state and to the demands of globalization.

Civil Society, *Paideia,* and Religious Education: Perspectives for the Future

The first two sections of this chapter lead to the conclusion that reconstituting the public role of Christian religious education is one of the central tasks for the future. Such a conclusion is certainly supported by the ongoing discussions on public theology, the public church, and public practical theology. I will here examine these discussions as a prelude to giving my own understanding of the task of reconstituting the public role of Christian religious education, noting especially the clear parallels between the discussions in the United States and Germany — parallels that may be surprising since there has been no immediate connection between these discussions.

In the United States, *paideia* has become a central concept in recent attempts to strengthen the public role of religious education. The term's present usage in this context goes back to L. A. Cremin's book on public education published in 1976, which defines *paideia* as the "social, political, or ethical aspiration" of a society.[24] Others, such as J. L. Seymour, R. T. O'Gor-

---

21. Robert Wuthnow, *Christianity and Civil Society: The Current Debate* (Valley Forge, Pa.: Trinity Press International, 1996).

22. José Casanova, *Public Religions in the Modern World* (Chicago: University of Chicago Press, 1994).

23. For example, Max L. Stackhouse et al., *Christian Social Ethics in a Global Era* (Nashville: Abingdon, 1995); Robert J. Schreiter, *The New Catholicity: Theology between the Global and the Local* (Maryknoll, N.Y.: Orbis Books, 1997).

24. L. A. Cremin, *Public Education* (New York: Basic Books, 1976), p. 39.

man, and C. R. Foster in 1984, and James Fowler in 1990, have subsequently combined the notion of *paideia* with the idea of a public church. According to these scholars, religious education should be reconceptualized in order to recapture its role in the education of the public:

> Therefore Christian religious education needs to become aware of its role in today's wider educational ecology. The nature of education and of religion, and their relationship, needs to be rethought. Education must be broadly seen in its variety of cultural manifestations, religion must be seen as the possibility for infusing transcendence into cultural life, and church education must be seen at the intersection of the cultural images and religious images that form persons and cultural life. Approaches are needed to enable church education to provide religious education in the midst of the culture's education.[25]

In several major statements, James Fowler has argued that there is a clear need for "reconstituting paideia in public education." He compares the concept of *paideia* to the German notion of *Bildung* in that it "involves all the intentional efforts of a community of shared meanings and practices to form and nurture the attitudes, dispositions, habits, and virtues — and in addition, the knowledge and skills — necessary to enable growing persons to become competent and reflective adult members of the community."[26] Addressing the situation in public education, Fowler has suggested that communities, instead of treating all perspectives on meaning and value as private matters, should make public dialogue about ethics the foundation of moral education. Addressing the situation of congregations in other writings, Fowler has suggested that one of their primary goals should be equipping children, adolescents, and adults for the task of being responsible citizens who, on the basis of their Christian faith, are committed to the common good.[27]

The current German discussion about the public role of Christian religious education has not used the term *paideia*, but it has used a parallel term — *kirchliche Bildungsverantwortung* — which means, literally, the responsibility for (public) education which the church should consider as one of its

25. J. L. Seymour, R. T. O'Gorman, and C. R. Foster, *The Church in the Education of the Public: Refocusing the Task of Religious Education* (Nashville: Abingdon, 1984), p. 29.

26. James W. Fowler, *Weaving the New Creation*, pp. 147ff. Also cf. his *Faithful Change: The Personal and Public Challenges of Postmodern Life* (Nashville: Abingdon, 1996), pp. 221ff.

27. James W. Fowler, "Reconstituting *Paideia* in Public Education," in *Caring for the Commonweal: Education for Religious and Public Life*, ed. P. J. Palmer, B. G. Wheeler, and James W. Fowler (Macon, Ga.: Mercer University Press, 1990), pp. 63-69.

tasks.[28] The church is seen as responsible for addressing not only the traditional fields of religious education in the congregation, family, and state school, but also for addressing education as a whole. There are various ways in which the church may fulfill the corresponding tasks. Participation in the public discourse on the meaning and purpose of education and schooling is one possibility. Another is sponsoring educational programs outside the congregation, for example, in public adult education programs. In all these cases, Christian ethics and anthropology are used as a basis for the public educational commitment of the church. Religiously affiliated schools, which have received new attention in Germany and the United States, are another example of a way the church can carry out its educational responsibility.[29] These schools are now seen as expressions of the church's interest in education, rather than as an expression of separatism or of religiously motivated isolation from public schools.

Having outlined both the current discussion of the possible contribution of religious education to reconstituting a public *paideia* and the current discussion of the church's responsibility for public education within its overall task of education, I will now state my own understanding of these tasks. The following six perspectives point out the general direction I believe future work should take.

1. *Both public education and religious education should endeavor to teach how to be a responsible citizen in a pluralistic society.*

Concepts such as *paideia* or civil society are often understood in a premodern sense to mean having a set of cultural ideals that unify society.[30] Given the impact of pluralization in modernity and of postmodernism in general, this understanding has become problematic. No unified set of ideals in the traditional sense can do justice to the democratic pluralism that must be the aim of public education.

Rather than trying to go back to a unified cultural situation in which all parts of society work together in socializing the next generation, we now

---

28. The major statement on this is K. E. Nipkow, *Bildung als Lebensbegleitung und Erneuerung. Kirchliche Bildungsverantwortung in Gemeinde, Schule und Gesellschaft* (Gütersloh: Gütersloher Verlagshaus, 1990).

29. See the new *International Journal of Education and Religion,* which has a strong focus on religiously affiliated schools; see in particular F. Schweitzer, "A Stronger Case for Religion: Perspectives on Multicultural Education and on Religiously Affiliated Schools," *International Journal of Education and Religion* 1 (2000): 47-63.

30. For a critical discussion cf. Adam B. Seligman, *The Idea of Civil Society* (Princeton, N.J.: Princeton University Press, 1995).

must prepare young people for responsible participation in a pluralistic world. The question the church and Christian religious education should address is not "How do we find ways to cooperate with other educational efforts in society?" It is instead, "How do we educate the public in light of the challenges it will face in the future?"

The idea of educating the public and of preparing people for responsible citizenship should not, therefore, be based on the model of a monolithic society but on the model of a true pluralism characterized by the cooperative efforts of different communities within society. This model differs clearly from the prevailing notion of pluralism based on the creation of a religiously neutral space as the common ground on which different groups can come together.

2. *The notion of a religiously neutral education has become contradictory.*
Ever since the separation of church and state, education has often been conceived in terms of religious neutrality. Religious convictions are seen as divisive, so religious neutrality in education, especially in public schools, is considered a prerequisite for peace and tolerance. The modern democratic ideal of equal rights for all citizens and nondiscrimination necessitates the religious neutrality of the state. But it is important to ask whether adhering to this ideal necessarily means that education must exclude all religious influences on education in the public sphere.

The two most important reasons for rejecting the idea of a religiously neutral education are the insufficiency of moral education alone and the negative effects of divorcing religion from education. Sometimes moral education is considered a viable alternative to religious education. For example, the influential models of Habermas and Kohlberg argue for a moral education based on universalist rather than religiously grounded values. It remains unclear, however, how the motivation for adopting and enacting such values can be developed if education does not make reference to overall worldviews, including worldviews based upon religious convictions. Discourse alone will hardly be enough to secure such motivation, especially in children and youth whose moral orientations are guided by groups and interpersonal relationships rather than by abstract moral principles.

The negative effects of religion without education can be seen, for example, in fundamentalist and extremist religious orientations. While such orientations clearly act as an obstacle to peaceful life in society, the removal of religion from the curriculum makes it impossible to work toward more tolerant forms of religion. In other words, the so-called peace that may be reached through religiously neutral education goes hand in hand with the privatization of religious conflicts — conflicts that may eventually become even stronger if they are not addressed in public education. Consequently, the inclusion of theology and of religious convictions in public education can serve to support dialogue and mutual understanding. The simplistic equation of religion and divisiveness does not take this into account.

3. *Worldviews are inevitably included in education.*

It is important to note that recent discussions have raised doubts as to whether any education can be neutral in the sense of not being based on some at least implicit worldview, such as a religious orientation.[31] All educational approaches in theory or practice necessarily make choices with respect to how they perceive and treat children and youth — or the learner in general. In this sense they presuppose an anthropology, and anthropologies are always related to religious outlooks or to other worldviews.

A similar point can be made concerning the moral norms and values implied by education. While it is true that many moral philosophers consider their work as independent of religious convictions or worldviews, it is also true that educators necessarily will contextualize the norms and values guiding their way of working with children and youth. Norms and values cannot be transmitted in the abstract. It is not effective merely to present them theoretically or to explain their usefulness (although explanations are a necessary part of moral education). Rather, norms and values are taught as part of a way of life that includes the experiences of belonging to a community, sharing the outlooks of this community, which are often related to narrative or myth, having certain traditions about how things are done, and so on. This cultural embeddedness of education clearly goes beyond — and must go beyond — what most current moral philosophers consider the religiously neutral grounds of their ethics. Seen in this light, it is clear that moral education is always related to religious orientations or to other worldviews.

Whether it is acknowledged or not, this relationship between education and religion or worldviews is, contrary to the assumptions of modern education, a given. A different role therefore seems appropriate for religious education theory than that prescribed by modern, so-called secular, philosophers of education. Rather than being confined to a specialized segment of education that is separate from general education, religious education — in the sense of the consideration of the religious implications and presuppositions

31. For an introduction to these discussions see Christoph Th. Scheilke and Friedrich Schweitzer, eds., *Religion, Ethik, Schule. Bildungspolitische Perspektiven in der pluralen Gesellschaft* (Münster: Waxmann, 1999).

of all education — should be a topic of general public interest. It does make a difference which anthropology or what kind of religious orientation and worldview guides education, particularly public education.

Religious education theory, as we now know it, is not fully prepared for this public task of being in critical dialogue with general education. It is clear that philosophers of education need to become aware of the religious implications of educational philosophies and to become open to a new dialogue with religious education. It is also clear that religious education theory needs to widen its scope beyond its traditional focus in order to reexamine what its role should be within the education of the general public.

In some ways this demand runs counter to the professional specialization of religious education which in Part II we discussed as a fundamental tendency in the twentieth century. But the return to a broader scope may be considered as another necessary step toward the development of a discipline of religious education that functions as a type of public practical theology.

4. Multicultural education in a religiously plural society must address not only cultural diversity but also religious diversity.
Globalization has made the need to come to terms with religious diversity even stronger because of the intercultural awareness fostered by migration, international travel, the media, and so on. This awareness makes people around the world more and more cognizant of different religions, beliefs, and religious lifestyles. Even if one does not expect a major conflict between the adherents of different religions, it is very likely that there is some correlation between a higher awareness of religious difference and internal and external tensions. Internally, this awareness may cause insecurity about one's own beliefs vis-à-vis other beliefs and consequently a relativization of all beliefs. Externally, the experience of religious plurality may lead to prejudice and intolerance.

Given this situation, it is surprising that while inter*cultural* or multi*cultural* education has received quite a bit of attention in the United States and Germany inter*religious* education is rarely addressed, especially in the United States. A public practical theology or Christian religious education that is interested in the education of the public should endeavor to broaden this limited interest in interreligious issues. It should develop models for helping Christians make sense of the multiplicity of religious presences surrounding them without giving up their own Christian faith. And it should design ways to support communities and societies in their search for ways to live together peacefully on the basis of mutual recognition and affirmation. It is easy to see why these tasks cannot even be approached in public as long as public education is required to stay clear of religious topics. Interreligious education is impossible without religious dialogue and conscious encounter with the other. Religiously neutral education is not a sufficient response to religious pluralism.

If we include religion in the public sphere, we will need to broaden the earlier understanding of *paideia*. As pointed out above, *paideia* has often been understood exclusively in moral terms. According to this perspective, Christianity should help reconstitute *paideia* by supporting certain norms and values. Although this support for public ethics remains important, the need for interreligious education forces us to realize that interreligious dialogue must be seen as a necessary component of *paideia*. If different religions are to play a public role, we need to learn civil ways of encountering different religious outlooks. How we can do this remains, admittedly, an open question; the respective models have yet to be developed. But it seems at least possible that religious education may contribute to this development.

5. Religiously affiliated schools can contribute to pluralism in education.
I mentioned above the new attention that religiously affiliated schools have received in Germany and Europe. These schools should no longer be considered only special interest schools that exclusively contribute to a privatized subculture. They offer an important contribution of the church and other religious communities toward fulfilling the educational responsibility that is shared among the state and the other institutions of civil society.

In countries like Germany where 95 percent of the students attend state schools, an increase in the number of religiously affiliated schools could clearly strengthen the influence of civil society vis-à-vis the state. It would counteract what, otherwise, comes close to a state monopoly of education. Religiously affiliated schools could, at the same time, become laboratories and models for developing new theories and methods for interreligious education and dialogue, responsible ways of dealing with pluralism and difference, and education for peace, tolerance, and mutual affirmation.

Strengthening religiously affiliated schools does not mean that all Christian children and youth should attend such schools, as traditional Roman Catholic teaching required them to do. What it does mean is that such schools should be seen as one important avenue by which the church can contribute to the education of the public — an avenue that in no way entails the church giving up its other avenues of educating the public through congregational education or through the church's relationship to public schools.

6. The public Christian educators must work toward is global civil society.
The last topic I will address is the most controversial. As mentioned above, some theorists suggest extending the idea of civil society to an international

level. The guiding ideal for this extension is international or global solidarity. In many ways, this can be seen as a secularized version of the theological concept of ecumenism, that is, the concept of worldwide justice and cooperation. If we want justice and cooperation to be the guiding norms of global solidarity, it becomes clear that the process of globalization should not be left solely in the hands of the economy and the governments of the different countries. Just as the widest possible public should be involved in the creation of societies within individual countries, a wider public should be involved in this process of globalization — a process that should be given a much broader participatory political basis. This process should be guided by both moral and political values.

While there can be no doubt that such an international public or civil society is highly desirable, many observers have raised doubts about the realism of this idea. Can there really be an international public in a serious sense or will it be, at best, an international reaction dependent on worldwide media reports, etc.? Is there a chance for global solidarity once the costly implications of this kind of thinking are taken into account (such as having to share one's resources not only with one's fellow citizens — through taxes, for example — but with everyone on earth)?

These and many other questions should caution us against unrealistic educational idealism. On the other hand, it is important to realize the implications of assuming that only a negative answer to these questions is possible. We must therefore consider whether or not there is a chance for humanity to survive if the different nations and groups around the globe do not cooperate. And we must consider whether or not it will be possible to realize the benefits of economic globalization if there is not a concomitant increase of political, social, and moral recognition of the people involved.

Global thinking is not just a product of an international market economy. The idea of a worldwide Christian *oikumene* — an all-inclusive household or economy transcending cultural boundaries — long pre-dated the idea of an international market, and could still serve as a model for global peace and solidarity.

Christian religious education should not be based on idealistic assumptions and expectations concerning the feasibility of an international civil society. But both the urgency of today's global problems and the theological rationale of ecumenicity give ample justification for including global perspectives in Christian education. If we want to be serious about a public theology and a public church, the public addressed by Christian education must be, increasingly, a truly global public.

7 Congregational Education and the Challenge of Cross-Disciplinary Thinking

This chapter focuses on congregations. As the previous chapter on *paideia* makes clear, we view congregations as only one setting that should be addressed in a comprehensive theory of Protestant religious education and in practical theology that is fully public. By limiting this chapter to congregations, I hope to bring into focus an issue emerging in our examination of paradigmatic figures of the twentieth century: cross-disciplinary thinking.

Questions from the Past; Questions for the Future

The issue of cross-disciplinary thinking emerged in the form of three basic questions in Part II of this book. These questions not only remain with us today but are questions with which religious education must grapple as it turns to the future:

1. Where does the praxis of Protestant religious education take place and what is its relationship to religious education theory?
2. What is the role of theology in Protestant religious education theory?
3. What role do the resources of cultural modernity play in the construction of Protestant religious education theory?

We will examine each of these briefly at the outset of this chapter and then offer a conceptual framework by which we might identify different types of cross-disciplinary thinking in religious education and practical theology. This will be followed by sections that explore cross-disciplinary thinking in a

231

practical theology of congregational education, attempting to illustrate some of the basic moves this sort of thinking might involve.

Let us begin with the first question bequeathed to us from the past century: *Where does the praxis of religious education take place and what is its relationship to religious education theory?* There are two sides to this question. One side focuses on the institutional settings in which we would expect Protestant religious education to occur. The second focuses on the relationship of religious educational praxis and religious education theory. One of the most obvious differences between religious education in Germany and the United States is the much broader scope of religious education in the former. Every German figure examined in the second part of this book viewed religious education as having a role in state-supported schools. In contrast, their counterparts in the United States focused almost exclusively on congregations as the site of religious education, arguing that religious education has no place in public education. The second dimension of this question emerged in a variety of ways in our historical overview. George Albert Coe, for example, viewed the relationship of religious education praxis and theory along the lines of philosophical pragmatism, which he blended with certain elements of personalism. Theory is *instrumental* to praxis, providing ideas that guide and criticize its various forms in particular social contexts. Religious education theory, as such, is tested against experience, both empirically and pragmatically.

Both sides of this question remain important as we enter the twenty-first century, though we might cast the question somewhat differently today: What role does religious education praxis play in the education of the public and how do the various theoretical models that reflect on this praxis take account of the changing role of religion in our contemporary global context? Obviously, I am recasting this question along the lines envisioned in the previous chapter. It is no longer adequate to think exclusively in terms of a few privileged *sites* of religious education, be they congregations, families, or state-supported schools. As our context has become more institutionally differentiated and more culturally diffuse, religious education can be seen as taking place across a wide variety of settings. For example, religiously affiliated schools, which are not related directly to congregations or the state, have come to play an increasingly important role in religious education. Likewise, religious education by parachurch organizations and special purpose groups has enormous significance today in the United States. New social movements, as well as contemporary music and literature, also have taken on a significant educational role vis-à-vis individuals who are loosely affiliated with religious institutions. Moreover, it is likely that traditional sites of religious education such as the family and congregations will become even more important in the twenty-first century. German religious education, for example, continued to rely on a partnership between the church and religious education in state schools over the past century. It is quite possible that congregations will be asked to place more emphasis on religious education in the future, as religious education classes in school settings become more marginalized in the school curriculum. At present, however, relatively little is offered to children and youth in this setting.

Taken together, religious education in all of these settings shapes the ways individuals and communities understand their life together — their life as a public. Thus it is important for contemporary Protestant religious education theory to locate its proposals in relation to a wide variety of settings that are educating the public, for better and for worse. This makes it important for religious education theory to articulate in a methodologically self-conscious fashion its relationship to the various forms of praxis taking place in a wide array of settings. Does the educational praxis of a new social movement, for example, provide the socioethical grounding of religious education theory? Some advocates of feminist and liberation religious education theory believe that it should. Or do the distinctive practices of the Christian community by which the Word is taught and embodied take methodological priority? Those developing communitarian theories of religious education argue that they should. Others argue for still a third perspective, sometimes identified as a public church position. Here, the distinctiveness of religious and moral communities within differentiated social contexts is affirmed but is not isolated from their location in and contribution to other spheres of life.

Clearly a range of perspectives is currently available in contemporary religious education. At this point, my purpose is not to advocate one or another of these perspectives but to make it clear why it is important for contemporary theories of religious education to articulate the relationship between religious education theory and religious education praxis, which can be conceptualized as taking place in a variety of possible settings. In order to do so, it will be necessary for religious education to give greater explicit attention to cross-disciplinary issues.

The second question that needs to be addressed is, *What is the role of theology in Protestant religious education theory?* This question was raised with particular force in the writings of Smart, Sherrill, von Tiling, Hammelsbeck, and Kittel, who focused on the recovery of the theological identity of the church. Evangelical instruction or Christian education, they argued, cannot be understood apart from theological reflection on the nature and purpose of the church. John Westerhoff, likewise, posed this question in the latter part of his work, beginning to use theological terms like "catechesis" and "faith formation" and adopting an Anglican-Episcopalian perspective to describe Protestant religious education.

Today, we might pose this question somewhat differently: In a social context that is religiously and culturally pluralistic, what role do the distinctive beliefs and practices of different religious communities play in the determination of the sort of education they offer? Christianity, Islam, Judaism, Hinduism, and Buddhism — to name but a few of the religious traditions found in Germany and the United States today — portray the ultimate purpose of the religious life quite differently, leading them to develop somewhat different forms of education. In seeking to justify and commend a particular pattern of the religious life, their theories of religious education articulate the self-understanding of their particular religious community.

In Christianity, this means that proposals about the education of congregations necessarily engage various theological arguments about the nature and purpose of the church. Throughout the modern period, this has involved a complex dialogue between biblical studies, dogmatic theology, church history, and practical theology. In our rapidly globalizing context, characterized by a high degree of postmodernism, this conversation is highly pluralistic. No consensus prevails, be it confessional or that of a dominant perspective like Christian realism or liberation theology. The task is not so much to justify an approach to Protestant religious education through appeals to *the* theological self-understanding of this community as it is to articulate good reasons a scholar finds a *particular* theological perspective most adequate.

A third important question emerged in our examination of representative figures in the second part of this book: *What role do the resources of cultural modernity play in the construction of Protestant religious education theory?* The reform movements emerging in both Germany and the United States in the first part of the twentieth century placed great emphasis on the insights of the social sciences. During the middle of the century, those figures preoccupied with the recovery of the church's theological identity (with the exception of Sherrill) cordoned off evangelical instruction or Christian education from a direct engagement of the social sciences. During the sixties and seventies, Westerhoff drew extensively on the resources of anthropology and socialization theory but never articulated an explicit method by which to understand their role in Protestant religious education theory of the figures examined, Sherrill and Nipkow brought theology into dialogue with the social sciences in a self-conscious fashion.

Today, we might pose this question somewhat differently: How is the dialogue between theology and the cultural resources of our present global context best conceptualized? Obviously, this way of posing the question grants an important role to theology in this dialogue. But how should this role be viewed? Should it be viewed as providing the answers to the questions these resources raise, or as an equal partner in a mutually influential learning process, or as setting the terms of the conversation, filtering out those aspects of these resources that are thought to contradict the fundamental convictions of theology? There is no single answer to these questions in contemporary Protestant religious education theory. Further complicating the task of bringing theology into conversation with the resources of culture is the remarkable pluralism characterizing the natural and human sciences in today's postmodern world. If modernity conceptualized science as a unitary set of operations leading to a universally established set of findings, such a view no longer exists. A range of disciplinary paradigms today characterizes virtually all fields. The task is no longer the dialogue between theology and science but between *a* particular theological perspective and *a* particular scientific perspective. Such conversations are, by necessity, local and particular, even if they seek to make broad generalizations about some aspect of our world.

Four Levels of Cross-Disciplinary Thinking

Obviously, the questions that have just been raised are complex. In focusing on congregational education, I am choosing to limit the discussion to the ways cross-disciplinary thinking takes place in relation to a single site of contemporary Protestant religious education, one that can be understood only in terms of the broader social analysis pointed to above. I will begin by attempting to develop a conceptual framework to describe various dimensions of cross-disciplinary thinking in Protestant religious education theory. In this framework, judgments about the relationship between theology and the cultural resources of our contemporary social context are portrayed as taking place at four levels of thinking.

Intradisciplinary thinking focuses on a practical theologian's evaluation of various options *within* a particular field. In virtually all fields today, more than one viable, theoretical approach is present. In contemporary psychology, for example, self, feminist, cognitive, and evolutionary psychologies represent viable options. Moreover, there is a range of positions within each of these perspectives. Within cognitive psychology, for example, the structural developmental psychology of Jean Piaget is quite different than the multiple intelligences approach of Howard Gardner. Thus practical theologians must make judgments about the perspective in a particular field they believe to be the most fruitful dialogue partner in shaping their proposals for congregational education. While this will involve grounds internal to that field, it also may involve theological precommitments as well. Such precommitments guide judgments about the quasi-ethical assumptions that often are embedded in other fields, especially the social sciences.

These kinds of intradisciplinary judgments rest on a set of prior decisions made at the level of *interdisciplinary* thinking. Here, the issue is not choice of dialogue partners *within* a particular field, but judgments about which fields *qua* fields are most germane to practical theology and about how they are properly engaged. With regard to congregational education, our historical investigation of twentieth-century American Protestant religious education is instructive. Sherrill viewed depth psychology as his most important dialogue partner; Westerhoff, cultural anthropology. Neither followed Coe in making modern educational theory primary. Moreover, Sherrill alone reflected systematically on how to conceptualize the relationship between theology and the cultural resources of modernity. Many new models of interdisciplinary thinking have emerged since Sherrill wrote: the revised correlational model of Tracy and Browning, the praxis correlational model of Chopp and Lamb, the ad hoc correlational model of Frei and Thiemann, the Chalcedonian model of Loder and Hunsinger, and the transversal model of van Huyssteen and Shults.[1] Each conceptualizes the dialogue between theology and the resources of culture along somewhat different lines.

Most proposals about congregational education in practical theology work on the two levels of cross-disciplinary thinking that have just been described. Both intra- and inter-disciplinary thinking, however, presuppose reflection on two additional questions that provide the larger frames in terms of which the more focused work of practical theology takes place: What is the place of theology amid human knowledge as a whole? What is the nature of a discipline? While these questions are closely related and are frequently treated

---

1. David Tracy, *Blessed Rage for Order: The New Pluralism in Theology* (Chicago: University of Chicago Press, 1996 [1975]); Don Browning, *A Fundamental Practical Theology: Descriptive and Strategic Proposals* (Minneapolis: Fortress, 1991); Rebecca Chopp, *The Power to Speak: Feminism, Language, God* (New York: Crossroad, 1989); Matthew Lamb, *Solidarity with Victims: Toward a Theology of Social Transformation* (New York: Crossroad, 1982); James Loder, *The Logic of the Spirit: Human Development in Theological Perspective* (San Francisco: Jossey-Bass, 1998); Deborah van Deusen Hunsinger, *Theology and Pastoral Counseling* (Grand Rapids: Eerdmans, 1995); Wentzel van Huyssteen, *The Shaping of Rationality: Toward Interdisciplinarity in Theology and Science* (Grand Rapids: Eerdmans, 1999); LeRon Shults, "Integrative Epistemology and the Search for Meaning," *Journal of Interdisciplinary Studies* 5, no. 1 (1993).

together, they can be distinguished for analytical purposes. The former can be described as *multidisciplinary* thinking; the latter, *metadisciplinary* thinking.

Multidisciplinary thinking attempts to describe the contribution of disciplined reflection by religious communities to human knowledge as a whole. If interdisciplinary thinking in practical theology focuses on an intense conversation between a limited number of fields, multidisciplinary thinking attempts to chart the larger landscape in which this more focused conversation takes place. During the early modern period, this sort of thinking occurred most frequently in theological encyclopedias that attempted to describe the various branches of theology in their relation both to one another and to the arts and sciences as a whole. Describing the "place" of theology was viewed as a crucial part of the task of making theology a fully public discipline. Contemporary exponents of this sort of thinking such as Nancey Murphy, George Ellis, and Stephen Jay Kline have eschewed the encyclopedic frame because of its close relationship to philosophical foundationalism.[2] They describe their endeavor as a historicist account of the present state of human knowledge. The disciplines are portrayed as evolving systems of knowledge with boundaries that are constantly shifting. This sort of thinking allows theology in general and practical theology in particular to describe its contribution to the larger conversation of humankind.

Metadisciplinary thinking focuses on the nature of the disciplines, exploring two questions: What constitutes a discipline sociologically, rhetorically, and epistemologically? What are the rational operations appropriate to different fields and various forums within a particular field? In our contemporary intellectual scene, characterized by a high degree of postmodernism, the very idea of a discipline has become the subject of serious debate.[3] Are the disciplines best conceptualized as argument fields (Toulmin and Perelman)?[4] Do they raise distinct validity claims that call for different patterns of warranting and modes of proof (Habermas)?[5] Do research programs across dif-

2. Nancey Murphy and George Ellis, *On the Moral Nature of the Universe: Theology, Cosmology, and Ethics* (Minneapolis: Fortress, 1996); Nancey Murphy, *Theology in the Age of Scientific Reasoning* (Ithaca: Cornell University Press, 1990); Stephen Jay Kline, *Conceptual Foundations for Multi-Disciplinary Thinking* (Stanford: Stanford University Press, 1995).

3. See, for example, J. Nelson, A. Megill, and D. McCloskey, eds., *The Rhetoric of the Human Sciences: Language and Argument in Scholarship and Public Affairs* (Madison: University of Wisconsin Press, 1987), and Alan Gross, *The Rhetoric of Science* (Cambridge: Harvard University Press, 1990).

4. Chaim Perelman and L. Olbrechts-Tyteca, *The New Rhetoric: A Treatise on Argumentation* (Notre Dame: University of Notre Dame Press, 1969); Stephen Toulmin, Richard Rieke, and Allan Janik, *An Introduction to Reasoning*, 2nd ed. (New York: Macmillan, 1984).

5. Jürgen Habermas, *The Theory of Communicative Action*, vol. 1: *Reason and the Rationalization of Society*, trans. T. McCarthy (Boston: Beacon, 1984).

ferent fields follow similar patterns (Lakatos and Murphy)?[6] Is the production of knowledge in the disciplines inevitably implicated in relations of power (Foucault)?[7] Contemporary metadisciplinary thinking grapples with these kinds of questions, setting forth the status of the disciplines as forms of knowledge, intersections of power, and forms of rational communication. It articulates the assumptions that guide cross-disciplinary work at other levels. Religious education theory grapples with issues of this sort, especially when it describes its relationship to praxis.

While much more could be said about each of these levels of cross-disciplinary thinking, enough has been offered to indicate the complexity of cross-disciplinary work and the different kinds of judgments involved in this sort of thinking. The remainder of this chapter is a kind of extended example of cross-disciplinary thinking in the construction of a theory of congregational education. It will proceed in two steps. First, it will explore cross-disciplinary dialogue *within* theology, focusing on the dialogue between dogmatic theology and practical theology. Not only will this clarify the differences between these fields, it will also indicate the importance of moving beyond the hyper-specialization of contemporary theology. Second, it will describe the importance of engaging the intellectual resources of contemporary culture in practical theology's construction of a theory of congregational education. In both cases, our task is to *illustrate* cross-disciplinary thinking, not to set forth a comprehensive theory of congregational education. Broadly speaking, Friedrich Schleiermacher's understanding of practical theology will be followed here; according to this perspective, practical theology is charged with constructing a theory of ecclesial practice in the context of modernity (now viewed in terms of globalization and postmodernism), issuing in "rules of art" that can guide both the leaders of the church and ordinary Christians in the pursuit of their worldly vocations.

Practical Theology in Dialogue with Dogmatic Theology

A recent book by Jeffrey Siker, *Scripture and Ethics: Twentieth-Century Portraits,* provides an in-depth analysis of the use of the Bible by eight important

6. Imre Lakatos, *The Methodology of Scientific Research Programmes: Philosophical Papers,* vol. 1, ed. J. Worrall and G. Currie (Cambridge: Cambridge University Press, 1978); Murphy, *Theology in the Age of Scientific Reasoning.*

7. Michel Foucault, *Power/Knowledge: Selected Interviews and Other Writings* (New York: Pantheon, 1980).

Christian ethicists over the past fifty years.[8] His findings are revealing. While all of these ethicists offered their own interpretation of the Bible in the development of their constructive ethics, they made virtually no use of the scholarship of professional biblical scholars. Dennis Olson describes a similar "chasm" between the work of contemporary dogmatic theology and modern biblical scholarship.[9] Both Siker and Olson point to a widespread trend in contemporary theology: an absence of cross-disciplinary dialogue across different fields of theological inquiry. Throughout the modern period, the specialized research programs of biblical studies, church history, dogmatic theology, and practical theology, frequently, have been pursued in relative isolation from one another.

In recent years, this sort of hyper-specialization of theology has been called into question in many quarters. In part, this questioning has been sparked by an awareness of the limits of the encyclopedic paradigm that structured theology for most of the modern period.[10] It has also been prompted by new interest in practice across many fields. Some biblical scholars, for example, have begun to explore the positive role of the theological convictions and practices of communities of faith in the interpretation of Scripture.[11] Similarly, some dogmatic theologians have begun to point to the "shaping function" of church doctrine in forming the actual beliefs of ordinary Christians and the ways such beliefs can function to shape their way of life.[12] In a variety of ways, the tight boundaries that have separated the theological disciplines from one another across the modern period have become more fluid, creating openings for conversation across disciplinary lines. In this section, we will explore the possibility of cross-disciplinary conversation between dogmatic and practical theology in the construction of a theory of congregational education. While our exploration, by necessity, will be relatively brief, the implications of this proposal point to a fuller program of cross-disciplinary conversation across the theological disciplines as a whole.

As noted at the beginning of this chapter, Protestant congregational edu-

---

8. Jeffrey Siker, *Scripture and Ethics: Twentieth-Century Portraits* (New York: Oxford University Press, 1997).

9. Dennis Olson, "The Bible and Theology: Problems, Proposals, Prospects," *Dialogue: A Journal of Theology* 37 (Spring 1998): 85-91.

10. Edward Farley, *Theologia: The Fragmentation and Unity of Theological Education* (Philadelphia: Fortress, 1983).

11. See, for example, Stephen Fowl, *Engaging Scripture* (Malden, Mass.: Blackwell, 1998).

12. Ellen T. Charry, *By the Renewing of Your Minds: The Pastoral Function of Christian Doctrine* (New York: Oxford University Press, 1997).

cation must take seriously theological argumentation about the nature and purpose of the church. In reflecting on the theological self-understanding of the Christian community, it finds important clues about the sort of education this community should offer. Some of the most important developments in the ecclesiologies of contemporary dogmatic theology have emerged in concert with new thinking about another doctrinal locus: the doctrine of God, or, more particularly, the doctrine of the Trinity.

Initially fostered by Karl Barth and Karl Rahner, this discussion has been taken up and developed in very different directions by process, feminist, and liberation theologians, as well as persons maintaining continuity with Barth's and Rahner's original proposals.[13] Common to all is a rejection of the substantialist metaphysics undergirding the doctrine of God for much of Western church history. In some cases, this has been coupled with a retrieval of insights from the Cappadocian Fathers, especially their portrayal of the oneness of God as a dynamic unity-in-diversity, as an outgrowth of the perichoretic relations of love between the divine Persons. This provides a way of describing how the eternal God can relate to the temporal world, both in the incarnation and providentially through the Holy Spirit.

Of special importance for our purposes is the influence of this recent Trinitarian discussion on the doctrines of humanity and the church. Some theologians like Moltmann, Pannenberg, and LaCugna have pointed out that this portrayal of the Godhead in terms of the perichoretic relations of the divine Persons has implications for the way we view humans, created in God's image. The *imago Dei,* they argue, is not best developed in terms of human rationality (setting humans "above" the animal world) or personal agency (allowing individuals to actualize themselves in freedom) but in terms of human relationality.[14] Human identity is inherently relational and exocentric. The human vocation is to mirror (image), in the manifold relations in which humans exist, the perichoretic love of the triune God. These theologians go on to argue that it is the distortion of this vocation that the narratives of Scripture portray God as addressing, first in the election of Israel and then in the sending of Jesus Christ. Christ's life of love in solidarity

13. Helpful overviews of this discussion are found in John Thompson, *Modern Trinitarian Perspectives* (New York: Oxford University Press, 1994), and Ted Peters, *God as Trinity: Relationality and Temporality in the Divine Life* (Louisville: Westminster/John Knox, 1993).

14. Jürgen Moltmann, *The Crucified God* (San Francisco: Harper and Row, 1973); Jürgen Moltmann, *The Trinity and the Kingdom: The Doctrine of God* (San Francisco: Harper and Row, 1981); Catherine Mowry LaCugna, *God for Us: The Trinity and Christian Life* (San Francisco: Harper and Row, 1973); Wolfhart Pannenberg, *Jesus: God and Man* (Philadelphia: Westminster, 1968).

with humanity and his sacrificial death on its behalf are simultaneously events in human history and within the Godhead, opening humans to the restoration of the communion between God, neighbor, and natural world for which they were created.

As many contemporary theologians have noted, this perspective has important ecclesiological implications.[15] The church serves as a sign of this communion, as a provisional representation of the human response to God's outreaching love for the world. The church thus finds its purpose and mission within the Trinitarian missions of God, existing not for itself but in love and service of the world that God has reconciled in Christ. To borrow Bonhoeffer's phrase, it is a church for others.[16] Or as more recent theologians have put it, it is a community of the *missio Dei,* a missionary church within the missions of God.[17]

Obviously, this brief sketch of a very complex discussion in contemporary dogmatic theology stands in need of further amplification. Is Barth's accent on the oneness of God to be preferred to Moltmann's social doctrine of the Trinity? Is LaCugna's elimination of the distinction between the economic and immanent Trinity preferable to Torrance's reworking of this traditional distinction? These are precisely the kinds of *intradisciplinary* judgments practical theologians will face as they engage this discussion. In part, they will make these judgments on grounds internal to dogmatic theology. Consideration will be given to the "governing doctrines" developed by this field. William Christian describes these as "doctrines about doctrine," doctrines that set forth the principles and rules by which primary or first order doctrines are developed.[18] Such norms guide dogmatic theologians in their judgments about matters of doctrinal authenticity, the ordering of doctrines in terms of their importance, consistency across a body of doctrines, and the scope of doctrinal teaching, including its relationship to the "alien claims" of

---

15. Jürgen Moltmann, *The Church in the Power of the Spirit: A Contribution to Messianic Ecclesiology,* trans. M. Kohl (New York: Harper and Row, 1977); Miroslav Volf, *After Our Likeness: The Church as the Image of the Trinity* (Grand Rapids: Eerdmans, 1998); Leonardo Boff, *Trinity and Society,* trans. P. Burns, Liberation and Theology Series (London: Burns and Oates, 1988).

16. Dietrich Bonhoeffer, "The Nature of the Church," in *A Testament to Freedom: The Essential Writings of Dietrich Bonhoeffer,* ed. G. Kelly and B. Nelson (San Francisco: HarperCollins, 1990), p. 89. See also in this same book Bonhoeffer's lecture "Worldliness and Christianity of the Church," p. 92.

17. For an overview of the *missio Dei* and the church, see David Bosch, *Transforming Mission: Paradigm Shifts in Theology of Mission* (Maryknoll, N.Y.: Orbis, 1991).

18. William Christian, *Doctrines of Religious Communities: A Philosophical Study* (New Haven: Yale University Press, 1987).

other forms of human knowledge. Significant differences on these matters distinguish the various perspectives found in dogmatic theology today.

Knowing what is at stake in these differences is an important part of a practical theologian's evaluation of the recent discussion of the doctrine of the Trinity on grounds internal to dogmatic theology. But this is not enough. It does not capture what is at stake in bringing dogmatic theology into dialogue with practical theology. Here the focus is on *interdisciplinary* dialogue, a conversation between two fields, each of which has distinctive subject matters, modes of inquiry, and goals. Practical theology has much at stake in how this conversation is conceptualized, for, too often, in the encyclopedic paradigm of theology, it has been portrayed as "applying" deductively the insights of dogmatic theology to the work of clergy or to the life of the church.

Practical Theology and the Construction of Models of Ecclesial Praxis

For this reason, it is important to pause and clarify the understanding of practical theology offered at an earlier point in this chapter. Drawing on Schleiermacher, I described practical theology as involving the construction of theories of ecclesial practice in the context of modernity (now viewed in terms of globalization and postmodernism), issuing in "rules of art" that can guide both the leaders of the church and ordinary Christians in the pursuit of their worldly vocations. Three aspects of this understanding of practical theology distinguish it from dogmatic theology: its subject matter or object, its rational modes of inquiry, and its goal.

First, practical theology's object of investigation is contemporary religious praxis, situated in a particular sociohistorical context. Ecclesiology, as such, is not investigated as one doctrine among others but in terms of its various empirical manifestations. This is the "living text" that practical theology exegetes, so to speak.[19] This point is made with particular force by two contemporary practical theologians, Hans van der Ven and Reiner Preul.[20] Both portray ecclesiology in practical theology as focusing on the praxis of the contemporary church. Van der Ven captures nicely the different levels of analysis involved in the investigation of this object:

19. Charles Gerkin uses the metaphor of "living text" to make this point in *The Living Human Document: Revisioning Pastoral Counseling in a Hermeneutical Mode* (Nashville: Abingdon, 1984).

20. Johannes van der Ven, *Ecclesiology in Context* (Grand Rapids: Eerdmans, 1996); Reiner Preul, *Kirchentheorie* (Berlin: de Gruyter, 1997).

The praxis of the church can be distinguished by the level at which it is given shape. The *micro level* has to do with the church insofar as it is developed in the local, regional environment. The *meso level* refers to the church insofar as it realizes itself in the national and continental environment. The *macro level* points to the church insofar as it takes shape in the intercontinental and global society.[21]

Preul locates this sort of empirical work in a complex cross-disciplinary dialogue between dogmatics, church history, practical theology, and the social sciences, including especially the sociology of religion and organizational theory. The intersection of this conversation is a special sphere of theological inquiry — what he calls *Kirchentheorie* (church-theory). He describes this as follows: "Church-theory relates the dogmatic understanding or essence of the church to a given church situation with the purpose of critical evaluation and, if possible, an improvement of this situation."[22] Within *Kirchentheorie,* practical theology has the special task of investigating the church in its various empirical manifestations, describing it as one social system among other social systems and bringing to expression its unique religious function within these systems. There are differences between van der Ven and Preul; Preul seems to grant a stronger normative role to dogmatics in *Kirchentheorie* and seeks the theological unity of the various functions of the church.[23] Both, however, describe the object of practical theology as the contemporary praxis of the Christian community. Moreover, both locate this praxis in broader interpretative frameworks.

Second, the forms of inquiry employed by practical theology include a strong component of empirical investigation. This has close analogies to the kind of empirical work undertaken by some of the figures examined in the second part of this book.[24] The point to be underscored is the importance of this sort of empirical investigation in practical theology, as well as its dialogue with research of cognate fields. If the object of investigation is the "living

21. Van der Ven, *Ecclesiology in Context,* p. xii.

22. Preul, *Kirchentheorie,* p. 3. Preul is drawing on Schleiermacher here, and his understanding of "essence" thus should not be construed as essentialism in the modern philosophical sense.

23. Preul portrays the foundations of church theory in Lutheran dogmatics, which serves as the all-important starting point of *Kirchentheorie.* It also provides the unity of the various functions investigated by practical theology, what he describes as the *cura anima,* the "cure of souls," and the *ordo salutis,* the order of salvation, which should animate every dimension of the church's life.

24. Coe, we can recall, carried out research on the psychology of conversion. Westerhoff explored the cultures of congregations, using the tools of cultural anthropology.

text" of contemporary religious praxis, then the rational operation appropriate to this object is empirical investigation, including clinical forms of inquiry.[25] Theories of modernization or globalization provide comprehensive interpretive frameworks of this more focused empirical work.

Third, the constructive dimension of practical theology is the formation of theories that can guide and transform religious praxis as it currently exists. Normative judgments are made about the adequacy of such practice and rules of art are developed to guide persons in concrete contexts of experience. It is at the point of making normative judgments about contemporary praxis that practical theology finds its dialogue with dogmatic theology most helpful, a point explicated by Preul in his description of *Kirchentheorie*. The perspective developed here differs with Preul on two significant points, however. First, the pluralism of contemporary dogmatic theology is taken more seriously. Practical theology's dialogue with this field does not assume a single dogmatic perspective (in Preul's case, a Lutheran perspective), but acknowledges a variety of positions within contemporary dogmatics. In the end, it must evaluate the range of ecclesiologies currently present in the field, which makes the intradisciplinary judgments it must form more complex. Second, practical theology's empirical and constructive work should be portrayed more forthrightly as "speaking back" to dogmatics. At times, it may challenge the eccesiologies of dogmatics in light of new forms of ecclesial practice discovered in its own empirical research or constructed in its own normative proposals. Only in this way can the conversation between these fields be genuinely interdisciplinary, moving back and forth in both directions.

Leaving these methodological considerations to one side, the important point to be made is practical theology's construction of a normative model of ecclesial practice, issuing in rules of art that can guide and critique contemporary religious praxis in its various manifestations. Here I agree with Preul, who makes this point quite nicely: "Even though the study of practical theology implies knowledge from all theological disciplines, and even though we produce theories ourselves, practical theology is — as Schleiermacher said — a technical discipline, the concern of which is the ongoing improvement of ecclesial activities."[26] What Preul is calling attention to here is Schleiermacher's de-

---

25. In the United States, the clinical dimension of practical theology has been given special attention in the work of Seward Hiltner, closely identified with the Clinical Pastoral Education movement. See *Preface to Pastoral Theology* (Nashville: Abingdon, 1958) and *The New Shape of Pastoral Theology: Essays in Honor of Seward Hiltner,* ed. W. Oglesby (Nashville: Abingdon, 1969). Rodney Hunter's essay in this volume is particularly helpful.

26. In Friedrich Schweitzer and Johannes van der Ven, eds., *Practical Theology: International Perspectives* (Frankfurt: Peter Lange, 1999), p. 149.

scription of the goal of practical theology in terms of the Greek term *techne*. In dynamic contexts of praxis, what is needed are open-ended guidelines that help leaders make normative and pragmatic judgments about how best to proceed. Schleiermacher sometimes referred to this sort of knowledge as "rules of art," harking back to the kind of knowledge constructed in classical rhetoric and ethics. Such guidelines assist leaders in making practical judgments about religious praxis in concrete contexts of experience.

An Illustration

By way of illustrating this approach to ecclesiology in practical theology and its role in the construction of a theory of congregational education, I will enter into a dialogue with a recent body of research on small groups in the United States by the sociologist Robert Wuthnow. It should be clear from the outset that we are focusing exclusively on the context of the United States and not on small groups like the base communities found in various parts of Latin America. In *Sharing the Journey,* Wuthnow investigates the importance of small groups of various sorts in contemporary American life.[27] These groups range from self-help groups like Alcoholics Anonymous to groups that are explicitly religious, such as neighborhood Bible studies and Sunday school classes. At the time of Wuthnow's investigation, four out of ten Americans participated in groups of this sort.[28] From interviews, surveys, and direct observation, he identified two primary needs drawing persons to such groups: a search for meaningful, face-to-face community in a highly differentiated social context with many large, impersonal institutions, and a spiritual quest for a personal encounter of the sacred.

While Wuthnow is appreciative of the ways small groups meet these needs, he raises critical questions about the long-term impact of this movement on Americans' understanding of community and spirituality. Among those involved in this movement, community comes to be closely identified with intimate, face-to-face encounters in relatively homogenous groups. Encounters "at a distance" among strangers who are culturally, racially, or ethnically diverse — long associated with normative descriptions of public life in pluralistic communities — give way to understandings of community based on closeness and similarity. Moreover, the community formed in small groups

27. Robert Wuthnow, *Sharing the Journey: Support Groups and America's New Quest for Community* (New York: Free Press, 1994).
28. Wuthnow, *Sharing the Journey,* p. 4.

is highly "portable," that is, individuals can join or depart at will. The more durable bonds of family, neighborhood, and civic association are not present.

Wuthnow also raises important questions about the ways the small group movement is reshaping Americans' understanding of the sacred. As he puts it,

> They are dramatically changing the way God is understood. God is now less of an external authority and more of an internal presence. The sacred becomes more personal but, in the process, also becomes more manageable, more serviceable in meeting individual needs, and more a feature of group processes themselves.[29]

Those participating in small groups tend to see as less important the received wisdom of religious communities embodied in their creeds, doctrines, and practices. Great emphasis is placed on the pragmatic dimensions of spirituality, such that people believe that "the best proof of God's existence is whether one has received an answer to some personal problem" and that "the Bible is true because it works in everyday life."[30]

Wuthnow's empirical investigation of the small group movement has important implications for ecclesiological reflection in practical theology and the construction of a theory of congregational education. Many congregations in the United States are deeply influenced by this movement. Indeed, many of the fastest growing churches in the United States place great emphasis on such groups, making them the cornerstone of their educational programs. What sort of ecclesiology is implicit in churches that define community and the sacred along the lines of the small group movement? A sort, perhaps, best described as an intimate community of the Spirit. Such ecclesiologies place the accent on building close-knit groups in which the members share common spiritual experiences and build intimate personal relationships. The educational programs of such churches follow suit. From the church school to parenting classes to neighborhood Bible studies to classes for new members, emphasis is placed on the development of close, interpersonal relationships that cultivate an intimate community, providing support for families and individuals. God is closely related to successful responses to the challenges of everyday life.

No doubt the success of these churches rests on their responsiveness to the deeply felt needs identified by Wuthnow. Normatively, however, they can be judged as theologically deficient in crucial ways. Recall our exploration of the doctrine of the Trinity in contemporary dogmatic theology and the important ecclesiological implications flowing from this discussion. What is

---

29. Wuthnow, *Sharing the Journey*, pp. 3-4.
30. Wuthnow, *Sharing the Journey*, pp. 4-5.

missing from these churches and their education is precisely what makes the church the church: its participation in the missionary God's outpouring of love for the world. Service and responsibility in the larger human community is replaced by fellowship within the church itself. The church is a haven in an impersonal, bureaucratic world rather than a servant of the world and a sign of the communion for which the world was created.

In making these kinds of normative judgments about the implicit ecclesiologies of churches shaped by the small group movement, practical theology can learn much from its dialogue with dogmatic theology. At the same time, its own task has a different focus, investigating empirically various forms of religious praxis — as we have done in our dialogue with Wuthnow — and projecting norms that can shape this praxis in concrete ways. It is to a concrete discussion of religious education praxis in the setting of Christian congregations that we now turn. Within this setting, we must ask, what shape might religious education take? Once again, I will point to the importance of cross-disciplinary thinking in the construction of a theory of congregational education.

Three Tasks of the Teaching Ministry of the Church: Catechesis, Exhortation, and Discernment

What would congregational education look like if informed by a *missio Dei* ecclesiology? What sort of rules of art would flow from this model? What forms of human knowledge might it engage? In the brief space of this chapter, we can offer only a general outline of our answer to these questions. We take our bearings from an understanding of the church that views the congregation normatively as finding its identity and mission within God's outpouring of love for the world — the Trinitarian missions of the Father in creating and sustaining the world, the Son in reconciling the world to God, and the Holy Spirit in restoring communion in ways that anticipate God's promised future for creation.[31] This locates the church in a complex series of relationships to the God in whom it believes, the fellowship *(koinonia)* of the church, and the world that it is called to serve. Three central educational tasks flow from this relational ecclesiology: catechesis, exhortation, and discernment. Each of

---

31. The three persons of the Trinity are all involved in the actions of creation/preservation, reconciliation, and transfiguration. I am following a long-standing tradition, articulated in the doctrine of appropriations, in which one of the persons of the Godhead is more closely identified with each action. Moltmann makes a similar point in his changing "grammar" of Trinitarian activity in *The Trinity and the Kingdom*.

these tasks can be found in the New Testament church but they have taken different forms across church history.[32]

The term "catechesis," as used here, refers to the task of handing on Christian Scripture and tradition in ways that allow the members of the Christian community to understand the God of whom they speak and to place their trust in this God.[33] While its goal is the cultivation of deeper, more complex forms of knowledge, catechesis should never lose sight of the fact that this knowledge finds its rightful place in a present relationship with the living God. It cultivates knowledge in the service of a relationship of *faith*. Simple transmission of information or socialization into the pre-existent beliefs and practices of a congregation are not adequate ways of conceptualizing this task. Handing on Scripture and Christian tradition ought to cultivate a freely chosen participation by the members of the congregation in the reconciling work of the Son and in the communion mediated by the Holy Spirit.

In the Pauline literature particularly, "exhortation" focuses on what we today would call moral formation and education. It is Paul's way of challenging his congregations to live lives that are pleasing to God. Recent work on the way this sort of moral formation took place in his congregations has uncovered parallels with the relations of censure and praise found among the schools of popular moral philosophy.[34] Moreover, it also has clarified the distinctiveness of the moral ethos of Paul's congregations in the Greco-Roman world.[35] Within the urban centers of the first century, Paul's congregations were virtually alone in bringing together women and men, rich and poor, slave and free for relatively egalitarian forms of social interaction on an ongoing basis.[36] For

---

32. I have described an earlier version of these three tasks more extensively elsewhere and, by necessity, my discussion in the present chapter will be brief. See Richard Osmer, "The Teaching Ministry in a Multicultural World," in *The Spirit and the Modern Authorities*, vol. 2: *God and Globalization*, ed. Max Stackhouse with Peter Paris (Harrisburg, Pa.: Trinity Press International, 2001).

33. Admittedly, many modern religious educators are ambivalent about the use of terms like "catechesis" and "catechetical instruction," because they believe they are closely associated with older forms of education focusing on information transmission. I am retrieving this term here for two reasons: (1) I do not believe this modernist view of catechesis does justice to the tradition of Christian education across history, and (2) its etymology (to answer back) captures nicely the nature of the Christian life as an active response to the self-giving of God.

34. Abraham Malherbe, *Paul and the Thessalonians: The Philosophic Tradition of Pastoral Care* (Philadelphia: Fortress, 1987).

35. Wayne Meeks, *The First Urban Christians: The Social World of the Apostle Paul* (New Haven: Yale University Press, 1983).

36. Elisabeth Schüssler Fiorenza, *Discipleship of Equals: A Feminist Ekklesia-logy of Liberation* (New York: Crossroad, 1993). See also Meeks, *The First Urban Christians*.

these reasons, the moral ethos of these communities — including moral exemplars, ethical teaching, and ongoing relations of support and accountability — played an all-important role in the sort of moral formation and education that was offered.

Within the context of a *missio Dei* ecclesiology, I would advocate the retrieval of this sort of Pauline emphasis by portraying moral formation and education as teaching the members of congregations how to participate in the outpouring of God's *love* for the world. Just as God loved the world in Jesus Christ, so too Christians are to learn how to practice self-giving love on the world's behalf — a love that strives to reconcile enemies, welcome the stranger, and seek justice for the dispossessed. This is the overriding ideal of the Christian moral life and the primary goal of contemporary forms of exhortation. Within the culturally pluralistic and institutionally differentiated social contexts of Germany and the United States today, educating the members of the Christian community toward the moral ideal of love both within and beyond the boundaries of the congregation is an exceedingly challenging task. At the least, it means helping the members of congregations learn how to communicate with empathy and understanding with others whose values and beliefs are often different than their own. Normatively, it means helping them acquire the cognitive, moral, and communicative competencies requisite to fair and open discussion across a range of publics.

"Discernment," as the term is being used here, refers to the educational task of teaching Christians how to read the signs of the times. Here too, the church's mission within the missions of God provides important clues for the conceptualization of congregational education. Christ did not come to save the church but the world. Education within the church is thus charged with helping the members of the Christian community learn how to discern what God is enabling and requiring them to do and be within the challenges and opportunities of their present social context.[37] The task of discernment, however, is more than learning to read the signs of the present time. More basically, it is one of learning how to interpret the present in light of God's promised future for creation. It is oriented toward Christian *hope*, discernment of the hidden possibilities of transformation in the present that anticipate the restored communion of creation promised in Jesus Christ.[38] The hard work of understanding the present through empirical and interpretive research is

37. This way of describing the ethical imperatives of the gospel is influenced by James Gustafson. See Richard Osmer, *A Teachable Spirit: Recovering the Teaching Office in the Church* (Louisville: Westminster/John Knox Press, 1990), pp. 169-72.

38. Jürgen Moltmann, *Theology of Hope: On the Ground and the Implications of a Christian Eschatology* (New York: Harper and Row, 1967).

included in this task. But it also includes the nurture of the imagination: education in the evocative contents of the church's eschatological symbols in order to project new possibilities for life in the present. In the face of the massive changes globalization is currently creating both within and between all nations of the world, teaching the members of congregations how to discern the present imaginatively in hope is surely one of the most important tasks of congregational education in the century that is just beginning.

Each of these three tasks has something to learn from an interdisciplinary dialogue with the various resources of contemporary culture: catechesis from science; exhortation from moral philosophy, critical social theory, and modern moral education; and discernment from aesthetics. Several examples can be given to illustrate what is at stake in this sort of dialogue. The challenge for practical theologians is to maintain the integrity of their own theological stance even as they engage with openness the insights of other fields.

Across the centuries, congregational catechesis at its best has been concerned with more than merely handing on the beliefs of the Christian faith. It has taken up the task of making these beliefs intelligible within the worldviews in which believers live. Especially across the modern period, this has included the cognitive challenges of science. By the time they reach adolescence, most Christian youth struggle with the relationship between science and faith. Can they believe in the Genesis account of creation, for example, and simultaneously believe in post-Darwinian theories of evolution? Can they affirm scientific accounts of causality and continue to believe that God is active in the course of human affairs? At the very least, practical theologians must assist congregational education in helping contemporary Christians in their struggle with these kinds of questions.

Most practical theologians recognize that they must go further, however, appropriating the insights of the natural and human sciences about human development and learning. Here, the challenge of maintaining consistency with their theological convictions comes to the fore. The relational anthropology and ecclesiology we have outlined above, for example, does not cohere well with highly individualistic forms of modern psychology that place the accent on self-actualization. In contrast, theories of cognitive psychology such as Gardner's theory of multiple intelligences cohere quite nicely, for they portray diverse forms of human cognition as inherently taking shape in relation to cultural contexts.[39] In dialogue with a theory like Gardner's, catechesis

---

39. Howard Gardner: *Frames of Mind: The Theory of Multiple Intelligences* (New York: Basic, 1983), and *The Disciplined Mind: What All Students Should Understand* (New York: Simon and Schuster, 1999).

learns that exclusive preoccupation with verbal and logical forms of intelligence — too often the focus of its teaching in catechetical instruction — excludes persons who learn best through musical, interpersonal, or spatial forms of intelligence. It appropriates the insight that Christian beliefs can be taught through songs, graphic representations, and interpersonal examples from everyday life. The findings of science inform catechesis in ways that do not inadvertently subvert understandings of the human formed theologically.

The task of exhortation, likewise, has much to learn from interdisciplinary dialogue, especially from contemporary philosophical ethics and social theory. Equipping persons for vocations and ministries of love in culturally pluralistic and institutionally differentiated social contexts must include attention to critical social analysis of these contexts. Many contemporary Christians, for example, have taken over uncritically the modern understanding of religion as located exclusively in the private sphere, concerned with personal morality and belief and the socialization of the young. Helping Christians to reclaim the concept of vocation as including every sphere of life and to understand the important role of congregations as "mediating structures" in civil society are merely two of the ways contemporary social analysis might inform the contents of exhortation directly. Likewise, practical theologians have much to learn from moral philosophy. Habermas's discourse ethic, for example, especially as reformulated by Seyla Benhabib,[40] has much to teach about the kinds of cognitive, moral, and communicative competencies important for ministries of love across public spheres in which culturally and religiously diverse actors are present.

Teaching the members of congregations how to discern the present in hope, likewise, has much to gain from interdisciplinary dialogue. Most obviously, reading the signs of the times involves forms of analysis and interpretation of the present context. Even more important, the task of projecting imaginative alternatives has much to gain from sustained dialogue with aesthetics, especially as formulated in critical social theory.[41] How do the aes-

---

40. Seyla Benhabib, *Situating the Self: Gender, Community and Postmodernism in Contemporary Ethics* (New York: Routledge, 1992).

41. Two of the most important recent books carrying out this dialogue are John de Gruchy, *Christianity, Art and Transformation: Theological Aesthetics in the Struggle for Justice* (Cambridge: Cambridge University Press, 2001), and Jeremy Begbie, *Theology, Music and Time* (Cambridge: Cambridge University Press, 2000). Some of the most important recent thinking about the role of art in education is found in the writing of Howard Gardner and David Perkins. See Gardner's *Art, Mind, and Brain* (New York: Basic, 1982) and, with Perkins, "Art, Mind, and Education," *Journal of Aesthetic Education* 22, no. 1 (1982). Contemporary research on the effects of the global media on adolescents is found in Quentin Schultze, Roy Anker, James Bratt, William

thetics of popular culture — especially television, music, and computers — shape human consciousness toward the demands of the global marketplace, evoking the needs and ideals of a consumer-driven culture? How might a congregation disrupt these cultural flows in its education and project alternative forms of beauty? Congregational education has much to learn from a dialogue with educators like Paulo Freire in answering these questions. But it must move beyond these educators' preoccupation with the cultivation of critical consciousness to a fuller appreciation of the ways the imagination is disrupted and reoriented in its encounter with the symbolic and artistic dimensions of culture and religion, in the graphic, literary, musical, and oral forms of artistic expression.

Toward a Theory and Praxis of Congregational Education: Practical Theology in Cross-Disciplinary Dialogue

As described in this chapter, models of congregational education are constructed through processes of thinking and dialogue that are inherently cross-disciplinary. Theology, as the reflective self-understanding of the Christian community, has been portrayed as an important participant in this dialogue. More particularly, practical theology has been viewed as the theological "home" of congregational education. This is not to imply that Protestant religious education theory should now retreat into an isolated theological ghetto. Rather, it must embrace an explicit program of cross-disciplinary thinking, a program not always pursued directly by Protestant religious education across the twentieth century in the United States and Germany. The constructive proposals outlined in this chapter have been offered as examples of a way practical theology might engage the cultural resources of our contemporary social context, as well as other theological disciplines. By necessity, these proposals have been brief and make no claim to comprehensiveness. They point to the kind of thinking that must be taken up more fully in theories of Protestant religious education as it enters the twenty-first century.

Romanowski, John Worst, and Lambert Zuidervaart, *Dancing in the Dark: Youth, Popular Culture and the Electronic Media* (Grand Rapids: Eerdmans, 1991). Some of the most important writings on aesthetics in the older critical social theory are Theodor Adorno, "How to Look at Television," *Quarterly of Film, Radio, and Television* 3 (Spring 1954) and Adorno's *Introduction to the Sociology of Music* (New York: Seabury, 1976); and Walter Benjamin, *Illuminations*, ed. H. Arendt (New York: Harcourt, Brace and World, 1968).

8   The Religious Dimension of the Self

Our analysis of twentieth-century religious education has shown that one of the central concerns that general education and religious education share is the development of the self. In fact, two of modern education's key questions are how the developing self should be understood and how its development can be supported through education.

Our discussion of twentieth-century psychological models of the development of the self has shown that these models have created an ambivalent situation for religious education. On the one hand, some of these models have been helpful in designing new approaches for religious education in congregations or schools. The fact that these new approaches were designed in light of the expectations and criteria of modern psychology has served in some ways to legitimate religious education. On the other hand, some of the most influential psychological and philosophical models have tended to weaken the position of religion by limiting its role to the time before or after adulthood or by conceptualizing the modern self as a post-religious self.

The idea that the self does not have to be rooted in a religious basis that gives it meaning, unity, and direction is closely connected to the tendencies of pluralization and individualization described in Part I. Modern philosophers and psychologists seem to assume that pluralization and individualization no longer allow a religious basis for identity because they see religion as divisive and are looking for something universal as a basis. Religious education and theology, therefore, find themselves faced with the question of why religion should still play a role in education. The advent of postmodernity has again changed perceptions of the self, making the question of religion's role in education even more pressing. The postmodern self, it is said, is no longer bound to the traditional ideals of unity and coherence. It is seen as flexible, ever-changing, and without temporal stability. Such views of the postmodern self are still highly tentative and hypothetical, however; it is an open question what religion means today.

This chapter contributes to our effort to construct what we called (in the first chapter of Part III) "a public practical theology in the context of *paideia*." In this present chapter we will move from addressing the meaning of religion within the *paideia* of the public to addressing the meaning of religion within the *paideia* of the individual person. The meaning of religion within the *paideia* of the individual must, however, be defended publicly — vis-à-vis the social sciences and other academic disciplines. Our task in this chapter will therefore be an exercise in multidisciplinary dialogue, a task that reflects the interdisciplinary and multidisciplinary character of practical theology as de-scribed in Chapter Seven. The following analysis may be read as a critical con-tribution to the emerging discussion about the postmodern self, an analysis that makes special reference to the religious dimensions of the self.

Conflicting Models of the Self: With or Without Religious Basis?

I will begin by attempting to clarify further the conflict between different views on the relationship between religion and the self or identity. For this purpose, I will first consider two influential theories: Erik H. Erikon's account of the for-mation of personal identity in the life cycle and Jürgen Habermas's model of the formation of postconventional identity or ego-identity. Both Erikson and Habermas see a place for religion in their normative understandings of identity, but, at least from my point of view, this place is not acceptable theologically. Both (to different degrees) adopt a reductionist position that can be challenged not only theologically but also on social scientific grounds. After examining Erikson and Habermas I will refer to alternative accounts of self and religion found in the social philosophies of Charles Taylor, Paul Ricoeur, Seyla Ben-habib, and others in order to gain a wider perspective on the self and to clarify how Erikson and Habermas can be critiqued from a social science perspective.

Erikson's work has been appreciated by many practical theologians and religious educators as an important contribution to the understanding of the role of religion in the life cycle. His account of the tension between basic trust and basic mistrust in early childhood as a basis for all religious development in later life has been especially widely accepted.[1] This perspective of Erikson's

1. For helpful accounts of Erikson's psychology of religion cf. J. Eugene Wright, *Erikson:*

has been used in approaches to theological anthropology written by Hans Küng, Wolfhart Pannenberg, and, most recently, James Loder.[2] In this respect, Erikson has become almost a classic for practical theology and religious education in many parts of the world.

Erikson theorizes that religion is the necessary basis for the achievement of personal identity in adolescence, a view that has also been widely accepted. In a famous quote from his *Young Man Luther,* he says that religion — which he includes in his understanding of "ideology" — "must do for the young person what the mother did for the infant: provide nutriment for the soul as well as for the stomach, and screen the environment so that vigorous growth may meet what it can manage."[3] The kind of meaning that a religious outlook may confer upon the adolescent is seen by Erikson as an important presupposition for healthy development.

Erikson's work has indeed advanced our understanding of religious development, and it is clear that his psychology has resonated with some theological points of view. But if we attempt to make Erikson our guide for the further trajectory of religion in the life cycle, we come to realize that he has little to say about the religious basis of the adult self.[4] According to Erikson's trajectory of religion in the life cycle, religion will not be a major factor in the time between adolescence and old age, except in the case of a "homo religiosus" — that is, a person with the extreme religious intensity of, for example, Martin Luther. In some ways, this map of religious development is quite contradictory. While religion is seen as playing a central role in making adolescent identity formation possible, it then recedes into the background during most of adulthood. It can be argued that this account of religion in the life cycle is empirically accurate because it corresponds to the widespread cultural perception that adults are focused on their rational capacities and that adulthood is defined by work, which emphasizes the full possession of one's rational capacities. But one can also argue that there is a difference between the culturally shaped self-understanding of modern adults and a more objec-

---

Identity and Religion (New York: Seabury, 1982), and Hetty Zock, *A Psychology of Ultimate Concern: Erik H. Erikson's Contribution to the Psychology of Religion* (Amsterdam: Rodopi, 1990).

2. Hans Küng, *Existiert Gott? Antwort auf die Gottesfrage der Neuzeit* (München: Piper, 1978); Wolfhart Pannenberg, *Anthroplogy in Theological Perspective* (Philadelphia: Westminster, 1985); James E. Loder, *The Logic of the Spirit: Human Development in Theological Perspective* (San Francisco: Jossey-Bass, 1998).

3. Erik H. Erikson, *Young Man Luther: A Study in Psychoanalysis and History* (New York: Norton, 1958), p. 118.

4. Although J. Eugene Wright was not outspoken about this, his interpretation *(Erikson: Identity and Religion)* does make this clear.

tive statement of the psychological facts about those modern adults. To some degree any model of human development, including Erikson's, contains normative aspects. Theories that prescribe the role religion should play in the human life cycle should be critical of the images that are operative in the everyday life of Western society. These "second thoughts" about Erikson's model of religious development become more obvious when we move on to the sociological and philosophical views of Habermas. Here, we return to issues initially raised in Chapter Two.

Habermas's theory of communicative action, which he develops in two volumes devoted to this subject[5] and in a number of other works published between the 1970s and 1990s, includes one of the most powerful and most influential statements on the relationship between modernization and religion. Habermas distinguishes four types of worldviews associated with four different stages of the role of religion in the development of social, cultural, and individual identity:

> *Stage One: Natural Identity.* Habermas describes religion in archaic societies characterized by tribal relationships as "mythical." He includes anthropomorphism, animism, and magic in this stage of early or primitive religion.
>
> *Stage Two: Role Identity.* This stage corresponds historically to the early high cultures. Here religion is the basis for a "clear-cut group identity." The identity of the individual is tied to "certain traditions, special roles or norms."[6]
>
> *Stage Three: Early Ego-Identity.* It is interesting to note that the world religions are seen as leading to this third developmental stage. The role-identity or group-identity is relativized — put into question — because now, through the relationship to God, the "development of an ego-identity" that is "detached from all concrete roles and norms" is anticipated. The individual ego-identity does not, however, really become dominant at this stage because the political circumstances of the times require a strong national identity. Habermas also attributes the suppression of individual ego-identity to remnants of earlier stages of religious development that are still contained within the world religions and that work against the more progressive universalizing po-

5. Jürgen Habermas, *The Theory of Communicative Action*, 2 vols. (Boston: Beacon, 1984, 1987).

6. Jürgen Habermas, *Zur Rekonstruktion des historischen Materialismus* (Frankfurt: Suhrkamp, 1976), pp. 94, 99.

tential of these religions. Habermas argues that it is the distinction between believers and nonbelievers that has prevented the world religions from the breakthrough to a truly humane, universal identity.[7]

Stage Four: True Ego-Identity. The development of true ego-identity associated with the advent of modernity is, Habermas argues, historically also influenced and supported by the universalizing potential of religion. But he also argues that religion eventually loses its influence on the formation of identity. According to Habermas, "not much more than the core of a universalist ethics" finally remains of the universal religions.[8]

It is clear, then, how Habermas views the transition from traditional religious worldviews to the modern position of discourse ethics and ego-identity. This transition depends on the departure from what, at earlier stages, used to be the religious basis of the self or of identity. Religion has its role to play in the early stages of human development, he accedes, but the more highly developed post-conventional ego-identity cannot be supported by religious worldviews or by religious traditions.

With this, I come back to Habermas's almost paradoxical view of the relationship between modernization and religion, discussed in Chapter Two. Habermas admits there are aspects of religion that cannot be transformed into rational discourse. He mentions, in passing, that there is at least the possibility of a permanent place for religion even at the most mature stages of human development. Nevertheless, the place he assigns to religion at these "mature" stages hardly leaves any room for what Christians could recognize as their faith, because during the process of religion's transformation into universal discourse or ethics "the mystical elements of an elementary experience, which is determined by non-action and which may not be transformed ethically, seem to be split off as a realm of their own."[9] This truncated sort of religion can have no influence on the universalist ethics that are seen as the basis for ego-identity. The role Habermas describes for "stage four" religion is thus in some ways close to what Friedrich Schleiermacher once ridiculed as a misconception of religion — a religious remnant of "mystical appearance" and occasional "attacks of religion."[10]

---

7. Habermas, *Zur Rekonstruktion*, pp. 99ff.

8. Habermas, *Zur Rekonstruktion*, p. 101.

9. Habermas, *Zur Rekonstruktion*, p. 101.

10. Friedrich Schleiermacher, *Über die Religion. Reden an die Gebildeten unter ihren Verächtern*, ed. R. Otto (Göttingen: Vandenhoeck und Ruprecht, 1967), p. 114.

Habermas's theory of the development of the self rejects the notion of basing identity on religious worldviews or traditions. Are there alternatives to this modernist understanding? The answer is clearly yes. Over the last two decades, a number of alternative models have been developed from different perspectives. In the following review of these perspectives we will limit ourselves to three such models, all of which show why religious education may have to play an important role in the formation of personal identity.

The philosophy of Seyla Benhabib combines feminist, communitarian, and postmodern arguments in order to challenge the assumption of an isolated and detached self, which she sees operative in the work of authors like Lawrence Kohlberg.[11] Against an abstract universalism, she insists on the need to include the other as a concrete person. Her plea for "situating the self" aims at a new appreciation of the contextual nature of all stages in the development of self or identity. Although Benhabib is not interested in the religious dimensions of such contexts, her work nevertheless opens up important possibilities for including religion as one of the constitutive factors of community, self, and identity.

Similarly, Paul Ricoeur has pointed out that the constitution of the self depends on narrative and story or, as he also puts it, on traditions that are encountered as texts. According to him, such texts are the basis of the self: "It is the text, with its universal power of unveiling, which gives a self to the ego."[12] The meaning contained by the text engenders "a new self-understanding." In this sense the self is a product of the text. For Ricoeur, the "constitution of the self" and of "personal identity" is closely related to narrative,[13] which can take many shapes. Personal identity in the sense of character emerges from narrative that takes the shape of "life plans."[14] "It is the identity of the story that makes the identity of the character."[15]

Ricoeur's theories of the development of the self are important to our argument, for they demonstrate an openness to tradition and religion. Unlike Habermas and Erikson, Ricoeur does not see the mature self as detached from all religious worldviews. Instead he takes seriously the role of tradition, including religious tradition, in the formation of the self. Although Ricoeur does not apply (at least not in this context of the self) his theory of narrative

11. Seyla Benhabib, *Situating the Self: Gender, Community, and Postmodernism in Contemporary Ethics* (New York: Routledge, 1992).

12. Paul Ricoeur, *Hermeneutics and the Human Sciences: Essays on Language, Action, and Interpretation* (Cambridge: Cambridge University Press, 1981), p. 193.

13. Paul Ricoeur, *Oneself as Another* (Chicago: University of Chicago Press, 1992), p. 114.

14. Ricoeur, *Oneself as Another*, p. 157.

15. Ricoeur, *Oneself as Another*, p. 148.

specifically to religious or biblical narrative, his theory offers a rationale for seeing religious education as playing a major role in the formation of identity. By introducing children and youth to the narratives of the Bible, religious education acquaints them not only with a different language but, more importantly, with meanings that enhance and challenge their self-understandings. At least in some sense it is the Bible as a text which can "give" them a self.

Next we turn to Charles Taylor's monumental analysis, *Sources of the Self,* in which he argues that the human self is not adequately understood if we do not include the cultural basis of human selfhood. Taylor speaks of the cultural and religious "frameworks" into which identity must be placed.[16] And since one is "a self only among other selves," identity implies the need for a "defining community." Like Ricoeur, Taylor also sees a place for narrative in the formation of the self. According to him, a "sense of our life as a whole" depends on grasping "our lives in a narrative."[17]

For Tayor, the separation that Habermas demands of a universalist ethic and the lifeworld or the good life appears questionable. Since Habermas does not respond to the question of the good because he sees no answer for it that can be universalized, he leaves the question of why we should be moral wide open.[18] According to Taylor, the formalism of this sort of universalist ethic, which refers only to procedures and not to material norms, remains powerless and uncritical vis-à-vis the fundamental challenge of self, identity, and ethics by a meaningless world.[19]

Taylor's account of the self and of its foundations does not treat the role of religion in the process of self-formation explicitly; it is only in the concluding section of the book that he mentions the need for a religious basis of the self.[20] But his whole argument makes it clear that his model of the self contradicts any attempt at reducing the self to a formal capacity of self-reflection which critically stands over and above all cultural traditions and contents. If the human self comes into being only through a vision of the good, and through narrative (which is always personal and may not be universalized), then the self must be seen much more contextually than Habermas's universalist ethics allows. Clearly religion represents one of these contexts — and an important one — because it offers visions of the good and because it formulates an answer to the question of why we should be moral.

16. Charles Taylor, *Sources of the Self: The Making of the Modern Identity* (Cambridge: Harvard University Press, 1989), p. 27.
17. Taylor, *Sources of the Self,* pp. 35, 41, 47.
18. Taylor, *Sources of the Self,* p. 87.
19. Taylor, *Sources of the Self,* p. 509.
20. Taylor, *Sources of the Self,* p. 495.

In short, even if none of these alternative accounts of self and identity is outspoken about the role of religion or religious education, their appreciation of the contextual and narrative character of the self makes it easy to conceptualize what this role should be. Following their lead, we may say that the self needs to be grounded in a vision of the good life as it arises from the community and tradition of which one is a part. Consequently religion and religious education must play an important role in the formation of self and identity.

The Child's Right to Religion

This chapter started with a theoretical debate on models of the self and on the role of religion within such models, yet the understanding of self and identity in education is first of all a practical question. How should education relate to the religious grounding of the self and how should it address the religious dimension of personal identity? And what should the contribution of religious education theory be in this context?[21]

When we argued in Chapter Six that religion has a public role to play in society's *paideia*, and when we insist that this role should not be limited to the support that moral education may receive from religion but should also include religious dialogue, we are working out of the assumption that religion is a necessary domain in education. We are convinced, in other words, that any kind of education that does not include religion is incomplete, and that any philosophy of education that does not address anthropological questions remains unaware of its own presuppositions.

In saying this, I am aware that not all parents, educators, or teachers would immediately agree with this view. Contemporary philosophers of education rarely even touch on religion as a dimension of education. When they do, religion is often treated only in connection with earlier historical periods or, if treated in a contemporary context, it is presented as a purely private matter. Many of today's parents are part of a generation whose ties to the church or to other religious communities are rather loose.[22] Consequently, they tend to be insecure about their role as religious educators in the family.

Against this background, religious education theory has to take on a new

21. For a more extensive treatment of this topic cf. Friedrich Schweitzer, *Das Recht des Kindes auf Religion. Ermutigungen für Eltern und Erzieher* (Gütersloh: Gütersloher Verlagshaus, 2000).

22. This has been established in the case of the so-called baby boom generation; cf. Wade Clark Roof, *A Generation of Seekers: The Spiritual Journeys of the Baby Boom Generation* (San Francisco: Harper, 1993).

task — the task of publicly advocating the human importance of religious education against its neglect in the philosophy of education as well as in the practice of education. One way to express this task is to say that the child has a right to religion. If it is true that religion should be acknowledged as an essential dimension of *all* education, one still cannot expect the inclusion of religion in education as an automatic consequence of the two primary rights concerning religion and children widely recognized in Western cultures today: the church's right to religious expression and the parents' right to determine their children's religious affiliation. Both of these rights may be guaranteed — and today they actually are guaranteed in the United States and in Germany — within the present system of religious privatism. As long as religion is considered only a private matter, these rights have no further implications for education in general. This situation cannot change until religion is recognized to be not only a right of the church — and not only a right of the parents — but a right of the child. In this view the child is entitled to his or her own religious expressions, and the support of religious education may be seen as a prerequisite for enabling the child to form these. In this case, any responsible educational agency has to make sure that this right of the child will actually be respected and fulfilled and that all children will have access to the kind of religious education and support they need in order to mature religiously.

It is interesting to note that the Geneva declaration on children's rights, passed by the League of Nations in 1924, includes the right of being enabled to develop "spiritually." And the United Nations' 1989 convention on children's rights includes (in article 14) the religious freedom of the child.[23] But even these attempts to establish legal rights for the child with respect to religion fall short of establishing a right to religious education and support. Only if it can be shown that children need educational support in order to take advantage of their religious freedom will it become plausible that they can have a right to religious education and support.

The field of philosophical anthropology cannot currently provide uncontestable proof that children have a right to religious education. There is no agreement between philosophers as to what a complete list of the various dimensions of human existence would have to include and if this list would have to include religion. So from a strictly philosophical point of view the child's right to religion may be considered only as a metaphorical way of

---

23. Cf. Ursula Carle, "75 Jahre Recht der Kinder: Was haben drei Generationen aus den Forderungen der Zwanzigerjahre gemacht?" in *Rechte der Kinder,* ed. Ursula Carle and Astrid Kaiser (Hohengehren: Schneider, 1998), pp. 12-23.

speaking. As theologians such as Wolfhart Pannenberg have shown, however, it makes sense to take the religious implications of philosophical and psychological theories of human development seriously.[24] In my own argument, I will follow this lead, not by reproducing Pannenberg's theological analysis but by looking at children themselves and at their own religious questions — for children and youth do ask religious questions.[25]

If we take our children seriously, we should take their questions seriously. And if we take their religious questions seriously, we should attempt to address them in as thoughtful a way as possible, in a way that draws upon the best of our collective resources as adult models, mentors, and teachers. Ultimately, the right of children to a religious education rests upon their right to have some of their most heartfelt inquiries about their world listened to with respect and responded to with care. This kind of care is costly to adults because the wide-eyed religious inquiries of young children and the all-too-pointed religious inquiries of youth often go to the heart of our own insecurities. They point out our mortality, our moral inconsistencies, and the enormity of our ignorance about the most important matters in human life. These questions make us uncomfortable. But showing care for our children as whole people demands that we honor their religious questions by responding to them with integrity — by giving them the most thoughtful and honest responses we can muster. We will look at five religious questions that almost inevitably emerge in children, questions that deal with death and dying, self and identity, morality, religious pluralism, and the idea of God.

1. Death and Dying

Children can hardly escape this question. Walking down the street they find a dead bird. In nursery school, they hear about the death of a friend's relative. Their own friends and family members die. Even if one wanted to keep death and dying away from one's children this would not be possible for long. How are we to respond to children's sometimes pressing questions about what happens to a dead animal or to a dead person? Is there life after death? Do you also have to die? And what will become of me when you die?

24. Wolfhart Pannenberg, *Anthropology in Theological Perspective* (Philadelphia: Westminster, 1985).

25. From a parental perspective Martha Fay reports similar experiences in her book *Do Children Need Religion? How Parents Today Are Thinking about the Big Questions* (New York: Pantheon, 1993).

It is certainly possible to answer all these questions without reference to God or even to personal faith. But is it sufficient to tell children that the person just had to die because he or she had cancer — that this is the reality of life and must be accepted? From my point of view, this kind of response clearly carries with it the danger of destroying all of the child's deep hopes and longings. If the world is "just like that," what sense then does it make to hope for anything different?

2. Self and Identity

Philosophers and psychologists widely agree that personal identity always depends on the affirmation of this identity by others. In the process of growing up, there are many "others" who may become sources of this affirmation — first parents, and later friends, colleagues, and teachers. Of course, children are not consciously aware of their need for affirmation, but through their behavior they make parents quite aware of this need. But can parents or educators really be the source of the child's or adolescent's identity? Would this not mean that children and adolescents are seen as ultimately dependent on certain adults for their deepest sense of self — thus putting their personal existence at the mercy of parents and educators? This is the point at which the question about a different, "higher" source of affirmation rises. Erik Erikson points to this sort of affirmation when he writes in a rarely quoted passage in his *Youth and Crisis,* "The counterplayer of the 'I' . . . can be, strictly speaking, only the deity who has lent this halo to a mortal and is Himself endowed with an eternal numinousness certified by all 'I's' who acknowledge this gift."[26]

3. Morality

"Why be moral?" is the question that, according to Lawrence Kohlberg, marks the dividing line between secular morality and religion.[27] In Kohlberg's understanding, this transition comes at the end of moral development — as a seventh stage beyond the well-known six stages of his model. For parents and educators, however, the question of the ultimate ground of moral behavior comes much

26. Erik H. Erikson, *Identity: Youth and Crisis* (New York: Norton, 1968), p. 220.

27. See esp. Lawrence Kohlberg, *The Philosophy of Moral Development: Moral Stages and the Idea of Justice,* Essays on Moral Development, vol. I (San Francisco: Harper and Row, 1981), pp. 307ff.

earlier. How can we explain to a child that he or she is supposed to be fair if others are unfair? Why be moral if being immoral seems much more promising in terms of social and material success? Of course, there are philosophical answers to such questions that do not rely on religious arguments. But is it really possible to introduce complex ethical systems such as discourse ethics or other nonreligious and nonfoundationalist ethical models to a young child? In my understanding, there is, rather, a need for an attitude toward the world which the child can share and actually experience — an attitude based on the hope that, in the end, the world is trustworthy and good because it is God's creation. In this basic sense, the question "Why be moral?" may be answered not so much directly and explicitly through explanations but rather through being part of a family or community that lives by this hope. There may be other possible sources for this kind of hope that are not based on the Christian faith or on any other religious faith. But it is clear that faith and religion can play an important role in establishing a firm basis for morality in an unjust world.

4. Religious Pluralism

Today's children are exposed to various religions, be it through personal encounter or through the media. They realize that some children have religious affiliations and go to a synagogue or temple or church and that some do not. They realize that some of the practices of other children's families are different from those of their own family and that this has something to do with religion. Growing up in today's world has come to mean growing up in a plural world, not only culturally plural but religiously plural. In Germany, with its growing Muslim population, kindergarten teachers report that children sometimes have fights over whose God is better — the Christian God or Allah. This may be a special case; such fights do not occur all the time. Nevertheless, it is clear that children have to make sense of the religious differences they encounter and the questions these differences engender. Does it matter to God which religious community one belongs to? Or (as they might put it later in adolescence) can religious affiliation be chalked up to a coincidence of birth since everything is relative and consequently not of ultimate importance? In light of such questions and experiences, it seems hard to deny that growing up in a multicultural and multireligious society makes it mandatory to stand alongside and accompany children in their attempts to make sense of their plural experiences. Children's inevitable encounter with the religious "other" is, therefore, another reason to argue for the child's right to religion and to religious education.

5. The Idea of God

Some psychoanalysts like Ana-Maria Rizzuto have claimed that no child in the Western world grows up without forming what she calls a God representation, because of the relational experiences in the nuclear family.[28] My own claim is more modest in that I only presuppose that Western culture — as well as cultures of many other parts of the world — makes it almost impossible for a child not to come across verbal or pictorial references to God. Children who have not been introduced to any understanding of God may then ask, "What is God? Who is that in the picture?" And parents or educators may respond to this question like a secular scientist by pointing out what people "once" believed. But is it really possible to explain the idea of God to a child with any sort of integrity without including the religious meaning of this idea? In any case, children will assimilate what they hear about God in their own ways. As we know from the psychology of religion, the idea of God living high up in the sky fits well with the worldview of children.

To summarize, this section on the child's right to religion considers the educational and practical ramifications of the philosophical and psychological debates on the formation of self and identity in relationship to religion. It claims that the emerging self is intrinsically related to religious questions in several ways, and that children almost inevitably raise questions that have, at least potentially, a religious meaning. In the next section we will place the issue of the right of children to religious education within the larger framework of this study. We will do so by considering this claim to children's religious rights in light of our prior discussion of modernization and postmodernism and in light of recent scholarship about the "plural" self.

Religion and the Plural Self

In the first two sections of this chapter we have explored the possible roles of religious education in the formation of individual identity, looking both at related scholarship in various fields and at the religious questions children ask. We have discussed several challenges to the assumption that personal identity needs a religious basis. In this final section we will examine another challenge to the notion that the self must be religiously grounded: the

---

28. Ana-Maria Rizzuto, *The Birth of the Living God: A Psychoanalytic Study* (Chicago: University of Chicago Press, 1979), p. 200.

postmodern experience of radical plurality and the way this experience manifests itself in identity formation in terms of the "plural self."

According to many observers, the experience of postmodern pluralism includes the emergence of a different kind of identity — an identity that is not based on lifelong commitments and cannot any longer even be called an integrated, unified, or coherent identity. The notion of the plural self is based on the assumption that over the lifespan and in various contexts, a person will construct and experience multiple identities. Some scholars have argued that since postmodernity has, according to Jean-François Lyotard, brought about the "end of all master stories," this means that postmodernity has also brought about the end of seeing one's life religiously. Religion is identified with a master story that serves as the basis of a unified self. So there is no more room for religion in connection to the plural self of postmodernity.

Quotations from adolescents are often cited in order to demonstrate the postmodern condition of religion in relationship to self and identity. Many of these adolescents consider all traditional religion as outdated. They have not, however, turned to secularism as was once predicted. Their religious interests are focused on a spirituality that is tied neither to the church nor to religious traditions. What they are looking for does not appear to them to be present in Christianity or the church but is something individual, something personal, something that makes sense within the context of their own lives and that appears meaningful in terms of their own personal experience. Using the language of postmodern philosophy, one could say they are not interested in having their lives framed by a "master story." Fitting one's identity into a master interpretation does not seem to make sense if one's day-to-day experience is that forming one's identity must be an *ongoing* personal project, that one has to construct and reconstruct one's own self. So personal identity formation becomes a matter of constructing a succession of selves over time or constructing various identities out of which one operates in different contexts. I call this type of identity the "plural self."

This kind of understanding of the postmodern self raises several different questions for religious education. Is it true that a plural self cannot be a religious self anymore? Is it accurate to identify the Christian faith with traditional ideas of personal unity and coherence? In addition to these two questions, which concern the effects that postmodernity may have on religion, we need to question the normative images of self and identity in postmodernism. Is the plural self really desirable? Is it even possible for the human person to give up all appeals to unity and coherence? Only after addressing these critical questions — as well as the impact of postmodernity on self-identity and religion — will it be possible to say how religious education should respond to the postmodern experience of plurality.

I will address these questions from two angles. First, by raising some challenges to the assumption that there are no positive points of contact between religion and this approach to identity, I will show how Christian theology might connect with the postmodern experience of the plural self in an affirming way. Second, by raising objections to some of the negative aspects of the experience of the plural self, I will point out how theology might consider the notion of the plural self in a critical way.

There are two assumptions that must be challenged: that religion in general can function only as a so-called master story by which a person's life history is transformed into a coherent unity, and that the Christian understanding of the person is limited to the unitary self. The core of Reformation theology is the doctrine of justification by faith, which sees the identity of the Christian not as a personal work of self-construction but as the work of God. This view finds its psychological expression not in a unitary self but rather in a fragmentary self.[29] The fact that we are not responsible for becoming acceptable to God on the basis of our human achievements opens up new possibilities for accepting the unfinished and imperfect character of one's own identity. If this is true, the experience of the plural self could actually be much closer to the Christian faith than is commonly assumed. Faith in God's justifying grace might be seen as supporting the inhabitants of postmodernity in their struggle to live with the plural self they experience.

In addition, the Christian faith need not be identified with a single "master story." Without doubt, the Bible is the first and canonical expression of the Christian faith. Yet there is definitely no "master story" in the Bible, at least not in the sense of a single story that governs all other narratives or expressions of faith in the Bible. Rather, there are many stories and many different points of view even in the New Testament. The New Testament begins with four (!) different Gospels and includes a variety of different voices in the letters included after the Gospels. All of them have a common reference point — faith in Christ as the messianic redeemer. But this reference is never superimposed on this textual variety in a way that screens out the richness of the different testimonies and theological interpretations. One positive way in which Christian educators could respond to one of postmodernism's pronouncements — the insistence that there are no longer any master stories — would be to hear this as a challenge to the church to develop a new appreciation for

---

29. Henning Luther, *Religion und Alltag. Bausteine zu einer Praktischen Theologie des Subjekts* (Stuttgart: Radius-Verlag, 1992), pp. 160ff.

the many stories of the Bible, an appreciation that serves as a point of connection to postmodern thinking.[30]

Such positive methods of correlating postmodern perspectives with theological perspectives are encouraging for religious educators struggling with the postmodern situation of plurality. It is important to note that postmodernity's plural nature does not imply the end of all attempts to give the self a religious basis nor of all attempts to draw on the biblical narrative.

It should also be clear, however, that the plural self cannot be accepted uncritically as a norm for religious education. Theological perspectives should also be connected with postmodernism in a critical fashion. The postmodern experience of personal discontinuity and incoherence is ambivalent. It can mean liberation from the pressures of social conformity and the constraints of having to present oneself or one's life as more continuous and unified than it really is. At the same time, an individual's experience of plural selves can mean suffering and loss. The person may feel homeless and without a sense of purpose or meaning in life. Social scientific research on postmodern identity points to a persisting need of a sense of personal coherence and unity, even if this need cannot anymore be described with the sociologically naive terminology of Erikson.[31] The context of postmodern pluralism certainly affects the ways in which coherence and unity are experienced, but individuals are still striving for coherence and unity in postmodernity no less than in modernity, even if in different ways.

The ambivalent character of a plural self can be critiqued in light of Christian theology on the basis of its lack of clear values. Building on H. Richard Niebuhr's work, James W. Fowler calls the postmodern plural self a polytheistic self — "a pattern of faith and identity that lacks any one center of value and power of sufficient transcendence to focus and order one's life."[32] From a Christian point of view this kind of ambivalent self, lacking in long-term commitments, cannot be accepted as a guiding ideal for education. It does not correspond to the biblical faith in a committed God, and it also is insufficient for moral education. The acknowledgement that postmodernity has in some ways changed popular thinking about the self is not sufficient

---

30. Cf. Walter Brueggemann's helpful statement, *Texts Under Negotiation: The Bible and Postmodern Imagination* (Minneapolis: Fortress, 1993).

31. Cf. Heiner Keupp and Renate Höfer, eds., *Identitätsarbeit heute. Klassische und aktuelle Perspektiven der Identitätsforschung* (Frankfurt: Suhrkamp, 1997); Heiner Keupp et al., *Identitätskonstruktionen. Das Patchwork der Identitäten in der Spätmoderne* (Reinbek: Rowohl, 1999).

32. James W. Fowler, *Stages of Faith: The Psychology of Human Development and the Quest for Meaning* (San Francisco: Harper and Row, 1981), p. 19.

grounds for justifying a normative vision of human identity in which the self adapts itself to the experience of plurality at the expense of all questions of truth and justice.

What should be the role of religious education vis-à-vis these challenges of postmodernism? The first task is to point out the persisting importance of religion in postmodernity. This entails public advocacy for the role of religion in the process of education and in the formation of self and identity. As parents, educators, and the general public become increasingly insecure about religion's role in these processes, we must demonstrate the various ways in which religion is a general issue in human development. We must also demonstrate that thinking about religious questions should not be limited to those who adhere to a particular religious faith. This task may be seen as a task of public theology.

The second task is for religious education to help give birth to — to help bring to light — the positive potentials of postmodernity. We mentioned above the ambivalence of the postmodern experience. This ambivalence arises from the tension between liberation, on the one hand, and the loss of direction and meaning, on the other. Both liberation and loss are connected to postmodernity, and there is little hope that its beneficial aspects will automatically overcome its drawbacks. Postmodern selves clearly need support and guidance to help them in their struggles with plurality. In this sense religious education could become a midwife for the positive potentials of postmodernity.

In concluding this chapter I want to mention two practical ways in which religious education could fulfill the task of being a postmodern midwife more effectively. The first way addresses the times of transition in people's lives. The emphasis on religious education at various stages in the life cycle has shown that these transitional times need to be a particularly important emphasis for religious education and youth ministry. Postmodernity has made this task even more pressing, but it has also changed the nature and meaning of these transitions. The traditional models of the human life cycle offered, for example, by theorists like Erik Erikson must be adapted to the changing situation. Are the standard accounts of the postmodern life cycle currently available in the academic literature adequately describing people's actual experience? And, if so, what descriptions are being offered? How can religious education address this life cycle and its transitions effectively? These are open questions that will be of central importance for the future of religious education.[33]

33. These questions will be addressed in a forthcoming publication on the postmodern life cycle by Friedrich Schweitzer (Chalice Press).

The second practical way in which religious education could bring out the positive potential of postmodernity is to take the individual more seriously. If educators, pastors, and youth workers really want to address the experiences that are connected to postmodernity, they first of all must create spaces in which young people can express and articulate their individual experiences, questions, hopes, and longings. Creating such spaces involves a willingness to be the target of a good deal of criticism, because many young people feel dissatisfied with what the church is offering them. As pointed out earlier, postmodern young people are not a hopeless case for religious educators, and postmodernity is not the end of religious life — but religious education will have a future only if educators are willing and able to take seriously the individual person.

9   The Family: The Rhetoric of Practical
Theology and the Engagement of Audience

Introductory Overview

Since the Reformation of the sixteenth century, Protestantism has viewed the family as an important site of Christian education. Luther, Calvin, and other early leaders of the reform movement wrote numerous tracts and treatises that addressed parents directly, exhorting them to take their teaching responsibilities in the home seriously. While several of the authors examined in the second part of this book focused on the important role of families in Protestant education, the relative paucity of literature on the family is noteworthy. The fact that this trend is evident in both Germany and the United States makes it even more striking. Within the framework developed over the course of this book, such a trend can be viewed against the backdrop of the social processes of modernization.

Across the modern period, the family, increasingly, has been located in the private sphere. With the rise of state-supported education, the family gradually came to be viewed as playing little or no role in the education of children, who are commonly seen as leaving the home and entering another institution — the public school — for that education. This social trend was accompanied by the professionalization of a number of fields, including those of teachers and religious educators. Academic discourse came to be directed at professionals, emphasizing a body of specialized knowledge and skills. Practical theology and religious education as disciplines have participated in this trend, focusing their attention on the construction of theories and rules of art that can guide the practice of professionals. The result has been a gradual "loss of audience," the disappearance of the family as an audience to be addressed directly by practical theology and Protestant religious education. Parents, after all, are not professionals.

Standing at the beginning of the twentieth-first century, we must view this relative inattention to the family in the rhetoric of practical theology and Protestant religious education as deeply problematic. As will become evident below, the family increasingly has come under pressure from a wide range of social forces. Some scholars go so far as to describe it as being in a state of decline. In failing to give sustained intellectual attention to the family, practical theology and Protestant religious education miss an opportunity to shape and, even, resist the social trends that have unfolded over the course of the past century. Matters of public policy, congregational practice, and family life have gone untreated. Inadvertently, the message has been sent that families are no longer important sites of Protestant religious education. From the perspective of the present, however, it is apparent that they do indeed play a crucial role in the religious education of children and youth, a role that cannot be captured adequately through the frame of socialization or enculturation alone. In the United States, which does not allow religious education in state-supported schools, the family is one of two institutions in which religious education can take place, the other being religious communities. In Germany, the increased presence of a variety of non-Christian religions and the reunification with East Germany are raising serious questions about religious education in state-supported schools. It is likely that families will be called on to play a more important role in religious education in the future.

These trends raise a number of important questions for practical theology as an academic discipline. Who is the audience of practical theology? Does it address exclusively the members of the academy and professionals or does its audience also include nonprofessionals such as parents, youth, and lay persons who are leading family-oriented ministries in congregations? Is an important part of its task the forging of a variety of rhetorics appropriate to a variety of publics? Are there models of rationality that would allow it to hold together its theoretical and practical interests and develop a variety of forms of discourse to address different audiences?

This chapter will proceed in three steps. It will begin by taking up briefly the questions that have just been raised, arguing that a rhetorical model of theological rationality allows practical theology to hold together a twofold interest in both theory and practice, while opening up a way of addressing a variety of publics beyond academics and professionals. It will, then, take up a sustained analysis of the family, arguing that this institution is best described as being in the midst of a transition from modern to postmodern family forms. By *postmodern* I mean both a shift beyond the modern structure of the family and the much higher degree of pluralism in family forms associated with cultural postmodernism. The chapter will conclude by commending certain lines of practice that congregations and families might put in place to strengthen religious education in families. Here, we will broaden Schleiermacher's understanding of rules of art — open-ended guidelines for the practice of the Christian life — to address both professionals and nonprofessionals alike.

Toward a Rhetorical Model of Practical Theology

To recall the nomenclature of cross-disciplinary thinking developed in our chapter on congregational education, the questions raised immediately above are *metadisciplinary* in nature. They are especially pressing for practical theology, for it has labored throughout the modern period within the constraints of the encyclopedic paradigm of theology that emerged in the modern university. In this paradigm, science — particularly natural science — was viewed as exemplary of rationality, reducing "practical" fields like medicine, ethics, and rhetoric to the application of theories and research emerging in "fully scientific" fields. When internalized by theology, this often placed practical theology in the position of "applying" to the church the insights of the other theological disciplines, which appropriated the scientific methodologies of cognate fields.

The recent recovery of practice in contemporary philosophy and science has called this paradigm into question.[1] A variety of models of the theory-practice relationship have emerged, from neo-Aristotelianism to critical social theory to neo-pragmatism. As noted in the chapter on congregations, each of these has left its mark on contemporary theology, contributing to the pluralism that currently characterizes this field. A metadisciplinary perspective of importance in this discussion has only recently been taken up by theology: a new appreciation of rhetoric, argumentation, and communicative models of rationality found in the writings of Toulmin, Perelmann, Habermas, and many others. This perspective challenges classical and modern models of rationality that conceptualize knowledge as secured by following universal rules that can be transported from one disciplinary context to another, the rules of good research or logic. The emerging rhetorical model of rationality breaks with this approach in three important ways.

---

1. See Don Browning's particularly helpful discussion of this recovery in *A Fundamental Practical Theology: Descriptive and Strategic Proposals* (Minneapolis: Fortress, 1991), chap. 2.

First, rationality is conceptualized as a special form of communicative action and as inherently social. Some scholars portray this communication along the lines of argumentation, as a dialogical exchange in which claims are put forward, challenged, and defended. Others contend that it is more adequately described as an open conversation in which the search for good reasons adopts the conflict orientation of argumentation in a more circumscribed fashion.[2] In both cases, rationality is described as a special form of communicative action and as inherently social. Second, rationality is broadened to include the rhetorical norms in which rational communication takes place, norms that differ from field to field and from one audience to another. One does not argue a legal case in court, for example, in the same way one writes up a scientific lab report for a journal. Third, rationality is viewed as informed by the epistemic values held by a particular argument field. As Toulmin points out, society's most important argument fields are located within relatively stable social systems designed to meet different human needs.[3] Accordingly, different "rational enterprises" pursue different social values and goals, from the prediction and control of science to an enhanced appreciation of beauty in aesthetics.

This rhetorical model of rationality poses three important metadisciplinary challenges to contemporary practical theology: (1) clarification of the epistemic values informing its work as a form of *theological* argumentation; (2) articulation of the role of research and theoretical reflection in its work, including their relationship to other fields; and (3) determination of modes of discourse (rhetorical norms) appropriate to the different audiences it addresses. We can very briefly indicate how our treatment of the family in this chapter makes certain assumptions about each of these issues.

To begin with the third, this chapter assumes an expansion of Schleiermacher's notion of rules of art, which tended to be oriented toward professionals. From the perspective of a rhetorical model of rationality, rules of art are those modes of discourse that address audiences actively involved in making judgments about practice in particular contexts of experience. They provide guidance in "how to" as well as "why to." If practical theology is to overcome the "loss of audience" pointed to above, it must forge a rhetoric appropriate to nonprofessionals such as parents, youth, and lay persons directly involved in the religious education of families. This will involve the de-

2. David Tracy, *Plurality and Ambiguity: Hermeneutics, Religion, and Hope* (San Francisco: Harper and Row, 1987).

3. Stephen Toulmin, Richard Rieke, and Allan Janik, *An Introduction to Reasoning,* second ed. (New York: Macmillan, 1984), chaps. 1, 23, and Part 4.

velopment of rules of art that do not presuppose a specialized professional education on the part of their target audience. As we shall see, the one form of academic discourse that has been particularly successful in addressing the family as an audience is deeply rooted in the contemporary practice of modern psychotherapy. While many gains have accrued to families from their encounter with this field, it is clear that Protestant religious education has a very different contribution to make to contemporary family life, one that is more directly rooted in the religious beliefs and ethical norms of the Christian community. Indeed, preoccupation with the therapeutic, to the exclusion of the more normative orientation of religious education, is somewhat problematic. Only a rhetorical "recovery of audience" by practical theologians, however, will allow religious education to guide families toward more normative ends.

This leads to consideration of the role of theory-construction and research in practical theology. A "recovery" of the family as an audience in practical theology does not entail inattention to these important dimensions of its work. Rules of art, even when directed at nonprofessionals, must be grounded in the more comprehensive perspectives of empirical research and theory. Otherwise, they will represent little more than intuitive guesswork about how families might best educate their young toward religious truth and goodness. Accordingly, matters that often lie in the background when addressing nonprofessionals come to the foreground when practical theologians seek to justify the theoretical and empirical presuppositions of their practical guidelines. At this point, they address other scholars in the field, both within and beyond their own particular discipline. In the following section, three comprehensive perspectives on contemporary family life will be engaged. While two have emerged from the social sciences, the most important has emerged from the research and reflection of a team of practical theologians. This underscores a point made most forcefully by Dutch practical theologians like Johannes van der Ven and Gerben Heitink: practical theology must undertake its own empirical research if it is to address the issues most pressing to religious communities.[4]

This sort of research and theoretical argumentation in practical theology opens out to the question of its epistemic focus. Here, a rhetorical model of rationality is particularly helpful, focusing attention on the social values and goals that inform all rational enterprises. What is the guiding purpose of prac-

4. Johannes van der Ven, *Practical Theology: An Empirical Approach,* trans. Barbara Schultz (Kampen: Kok Pharos, 1993); Gerben Heitink, *Practical Theology* (Grand Rapids: Eerdmans, 1999).

tical theology as a knowledge-producing enterprise? Does it construe its primary goal as service to the church or to the church's public role in a particular social context? If the former, its focus will be on families affiliated with Christian congregations. If the latter, its focus will include public policies, cultural trends, and social movements that influence all families in a particular society, addressing a much wider array of audiences. In our chapter on *paideia*, we argued for an understanding of practical theology that is fully public. It is this perspective that informs the following analysis of the postmodern family and the rules of art commended in the final part of this chapter.

From the Modern to the Postmodern Family

The rise of the modern family is commonly viewed as taking place during the eighteenth and nineteenth centuries in conjunction with the emergence of a wage economy and industrialization. Prior to these changes, families remained centers of economic production in which all family members contributed to its financial well-being by their participation in farming, family-centered shops, domestic crafts and cooking, and home-based trades like carpentry, masonry, and smithing. The emergence of a wage economy and industrialization gradually altered this pattern, giving rise to a new family form and ideals largely centered in the experience of the expanding middle class.

In the modern, bourgeois family, fathers now left the home for employment, while mothers remained in the domestic sphere to care for children and to carry out a shrinking set of responsibilities. The family thus came to be associated with the private sphere, a domain of modern life relatively isolated from the "rough and tumble" worlds of politics and economics. Three important cultural trends were closely associated with this family form: the identification of childhood as a time of innocence and vulnerability in the life cycle; the cult of domesticity in which the role of mothers was idealized and portrayed as having especially close ties to religion and virtue; and the redefinition of the companionate marriage in terms of psychological intimacy and personal expressivity. In each case, the relative isolation of the family in the private sphere was viewed positively, as protecting children from premature exposure to the morally ambiguous transactions of public life and as providing a respite from the demands of the marketplace for men upon their return home.

Ironically, the "private" family was surrounded by a network of social and institutional supports throughout the modern period. These included the following: (1) the physical proximity of extended families; (2) networks of friendship, civic associations, and local business relationships located primarily in small towns and urban neighborhoods; (3) schools with strong links to their immediate neighborhood; and (4) religious congregations and parishes actively involved in supporting families in the tasks of moral and Christian education and serving as sites of voluntary activity and social support for many adult women.

Many social scientists believe the modern family is giving way to a postmodern family form. This shift involves the intensification of certain features of the modern family and the transformation of others. One of the most significant factors marking the shift to the postmodern family is the entry of large numbers of women into the labor force. In the United States, the Bureau of Labor Statistics indicates that in 1992, 75 percent of all mothers with children under eighteen and 55 percent with children under three were employed outside the home.[5] The overall percentage of women working in the wage economy rose from just under 40 percent in 1960 to almost 60 percent in 1990.[6] In West Germany in 1988, 51 percent of all mothers with children under eighteen and 28 percent with children under three were employed outside the home.[7] In 1970, the number of all women in the wage economy was 46 percent in Germany; in 1990 it was up to 60 percent.[8] With the entry of large numbers of women into the workforce, the modern family form, organized around the wage-earning father and stay-at-home mother, became one lifestyle option among many. This points to the most significant characteristic of the postmodern family: *the experience of choice in the face of the pluralization of family forms.*

Four highly visible signs of this pluralization can be noted. First, the entry of women into the workforce has given rise to greater flexibility in the division of labor in families. This is due in part to the widespread influence of feminism since the 1960s. Research indicates that many women who do not explicitly identify themselves as feminists share many of feminism's goals, such as the abandonment of sex-role stereotypes, equal opportunity and pay for women in the workplace, and the elimination of domestic violence.[9] One important

5. Cited in Don Browning et al., *From Culture Wars to Common Ground: Religion and the American Family Debate* (Louisville: Westminster/John Knox Press, 1997), p. 55.

6. Browning et al., *From Culture Wars to Common Ground,* p. 55.

7. Rüdiger Peuckert, *Familienformen im sozialen Wandel,* second ed. (Opladen: Leske und Budrich, 1996), p. 201. We are limiting ourselves to West Germany, since East Germany was in a very different context to this point, still a part of the Soviet bloc.

8. Peuckert, *Familienformen im sozialen Wandel,* p. 199.

9. This is evident, for example, in the discussion of the various cases offered in Browning, *From Culture Wars to Common Ground.* Women and men who did not directly identify with feminist ideology frequently articulated family ideals consistent with feminism's egalitarian emphasis.

by-product of feminism's broad influence has been a sustained critique of the modern family's division of labor between men and women. In the post-modern family, couples no longer assume that men will work and women stay at home. They negotiate how they will share the tasks of parenting, wage-earning, and household maintenance. In other words, the form their particular family life will take is a matter of their own values and decisions.

A second sign of pluralization is the increasingly widespread practice of cohabitation and delay of marriage among young adults. Entry into adult roles in effect has become disconnected from marriage. The launching of one's career, entry into a long-term sexual relationship, and bearing of children no longer are viewed as necessarily accompanied by entry into a legal marriage. Growing up, getting married, and settling down holds little normative import today. They are matters of choice amid a variety of family forms.

A third sign of pluralization is the increased prevalence of divorce and out-of-wedlock births, making single-parent families a common family form. The divorce rate has risen steadily in the United States for the past one hundred years, accelerating rapidly since the 1960s. In 1860, only 7 percent of all marriages ended in divorce. Today, slightly more than 50 percent of all marriages do.[10] In Germany, divorce rates rose dramatically after 1970 — from 15 percent in that year to 30 percent in 1990.[11] The rise of out-of-wedlock births in the United States is a more recent phenomenon. In the early 1960s, only 5 percent of all births fell into this category. Today, more than 30 percent of all births are out of wedlock. The highest rate of growth has taken place among women with college and graduate education.[12] While the percentage of births to never-married mothers has grown rapidly among the inner-city black population (from 22 percent in the 1960s to 68 percent in 1994), the rate of increase among the white community has been even greater (rising to 23 percent in 1994).[13] As a result of these two trends, 27 percent of all children in the United States were living in single-parent families by the late 1980s. It was estimated that 44 percent of all children born between 1970 and 1984 would live with a single parent before reaching the age of sixteen.[14] In Germany, as of 1990, almost 90 percent of all children under eighteen still lived with both parents.[15] This is true even though single-parent households were gradually

10. Browning et al., *From Culture Wars to Common Ground*, p. 52.
11. Peuckert, *Familienformen im sozialen Wandel*, pp. 146f.
12. Browning et al., *From Culture Wars to Common Ground*, p. 52.
13. Browning et al., *From Culture Wars to Common Ground*, p. 52.
14. Browning et al., *From Culture Wars to Common Ground*, p. 53.
15. Rosemarie Nave-Herz, *Familie Heute: Wandel der Familienstrukturen und Folgen für die Erziehung* (Darmstadt: Wissenschaftliche Buchgesellschaft, 1994), p. 13.

becoming more widespread. In 1995, 13 percent of all children were born out of wedlock.[16] Obviously, many single-parent families become blended families at some point through remarriage. This too gives rise to variety in family forms, as many children spend a portion of their time in several family situations over the course of a given year.

A final sign of the pluralization of family forms is the highly visible rise of the gay and lesbian movement. While the legal status of homosexual partners varies widely from one state to another in the United States in terms of inheritance, insurance coverage, and so forth, it is now possible in some states for gay and lesbian couples to legally adopt children. When this fact is viewed alongside advances in reproductive technologies affording infertile couples and single women the opportunity to have children through *in vitro* fertilization and other means, it becomes clear the link between heterosexual sexual relations and reproduction has been broken. It is one facet of the "end of nature" poignantly described by Anthony Giddens: the elimination of "nature" as a fixed set of constraints to which humans must adapt.[17] For most of human history, childbearing has been viewed as the exclusive "natural" by-product of sexual relations between men and women, normatively organized within stable family forms. With sex, reproduction, and childrearing now detached, bearing children has become a choice consistent with a variety of family forms.

While the pluralization of family forms is undoubtedly the single most important marker of the transition to the postmodern family, two additional features can also be noted. The first is the widely shared belief that the ecology of institutions supporting the family across the modern period has deteriorated sharply. One of the unexpected findings of an empirical study conducted by Don Browning and his colleagues in the Religion, Culture, and Family Project was the discovery of a widely shared perception on the part of parents that they receive much less support from institutions outside the home in raising their children than did their parents.[18] Such institutions include churches, schools, neighborhoods, and civic associations. Some social scientists confirm this perception, pointing to the decline in religious attendance and participation in voluntary associations as indicative of a decline in the social supports lying at the heart of civil society.[19]

16. Deutscher Bundestag (ed.), *Zehnter Kinder und Jugendbericht vom 25.8. 1998* (Bonn: Deutscher Bundestag, 1998), p. 23.

17. Anthony Giddens, *Modernity and Self-Identity: Self and Society in the Late Modern Age* (Stanford: Stanford University Press, 1991), pp. 137, 165-66.

18. Giddens, *Modernity and Self-Identity*, p. 9.

19. Robert Putnam drew attention to this issue in his well-known article, "Bowling Alone:

Closely related is another trend contributing to the emergence of the postmodern family: the appearance of what is sometimes called the public-private family form.[20] If one of the most important features of the modern family was its relative insulation in the private sphere, the postmodern, public-private family is characterized by a large number of overlaps between the public and private spheres. These overlaps are evident in a number of areas. One of the most important is the blurring of the boundaries between family and work. Some companies now sponsor on-site daycare and allow time off for the birth or sickness of a child. In order to cut back on highly expensive office space, others are now encouraging employees to work out of the home, linking with corporate offices by computers. The negotiation of flextime in which work and parenting responsibilities are handled with greater fluidity has become more prevalent. While these trends are by no means universal, they are common enough to indicate greater permeability between work and home than was common during the modern period.

The boundaries between the family and other spheres of life have become more permeable in additional ways as well. Television represents an important intrusion of the marketplace into family life, being widely used for commercials that target particular age groups. Moreover, it has come to be an important part of children's everyday lives, along with other electronic media like computers, video games, and compact disk players. American preschool children watch an average of four hours of television every day; elementary-school children watch thirty hours per week; junior high children watch even more.[21] In Germany, the corresponding data are one hour per day for children between ages three and five in 1991.[22] In 1995, children between the ages of three and thirteen watched about 95 minutes of TV per day.[23] While it is

---

America's Declining Social Capital," *Journal of Democracy* 6, no. 1 (January 1995): 65-78. See also his article "The Strange Disappearance of Civic America," *American Prospect* 24 (Winter 1996): pp. 34-49.

20. An early exploration of the public-private family form is found in the writings of Jean Bethke Elshtain: *Public Man, Private Woman: Women in Social and Political Thought* (Princeton, N.J.: Princeton University Press, 1981); and "The Family and Civic Life," in *Rebuilding the Nest: A New Commitment to the American Family*, ed. Elshtain, David Blankenhorn, and Steven Bayme (Milwaukee: Family Service America, 1990). The concept is used somewhat differently in Browning et al., *From Culture Wars to Common Ground*, p. 2.

21. Thomas Lickona, *Raising Good Children: Helping Your Child Through the Stages of Moral Development* (New York: Bantam, 1983), pp. 350-51.

22. Christine Feil, "Das kindliche Fernsehpublikum. Gespräche und Spiele im Kindergarten," in *Was für Kinder. Aufwachsen in Deutschland. Ein Handbuch*, ed. Deutsches Jugendinstitut (München: Kösel, 1993), pp. 392-401, 393.

23. Bundesministerium für Familie, Senioren, Frauen und Jugend, *Kinder und ihre*

difficult to assess the impact this has on children, it is safe to say that the media reaches into the lives of postmodern families in ways that were unimaginable at the turn of the twentieth century. It plays a role in socialization that it did not play in the modern era.

The Postmodern Family: Changing or Declining?

What sense are we to make of this shift from the modern to the postmodern family? Here comparisons between the American and German situations prove to be quite helpful, bringing into focus both the consequences of different governmental policies and trends that appear to cross national lines. Let us begin with the situation in the United States. In this country, a highly charged national political debate over the family has unfolded since the early 1980s, with conservative and evangelical Protestants generally aligning with those political forces calling for the reaffirmation of traditional (i.e., modern) family values and liberal Protestants aligning with those forces calling for governmental support of single-parent families, abortion rights, and expansion of the legal rights of gays and lesbians. A survey of social teachings on the family developed in national policy statements of mainline American Protestant denominations since the 1960s finds them strongly identified with liberal Protestantism.[24] Almost across the board, these statements affirm the pluralization of family forms we have traced above. The language of committed relationships between just and loving partners consistently blurs distinctions between "nonsexual friendships, sexual friendships, cohabiting couples, legally contracted marital couples, and couples both legally contracted and covenantally or sacramentally sanctioned."[25] Moreover, little criticism or social analysis is offered in these social teachings of the ambiguities present in the postmodern family form. From the vantage point of the late 1990s, these statements look terribly out of date, a classic case of misreading the signs of the times. A large body of social scientific research has now begun to document the darker side of the postmodern family, making it clear that many families are not merely changing but in a full-blown state of crisis.

Some of the most important research in the United States focuses on the

---

Kindheit in Deutschland. Eine Politik für Kinder im Kontext von Familienpolitik. Wissenschaftlicher Beirat für Familienfragen (Stuttgart: Kohlhammer, 1998), p. 215.

24. Most of these teachings are discussed in *Faith Traditions and the Family,* ed. Phyllis D. Airhart and Margaret Lamberts Bendroth (Louisville: Westminster/John Knox Press, 1996). A nice summary is found in Browning et al., *From Culture Wars to Common Ground,* pp. 43-48.

25. Browning et al., *From Culture Wars to Common Ground,* p. 45.

deleterious effects on children of divorce and those in single-parent families.[26] Sara McLanahan and Gary Sandefur's *Growing Up with a Single Parent* appeared in 1994 and laid out the results of a statistical analysis of four major national studies of families, three of which were longitudinal. McLanahan and Sandefur summarized their findings as follows:

> Compared with teenagers of similar background who grow up with both parents at home, adolescents who have lived apart from one of their parents during some period of childhood are twice as likely to drop out of high school, twice as likely to have a child before age twenty, and one and a half times as likely to be "idle" — out of school and out of work — in their late teens and early twenties.[27]

Overall, the studies found that children of single parents do worse on four of five measures of high school performance: grade point average, school attendance, test scores, and college expectations.[28]

Closely related is research on the economic status of single-parent families, especially households headed by mothers. On average, single-parent families have less than half the income of two-parent families.[29] According to the United States Census Bureau, around 47 percent of families headed by a single mother lived in poverty in the early 1990s, compared with 8.3 percent of two-parent families.[30] In part, this was due to the fact that during this period only 31 percent of households headed by single mothers received any child support or alimony.[31] Less than one-third of all children of divorced families received the full amount of child support to which they were legally entitled.

This is closely related to another area of research: the diminishment of

---

26. This chapter will focus on only a small part of this growing body of research. See also the following: David Popenoe, *Disturbing the Nest* (New York: Walter de Gruyter, 1988); Judith Wallerstein and Joan Kelly, *Surviving the Breakup: How Children and Parents Cope with Divorce* (New York: Basic, 1980); Judith Wallerstein and Sandra Blakeslee, *Second Chances: Men, Women, and Children a Decade after Divorce: Who Wins, Who Loses, and Why* (New York: Ticknor and Fields, 1989); and E. Mavis Hetherington, "Family Relations Six Years after Divorce," in *Remarriage and Stepparenting: Current Research and Theory,* ed. Kay Pasley and Marilyn Ihinger-Tallman (New York: Guilford, 1987), pp. 185-205.

27. Sara McLanahan and Gary Sandefur, *Growing Up with a Single Parent: What Hurts, What Helps* (Cambridge: Harvard University Press, 1994), pp. 1-2.

28. McLanahan and Sandefur, *Growing Up,* p. 44.

29. McLanahan and Sandefur, *Growing Up,* p. 81.

30. Cited in Browning et al., *From Culture Wars to Common Ground,* p. 53.

31. Browning et al., *From Culture Wars to Common Ground,* p. 53.

parental investment in childrearing. Fathers' lack of economic support of their children after divorce is only one facet of this trend. National studies in the United States since the 1980s have found that divorced fathers spend little time with their children. One national survey found that only one child in six visited his or her father once a week and that close to 50 percent had not seen their fathers at all during the past year.[32] Even in those situations in which fathers do spend time with their children regularly, they play a minimal role in their day-to-day nurture. As many social scientists point out, the absence of the father in situations of divorce is only one part of a much larger phenomenon, sometimes referred to as the parenting deficit: "the diminished capacity of parents to spend sufficient time with the children."[33] In recent years the work week has been extended, women have entered the workforce in larger numbers, take-home pay has diminished, and parents are working longer hours and, consequently, spending less time with their children.[34] In one study cited by Browning and his colleagues, parents in the mid 1980s were found to spend an average of seventeen hours per week with their children in comparison with thirty hours in 1965.[35]

As we reflect on this research in the United States and Germany, it is evident that the postmodern family is ambiguous in its effects on the well-being of children. While many gains can be pointed to, there also is an increasing number of signs that the emergence of this family form has created problems for children and youth. Three important interpretive frameworks point to factors that seem to be important across the United States and Germany.

One of the most influential frameworks to emerge in recent social scientific research is the social capital theory of James Coleman.[36] Parents, he argues, mediate social capital to their children — social networks, cultural and

32. Reported in Frank Furstenberg and Andrew Cherlin, *Divided Families* (Cambridge, Mass.: Harvard University Press, 1991), pp. 35-36.

33. Browning et al., *From Culture Wars to Common Ground*, p. 55.

34. Browning et al., *From Culture Wars to Common Ground*, p. 55, citing Juliet B, Schor, *The Overworked American: The Unexpected Decline of Leisure* (New York: Basic, 1991).

35. Schor, *The Overworked American*, p. 55.

36. James Coleman, "Social Capital and the Creation of Human Capital," *American Journal of Sociology* 94 (1988): 95-120. Social capital theory is an important aspect of the explanatory frameworks found in McLanahan and Sandefur, *Growing Up*, and of Browning et al., *From Culture Wars to Common Ground*, as well as of rational choice economic theorists who focus on the family such as Francis Fukuyama, *Trust: The Social Virtues and the Creation of Prosperity* (New York: Free Press, 1995); Gary Becker, *A Treatise on the Family* (Cambridge, Mass.: Harvard University Press, 1991); and Richard Posner, *Sex and Reason* (Cambridge, Mass.: Harvard University Press, 1992).

economic resources, and moral norms. When fathers are absent from families, as in situations of divorce and out-of-wedlock births, children are likely to receive less of this social capital than in families in which both parents are present and invested in their children. Coleman's point goes beyond single-parent families, however. The same dynamics are operative in two-parent families as well. In his research on American public education, he discovered that the economic well-being of a public school does not, in itself, guarantee that a child will receive a good education.[37] Parental investment in a child's education was found to be the single most important factor in school success. When this is lacking, as it often is even in two-parent families, social capital does not get transmitted to children. A corollary of Coleman's theory, moreover, focuses less on parents than on the ecology of social supports that surrounds families. These are the formal and informal networks of families, schools, neighbors, civic associations, and religious communities that characterize a healthy civil society. If these networks are weak, the task of transmitting social capital to children becomes much more difficult. Governmental policies more supportive of families, such as those found in Germany, cannot alone fill this void.

A second interpretive framework focuses on the cultural and moral meanings by which couples understand their life together and their responsibilities as parents, giving special attention to the pernicious effects of new forms of individualism. This perspective was articulated by Robert Bellah and his co-authors in *Habits of the Heart*. This book did not focus primarily on families. It made a broader argument, namely, that the 1960s represented a watershed in modern (American) culture, marking the spread of two new forms of individualism — one focusing on the expressive and the other on utilitarian dimensions of individual life. By implication, however, the book offers a devastating critique of the inadequacy of these forms of moral meaning for the conduct of marriage and family life.

Expressive individualism views intimate relations as a primary locus for the discovery and actualization of one's "true" or "authentic" inner self. Utilitarian individualism draws on the cost/benefit logic of the marketplace, viewing marital and family relations along the lines of a limited contract in which parties negotiate the fair exchange of goods. Neither form of individualism, Bellah and his colleagues argue, provides an adequate moral language with which to grasp the responsibilities and goods of communities transcending the individual, from the social commons to marriage and family. At least in

---

37. James Coleman et al., *Equality of Educational Opportunity* (Washington, D.C.: U.S. Department of Health, Education, and Welfare, Office of Education, 1966).

part, the various problems of the postmodern family are due to a failure of the moral imagination, the inadequacy of the moral models and metaphors by which adults understand their most intimate relationships and their responsibilities to dependent children and aging parents.

A third interpretive framework draws together the insights of critical social theory, contemporary feminism, and evolutionary psychology to offer a multidimensional interpretation of the contemporary crisis of the family. This perspective is developed by Don Browning and his co-authors in *From Culture Wars to Common Ground: Religion and the American Family Debate*. While acknowledging the insights of Coleman and Bellah, this team of practical theologians directs its attention outward to broader transnational, socio-economic forces and inward to the needs and tendencies of the human evolutionary heritage. The former are largely cast in a Habermasian interpretation of the family developed by Alan Wolfe. The sort of cultural analysis offered in *Habits of the Heart* is now conceptualized as the colonization of the family, along with other spheres of the lifeworld, by the "logics" of the marketplace and state bureaucracies. The use of technical rationality in family life and the shaping of "desire" toward patterns of consumption are but two of the ways these institutions have invaded the domestic sphere in late modernity. The "lifestyle pluralism" of the postmodern family, thus, must be viewed critically in relation to the global market forces that have a stake in evoking ever-changing constellations of personal preference.

These social forces are portrayed as interacting with psycho-biological needs and tendencies illumined by contemporary feminism and evolutionary psychology. Feminism's interest in unmasking the dynamics of patriarchy in families is conjoined to an analysis of the asymmetrical reproductive strategies of men and women described by evolutionary psychology. Women are portrayed as biologically and psychologically potentiated for investment in the tasks of child-rearing and monogamous sexual exchange. Men, in contrast, are characterized by the "male problematic": the tendency to invest little in child-rearing and a readiness to engage multiple sexual partners outside of a committed relationship to ensure the maximum number of offspring. Thus, contemporary expressions of this problematic — the absent father of divorce and the uninvested father of intact marriages — must be seen against a backdrop of deep-seated, psycho-biological tendencies. When located in a social context that relies heavily on the market-driven logics of technical rationality and personal consumption, these proclivities are not offset by moral norms that encourage men to invest in the demanding project of sharing equally with women in the activities of child-rearing and wage-earning.

Browning and his colleagues do not portray either the social or psychoevolutionary forces they explore in deterministic terms. Men and women have a measure of freedom in how they will respond to the inner and outer forces that impinge upon their lives. To take advantage of this freedom, however, they need far more assistance than they currently are receiving from the ecology of supports located in civil society and the political policies of the state. The authors give special attention to the potential role of religious communities in providing both their members and society in general with a new family ethic. New forms of moral discourse are needed to guide postmodern families in the face of the multiple cultural options before them and the various social and psycho-biological forces that are shaping them, often outside their awareness.

Obviously, each of these interpretive frameworks is more complex than can be presented in the brief space of this chapter. Taken together, however, they raise significant questions about the postmodern family form. Is the family changing or declining? The final answer, we believe, cannot yet be given. The postmodern family is in an early stage of evolution. While signs of distress are readily apparent, they should not completely overshadow the gains this family form represents. The democratization of family life that has followed the widespread entry of women into the workforce and the acceptance of greater diversity in the ways families handle the tasks of child-rearing and wage-earning are surely to be seen in a positive light. The decline of patriarchy found in some forms of the postmodern family, likewise, must be evaluated positively.

At the same time, it is apparent that the emergence of the postmodern family has been accompanied by a host of problems. The social instability of this family form often has devastating consequences for women and children as they are thrust into poverty following divorce or out-of-wedlock births. Many men now live much of their lives outside the context of committed and supportive family relations, a situation that undoubtedly is psychologically crippling for many. The widely perceived loss of a supportive family ecology in civil society raises far-reaching questions about the moral logics shaping American and German societies in the face of a global market economy. The church alone cannot provide solutions to problems this far-reaching. It can, however, do three important things: (1) prepare its members to add their voices to public debate over the kinds of social, educational, economic, and political supports postmodern families need; (2) reach out to families in civil society, providing them with the kinds of supports that no longer seem readily available from schools, neighborhoods, and civic associations; and (3) give special attention to families in their teaching ministries, including support of religious education in the home. Each of these tasks will be described briefly in the final part of this chapter, pointing to the kinds of rules of art that can guide judgments of practice in concrete contexts of experience. Protestant religious education must not view these as directed exclusively to policy-makers or professional church leaders. It must recover the family as an audience, addressing parents, youth, and even children as significant actors in the shaping of their life together.

The Contribution of the Church

Educating for Public Voice

An important question to emerge from our comparison of research on the family in Germany and the United States is the effect of different governmental family policies. It is difficult to make comparisons for various reasons. Often, the data is gathered and interpreted differently. In the United States, moreover, many governmental programs for low-income families are now administered at the state level and vary widely. Comparisons of family policies in Europe, likewise, reveal trends that are quite diverse. Denmark, with its strong governmental support for families with children, has 80 percent of its mothers in the workforce; the Netherlands, with similar programs, only 32 percent. As noted above, Germany, with comparable programs, has 60 percent. It is difficult to know what to make of these differences.

The point to underscore is the important role government policies and legal statutes play in maintaining the well-being of families. With the less extensive governmental safety net for families in the United States, divorce commonly thrusts young mothers and their children into dire economic circumstances. The implication for the church is readily apparent. If it is committed to helping the postmodern family realize its latent potential, then it must take very seriously the task of educating both its own members and the broader public about the choices they face as citizens. It must educate for public voice.

A high degree of pluralism currently characterizes congregations in their handling of this task. Some take a stance of advocacy, strongly commending certain policies and laws in light of a clear set of theological and moral convictions. Abortion, reproductive rights, and the legal status of gay and lesbian partnerships are examples of family-oriented issues around which some congregations take advocacy stances. Unfortunately, these congregations often fail to grant even a minimal amount of legitimacy to opposing views. Without denigrating this approach, we are more supportive of one in which the task of educating Christians for public voice intentionally sponsors a wide diversity of perspectives. Differing points of view are not merely tolerated but are actively sought out, both to foster genuine understanding and to give persons the opportunity to learn and practice the communicative competencies necessary for participation in democratic political processes.

How this is best achieved no doubt will vary from one congregation and parish to another in light of the expertise of members, financial resources, proximity to academic and medical institutions, and other factors. Minimally, however, this sort of education for public voice on family issues should include the following: (1) cultivation of a group of leaders committed to studying family issues in an ongoing fashion, a group that can educate the congregation about important issues currently receiving legislative attention; (2) periodic forums in which hot-button issues are debated and discussed from a variety of perspectives, with congregational members actively involved not only in studying the issue at hand but also in learning how to articulate their own stance in democratic public forums; and (3) education in how to influence the political process on family issues both as individuals and through participation in extra-church movements and organizations.

Actively Supporting Families in Civil Society

One of the most important insights found in each of the interpretive frameworks examined in the previous section is the crucial role of an ecology of supports for families in civil society. If it is true that these supports have declined in recent decades, then it is imperative that congregations view their ministries to postmodern families as extending beyond their own members. This will stretch the self-understanding of many congregations and parishes, which tend to focus first on the needs of their own members and only incidentally on those of nonmember families. A major task of the leadership of the church is to develop sound theological, ethical, and social scientific reasons by which to persuade church members to move beyond this limited point of view. At the very least, this involves helping congregations rethink their mission in democratic social contexts like the United States and Germany. Their mission, in part, is to help strengthen the social fabric of civil society as one religious community among many in a pluralistic context. As such, their stance should be one of service and education, not exclusively evangelism or the imposition of a monolithic "Christian" point of view on the social whole.

What does this mean concretely? Two general lines of practice can be pointed to. First, the church must expand its educational program to include offerings that are not directed primarily to its own members but to all interested families within its orbit of influence. The topics of such programs should focus on perceived needs of these families and should not be cast in explicitly Christian terms. They might include general topics like sex education in the home, improving communication skills in families, coping with divorce, signs of drug and alcohol abuse among teens, and making retirement meaningful. They might also include topics that are more context-specific. Many congregations, for example, now have immigrant populations located nearby. In partnership with leaders of these communities, congregations might sponsor educational programs specifically oriented to their needs. They might focus, for instance, on helping immigrant parents better understand the local school system and how they can support their children in this setting. Recent research has pointed to this sort of "brokering" between school and home as crucial to the successful integration of immigrant children into the school system.[38]

Congregations can also support families at the level of civil society in ways that link action/reflection models of education with specific programs of social service. Here, the goal is to provide supports for families that might otherwise not be available and, educationally, to help those involved to reflect on the social and ethical issues at stake. The goal is not to replace government programs that should be available if the state is actively pursuing pro-family policies. It is increasingly evident, however, that the bureaucratic organization of government-sponsored programs often works against the kind of local knowledge and personal care most helpful to families in need. In the United States, a variety of faith-based initiatives have emerged in recent years, sometimes partnering with governmental agencies to provide support for families. In the Boston area, for example, congregations have banded together to provide mentoring for youth involved in the criminal justice system. In other parts of the United States, congregations have refurbished inner city apartment buildings to provide low-income housing and have built retirement communities for seniors. Some congregations have created job training and relocation centers, counseling centers with sliding scales, shelters for abused women, low-cost childcare programs, and crisis-intervention centers. These are but a sampling of the ways congregations can support families at the level of civil society, providing a network of supports which complement, not replace, governmental programs at local, state, and national levels. When linked to action/reflection models of education, they have the additional ben-

---

38. Wendy Walker-Moffat, *The Other Side of the Asian American Success Story* (San Francisco: Jossey-Bass, 1995).

efit of helping congregation members gain a deeper understanding of the social trends to which such programs are responsive and the ethical reasons for
the church's involvement.

Congregational Family Ministries

This task focuses on educational programs aimed directly at families who belong to congregations and parishes. If the primary reality of the postmodern
family is the experience of choice in the face of the pluralization of family
forms, then it is crucial for congregations to help family members of all ages
make choices that are informed by their religious convictions. Three lines of
education are particularly important.

The team of practical theologians writing *From Culture Wars to Common
Ground* points to the first and, perhaps, most important line of education:
helping the members of Protestant congregations construct a new family
ethic. The myriad changes of the postmodern family have left many adults
confused about the roles they should play and the commitments they should
make as marital partners and parents. Neither the new individualism of the
hyper-differentiated global marketplace nor the old traditionalism of conservative religion represents an ethical framework that can help families grapple
with the problems and possibilities of the emerging postmodern family form.
The former sees only possibilities (enhanced freedom and relational experi-
mentation) while the latter sees only problems (broken relationships, loss of
social and economic capital, and moral decline). The family-oriented ministries of Protestant churches in Germany and the United States must explore
alternatives to both of these ethical positions. Whether this is the ethic of
equal regard articulated by Browning and his colleagues or a more explicitly
covenantal ethic, long central to Reformed Protestantism, the primary goal is
to help the present and future members of families develop an explicit moral
framework with which they can understand their choices and commitments.

At the very least, a new Christian family ethic must provide guidance in
the face of three important questions coming to the fore in the postmodern
family: How can marital partners share power in ways that are just, achieving
a measure of fairness in the difficult balancing act between individual aspirations and the responsibilities of household care and parenting? How can the
well-being of children be protected in the face of the increasing demands and
reach of a globalized economy and the choices made possible by advances in
reproductive technology? How can the importance of long-term commitment to spouse and children be given moral weight without inadvertently en-

couraging persons to remain in abusive relationships or discouraging single parents and the divorced from affiliating with the church? A range of ethical frameworks have emerged in recent years that respond to these questions somewhat differently, and pastors and educators must become fully conversant with these alternatives if they are to make them a part of congregational teaching.

It is no accident that these questions have been cast in terms of "how" and not exclusively in terms of "ought," the primary focus of modern Christian ethics. It is precisely at the intersection of "how to" and "why to" or, more traditionally, means and ends that practical theology moves from the kind of theoretical interpretation of the previous section to the construction of rules of art that can guide the judgments of practice. Here, practical theology moves beyond the more limited scope of modern ethics. It is not enough for Protestant religious education to encourage marital partners to adopt more egalitarian attitudes, for example. It must also help them learn the communicative competencies requisite to the ongoing negotiation of their roles and commitments in a fair manner. In developing rules of art for this sort of task, practical theology must do more than address the professional leadership of the church. It must develop resources that can be understood and used by a nonspecialist audience, those adults directly involved in creating rules and roles for their life together.

A second line of education is support of the teaching ministry within the home, the so-called "domestic church" of older theological writings. In spite of the many ways the postmodern family has been decentered as the exclusive agent of socialization — from the intrusion of the electronic media and workplace into the home to the increased role of "peers" and school — families still remain one of the most important centers of moral and religious identity formation. The rapidity of change and the pluralism of postmodern family forms, however, threaten to overwhelm parents. Generational discontinuity in many spheres of life — from computer literacy to sexual mores — leave many parents uncertain about their roles as religious and moral educators.

Congregational education can play an extremely important role in helping parents both reflect on the kinds of concrete choices they face (the choice between career advancement and parental investment, for example) and develop styles of parenting that reflect their deepest religious and ethical convictions. While both of these are dependent on the construction of a family ethic, they go beyond this task in focusing on the highly processive nature of moral and religious education in the postmodern family. The role of parents in moral and Christian education shifts markedly across the family life cycle. Parents, moreover, must guide their children in situations that are quite different than those they encountered while growing up. The challenge before congregations is to develop educational programs that support parents in an *ongoing process* of moral and religious education, targeting parents of different age groups who face very specific challenges, such as the prevalence of drugs in high school, the lure of "virtual" relationships over real ones, or the presence of racist hate groups in the immediate community. Such issues are local and particular. They can shift markedly in a short period of time.

A third line of Protestant religious education flows from the recognition that the teaching ministry of families takes place within the broader context of the congregation. The "domestic church" is no substitute for the church community as a whole. It is not difficult to point to many ways Christian parents are dependent on their congregation to offer moral and Christian education that they are unable to provide themselves. Most are ill-equipped to provide systematic instruction in the stories of the Bible that a good Sunday school or religious education class can offer. Likewise, they must trust that their congregation will offer programs and relationships that will support their adolescents' struggle with personal identity issues, a struggle that often places young persons over against their parents. At such points, the congregation as a whole must take seriously the promise made at baptism, that all members of a congregation, not parents alone, are responsible for the education and care of its young.

In Closing

In coming to the end of this chapter, we also arrive at the end of this book. It is fitting that we should draw together issues that have emerged in our examination of the family as a way of reminding the reader of broader themes that have come to the fore over the course of this project as a whole. Three themes are readily apparent.

First, the family is a striking example of our basic thesis. *Religious education stands in an interdependent relationship to its social context and if it is to play a role in shaping this context toward a more desirable future, then it must seek to both understand and respond to the particular challenges it poses.* Over the course of this book, we have drawn on three historical-interpretive frameworks with which religious education might understand its context: modernization, globalization, and postmodernism. In this particular chapter, we have pointed to many signs that the family presently is undergoing massive change, something we have characterized as the emergence of postmodern family forms in an emerging global context. While these changes hold many promising possibilities, they also hold many real dangers. Religious education cannot afford to ignore the threats and possibilities of this present context. It must seek to investigate and understand the changing context of the postmodern family and attempt to shape this context in ways that promote the well-being of families — both in the church and in our national and global communities. In short, religious education stands in an interdependent relationship to its context. This is true not only with regard to the family but also to the other areas we have examined in this part of the book: the changing context of public *paideia,* the church, and the individual self.

Second, our reflection on the family in this chapter has led us to point to the possibilities of a rhetorical model of practical theology that is supple enough to address a variety of audiences. It is not enough for practical theology and religious education simply to address a professional audience of church leaders and teachers of religious education. They must also take seriously the rhetorical challenge of addressing non-specialist audiences: parents, policymakers, and the broader public. They, too, have a stake in promoting the well-being of families. This reflects an important theme that has emerged over the course of this book: *the loss of an audience in practical theology and religious education during the twentieth century.* Over the course of modernization during this period, these fields have taken the form of specialized academic disciplines that direct their primary research and writing to a professional audience. In a differentiated social context in which religion is one subsystem among many and commonly confined to the private sphere, this has led prominent religious education theorists to address their writings almost exclusively to the church (especially its professional leaders) and, in Germany, to teachers of religious education in the school. A narrowing of audience has taken place, and the task of addressing audiences beyond these two target groups has been neglected. In this chapter and throughout the book as a whole, it has gradually become clear that we do not believe this loss of audience to be a salutary development. We have advocated the recovery of an audience as an essential part of the program of public practical theology. This does not preclude addressing professional church leaders and teachers of religious education. But it does involve contributing to the discourse of groups and institutions beyond the church and adding its own voice to public discourse about the present and future of the common good of our national and global communities.

Third, this chapter has pointed to the importance of cross-disciplinary thinking, a theme that also has emerged over the course of this book. Research and theorizing by the social sciences and social ethics were an important dialogue partner in our understanding of the threats and possibilities of the postmodern family form. A broader point is at stake here. It is simply not possible for practical theology and religious education to grasp the challenges of their present social context or make their own distinctive contribution to the public discourse of the academy and public life unless they are willing to enter into critical dialogue with other fields. The paradigmatic figures and texts examined in the second part of this book reveal a problematic legacy in this regard. The early reformers of the past century took up the challenges of the newly emerging social sciences but, at least in the United States, had great difficulty conceptualizing the continuing role of theology in this dialogue. In both Germany and the United States, the shift toward a recovery of theological identity in religious education accentuated theology's role in religious education but at the expense of really grappling with the positive contribution of nontheological disciplines to this field — with a few notable exceptions. The ecumenicity and pluralism of religious education and practical theology emerging in the 1960s gradually gave rise to a number of models of cross-disciplinary work in which theology entered into dialogue with other fields. Nipkow is exemplary in this regard. While Westerhoff never offered an explicit model of cross-disciplinary work, he did reintroduce the language of practical theology into religious education in the United States and was quite creative in his use of the tools of cultural anthropology and developmental psychology within his theories of catechesis and faith formation. In recent decades, cross-disciplinary thinking has become even more important and more complex through the challenges of postmodernism. The pluralism beginning to emerge in the 1960s has now become a characteristic of virtually every field today — not only religious education and practical theology but also psychology, sociology, philosophical ethics, and so forth. In a religiously plural context, moreover, different religious communities have come to feel more free to draw on their own distinctive understandings of the ultimate context of human existence. There is no one, normative "master story" that will characterize all forms of religious education in all communities. At the same time, it is equally clear that religious communities are squarely situated in a context where dialogue with other perspectives — including those of other religions and other disciplines — is not only possible but imperative.

Three themes have therefore come to the fore over the course of this book. The unique perspective afforded by international-comparative work has allowed us to identify these themes and to place them against the backdrop of modernization, globalization, and postmodernism. As religious education and practical theology look to the future, it is our hope that this sort of international-comparative work will become more common. Our contribution is a modest first step in the direction of research that is likely to become increasingly important in a world that is rapidly developing systemic connections drawing our various national cultures and societies into an interconnected global whole.

Bibliography for Paradigmatic
Figures and Texts, Chapters 3-5

Chapter Three: The Religious Education Reform Movements

The United States

PRIMARY

Bower, William C. 1919. *A Survey of Religious Education in the Local Church*. Chicago: University of Chicago Press.

————. 1925. *The Curriculum of Religious Education*. New York: C. Scribner's Sons.

————. 1930. *Character Through Creative Experience*. Chicago: University of Chicago Press.

————. 1933. *Religion and the Good Life*. New York: Abingdon.

————. 1936. *The Living Bible*. New York, London: Harper and Brothers.

Coe, George A. 1900. *The Spiritual Life: Studies in the Science of Religion*. New York: Eaton and Mains.

————. 1902. *The Religion of a Mature Mind*. Chicago: Fleming H. Revell.

————. 1904. *Education in Religion and Morals*. Chicago: Fleming H. Revell.

————. 1909. *Can Religion Be Taught?* New York: Union Theological Seminary.

————. 1912. *The Core of Good Teaching*. New York: C. Scribner's Sons.

————. 1916. *The Psychology of Religion*. Chicago: University of Chicago Press.

————. 1917. *A Social Theory of Religious Education*. New York: C. Scribner's Sons.

————. 1924. *Law and Freedom in the School*. Chicago: University of Chicago Press.

————. 1925. *What Ails Our Youth?* New York: C. Scribner's Sons.

————. 1929. *What Is Christian Education?* New York: C. Scribner's Sons.

————. 1929. *Am I Getting an Education?* Garden City, N.Y.: Doubleday and Doran.

————. 1932. *Educating for Citizenship: The Sovereign State as Ruler and as Teacher*. New York: C. Scribner's Sons.

————. 1937. *Religion in Transition*. London: George Allen and Unwin.

————. 1943. *What Is Religion Doing to Our Consciences?* New York: C. Scribner's Sons.

————. 1977. *George Albert Coe Papers.* Yale University Library.

Elliott, Harrison S. 1927. *The Bearing of Psychology Upon Religion.* New York: Association Press.

————. 1939. *Group Discussion in Religious Education.* New York: Association Press.

————. 1940. *Can Religious Education Be Christian?* New York: Macmillan.

Fahs, Sophia L. 1923. *Racial Relations and the Christian Ideal: A Discussion Course for College Students.* New York: Council of Christian Associations.

————. 1930. "The Beginnings of Religion in Baby Behavior." *Religious Education* 25, no. 10, p. 896.

————. 1942. "Religion in the Public Schools . . . Values at Stake." *Childhood Education* 18, no. 6, pp. 245-46.

————. 1950. *Jesus, the Carpenter's Son.* Boston: Skinner House Books.

————. 1952. *Today's Children and Yesterday's Heritage: A Philosophy of Creative Religious Development.* Boston: Beacon.

————. 1955. *The Old Story of Salvation.* Boston: Starr King Press.

————. 1965. *Worshipping Together with Questioning Minds.* Boston: Beacon.

————. 1971. "The Future and Religious Education." *Religious Education* 66, no. 6, p. 457.

————. *Papers.* Andover-Harvard Theological Library.

Fahs, Sophia L., and Helen F. Sweet. 1930. *Exploring Religion with Eight-Year-Olds.* New York: H. Holt and Company.

Fahs, Sophia L., and Elizabeth S. M. Manwell. 1940. *Consider the Children — How They Grow.* Boston: Beacon.

Henderlite, Rachel. 1961. *Forgiveness and Hope: Toward a Theology for Protestant Christian Education.* Richmond: John Knox.

————. 1964. *The Holy Spirit in Christian Education.* Philadelphia: Westminster.

SECONDARY ON COE

Archibald, Hellen A. 1975. "George Albert Coe: Theorist for Religious Education in the Twentieth Century." Diss., University of Illinois.

Bremer, David H. 1949. "George Albert Coe's Contribution to the Psychology of Religion." Diss., Boston University.

Campbell, Eldrich C., Jr. 1970. "A Comparative Study of the Role of the Church in Christian Education as Viewed by George Albert Coe with Selected Contemporary Religious Educators." Diss., New York University.

Channels, Lloyd V. 1940. "The Contribution of George Albert Coe to Religious Education." Diss., University of Chicago.

Haney, John C. 1959. "A Critical Comparison of the Educational Philosophies of John Dewey and George Albert Coe." Diss., Boston University.

McCaffrey, Jane De Chantal. 1979. "The Relationship Between Moral Education and Religious Education in the Writings of George Albert Coe." Diss., Catholic University of America.

Moore, A. 1987. "A Social Theory of Religious Education." *Religious Education* 82, no. 3, pp. 415-25.

Nicholson, I. 1994. "Academic Professionalization and Protestant Reconstruction, 1890-

1902: George Albert Coe's Psychology of Religion." *Journal of the History of the Behavioral Sciences* 30, no. 4, pp. 348-68.

Osmer, Richard R. 1985. Vol. 1, chap. 1 of "Practical Theology and Contemporary Christian Education: An Historical and Constructive Analysis." Diss., Emory University.

Swatos, W. 1989. "Religious Sociology and the Sociology of Religion in America at the Turn of the 20th Century: Divergencies from a Common Theme." *Sociological Analysis* 50, no. 4, pp. 363-75.

Tippen, Brian A. 1989. "Transitions in 20th-Century Religious Education: An Intellectual History of the Succession of Five Professors of Religious Education at Union Theological Seminary in New York." Diss., Columbia University.

Warren, H. 1997. "Character, Public Schooling and Religious Education, 1920-1934." *Religion and American Culture: A Journal of Interpretation* 7, no. 1, pp. 61-80.

SECONDARY ON FAHS

Beck, D. 1978. "Sophia Lyon Fahs: Militant Liberal and Lover of Children." *Religious Education* 73, no. 6, pp. 714-20.

Boys, Mary C. 1984. "Teaching, the Heart of Religious Education." *Religious Education* 79, no. 2, pp. 252-72.

Chandler, Daniel. 1989. "Sophia Lyon Fahs." *Religious Education* 84, no. 4, pp. 538-52.

Crandall, Robert A. 1977. "The Sunday School As an Instructional Agency for Religious Instruction in American Protestantism, 1872-1922." Diss., University of Notre Dame.

Hunter, Edith. 1966. *Sophia Lyon Fahs.* Boston: Beacon.

Keely, Barbara A., ed. 1997. *Faith of Our Foremothers: Women Changing Religious Education.* Louisville: John Knox.

Little, Lawrence C. 1966. *Religion and Public Education: A Bibliography.* Pittsburgh: University of Pittsburgh.

Lotz, Philip H. 1931. *Studies in Religious Education: A Source and Textbook for Colleges, Universities, Seminaries.* Nashville: Cokesbury.

McClellan, Edward B. 1992. *Schools and the Shaping Character: Moral Education in America, 1607-Present.* Bloomington: Indiana University Press.

VanDyk, Gerard. 1979. "A Study of the History and Development of the Sunday School in the Reformed Church in America: An Examination of the Influences of Secular Educational Developments on Religious Education from 1870-1910." Diss., Rutgers University.

Weeks, L. 1991. "The Incorporation of American Religion: The Case of the Presbyterians." *Religion and American Culture* 1, no. 1, pp. 101-18.

Germany

PRIMARY

Baumgarten, Otto. 1903. *Neue Bahnen. Der Unterricht in der christlichen Religion im Geist der modernen Theologie.* Tübingen: Mohr.

————. 1905. *Über Kindererziehung. Erlebtes und Gedachtes.* Tübingen: Mohr.

————. 1917. *Erziehungsaufgaben des Neuen Deutschland.* Tübingen: Mohr.

————. 1922. *Die religiöse Erziehung im Neuen Deutschland*. Tübingen: Mohr.

Eberhard, Otto. 1908. *Die wichtigsten Reformbestrebungen der Gegenwart auf dem Gebiete des Religionsunterrichts in der Schule*. Leipzig: Dörffling und Franke.

————. 1910. *Brennende Fragen des Religionsunterrichts der Volksschule in der Gegenwart*. Altenburg: S. Geibel.

————. 1921 (second ed.). *Arbeitsschule, Religionsunterricht und Gemeinschaftserziehung. Ein Beitrag zur Tat- und Lebenserziehung*. Berlin: Union Deutsche Verlagsgesellschaft.

————. 1923. *Wie lassen sich die modernen pädagogischen Bestrebungen für die evangelische Erziehungsschule fruchtbar machen?* Langensalza: H. Beyer.

————. 1924. *Neuzeitlicher Religionsunterricht und Handreichung evangelischer Jugenderziehung*. Mannheim: J. Bensheimer.

————. 1925. *Von der Arbeitsschule zur Lebensschule*. Berlin: Union Deutsche Verlagsgesellschaft.

————. 1932. *Evangelischer Religionsunterricht an der Zeitenwende. Einblicke und Ausblicke*. Tübingen: Mohr.

————. 1961. *Evangelischer Unterricht und Reformpädagogik. Ein Beitrag zur Geschichte der Religionspädagogik seit der Jahrhundertwende*. München: Ev. Presseverband f. Bayern.

Kabisch, Richard. 1910. *Wie lehren wir Religion? Versuch einer Methodik des evangelischen Religionsunterrichts für alle Schulen auf psychologischer Grundlage*. Göttingen: Vandenhoeck und Ruprecht.

————. 1913. *Das neue Geschlecht. Ein Erziehungsbuch*. Göttingen: Vandenhoeck und Ruprecht.

Niebergall, Friedrich. 1902. *Wie predigen wir dem modernen Menschen? I. Eine Untersuchung über Motive und Quietive*. Leipzig: Mohr.

————. 1908. *Die evangelische Kirche und ihre Reformen*. Leipzig: Quelle und Meyer.

————. 1910. *Jesus im Unterricht*. Göttingen: Vandenhoeck und Ruprecht.

————. 1912. *Der Schulreligions- und der Konfirmandenunterricht*. Leipzig: J. Klinkhardt.

————. 1913. *Jesus im Unterricht auf gefühlspsychologischer Grundlage*. Leipzig: J. Klinkhardt.

————. 1918-1919. *Praktische Theologie*. 2 vols. Tübingen: Mohr.

————. 1921. *Zur Reform des Religionsunterrichts*. Langensalza: Beltz.

————. 1922. *Der neue Religionsunterricht*. Langensalza: Beltz.

————. 1924. *Christliche Jugend- und Volkserziehung. Eine Religionspädagogik auf religionspsychologischer Grundlage*. Göttingen: Vandenhoeck und Ruprecht.

SECONDARY ON NIEBERGALL

Luther, Henning. 1984. *Religion, Subjekt, Erziehung. Grundbegriffe der Erwachsenenbildung am Beispiel der Praktischen Theologie Friedrich Niebergalls*. München: Kaiser.

Sandberger, Jörg Viktor. 1972. *Pädagogische Theologie. Friedrich Niebergalls Praktische Theologie als Erziehungslehre*. Göttingen: Vandenhoeck und Ruprecht.

Steck, Wolfgang. 1974. *Das homiletische Verfahren*. Göttingen: Vandenhoeck und Ruprecht.

Zillessen, Dietrich. 1989. "Friedrich Niebergall (1966-1932)." Pages 161-80 in *Klassiker der Religionspädagogik*, ed. Henning Schroer and Dietrich Zillessen. Frankfurt am Main: Diesterweg.

SECONDARY ON THE PERIOD

Bockwoldt, Gerd. 1977. *Religionspädagogik. Eine Problemgeschichte.* Stuttgart: Kohlhammer.

Bloth, Peter C. 1968. *Religion in den Schulen Preußens.* Heidelberg: Quelle und Meyer.

Fraund, Hans Martin. 1980. *Die Geschichte des Religionsunterrichts zwischen 1848 und 1933 am Beispiel ausgewählter Krisen- und Knotenpunkte und die Frage nach Freiheit, Konfessionalität und Wissenschaftlichkeit.* Dissertation.

Kahrs, Christian. 1995. *Evangelische Erziehung in der Moderne. Eine historische Untersuchung ihrer erziehungstheoretischen Systematik.* Weinheim: Deutscher Studien-Verlag (DSV).

Kling de Lazzer, Marie-Luise. 1982. *Thematisch-problemorientierter Religionsunterricht. Eine historisch-systematische Untersuchung zur Religionsdidaktik.* Gütersloh: Gütersloher Verlagshaus.

Koerrenz, Ralf, and Norbert Collmar, eds. 1994. *Die Religion der Reformpädagogen.* Weinheim: DSV.

Lachmann, Rainer. 1996. *Religionsunterricht in der Weimarer Republik.* Würzburg: Stephans-Buchhandlung.

Lämmermann, Godwin. 1994. *Religionspädagogik im 20. Jahrhundert.* Gütersloh: Gütersloher.

Müller-Rolli, Sebastian, ed. 1999. *Evangelische Schulpolitik in Deutschland 1918-1958.* Göttingen: Vandenhoeck und Ruprecht.

Nipkow, Karl Ernst, and Friedrich Schweitzer, eds. 1994. *Religionspädagogik. Texte zur evangelischen Erziehungs- und Bildungsverantwortung seit der Reformation.* Vols. 2/1, 2/2. Gütersloh: Gütersloher Verlagshaus.

Schelander, Robert. 1993. *Religionstheorie und Reformbewegung. Eine Untersuchung zur liberalen Religionspädagogik.* Würzburg: Stephans-Buchhandlung.

Chapter 4: The Reaffirmation of Theological Identity

The United States

PRIMARY

Henderlite, Rachel. 1959. "Elements of Unpredictability Which Create Difficulties in a Precise Definition of Christian Education." *Religious Education* 54 (September-October): 489-96.

Homrighausen, Elmer G. 1931. "Barthianism and the Kingdom." *Christian Century* 48, pp. 922-25.

———. 1937. *Current Trends in Theological Thought.* Philadelphia: Board of Christian Education.

———. 1940. *Let the Church Be the Church.* New York: Abingdon.

———. 1959. *I Believe in the Church.* New York: Abingdon.

Little, Sara. 1961. *The Role of the Bible in Contemporary Christian Education.* Richmond: John Knox.

Lynn, Robert W. 1964. *Protestant Strategies in Education.* New York: Association Press.

Miller, Randolph Crump. 1941. *What We Can Believe*. New York: C. Scribner's Sons.

————. 1950. *The Clue to Christian Education*. New York: C. Scribner's Sons.

————. 1950. *Religion Makes Sense*. Chicago: Wilcox and Follett.

————. 1956. *Biblical Theology and Christian Education*. New York: C. Scribner's Sons.

————. 1961. *Christian Nurture and the Church*. New York: C. Scribner's Sons.

————. 1963 (second ed.). *Education for Christian Living*. Englewood Cliffs, N.J.: Prentice-Hall.

————. 1982. "Theology in the Background." In *Religious Education and Theology*, ed. N. Thompson. Birmingham, Ala.: Religious Education Press.

————. 1983. "How I Became a Religious Educator — Or Did I?" In *Modern Masters of Religious Education*, ed. M. Mayr. Birmingham, Ala.: Religious Education Press.

Niebuhr, Hulda. 1935. *Ventures in Dramatics with Boys and Girls of the Church School*. New York: C. Scribner's Sons.

————. 1949. *The One Story*. Philadelphia: Westminster.

Sherrill, Lewis Joseph. 1926. "Religious Education Yesterday and Today." *The Register* 15 (July, August, September): 2-10.

————. 1928. "Changes in Religious Education." *Union Seminary Review* 40 (October): 10-16.

————. 1932. *Religious Education in the Small Church*. Philadelphia: Westminster.

————. 1936. *Adult Education in the Church*. Richmond: Presbyterian Committee of Publication.

————. 1939. *Understanding Children*. New York: Abingdon-Cokesbury.

————. 1939. *The Opening Doors of Childhood*. New York: Macmillan.

————. 1943. *Becoming a Christian*. Richmond: John Knox.

————. 1944. *The Rise of Christian Education*. New York: Macmillan.

————. 1945. *Guilt and Redemption*. Richmond: John Knox. (A revised edition of this work was published in 1957.)

————. 1949. *Lift Up Your Eyes: A Report to the Churches on the Religious Education Re-Study*. Richmond: John Knox.

————. 1950. "A Historical Study of the Religious Education Movement." In *Orientation in Religious Education*, ed. Philip H. Lotz. New York: Abingdon-Cokesbury.

————. 1953. *The Struggle of the Soul*. New York: Macmillan.

————. 1955. *The Gift of Power*. New York: Macmillan.

Smart, James D. 1943. *What a Man Can Believe*. Philadelphia: Westminster.

————. 1947. *The Church Must Teach — or Die: A Five Chapter Study Course to Prepare Local Churches for a New Day in Christian Education, and Introducing the New Curriculum*. Board of Christian Education of the Presbyterian Church in the United States of America.

————. 1948. *Jesus: Stories for Children*. Philadelphia: Westminster.

————. 1949. *A Promise to Keep*. Philadelphia: Westminster.

————. 1953. *The Recovery of Humanity*. Philadelphia: Westminster.

————. 1954. *The Teaching Ministry of the Church: An Examination of the Basic Principles of Christian Education*. Philadelphia: Westminster.

————. 1960. *The Rebirth of Ministry: A Study of the Biblical Character of the Church's Ministry*. Philadelphia: Westminster.

————. 1961. *The Interpretation of Scripture*. Philadelphia: Westminster.

————. 1962. *The Creed in Christian Teaching*. Philadelphia: Westminster.

————. 1964. *The Old Testament in Dialogue with Modern Man*. Philadelphia: Westminster.

————. 1968. *The ABC's of Christian Faith*. Philadelphia: Westminster.

————. 1969. *The Quiet Revolution: The Radical Impact of Jesus on Men of His Time*. Philadelphia: Westminster.

————. 1970. *The Strange Silence of the Bible in the Church: A Study in Hermeneutics*. Philadelphia: Westminster.

————. 1977. *The Cultural Subversion of the Biblical Faith: Life in the 20th Century under the Sign of the Cross*. Philadelphia: Westminster.

————. 1979. *The Past, Present, and Future of Biblical Theology*. Philadelphia: Westminster.

Smith, Shelton H. 1941. *Faith and Nurture*. New York: C. Scribner's Sons.

————. 1951. "Christian Education." In *Protestant Thought in the Twentieth Century*, ed. Arnold S. Nash. New York: Macmillan.

————. 1951. "Christian Education: Do Progressive Religious Educators Have a Theology?" In *America at the End of the Protestant Era*, ed. Arnold S. Nash. New York: Macmillan.

————. 1955. *Changing Conceptions of Original Sin*. New York: C. Scribner's Sons.

————. 1978. "Let Religious Educators Reckon with the Barthians." In *Who Are We? The Quest for a Religious Education*, ed. John H. Westerhoff III. Birmingham, Ala.: Religious Education Press.

————, ed. 1965. *Horace Bushnell: A Library of Protestant Thought*. New York: Oxford University Press.

Wyckoff, Campbell D. 1955. *The Task of Christian Education*. Philadelphia: Westminster.

————. 1958. *In One Spirit: Senior Highs and Missions*. New York: Friendship.

————. 1959. *The Gospel and Christian Education: A Theory of Christian Education for Our Times*. Philadelphia: Westminster.

————. 1961. *Theory and Design of Christian Education Curriculum*. Philadelphia: Westminster.

————. 1983. "From Practice to Theory — and Back Again." In *Modern Masters of Religious Education*, ed. M. Mayr. Birmingham, Ala.: Religious Education Press.

SECONDARY ON SMART AND SHERRILL

Boys, Mary C. 1979. "Religious Education and Contemporary Biblical Scholarship." *Religious Education* 74, no. 2, pp. 182-97.

Campbell, Eldrich C., Jr. 1970. "A Comparative Study of the Role of the Church in Christian Education as Viewed by George Albert Coe with Selected Contemporary Religious Educators." Diss., New York University.

Fairchild, Roy W. 1958. "The Contributions of Lewis J. Sherrill to Christian Education." *Religious Education* 53 (September-October): 403-11.

Goodykoontz, Harry G. 1957. "Dr. Sherrill as an Author." In *A Volume of Memorials*. Louisville: Louisville Presbyterian Theological Seminary.

Kao, Charles C. L. 1969. "The View of Man and the Philosophy of Christian Education in the Thought of Harrison Sacket Elliot and of Lewis Joseph Sherrill." Diss., Boston University.

Kinsinger, Lora P. 1956. "The Theological Presuppositions of Lewis J. Sherrill's Philosophy of Christian Education." Diss., Union-PSCE.

Lee, Kyoo-Min. 1996. "Koinonia: A Critical Study of Lewis Sherrill's Concept of Koinonia and Jürgen Moltmann's Social Understanding of the Trinity as an Attempt to Provide a Corrective to the Problems of the Korean Church and Its Educational Ministry." Diss., Princeton Theological Seminary.

Louisville Presbyterian Theological Seminary. 1957. *A Volume of Memorials: Lewis Joseph Sherrill.* Louisville: Lousiville Presbyterian Theological Seminary.

Nabekura, Isao. 1970. "The Relevancy of Lewis J. Sherrill to Christian Education in Japan." Diss., Southern Baptist Theological Seminary.

Nyberg, Walter L. 1966. "A Comparative Study of Key Concepts in the Theories of Religious Education Advocated by George Albert Coe and Lewis Joseph Sherrill." Diss., New York University.

Osmer, Richard R. 1985. Vol. 1, chap. 3 of "Practical Theology and Contemporary Christian Education: An Historical and Constructive Analysis." Diss., Emory University.

Parsons, G. 1983. "Reforming the Tradition, a Forgotten Dimension of Liberal Protestantism." *Religion* 13, no. 3, pp. 257-71.

Stoecker, J. 1989. "Persistence in Higher Education: A 9-Year Test of a Theoretical Model." *Journal of College Student Development* 29, no. 3, pp. 196-209.

Thistlethwaite, Susan. 1980. "H. Shelton Smith: Critic of the Theological Perspective of Progressive Religious Education." Diss., Duke University.

Tippen, Brian A. 1989. "Transitions in 20th-Century Religious Education: An Intellectual History of the Succession of Five Professors of Religious Education at Union Theological Seminary in New York." Diss., Columbia University.

SECONDARY ON THE PERIOD

Benton, Charles E. 1964. *History of Christian Education.* Chicago: Moody.

Carmichael, P. H. 1936. "Trends in Religious Education." *Union Seminary Review* 47 *(April): 189-99.*

Chave, Ernest J. 1947. *A Functional Approach to Religious Education.* Chicago: University of Chicago Press.

Childs, John L. 1931. *Education and the Philosophy of Experimentalism.* New York: The Century Company.

Cully, Kendig B. 1959. "Two Decades of Thinking Concerning Christian Nurture." *Religious Education* 54 (November-December): 481-89.

———. ed. 1960. *Basic Writings in Christian Education.* Philadelphia: Westminster.

Dent, Frank L. 1989. "Motive Magazine: Advocating the Arts and Empowering the Imagination in the Life of the Church." Diss., Columbia University Teachers College.

Devitt, Patrick M. 1992. *That You May Believe: A Brief History of Religious Education.* Dublin: Dominican Publications.

Fergusson, Edmund M. 1935. *Historic Chapters in Christian Education in America: A Brief History of the American Sunday School.* New York: Fleming H. Revell.

Gleason, Philip. 1977. "Blurring the Line of Separation: Education, Civil Religion, and Teaching about Religion." *Journal of Church and State* 19, no. 3, pp. 517-38.

Howe, Reuel L. 1959. "A Theology for Education." *Religious Education* 54 (November-December): 489-96.

Hunter, Edith. 1950-1951. "Neo-Orthodoxy Goes to Kindergarten." *Religion in Life* 20 (Winter): 3-14.

Kalmijn, Matthijs. 1991. "Shifting Boundaries: Trends in Religious and Educational Homogamy." *American Sociological Review* 56, no. 6, pp. 786-800.

Kennedy, William B. 1998. "Neo-Orthodoxy Goes to Sunday School: The Christian Faith and Life Curriculum." *Journal of Presbyterian History* 76, no. 1, pp. 81-109.

McMurry, Richey S. 1963. "Toward the Renewal of Faith and Nurture." *The Duke Divinity School Bulletin* (May).

Mize, Richard L. 1980. "The Legal Aspects of Religious Instruction in Public Schools." Diss., University of North Carolina.

Murch, J. DeForest. 1943. *Christian Education and the Local Church: History, Principles, Practice.* Cincinnati: Standard Publishing.

Taylor, Marvin J., ed. 1966. *An Introduction to Christian Education.* Nashville: Abingdon.

Vieth, Paul H. 1930. *Objectives in Religious Education.* New York: Harper and Brothers.

———. 1947. *The Church and Christian Education.* St. Louis: Bethany.

Warren, Heather A. 1997. "Character, Public Schooling, and Religious Education, 1920-1934." *Religion and American Culture* 7, no. 1, pp. 61-80.

Weigle, Luther A. 1933. "The Religious Education of a Protestant." In *Contemporary American Theology,* ed. V. Ferm. Second series. New York: Round Table Press.

———. 1936. "The International Sunday School Lesson System." *Union Seminary Review* 47 (April): 180-89.

Wood, James E., Jr. 1984. "Religion and Education in American Church-State Relations." *Journal of Church and State* 26, no. 1, pp. 31-54.

Young, Norman. 1965. "Some Implications in Tillich's Theology for Christian Education." *Religious Education* 60 (May-June): 230-37.

Germany

PRIMARY

Bohne, Gerhard. 1922. *Die religiöse Entwicklung der Jugend in der Reifezeit. Auf Grund autobiographischer Zeugnisse.* Leipzig: Hinrichs.

———. 1929. *Das Wort Gottes und der Unterricht. Zur Grundlegung einer evangelischen Pädaogogik.* Berlin: Furche.

———. 1934. *Evangelische Religion. Gegenstand und Gestaltung.* Leipzig: J. Klinkhardt.

———. 1951/1953. *Grundlagen der Erziehung. Die Pädagogik in der Verantwortung vor Gott.* 2 vols. Hamburg: Furche.

Hammelsbeck, Oskar. 1938. *Leben unter dem Wort als Frage des kirchlichen Unterrichts.* München: Kaiser.

———. 1939. *Der kirchliche Unterricht. Aufgabe — Umfang — Einheit.* München: Kaiser.

———. 1940. *Glaube und Bildung.* München: Kaiser.

———. 1946. *Die kulturpolitische Verantwortung der Kirche.* München: Kaiser.

———. 1946. *Kirche — Schule — Lehrerschaft.* Gütersloh: Bertelsmann.

———. 1946. *Um Heil oder Unheil im öffentlichen Leben.* München: Kaiser.

———. 1947. *Der heilige Ruf.* Gütersloh: Rufer.

———. 1950. *Evangelische Lehre von der Erziehung.* München: Kaiser.

———. 1954. *Glaube — Welt — Erziehung.* Mülheim: Setzkorn-Scheifhacken.

———. 1962. *Volksschule in evangelischer Verantwortung.* Bochum: Kamp.

Kittel, Helmuth. 1947. *Vom Religionsunterricht zur Evangelischen Unterweisung.* Wolfenbüttel: Wolfenbütteler Verlagsanstalt.

———. 1947. *Evangelische Unterweisung und Reformpädagogik. Eine Untersuchung zur Methodenlehre evangelischer Unterweisung.* Lüneburg: Heliand.

———. 1949. *Schule unter dem Evangelium. Zum Problem der Konfessionalität im Schulwesen.* Braunschweig: Westermann.

———. 1951. *Der Erzieher als Christ.* Göttingen: Vandenhoeck und Ruprecht.

———. 1970. *Evangelische Religionspädagogik.* Berlin: de Gruyter.

Rang, Martin. 1936. *Biblischer Unterricht. Theoretische Grundlegung und praktische Handreichung für den Religionsunterricht in Schule, Kirche und Familie.* Berlin: Furche.

———. 1939. *Handbuch für den biblischen Unterricht. Theoretische Grundlegung und praktische Handreichung für die christliche Unterweisung der evangelischen Jugend.* 2 vols. Berlin: Furche.

Tiling, Magdalene von. 1932. *Grundlagen pädagogischen Denkens.* Stuttgart: Steinkopf.

———. 1948. *Der Unterricht im Neuen Testament auf der Unter- und Mittelstufe.* Berlin: Haus und Schule.

———. 1955. *Wir und unsere Kinder. Eine Pädagogik der Altersstufen für evangelische Erzieher in Familie, Heim und Schule.* Stuttgart: Steinkopf.

SECONDARY ON HAMMELSBECK, KITTEL, AND VON TILING

Adam, Gottfried. 1989. "Oskar Hammelsbeck (1899-1975)." Pages 236-49 in *Klassiker der Religionspädagogik,* ed. Henning Schröer and Dietrich Zillessen. Frankfurt am Main: Diesterweg.

Crimmann, Ralph P. 1986. *Erich Weniger und Oskar Hammelsbeck.* Weinheim: Beltz.

Herkenrath, Liese-Lotte. 1972. *Politik, Theologie und Erziehung. Untersuchungen zu Magdalene von Tilings Pädagogik.* Heidelberg: Quelle und Meyer.

Lähnemann, Johannes. 1989. "Helmuth Kittel (1902-1984)." Pages 250-66 in *Klassiker der Religionspädagogik,* ed. Henning Schröer and Dietrich Zillessen. Frankfurt am Main: Diesterweg.

Reimers, E. 1958. *Recht und Grenzen einer Berufung auf Luther in den neueren Bemühungen um eine evangelische Erziehung.* Weinheim: Beltz.

Schneider-Ludorff, Gury. 2001. *Magdalene von Tiling (1877-1974).* Göttingen: Vandenhoeck und Ruprecht.

SECONDARY ON THE PERIOD

Dross, Reinhard. 1970. *Zur Neukonzeption des Religionsunterrichts.* Gütersloh: Mohn.

Krotz, Fritz. 1982. *Die religionspädagogische Neubesinnung. Zur Rezeption der Theologie K. Barths in den Jahren 1924 bis 1933.* Göttingen: Vandenhoeck und Ruprecht.

Lämmermann, Godwin. 1994. *Religionspädagogik im 20. Jahrhundert.* Gütersloh: Gütersloher Verlagshaus.

Nipkow, Karl Ernst, and Friedrich Schweitzer, eds. 1994. *Religionspädagogik. Texte zur evangelischen Erziehungs- und Bildungsverantwortung seit der Reformations.* Vol. 2/2. Gütersloh: Gütersloher Verlagshaus.

Rickers, Folkert. 1995. *Zwischen Kreuz und Hakenkreuz. Untersuchungen zur Religionspädagogik im "Dritten Reich."* Neukirchen-Vluyn: Neukirchener.

Schweitzer, Friedrich. 1992. *Die Religion des Kindes. Zur Problemgeschichte einer religionspädagogischen Grundfrage.* Gütersloh: Gütersloher Verlagshaus.

Sturm, Wilhelm. 1971. *Religionsunterricht — gestern — heute — morgen.* Stuttgart: Calwer.

Wegenast, Klaus, ed. 1981/1983. *Religionspädagogik.* 2 vols. Darmstadt: Wissenschaftliche Buchgesellschaft.

Chapter 5: Protestant Religious Education after the 1960s

The United States

PRIMARY

Durka, Gloria. 1976. *Modeling God: Religious Education for Tomorrow.* New York: Paulist.

Durka, Gloria, and J. Smith, eds. 1976. *Emerging Issues in Religious Education.* New York: Paulist.

————, eds. 1979. *Aesthetic Dimensions of Religious Education.* New York: Paulist.

————, eds. 1980. *Family Ministry.* Minneapolis: Winston.

Foster, Charles R. 1982. *Teaching in the Community of Faith.* Nashville: Abingdon.

————. 1994. *Educating Congregations: The Future of Christian Education.* Nashville: Abingdon.

————. 1996. *We Are the Church Together: Cultural Diversity in Congregational Life.* Valley Forge, Pa.: Trinity Press International.

————. 1997. *Embracing Diversity: Leadership in Multicultural Congregations.* Bethesda, Md.: Alban Institute.

————, ed. 1987. *Ethnicity in the Education of the Church.* Nashville: Scarritt.

Fowler, James W. 1974. *To See the Kingdom: The Theological Vision of H. Richard Niebuhr.* Nashville: Abingdon.

————. 1978. *Life Maps: Conversations on the Journey of Faith,* ed. J. Berryman. Waco, Tex.: Word Books.

————. 1980. *Trajectories in Faith: Five Life Stories.* Nashville: Abingdon.

————. 1981. *Stages of Faith: The Psychology of Human Development and the Quest for Meaning.* San Francisco: Harper and Row.

————. 1984. *Becoming Adult, Becoming Christian: Adult Development and Christian Faith.* San Francisco: Harper and Row.

————. 1991. *How Faith Grows: Faith Development and Christian Education.* London: National Society/Church House Publishing.

————. 1991. *Weaving the New Creation: Stages of Faith and the Public Church.* San Francisco: HarperSanFrancisco.

————. 1996. *Faithful Change: The Personal and Public Challenges of Postmodern Life.* Nashville: Abingdon.

————, ed. 1991. *Stages of Faith and Religious Development: Implications for Church, Education, and Society.* New York: Crossroad.

Freire, Paulo. 1973. *Education for Critical Consciousness.* New York: Continuum.

————. 1974. "Conscientization." *Cross Currents* 23, pp. 23-31.

————. 1974. *Pedagogy of the Oppressed.* New York: Seabury.

————. 1978. *Pedagogy in Process.* New York: Seabury.

Groome, Thomas. 1980. *Christian Religious Education: Sharing Our Story and Vision.* San Francisco: Harper and Row.

————. 1991. *Language for a "Catholic" Church: A Program of Study.* Kansas City, Mo.: Sheed and Ward.

————. 1991. *Sharing Faith: A Comprehensive Approach to Religious Education and Pastoral Ministry: The Way of Shared Praxis.* San Francisco: Harper and Row.

————. 1998. *Educating for Life: A Spiritual Vision for Every Teacher and Parent.* Allen, Tex.: T. More.

Harris, Maria. 1978. *Parish Religious Education.* New York: Paulist.

————. 1981. *Portrait of Youth Ministry.* New York: Paulist.

————. 1987. *Teaching and Religious Imagination.* San Francisco: Harper and Row.

————. 1989. *Fashion Me a People.* Louisville: Westminster/John Knox.

————. 1995. *Jubilee Time: Celebrating Women, Spirit, and the Advent of Age.* New York: Bantam.

————. 1996. *Proclaim Jubilee: A Spirituality for the Twenty-First Century.* Louisville: Westminster/John Knox.

————. 1998. *Reshaping Religious Education: Conversations on Contemporary Practice.* Louisville: Westminster/John Knox.

Kegan, R. 1982. *The Evolving Self: Problem and Process in Human Development.* Cambridge: Harvard University Press.

————. 1994. *In Over Our Heads: The Mental Demands of Modern Life.* Cambridge: Harvard University Press.

Kennedy, William B. 1957. "The Genesis and Development of the Christian Faith and Life Series." Diss., Yale University.

————. 1966. *The Shaping of Protestant Education: An Interpretation of the Sunday School and Development of Protestant Educational Strategy in the United States, 1789-1860.* New York: Association Press.

Kohlberg, Lawrence. 1981. *The Meaning and Measurement of Moral Development.* Worcester, Mass.: Clark University Press.

————. 1981. *The Philosophy of Moral Development. Moral Stages and the Idea of Justice.* San Francisco: Harper and Row.

————. 1984. *The Psychology of Moral Development: The Nature and Validity of Moral Styles.* San Francisco: Harper and Row.

Lee, James M. 1973. *The Flow of Religious Instruction: A Social-Science Approach.* Dayton, Ohio: Pflaum/Standard.

————. 1985. *The Content of Religious Instruction: A Social Science Approach.* Birmingham, Ala.: Religious Education Press.

————. 1999. *The Sacrament of Teaching: A Social Science Approach.* Birmingham, Ala.: Religious Education Press.

————, ed. 1967. *Catholic Education in the Western World.* Notre Dame: University of Notre Dame Press.

————, ed. 1977. *The Religious Education We Need: Toward the Renewal of Christian Education.* Mishawaka, Ind.: Religious Education Press.

————, ed. 1985. *The Spirituality of the Religious Educator.* Birmingham, Ala.: Religious Education Press.

————, ed. 2000. *Forging a Better Religious Education in the Third Millennium.* Birmingham, Ala.: Religious Education Press.

Lee, James M., and Patrick C. Rooney, eds. 1970. *Toward a Future for Religious Education.* Dayton, Ohio: Pflaum Press.

Little, Sara. 1956. *Learning Together in the Christian Fellowship.* Richmond: John Knox.

————. 1961. *The Role of the Bible in Contemporary Christian Education.* Richmond: John Knox.

————. 1968. *Youth, World, and the Church.* Richmond: John Knox.

————. 1983. *To Set One's Heart: Belief and Teaching in the Church.* Atlanta: John Knox.

Loder, James E. 1965. *Religion and the Public Schools.* New York: Association Press.

————. 1966. *Religious Pathology and Christian Faith.* Philadelphia: Westminster.

————. 1969. *Adults in Crisis.* New York: Fifth Avenue Presbyterian Church.

————. 1981. "Transformation in Christian Education." *Religious Education* 76 (March-April): 204-21.

————. 1981. *The Transforming Moment: Understanding Convictional Experience.* San Francisco: Harper and Row.

————. 1992. *The Knight's Move: The Relational Logic of the Spirit in Theology and Science.* Colorado Springs: Helmers and Howard.

————. 1998. *The Logic of the Spirit.* San Francisco: Jossey-Bass.

Lynn, Robert. 1990. *Caring for the Commonweal: Education for Religious and Public Life,* ed. P. Palmer, B. Wheeler, and J. Fowler. Macon, Ga.: Mercer University Press.

Lynn, Robert, and Elliott Wright. 1980. *The Big Little School: Two Hundred Years of the Sunday School.* Rev. ed. Birmingham, Ala.: Religious Education Press.

Marthaler, Berard L. 1993. *The Creed: The Apostolic Faith in Contemporary Theology.* Mystic, Conn.: Twenty-Third Publications.

————. 1995. *The Catechism Yesterday and Today: The Evolution of a Genre.* Collegeville, Minn.: Liturgical Press.

————, ed. 1994. *Introducing the Catechism of the Catholic Church: Traditional Themes and Contemporary Issues.* New York: Paulist.

Melchert, Charles F. 1969. "An Exploration in the Presuppositions of Objective Formation for Contemporary Protestant Christian Educational Ministry." Diss., Yale University.

————. 1977. "What Is Religious Education?" *Living Light* (Fall): 339-52.

————. 1978. "Understanding in Religious Education." In *Process and Relationship: Issues in Theology, Philosophy and Education,* ed. K. Cully and I. Cully. Mishawaka, Ind.: Religious Education Press.

————. 1998. *Wise Teaching: Biblical Wisdom and Educational Ministry.* Harrisburg, Pa.: Trinity Press International.

Moore, Mary E. 1983. *Education for Continuity and Change: A New Model for Christian Religious Education.* Nashville: Abingdon.

————. 1991. *Teaching from the Heart: Theology and Educational Method.* Minneapolis: Fortress.

————. 1998. *Ministering with the Earth.* St. Louis, Mo.: Chalice.

Moran, Gabriel. 1963. *Scripture and Tradition: A Survey of the Controversy.* New York: Herder and Herder.

————. 1966. *Theology of Revelation.* New York: Herder and Herder.

————. 1967. *Where There's Life.* Dayton, Ohio: Pflaum.

————. 1968. *Vision and Tactics: Toward an Adult Church.* New York: Herder and Herder.

————. 1970. *Design for Religion: Toward Ecumenical Education.* New York: Herder and Herder.

————. 1970. *The New Community: Religious Life in an Era of Change.* New York: Herder and Herder.

————. 1972. *The Present Revelation: The Search for Religious Foundations.* New York: Herder and Herder.

————. 1973. *Catechesis of Revelation.* New York: Seabury.

————. 1979. *Education Toward Adulthood.* New York: Paulist.

————. 1989. *Religious Education as a Second Language.* Birmingham, Ala.: Religious Education Press.

Moran, Gabriel, and Maria Harris. 1968. *Experiences in Community: Should Religious Life Survive?* New York: Herder and Herder.

Nelson, C. Ellis. 1967. *Where Faith Begins.* Richmond: John Knox.

————. 1989. *How Faith Matures.* Louisville: John Knox.

————, ed. 1988. *Congregations: Their Power to Form and Transform.* Atlanta: John Knox.

Piaget, J. 1932. *The Moral Judgement of the Child,* trans. M. Gabain. New York: Harcourt, Brace.

————. 1952. *The Origins of Intelligence in Children,* trans. M. Cook. New York: International Universities Press.

————. 1963. *The Language and Thought of the Child,* trans. M. Gabain. Cleveland: World.

————. 1967. *Six Psychological Studies,* trans. A. Tenzer, ed. D. Elkind. New York: Random House.

————. 1970. *Genetic Epistemology,* trans. E. Duckworth. New York: Columbia University Press.

————. 1971. *Structuralism,* trans. and ed. Chaninah Maschler. London: Routledge.

————. 1972. *The Principles of Genetic Epistemology,* trans. W. Mays. London: Routledge.

Schipani, Daniel S. 1981. "Conscientization and Creativity: A Reinterpretation of Paulo Freire, Focused on His Epistemology and Theological Foundations with Implications for Christian Education Theory." Diss., Princeton Theological Seminary.

————. 1984. *Conscientization and Creativity: Paulo Freire and Christian Education.* Lanham: University Press of America.

————. 1988. *Religious Education Encounters Liberation Theology.* Birmingham, Ala.: Religious Education Press.

————, ed. 1989. *Freedom and Discipleship: Liberation Theology in an Anabaptist Perspective*. Maryknoll, N.Y.: Orbis.

Warren, Michael. 1975. *A Future for Youth Catechesis*. New York: Paulist.

————. 1982. *Youth and the Future of the Church: Ministry with Youth and Young Adults*. New York: Seabury.

————. 1987. *Youth, Gospel, Liberation*. San Francisco: Harper and Row.

————, ed. 1977. *Youth Ministry: A Book of Readings*. New York: Paulist.

————, ed. 1978. *Resources for Youth Ministry*. New York: Paulist.

————, ed. 1983. *Sourcebook for Modern Catechetics*. Winona, Minn.: St. Mary's.

Westerhoff, John H. 1970. *Values for Tomorrow's Children: An Alternative Future for Education in the Church*. Philadelphia: Pilgrim.

————. 1972. *A Colloquy on Christian Education*. Philadelphia: United Church Press.

————. 1972. *Learning to Be Free*. Philadelphia: United Church Press.

————. 1976. *Tomorrow's Church: A Community of Change*. Waco, Tex.: Word.

————. 1976. *Will Our Children Have Faith?* New York: Seabury.

————. 1978. *McGuffey and His Readers: Piety, Morality, and Education in 19th Century America*. Nashville: Abingdon.

————. 1978. "Necessary Paradox: Catechesis and Evangelism, Nurture and Conversion." *Religious Education* 73, no. 4, pp. 409-16.

————. 1978. *Who Are We?: The Quest for a Religious Education*. Birmingham, Ala.: Religious Education Press.

————. 1979. "A Discipline in Crisis." *Religious Education* 74, no. 1, pp. 7-15.

————. 1979. *Inner Growth, Outer Change: An Educational Guide to Church Renewal*. New York: Seabury.

————. 1980. *Bringing Up Children in the Christian Faith*. Minneapolis: Winston.

————. 1982. *The Spiritual Life: Learning East and West*. New York: Seabury.

————. 1983. *Building God's People in a Materialistic Society*. New York: Seabury.

————. 1984. *A Pilgrim People: Learning Through the Church Year*. New York: Seabury.

————. 1985. *Living the Faith Community: The Church That Makes a Difference*. Minneapolis: Winston.

————. 1986. *On the Threshold of God's Future*. San Francisco: Harper and Row.

————. 1987. "Formation, Education, Instruction." *Religious Education* 82, no. 4, pp. 578-91.

————. 1994. "Evangelism, Evangelization, and Catechesis: Defining Terms and Making the Case for Evangelization." *Interpretational Journal of Bible and Theology* 48, no. 2, pp. 156-65.

————. 1994. *Spiritual Life: The Foundation for Preaching and Teaching*. Louisville: Westminster/John Knox.

Westerhoff, John H., and Gwen K. Neville. 1974. *Generation to Generation: Conversations on Religious Education and Culture*. Philadelphia: United Church Press.

Westerhoff, John H., and W. H. Willimon. 1980. *Liturgy and Learning through the Life Cycle*. New York: Seabury.

Westerhoff, John H., and C. O. Edwards, Jr., eds. 1981. *A Faithful Church: Issues in the History of Catechesis*. Wilton, Conn.: Morehouse-Barlow.

Westerhoff, John H., and Stanley Hauerwas, eds. 1992. *Schooling Christians: "Holy Experiments" in American Education.* Grand Rapids: Eerdmans.

SECONDARY ON WESTERHOFF

Asali, Mona Abou. 1989. "Westerhoff on Faith Enculturation." *Chicago Theological Seminary Register* 79, pp. 17-22.

Au, Wilkie. 1991. "Holistic Catechesis: Keeping Our Balance in the 1990s." *Religious Education* 86, pp. 347-60.

Boys, Mary C. 1984. "The Role of Theology in Religious Education." *Horizons* 11, no. 1, pp. 61-85.

Browning, Don. 1985. "Practical Theology and Political Theology." *Theology Today* 42, no. 1, pp. 15-33.

Cully, Kendig B. 1978. "An Applied Theoretician: John H. Westerhoff III." *New Review of Books and Religion* 3, pp. 4, 24.

Gobbell, A. 1980. "On Constructing Spirituality." *Religious Education* 75, no. 4, pp. 409-21.

Heywood, David. 1988. "Christian Education as Enculturation: The Life of the Community and Its Place in Christian Education in the Work of John H. Westerhoff III." *British Journal of Religious Education* 10, pp. 65-71.

Lee, James M. 1982. "From Theory to Practice: Curriculum — Reflective Response." *Religious Education* 77, no. 4, pp. 383-95.

Lim, Adynna Y. 1982. "A Comparative Study of the Socialization Models of Christian Education by John H. Westerhoff III and Lawrence O. Richards." Diss., New York University.

Llovio, Kay. 1984. "Toward a Definition of Christian Education: A Comparison of Richards and Westerhoff." *Christian Education Journal* 5, no. 2, pp. 15-23.

Nicholson, John P. 1982. "Analysis of Theological, Sociological, Educational, Organizational Dimensions of Westerhoff's Socialization-Enculturation Paradigm." *Religious Education* 77.

Schmidt, S. 1985. "The Uses of History and Religious Education." *Religious Education* 80, no. 3, pp. 345-72.

Thistlethwaite, Susan. 1981. "Feminization of American Religious Education." *Religious Education* 76, no. 4, pp. 391-402.

SECONDARY ON PERIOD

Boys, Mary C. 1989. *Educating in Faith: Maps and Visions.* San Francisco: Harper & Row.

Carper, James C., and Thomas C. Hunt, eds. 1984. *Religious Schooling in America.* Birmingham, Ala.: Religious Education Press.

Collins, Denis E. 1977. *Paulo Freire: His Life, Works and Thought.* New York: Paulist.

Dudley, C., C. Jackson, and J. Wind, eds. 1991. *Carriers of Faith: Lessons from Congregational Studies: A Festschrift in Honor of Robert W. Lynn.* Louisville: John Knox.

Dykstra, C., and Sharon Parks, eds. 1986. *Faith Development and Fowler.* Birmingham, Ala.: Religious Education Press.

Eisner, Elliot. 1982. *Cognition and Curriculum.* New York: Longman.

———. 1985. *The Educational Imagination.* Second rev. ed. New York: Macmillan.

Fowler, James W. 1984. "Pluralism, Particularity and Paideia." *Journal of Law and Religion* 2, no. 2.

Giltner, Fern M., ed. 1985. *Women's Issues in Religious Education.* Birmingham, Ala.: Religious Education Press.

Koper, Paul W. 1981. "The United Presbyterian Church and Christian Education: An Historical Overview." *Journal of Presbyterian History* 59, no. 3, pp. 288-308.

Lerner, Gerda. 1986. *The Creation of Patriarchy.* Vol. 1 of *Women and History.* New York: Oxford University Press.

Lines, Timothy A. 1987. *Systematic Religious Education.* Birmingham, Ala.: Religious Education Press.

Lovin, Robin W., ed. 1986. *Religion and American Public Life.* New York: Paulist.

Lynn, Robert W. 1964. *Protestant Strategies in Education.* New York: Association Press.

Marty, Martin E. 1981. *The Public Church: Mainline, Evangelical, Catholic.* New York: Crossroad.

———. 1987. *Religion and Republic: The American Circumstance.* Boston: Beacon.

McCluskey, Neil G., S.J. 1962. *Catholic Viewpoint on Education.* Rev. ed. Garden City: Doubleday and Company.

Murray, John C. 1960. *We Hold These Truths: Catholic Reflections on the American Proposition.* New York: Sheed and Ward.

Reichley, James A. 1985. *Religion in American Public life.* Washington, D.C.: Brookings Institute.

Rich, Lee Sharon, and Ariel Phillips, eds. 1985. *Women's Experience and Education.* Harvard Educational Review Reprint Series no. 17. Cambridge, Mass.: Harvard University Press.

Rood, Wayne R. 1970. *Understanding Christian Education.* Nashville: Abingdon.

Schuster, Marylin R., and Susan R. Van Dyne. 1985. *Women's Place in Academy: Transforming the Liberal Arts Curriculum.* Totowa, N.J.: Rowman Allanheld.

Seymour, Jack L. 1982. *Contemporary Approaches to Christian Education.* Nashville: Abingdon.

Seymour, Jack L., R. T. O'Gorman, and C. R. Foster. 1984. *The Church in the Education of the Public: Refocusing the Task of Religious Education.* Nashville: Abingdon.

Seymour, Jack L., and Donald E. Miller, eds. 1990. *Theological Approaches to Christian Education.* Nashville: Abingdon.

Stackhouse, Max L. 1987. *Public Theology and Political Life.* Grand Rapids: Eerdmans.

Taylor, Marvin J., ed. 1960. *Religious Education: A Comprehensive Introduction.* New York: Abingdon.

———. 1966. *An Introduction to Christian Education.* New York: Abingdon.

Tracy, David. 1986. "Social Contract or a Public Covenant?" In *Religion and American Public Life,* ed. R. Lovin. New York: Paulist.

Wilhoit, Jim. 1986. *Christian Education and the Search for Meaning.* Grand Rapids: Baker.

Germany

PRIMARY

Nipkow, Karl Ernst. 1960. *Die Individualität als pädagogisches Problem bei Pestalozzi, Humboldt und Schleiermacher.* Weinheim: Beltz.

————. 1963. *Evangelische Unterweisung oder evangelischer Religionsunterricht?* Essen: Neue Deutsche Schule.

————. 1967. *Grundfragen des Religionsunterrichts in der Gegenwart.* Heidelberg: Quelle und Meyer.

————. 1969. *Christliche Bildungstheorie und Schulpolitik. Deutsches Institut für Bildung und Wissen 1958-1968.* Gütersloh: Mohn.

————. 1971. *Schule und Religionsunterricht im Wandel. Ausgewählte Studien zur Pädagogik und Religionspädagogik.* Heidelberg: Quelle und Meyer.

————. 1975-1982. *Grundfragen der Religionspädagogik.* 3 vols. Gütersloh: Gütersloher Verlagshaus.

————. 1979. *Religionsunterricht in der Leistungsschule. Gutachten — Dokumente.* Gütersloh: Gütersloher Verlagshaus.

————. 1981. *Moralerziehung. Pädagogische und theologische Antworten.* Gütersloh: Gütersloher Verlagshaus.

————. 1987. *Erwachsenwerden ohne Gott? Gotteserfahrung im Lebenslauf.* München: Kaiser.

————. 1990. *Bildung als Lebensbegleitung und Erneuerung. Kirchliche Bildungsverantwortung in Gemeinde, Schule und Gesellschaft.* Gütersloh: Gütersloher Verlagshaus.

————. 1998. *Bildung in einer pluralen Welt.* 2 vols. Gütersloh: Gütersloher Verlagshaus.

Nipkow, Karl Ernst, and Friedrich Schweitzer, eds. 1991-1994. *Religionspädagogik. Texte zur evangelischen Erziehungs- und Bildungsverantwortung seit der Reformation.* 3 vols. München/Gütersloh: Kaiser/Gütersloher Verlagshaus.

Stallmann, Martin. 1963. *Die biblische Geschichte im Unterricht. Katechetische Beiträge.* Göttingen: Vandenhoeck und Ruprecht.

Stock, Hans. 1959. *Studien zur Auslegung der synoptischen Evangelien im Unterricht.* Gütersloh: Gütersloher.

SECONDARY

Grethlein, Christian. 1998. *Religionspädagogik.* Berlin: de Gruyter.

Kaufmann, Hans-Bernhard, ed. 1973. *Streit um den problemorientierten Unterricht in Schule und Kirche.* Frankfurt am Main: Diesterweg.

Lämmermann, Godwin. 1994. *Religionspädagogik im 20. Jahrhundert.* Gütersloh: Gütersloher Verlagshaus.

Mette, Norbert, and Folkert Rickers, eds. 2001. *Lexikon der Religionspädagogik.* Neukirchen-Vluyn: Neukirchener.

"Religionspädagogik seit 1945. Bilanz und Perspektiven." 1996. In *Jahrbuch der Religionspädagogik,* ed. Peter Biehl et al. Vol. 12. Neukirchen-Vluyn: Neukirchener.

Wegenast, Klaus, ed. 1971. *Religionsunterricht — wohin? Neue Stimmen zum Religionsunterricht an öffentlichen Schulen.* Gütersloh: Mohn.

————. 1981-1983. *Religionspädagogik.* Darmstadt: Wissenschaftliche Buchgesellschaft.

Ziebertz, Hans-Georg, and Werner Simon, eds. 1995. *Bilanz der Religionspädagogik.* Düsseldorf: Patmos.

Index of Authors

Adorno, Theodor, 252n.41
Ammerman, Nancy Tatom, 185, 186
Appadurai, Arjun, 61
Arato, Andrew, 59, 222

Barber, Benjamin, 67
Bar-Lev, Mordechai, xiin.1
Bauman, Zygmunt, 67
Beck, Ulrich, 4, 16n.18, 39, 60n.39, 61, 69, 97, 161n.97
Becker, Gary, 61, 283n.36
Bellah, N. Robert, 11n.10, 127n.24, 183, 221, 284, 285
Benhabib, Seyla, 5n.2, 48n.17, 54, 251, 258
Berger, Johannes, 35, 39
Berger, Peter, 4, 37, 38n.9, 43n.13
Beyer, Peter, 59n.33
Bohne, Gerhard, 141
Bonhoeffer, Dietrich, 16, 57, 140, 217, 241n.16
Boys, C. Mary, 18n.21
Browning, Don, 205, 218, 236n.1, 273n.1, 277n.5, 279, 285

Carroll, Jackson, 186n.59
Casanova, José, 22, 223n.22
Chopp, Rebecca S., 216, 236n.1
Christian, William, 241
Coe, George Albert, 24, 25n.37, 114n.74, 232; contextual assessment, 91-98; Edu-
cating for Citizenship, 87; life of, 81-82; overview of intellectual contribution, 82; *The Psychology of Religion,* 86; *A Social Theology of Religious Education,* 83-87

Cohen, Jean, 59
Coleman, James S., 35, 283n.36
Cremin, Lawrence, 8, 173, 175

De Gruchy, John, 251n.41
Dewey, John, xi, 30n.1, 53n.23, 80, 82, 84, 88, 94, 98, 116, 220

Eberhard, Otto, 25n.37, 98, 113, 116
Eisenstadt, Samuel N., 35n.4
Elliott, Harrison, 80, 88, 120, 128
Erikson, Erik H., 15n.17, 71, 203, 205, 255n.1, 263, 269

Fahs, Sophia Lyon: *Consider the Children,* 88, 90; contextual assessment, 91-98; life of, 87-88; overview of intellectual contribution, 88-91; *Today's Children and Yesterday's Heritage,* 88-91
Farley, Edward, 239n.10
Fiorenza, Francis Schüssler, 5n.2, 59
Foster, Charles R., 20, 170
Foucault, Michel, 238n.7
Fowler, James W., 20, 56, 170, 171n.9, 173,

Index of Subjects

adolescence, 15, 147, 148, 197, 205, 255, 264; late, 71

anthropology, 212, 225, 227, 228, 234; cultural, 205, 236; of religion, 102; philosophical, 261; theological, 145, 212, 255

catechesis, 7, 174, 175, 176, 185, 187, 234, 250, 251; congregational, 250; definition of, 248

childhood, xii, 15, 107, 276, 282; developmental stages of, 147, 148, 254

children's right to religion, 260-65

civil society, 5, 11, 14, 27, 43, 59, 217, 221, 222, 223, 279, 284, 286, 288, 289; definition of, 40; global, 229

church and state, separation of, 10, 20, 87, 104, 105, 107, 109, 111, 114, 115, 157, 164, 217, 220, 221, 223, 226

congregations: as the center of the religious life, 186; education in ethnic, 177; educational ministries of, 81, 173; teaching ministry of, 247-52

context, 18

Christian education: aim of, 85; Barthian, 120; and evangelical instruction, 162; global perspective in, 230; ministers and directors of, 124; Protestant theory and practice, 175; theory of, 120; World Council of, 161

Christian realism, 121, 122, 134, 170, 234; new, 161; rhetoric of, 128

cross-disciplinary thinking, 213, 231: Chopp and Lamb's praxis correlational model, 236; Frei and Thiemann's *ad hoc* correlational model, 236; levels of, 235-38; Loder and Hunsinger's Chalcedonian model, 236; Sherrill's method of correspondence, 132; Tillich's method of correlation, 116, 121, 129, 131, 137; Tracy and Browning's revised correlational model, 236; Van Huyssteen and Shults's transversal model, 236

differentiation, 39; cultural, 22; functional, 36, 41; institutional, 39; internal, 105; pluralizing and individualizing effects of, 71; process of, 35; of religion in modern societies, 44; social, 36; and specialization, 40; theory of and religious education, 40

discernment, 247, 250; definition of, 249; task of, 249

discourse ethic, 51-52

ecumenism, 230

education: confessional, 20-21; ecology of, 44; multicultural, 228; post–World

DATE DUE

The Library Store   #47-0103